Extremist for Love

EXTREMIST FOR LOVE

MARTIN LUTHER KING JR., MAN OF IDEAS AND NONVIOLENT SOCIAL ACTION

RUFUS BURROW JR.

Fortress Press
Minneapolis

EXTREMIST FOR LOVE

Martin Luther King Jr., Man of Ideas and Nonviolent Social Action

Cover photo by Francis Miller / Time Life Pictures / Getty Images

Cover design: Laurie Ingram

Library of Congress Cataloging-in-Publication Data

Burrow, Rufus, 1951–

Martin Luther King Jr., man of ideas and nonviolent social action / Rufus Burrow, Jr.

pages cm

Includes bibliographical references and index.

ISBN 978-1-4514-7020-8 (pbk. : alk. paper) — ISBN 978-1-4514-8027-6 (ebook)

1. King, Martin Luther, Jr., 1929-1968. 2. King, Martin Luther, Jr., 1929-1968–Political and social views. 3. Nonviolence–United States–History–20th century. 4. Social action–United States–History–20th century. 5. African Americans–Biography. 6. Civil rights workers–United States–Biography. 7. Baptists–United States–Clergy–Biography. 8. African Americans–Civil rights–History–20th century. 9. Civil rights movements–United States–History–20th century. 10. United States–Race relations–History–20th century–Sources. I. Title.

E185.97.K5B7995 2014

323.092–dc23   [B]   2013034955

The paper used in this publication meets the minimum requirements of American National Standard for Information Sciences — Permanence of Paper for Printed Library Materials, ANSI Z329.48-1984.

Manufactured in the U.S.A.

This book was produced using PressBooks.com, and PDF rendering was done by PrinceXML.

To the memory of my son-in-love, Mr. David Todd Anderson (1966–2012), who had the audacity to believe that people whose humanity and dignity are systematically undermined by those who control and benefit mightily from unjust systems will overcome when they make up their minds to organize and take on the powers that be. He believed we can all be better than we are, but had an uncanny sense that we sometimes have to be pushed and prodded in this regard. In the best sense, and in the spirit of Martin Luther King Jr., David too was a man of ideas and ideals who had a deep faith in nonviolent direct action.

CONTENTS

Foreword

Martin Luther King Jr. was the most influential civil rights activist in the United States in the twentieth century. This point is well established in the growing body of scholarship on this phenomenal figure. But King was far more than a celebrated civil rights activist who gave dynamic speeches, led nonviolent demonstrations, and engaged in creative acts of civil disobedience. He was also a great thinker and man of ideas and letters, and the scope and vitality of his mind were such that he should be considered a part of that rich story that constitutes American intellectual history.

Rufus Burrow Jr. traces King's metamorphosis as both an intellectual and activist, noting that in both categories his life was filled with incredible fulfillment and achievement. For Burrow, the arresting power of King's ideas and idealism, and the ways in which this grounded his quest for social change, cast him in the image of the quintessential *organic intellectual*. Burrow teases out and analyzes the major features of King's thought and intellectual sources and categories, while also linking his life to the broader cultural and political contexts that surrounded him. The finished product is a King who has been elusive and largely unknown to much of this nation and the world.

An Extremist for Love is a superb work in several respects. First, it is a vivid character assessment of a complex individual who thought and acted out of the proud heritage of his southern forefathers and mothers. Burrow reminds us that King's thinking and activism were pervaded by the same visions that caught the imaginations of his grandparents and parents. The contention, then, is that the familial roots of King's nonviolence and protest activities constitute the proper point of departure in any credible reconstruction of King's public career as a thinker, idealist, and social activist.

Second, Burrow has given us perhaps the most extensive examination of King's key ideas and concepts, such as the love and rationality of God, the dignity and worth of human personality, the essentiality of the love ethic, the communitarian nature of persons, and human freedom and sin. Careful attention is also devoted to Mohandas K. Gandhi, Walter Rauschenbusch, Reinhold Niebuhr, and other formal intellectual influences, which provided King with intellectual categories, interpretive models, and a conceptual framework to articulate many of these ideas. At the same time, Burrow reminds us of King's amazing creativity in translating ideas into practical action and reality.

Third, Burrow highlights King's connections and indebtedness to some of his most progressive-minded and socially active contemporaries, such as Vernon Johns, Jo Ann Robinson, James M. Lawson, Ella J. Baker, Bayard Rustin, and Glenn Smiley. Although these figures loomed large in King's early development as a thinker and practitioner of creative nonviolent dissent and protest, they have, up to this point, received little attention in studies of King. Burrow corrects this pattern of neglect while establishing King's rightful place in a movement that included numerous thinkers and courageous activists.

Finally, Burrow offers a fresh perspective on King's legacy and what it means for our times, especially as we continue to grapple with the enduring problems of white supremacy, black intracommunal crime and violence, sexism, and other social ills. We are thus challenged to read and understand King not only *in context*, but also *beyond context*. Although much is revealed about King's relevance and meaningfulness as a cultural and political icon for this age, Burrow also gives some indication as to why the intellectual legacy of King promises to be richer as time goes on. There is already a notable increase in interest in that part of King's legacy.

But we are also confronted with caricatures of King that arise not only from a procrustean attitude toward figures of the past, but also from a lack of acquaintance with his words and ideas. Thus, it is not surprising that we are increasingly confronted with the image of the gentle, harmless southern black Baptist preacher who made love, nonviolence, and redemptive suffering the heart of the Christian faith. Images routinely fix themselves in the public consciousness, and this image of King is not easily shattered. In such a climate, Burrow's book should be seen as part of a breakthrough toward a more enlightened understanding of King. With an admirable grasp of King's thought and social activism in all of their depth and scope, Burrow has performed a significant measure of iconoclasm in the process of projecting a more accurate and balanced portrayal of King the man and his times.

Lewis V. Baldwin
Vanderbilt University
May 2013

Preface

So great a person was Martin Luther King Jr., and so profound were his contributions and legacy to this country and the world, that volumes of books have been and will be written on him. There was a time when I believed that the market could not contain more publications on King. I therefore concluded that there was nothing I could add that had not already been said or was being said about King and his civil rights ministry. However, when I began reading book after book after book on King, I discovered one of two things to be true: either no one was actually addressing the issues that most interested me or seemed most important to me, or no one approached a given topic on him in quite the way I would. In either case, I soon concluded that, owing to his monumental contributions toward the improvement of individuals and communities, areas of the life of Martin Luther King Jr. will continue to cry out for exploration.

Indeed, I came to believe, along with renowned King scholar Lewis V. Baldwin of Vanderbilt University, that if one takes a topic-specific approach to King the field is fertile and wide open to the curious, creative, energetic mind. I do not know how creative I am in this regard, but over the past two decades one of the two most interesting and significant persons in theological and ethical studies to me has been Martin Luther King Jr.[1] This is why I continue to study, teach, and write about King, and why I have written this book, with its focus on King as man of ideas and nonviolent direct social action.

In all of my years of teaching, thinking, and writing about King, I have been mindful that he was an imperfect earthen vessel who, given his particular set of strengths and limitations, was able to provide such significant leadership

---

1. The other significant person of interest is Rabbi Abraham Joshua Heschel (1907–1972). King and Heschel met for the first time in 1963 at the National Conference on Religion and Race in Chicago. Both men delivered keynote addresses in which they revealed the strong influence of the Hebrew prophets, most especially Amos. Both expressed their commitment and determination to fighting for justice and civil rights for blacks. The two men became fast friends and colleagues in the civil rights struggle, as King later appealed to Heschel to join him and SCLC in the famous march from Selma to Montgomery, Alabama in 1965. Although I have not written as much on Heschel to this point, my co-authored book with Mary Alice Mulligan, *Daring to Speak in God's Name: Ethical Prophecy in Ministry* (Pilgrim, 2002), is heavily influenced by his ideas on the Hebrew prophets and their meaning for us today. In addition, there are so many similarities between Heschel and King that I hope to write a book on the two men.

and contributions to what came to be the civil rights movement. His determination to be faithful to his ministerial call and his willingness, right or wrong, to sacrifice all to this end—including responsibilities to wife and children—has been a constant reminder of just how important is the vocation of ministry—the most important in the world according to King—and what is required of those who are called by God. To a large extent, King set the standard in this regard.

Over the years, I have been fond of telling my students in the class I teach annually on King that he was an ordinary human being who did some very extraordinary things as he endeavored to be true to his calling from God. I like putting it this way because it is true to the facts about the man—the human being. He was not perfect, and did not pretend or presume to be. He was not a saint, did not want to be, and insisted that the Ebenezer Baptist Church congregation not think of him as such. He had no desire to be placed on a pedestal of any kind. He was born of a woman and a man, and thus was thoroughly human, with strengths and weaknesses similar to those of other human beings. He was an earthen vessel, and thus in any given moment could be weak or strong. He was a sinner like every human being, missing the mark, despite how vigilant he was in trying to hit it. And yet, he stood out from most human beings because in the barely thirty-nine years he lived he refused to give up trying to hit the mark—sometimes coming quite close, and at other times missing the moral mark wide of center. Indeed, theologian Cheryl Kirk-Duggan has rightly observed: "King had unique gifts; King was human. Like many leaders, he left powerful legacies and was a flawed person. People who live large, often have considerable flaws."[2]

From the time that Martin Luther King Jr. was a little boy he exhibited signs of precociousness as well as a desire to help his father to fight racism. When a white Atlanta policeman tried to insult his father by referring to him as "boy," the younger King, who was beside him in the car, knew from his father's reaction that something very serious had just occurred that elicited both anger and resistance from Daddy King. In addition, King Jr. observed that the policeman himself was so shocked by Daddy King's reaction that he failed to complete his business and left the scene. When Daddy King explained to his son that he would never passively accept such treatment, and that he would always resist it, King Jr. responded that he would do what he could to help

2. Cheryl Kirk-Duggan, "Drum Major for Justice or Dilettante of Dishonesty: Martin Luther King, Jr., Moral Capital, and Hypocrisy of Embodied Messianic Myths," in *The Domestication of Martin Luther King, Jr.: Clarence B. Jones, Right-Wing Conservatism, and the Manipulation of the King Legacy*, ed. Lewis V. Baldwin and Rufus Burrow Jr. Foreword by Adam Fairclough (Eugene, OR: Cascade, 2013), 100.

him eradicate racism. On the surface, this seemed innocent enough coming from a young boy. But this particular boy had both witnessed many other acts of racism and had been on the receiving end of it multiple times as a child. Although just a boy when he told his father he would help him fight racism, Martin Luther King had actually been quite serious. Because he and his siblings were early taught the value of education, as well as the obligation to resist anything that undermined their sense of humanity and dignity, there is every reason to believe that even as a young boy King sensed that there was a connection between ideas gleaned from a good education and the liberation of his people from segregation and deeply entrenched racism.

For a long time in King Studies, the tendency for most scholars and others who wrote on Martin Luther King was to present him as the quintessential Christian social activist in the civil rights movement. He was social activist, not "theologian" (read *man of ideas*) as such. The thinking seemed to be that although King earned the Ph.D. in systematic theology from Boston University, his primary work was in social activism rather than the typical activities of the traditional theologian, for example, teaching in the academy and writing esoteric articles and books, which often have little to do with human beings' daily life struggles and God's expectation that justice be done. In part, this view of King was due to narrow thinking about what it means to be a theologian. But it was also due to racism in the theological academy and the sense that blacks could be appointed to every position in a school's curriculum except systematic or philosophical theology, an area reserved primarily for white men. I have known many blacks and a number of Hispanics who were formally trained in theology, but found themselves in positions such as ethics, theology and culture, theology and ethics, and so on, but not theology or systematic theology. Only in fairly recent years has this practice changed.

Martin Luther King Jr. acknowledged being many things: father, husband, civil rights leader, author, recipient of the Ph.D. and dozens of honorary degrees, the Nobel Peace Prize, and so on. More important than all of these, he made it crystal clear that he was fundamentally a Baptist preacher; a man of the cloth; "a religious man, formed to the bone marrow in the Christian faith of his black Baptist tradition."[3] At the very center of King's life and civil rights ministry were his religious faith and theological convictions, most particularly his sense of God as personal, just, and loving creator and the source of the inviolable sacredness of human beings as such. Inherent in this is also King's sense that God is concerned about both the spiritual and material condition of

3. James W. Fowler, Foreword, in *To See the Promised Land: The Faith Pilgrimage of Martin Luther King, Jr.* by Frederick L. Downing (Macon, GA: Mercer University Press, 1986), ix.

human beings, most particularly those counted among the least of the sisters and brothers. This book takes that stance for granted, focusing as it does, on Martin Luther King as man of ideas *and* nonviolent social activism.

Much of my previous writing on King has focused on what I call the *man of ideas* genre. I have focused on this primarily because I have not been satisfied with much of past and present scholarship on King, which has not given enough attention to him as a thinker-theologian who loved ideas. Indeed, when Kenneth L. Smith, Ira Zepp Jr., and John J. Ansbro did stress the intellectual influences on King in 1974 and 1982, respectively, they implied but did not expressly present him as a man of ideas. Their emphasis was primarily on how European and European American thinkers influenced his intellectual maturation. Moreover, they failed to include the informal influences from King's family and black church upbringing, as well as the influence of the southern black cultural environment that he loved so much. Nor did they consider the influences of historically black Morehouse College. The fact that King learned the importance of thinking about his faith-claims at Morehouse, for example, gave him a considerable academic advantage over most southern Baptist students he met when he entered the predominantly white Crozer Theological Seminary. To address this and other limitations I wrote *God and Human Dignity: The Personalism, Theology, and Ethics of Martin Luther King, Jr.* (University of Notre Dame Press, 2006) and later, *Martin Luther King, Jr. for Armchair Theologians* (Westminster John Knox, 2009). However, neither of these books stressed the theme of King as man of ideas *and* nonviolent social activism. The present book aims, in part, to fill the gap left by my previous books on King. It gives more attention to the family roots of King's commitment to nonviolent protest against dehumanizing treatment, and examines the contributions of some of those who paved the way for him in Montgomery, the beginning of his civil rights ministry.

Much of pre-1980s scholarship on King, such as the work of August Meier and David L. Lewis, was typical of the concern expressed above in that it focused primarily on his contributions as social activist, with little positive acknowledgment and attention to the fact that he was also a first-rate theologian and a very good thinker, although of a different type than theologians, ethicists, and philosophers who influenced him during his formal intellectual pilgrimage. A number of those thinkers, whose ideas and what they meant to King will be examined at some length in this book, were strong advocates for social justice and provided helpful ideas that the student King would appeal to in an effort to ground his social conscience theologically. It was left to Mahatma Gandhi, however, to provide a method or technique to actually resist injustice; a method that King honed and made his own. The white thinkers who influenced King's thought did not, like King, literally and systematically apply and refine their ideas through nonviolent direct action campaigns to set at liberty oppressed black people.

Pre-1980s studies on King generally highlighted his contributions as social activist but to the exclusion of his ability and contributions as thinker and lover of ideas and ideals. King was not only influenced by the ideas of a number of Western thinkers. He was himself a man of ideas who creatively melded together what he considered the best in the ideas of others with his own ideas and experiences and produced a theology that was reflective of, but in some ways went well beyond the contribution of others. He was able to do this in large part because of his direct engagement in the struggle for justice as he sought to apply his best ideas to the civil rights struggle. Without question, King learned much about the theory of love and justice during his formal academic preparation, but these took on a deeper meaning when he sought to apply them through nonviolent direct action campaigns. At the very least, he had to adjust his understanding of love and justice and what was possible to achieve through their application. He learned firsthand (in the hot furnace of the civil rights struggle) that love is very nearly an impossible ideal to actualize in group relations, and yet unlike some thinkers who influenced him (e.g., Reinhold Niebuhr), King insisted on its applicability to individuals as well as groups of all sizes, including the largest, most complex of all—nations.

More than anything else, Martin Luther King's love for ideas had to do with what he believed they could contribute toward making the most of persons-in-community, and because of what he knew the best ideas and ideals actually require of human beings as they relate together in community. What can ideas contribute toward helping us to live together in civilized and beloved community-making ways? This is what intrigued and energized Martin Luther King. For in his view, it was not enough to merely be the recipient of a quality education from a top university, for example. Vast numbers of people are formally educated, and yet seem to have no moral qualms with racism, inequality, and other forms of systemic oppression. They are more committed to political correctness than to moral rightness. King believed that the truly educated person is aware of her responsibility to do all in her power to be a good citizen and to make better persons and communities. Minimally, this means that one should do all in her power to resist and eradicate whatever undermines human dignity. It is wonderful to be able to say that one has earned the doctor of philosophy degree in systematic theology from a prestigious university as King had, but at the end of the day he believed that it was more important to know what difference having such a degree could make in a society where people of Afrikan descent are systematically beaten and crushed to the earth in what is ostensibly the greatest democratic nation in the world.[4] The values instilled in King by his parents and maternal grandmother, his observation of how his father and other southern black preachers did ministry, as well as how two of his mentors in college represented the Christian ministry, convinced him that as important as education and ideas are, they mean little if one does not put them to the task of making persons and the world better than they were before one was born. Moreover, as literary artist James Arthur Baldwin tried to teach, we humans can be better than we are, and we do not have to leave the world in the same condition we found it when we came into it.

Because Martin Luther King was an Afrikan American who grew up in the blatantly racist and violent Deep South and experienced racism and racial discrimination firsthand, it is important to remember that in virtually every case, he filtered the ideas gleaned from formal academic training through his own sociocultural grid, thus making them more relevant to his context and that of his people. Only in this way could he adapt these ideas to what he and his people confronted on a daily basis in a nation that was essentially hostile toward them. For King, the ideas must aid in the quest to help liberate his people from racial and other forms of oppression.

For all the publicity that was his from Montgomery, Alabama to Memphis, Tennessee, King did not act alone. Although the media and others sometimes erroneously implied otherwise, King himself never pretended that he either started the civil rights movement or that he was its sole, or even its most important leader. Rather, he acknowledged on more than one occasion that in Montgomery, for example, circumstances and the sweep of history were such that the boycott in that city would have occurred even had he not appeared on the scene. Nor did he hesitate to praise the contributions of other leaders, including student activists and local grassroots leaders. King was aware that others fallowed the ground for him, an important point that seems often to elude people who talk about him and the civil rights movement today. In

---

4. The use of "c" in the spelling of "Africa" is the Anglicized spelling: that letter does not exist in West Afrikan languages. I use the "k" out of homage and respect for those who struggled for freedom and liberation in the 1960s. During the Black Consciousness Movement of this period, a number of proponents adopted the use of "k," which was consistent with the usage of many groups on the Afrikan continent. The spelling is still prevalent among some Afrikans on the continent and in diaspora. For example, this is the preferred spelling in a publication I received from Accra, Ghana (*The Afrikan Crusader*), where on every page the spelling is "Afrikan." I adopted this spelling for my own writing after the publication of my first book in 1994 and have consistently used it in my writing.

this regard, this book will discuss and analyze—among others—the role of the Rev. Vernon Johns, and the women of the Women's Political Council (WPC), since only in fairly recent years has attention been given their outstanding contributions.

This book takes for granted that in many instances there were phases of the movement that developed and flourished without King's leadership. Examples include the contributions of black youths as illustrated by the student sit-ins and Freedom Rides in early 1960 and mid-1961, respectively. In addition, it was the young people in the Student Nonviolent Coordinating Committee (SNCC) that launched the voter education-registration campaigns in the very dangerous Mississippi Delta and Selma, Alabama. On more than one occasion, King found himself in the position of having to publicly defend the contributions and technique of nonviolent civil disobedience advanced by the students and other youths. Furthermore, it is noteworthy that King was never eager to engage in public confrontation with his youthful colleagues in the movement, but generally preferred to iron out differences behind closed doors.

For Martin Luther King Jr., then, ideas and nonviolent social activism went hand in hand. Indeed, King's daily living was a creative admixture of both, and in my estimation he actually wrote the book on what it truly means to be a theological social ethicist who is in touch with the everydayness of life, and thus understands that theory and ideas mean little if their purpose is not to make people and the world better. King was also unequaled when it came to modeling what it means for the theologian to be actively involved in resistance to injustice, thus testing his basic ideas in the fire of the struggle for racial equality. This is what set him apart from other theologians who also staunchly advocated the relevance of the Christian ethic to the social question and the obligation to apply its principles to solving social problems. No theologian whose ideas had a deep impact on King came close to the way he did this—not Walter Rauschenbusch, not Reinhold Niebuhr, not L. Harold DeWolf (his teacher-mentor in personalistic studies at Boston University). King organized and led nonviolent direct action demonstrations against social injustice, putting his ideas to work and his life in jeopardy each and every time.

Because I actually see an ongoing dance between King's ideas and his nonviolent social activism, I presently find it impossible to speak and write about him without making it unequivocally clear that he was at once a man of ideas *and* a man of relentless nonviolent social activism. Therefore, he had no choice but to seek justice and righteousness for systematically oppressed people. A number of important ideas affiliated with social gospel Christianity, Christian realism, Christian agape, and the philosophy of nonviolence influenced the development of King's social ethics and how he put these ideas to work in his civil rights ministry. This book will provide a deeper and more informed discussion on these intellectual sources and how they affected King's thought and practice than appears in my previous writings, and in the writings of an earlier generation of scholars who addressed this topic, but for whom King's unpublished papers were not as readily accessible as today. Although references are made in this book to the philosophy of personalism and some of its basic ideas, there is no in-depth discussion of it here. The influence of the philosophy of personalism on King is taken for granted in this text, since I have written two books on the subject. My introductory text on personalism situates King in the moral law tradition of his personalist teachers at Boston University.[5] The other book focuses explicitly on the mutual influence between King and personalism and how he sought to apply it in his civil rights ministry.[6]

5. See Rufus Burrow Jr., *Personalism: A Critical Introduction* (St. Louis: Chalice, 1999), 218–22.

6. Burrow, *God and Human Dignity: The Personalism, Theology, and Ethics of Martin Luther King, Jr.* (Notre Dame: University of Notre Dame Press, 2006).

Acknowledgements

I have read many volumes of books on the life, teachings, and nonviolent philosophy of Martin Luther King Jr. It is important that readers know that I consider Professor Lewis V. Baldwin of Vanderbilt University and Clayborne Carson, Director of the King Papers Project and Professor of History at Stanford University, to be *King scholars extraordinaire*. There may be others. These are two of the most distinguished. The breadth, depth, and precision of their knowledge about King is second to no other in the world. My own study, reflection, and interpretation of King has been much influenced by the meticulous and creative work produced by these two superb scholars. There are no adequate words to express the depth of my appreciation for their contributions to King Studies. They have been Teachers.

Although it has not often enough been an easy place to do the work I have long felt *called* to do, Christian Theological Seminary in Indianapolis, Indiana has been my home base. Oddly, of late, I find myself reminiscing about a number of white colleagues who did their part as participants and sympathizers of the civil rights movement to unlock the seminary's doors from the inside in order to begin in a new way the difficult, painful, and challenging task of creating a faculty, staff, administration, and student body that looks more like the people that the God of the Hebrew prophets and Jesus Christ actually created. The "fathers" and "mothers" as I affectionately refer to them were not by any means perfect, and not all of them always did everything they could in the cause of establishing and maintaining a colorful, multicultural seminary community where power is shared more equitably than in much of the theological academy. In short, I am truly grateful for parts of the journey with the "mothers" and "fathers" of CTS, although along the way I always remembered a good piece of advice given me by my mother: "Always keep a rake and shovel handy," she said. "That way, you can rake in what you need, and shovel out the fecal matter." God knows I've done my share of shoveling over thirty years.

To be granted a yearlong research leave to write this book and to make substantial progress on another is no small blessing, for which I am thankful. I am a better King scholar and feel myself to be a better theological educator for having been granted and taken advantage of this gift.

I wrote several key sections of this book at the home of my daughter, Sheronn Lynn, in Chester, Pennsylvania (where Martin Luther King attended seminary). My four-year-old granddaughter, Bailey Reign, had a thing or two to say about that. We bonded as I tried to write, and she insisted that I give her my undivided attention, whenever she wanted it, which was whenever she saw me sitting at the dining room table trying to write. I have no doubt that those pages are among the most interesting to read, and perhaps even the best in the book.

My students over the years have always played an important part in what I write, particularly since many of my ideas for writing projects arise out of course lectures, discussions, and calls (from students) for clarity. The present book is no exception. I often find that students contribute much toward helping me understand my own ideas and arguments better, which in turn leads to ideas and arguments that are more cogently stated. I wish to convey my deepest thanks to the groups of students who have put up with me, in addition to reading and studying the writings of Martin Luther King Jr. with me. I have no doubt that some will recognize in these pages the fruits of some of our discussions and disagreements from the class. Others will see that no matter how hard they tried, I still didn't get it. And yet, they will know from these pages that I tried.

Introduction

This book is comprised of five parts, with a total of ten chapters. Each part introduces the major subject to be discussed and provides an overview of the chapter(s) therein. Part 1 focuses on the family roots of the protest tradition of Martin Luther King. Did King come from a family that was steeped in the tradition of nonviolence? Many, including Coretta Scott King, have given a negative answer to that question, especially if they heard the story of King's paternal grandmother's violent encounter with a white man who beat her young son (Daddy King). But can we reasonably conclude from this incident that the spirit and practice of nonviolence was absent from King's entire family lineage? The three chapters in Part 1 address this and the related question: What, if anything, did King's paternal grandparents (chapter one), maternal grandparents (chapter two), and parents (chapter three) contribute to the protest and nonviolence traditions that were so important to his adult life and civil rights ministry? We will see that the family influences contributed much to making King who he came to be, and also helped to lay the foundation for his moral conviction that we ought to protest injustice, but *only* by engaging in nonviolent direct action as the sole means. King's family also nurtured and influenced his intellectual development and his burning desire to help eradicate the injustices that were undermining the humanity and dignity of his people. Martin Luther King was an ordinary human being who did some very extraordinary things, a theme that permeates this book.

In Part 2, we turn to an in-depth discussion of some of the formal intellectual influences on King. Because of my firm conviction that Martin Luther King was a man of ideas and ideals, and that this warrants even more attention in King studies, the two chapters in Part 2 (four–five) are devoted to a deeper examination of two thinkers who influenced his developing theology and philosophy, as well as how he thought about socio-ethical practice. Chapter four is devoted to a careful examination of the social gospel ideas of Walter Rauschenbusch and King's claim to have been a staunch advocator of the social gospel even before reading Rauschenbusch. In chapter five, I engage in an extensive discussion of the Christian realism of Reinhold Niebuhr and how it influenced the theology and social ethics of King. In each case, the reader will be reminded that these formal ideas actually had their beginnings in teachings and practices that King was exposed to during his family upbringing, in religious instruction at the Ebenezer Baptist Church where his father was senior minister, in conversations with his father and in observing him do ministry, as well as in the contributions of his teachers and mentors at Morehouse College. Therefore, when King was formally introduced in seminary to liberal theological ideas such as the significance of subjecting all things to reason, the inherent goodness of human nature, God as personal, and the application of the historical-critical method to the study of the Bible, he easily resonated to these because of what he had already been exposed to at home, in church, and at Morehouse. When he arrived at Crozer Theological Seminary in Chester, Pennsylvania in the fall of 1948, his mind was not a *tabula rasa* or blank sheet, and he was already developing into a serious thinker, willing to subject his own long-held faith claims to critique.

In the two chapters in Part 3 (six–seven), we take up the important idea that King did not begin his civil rights ministry in a vacuum, a point that he himself acknowledged many times during and after the Montgomery bus boycott. He made no effort to get the media and other forces to focus on him as a kind of "great man" as the source and sole driving spirit of the movement. King did not initiate the Montgomery struggle. Instead, he was happy to point out that there were forerunners or trailblazers who paved the way, and that he just happened to be in Montgomery and was able and willing to carry out the leadership role into which he was cast. However, unlike the claim of some writers on King, such as Peter J. Ling, as well as civil rights activists Ella Baker and Edwin D. Nixon, this should not be taken to mean that Montgomery or the movement *made* King. This is at best a half-truth. The larger, broader truth is that King both made, *and* was made by, the movement. Indeed, in many ways he contributed as much to the movement as it contributed to him. Thus, it seems to me that one positions self to get the best and fullest understanding of King and the movement by focusing not on one or the other—King "the great man" *or* the movement—but both. King himself always seemed aware that both he *and* local movements were making significant contributions to the civil rights of blacks, although his tendency was to downplay his own role.[1]

1. See Clayborne Carson, "Martin Luther King, Jr.: Charismatic Leadership in a Mass Struggle," *The Journal of American History* 74 (September 1987): 448–56, and Nathan I. Huggins, "Martin Luther King, Jr.: Charisma and Leadership," *The Journal of American History* 74 (September 1987): 477–81. Carson, Huggins, and others discuss whether the focus should be on King or the movement. Most of the contributors, including Carson, rejected the "great man" approach, preferring that emphasis be placed on the movement, since this would mean that more focus could be placed on local grassroots leaders who contributed greatly to the struggle for freedom and civil rights. Huggins concluded that the emphasis should be placed on King, which need not preclude stressing the contributions of grassroots local leaders

Chapters six and seven, then, focus on the contributions of some key forerunners of the movement: the venerable Rev. Vernon Napoleon Johns, and black women trailblazers, respectively. Johns was King's immediate predecessor at Dexter Avenue Baptist Church in Montgomery, Alabama. He was intellectually brilliant, inimitable, prophetic, sometimes eccentric, and he paved the way for King like no other single individual. To date, not much has been written on Johns, and yet what is known about him is quite a fascinating story that deserves to be told. But in the present book, Johns is presented as only one of the primary characters who actually broke ground for and paved the way for Martin Luther King and the work that lay ahead of him. We will see that although King had occasion to meet Johns just prior to succeeding him as pastor at Dexter, most of what he knew about him was secondhand, based on the stories of other black preachers. Nevertheless, the reputation of Johns convinced King that he was not only one of God's "bad boy" preachers, but a fearless and passionate pastor in the tradition of the Hebrew prophets of the eighth century bce, and that he never backed away from a good fight, especially when it had to do with working for justice for those counted among the least of these. Indeed, Johns was often heard saying: "If you see a good fight, get in it," advice he claimed to have gotten from his mother.[2]

For far too long, the contributions of black women to the civil rights movement from Montgomery onward were not given the attention they deserved in books and articles by scholars and popular writers. When this pattern of neglect began to be broken, the effort, not surprisingly, was led by black and other women themselves.[3] Although King himself was not always forthcoming about the significant roles that women played from the time he was cast upon the stage as a leader, there is no question that he had some awareness of this, and periodically said so. Chapter seven, then, considers the

who might also possess charisma. He was careful to point out: "There is as much danger in romanticizing movements as in romanticizing individual leaders" (481). It seems to me that the richest, fullest understanding will come from seeing the two in dialectical relationship, which is consistent with King's method. As far as possible, the effort should be made to place equal emphasis on both King (the great man) *and* the movement.

2. Houston Bryan Roberson, *Fighting the Good Fight: The Story of the Dexter Avenue King Memorial Baptist Church, 1865-1977* (New York: Routledge, 2005), 88.

3. For example, see Zita Allen, *Black Women Leaders of the Civil Rights Movement* (New York: Franklin Watts, 1996); Belinda Robnett, *How Long? How Long?: African-American Women in the Struggle for Civil Rights* (New York: Oxford University Press, 1997); Lynne Olson, *Freedom's Daughters: The Unsung Heroines of the Civil Rights Movement from 1830 to 1970* (New York: Scribner, 2001); and Rosetta E. Ross, *Witnessing & Testifying: Black Women, Religion, and Civil Rights* (Minneapolis: Augsburg Fortress Press, 2003). Allen, Robnett, and Ross are Afrikan American writers and scholars; Olson is an Anglo one.

woman factor in paving the way to the civil rights movement commencing in Montgomery. The focus is primarily on the contributions of black women, a number of whom were influenced by their pastor, Vernon Johns. However, the chapter also considers the contributions of a couple of southern white women as well, especially during the Montgomery bus boycott. Who were some of these black and white women? They include members of the Women's Political Council, such as Mary Fair Burks and Jo Ann Robinson, two teenagers who in March and October of 1955, respectively, were arrested on buses for violating Montgomery's segregation ordinance (the same year of Rosa Parks's arrest on December 5), and a librarian who was openly friendly to blacks' struggle. While the chapter will cite other Montgomery residents who helped to break ground for King, the focus is on the contributions of black women, since it is only in fairly recent civil rights scholarship that they have been made more visible and given their much-deserved recognition and credit.

The purpose of including the contributions of the two teens, Claudette Colvin and Mary Louise Smith, is to show that black youths were involved in a significant way in the movement from start to finish. This means, among other things, that the contributions of black children and youths did not begin with the sit-in movement and the Freedom Rides of 1960 and 1961, respectively. Rather, they were involved and active in the struggle for freedom and liberation from Montgomery to Memphis, and beyond. This chapter also aims to provide a sense of King's reaction to the woman factor and how (or whether) he was influenced by it in any significant way(s). This is a topic that screams for deeper, systematic exploration. While I am convinced that male writers can, and should, explore this in attempts to tell more of the untold stories about the contributions of women to the civil rights movement, my hope is that discussions like the one in this chapter will generate increasing interest among women scholars such that growing numbers will begin devoting even more of their genius and way of seeing and being to scholarship on King and the movement, including the role that women have, and must continue to play. Although at this writing, no book-length text has been written on King by a woman,[4] in recent years, second-generation womanist religious scholars such as Cheryl Kirk-Duggan of Shaw University Divinity School and Traci West of

---

4. It should be noted, however, that two important comparative books have been written on King by white women, one from the United States, and the other from Germany. See Mary E. King (former leader in the Student Nonviolent Coordinating Committee), *Mahatma Gandhi and Martin Luther King, Jr: The Power of Nonviolent Action* (Paris: UNESCO, 1999), and Britta Waldschmidt-Nelson, *Dreams and Nightmares: Martin Luther King, Jr., Malcolm X, and the Struggle for Black Equality in America* (Gainesville: University Press of Florida, 2012).

Drew Theological School have begun devoting significant space and attention to King in the context of some of their publications.[5] First-generation womanist ethicist Katie G. Cannon devoted a strong comparative chapter on King and Howard Thurman in her seminal book, *Black Womanist Ethics*.[6]

Part 4 brings us to a consideration of Christian love and Gandhian nonviolence, and especially on how these influenced King and what he contributed to them as he sought the *practiced* use of his ideas in nonviolent direct action campaigns throughout the South and in some places in the North as well. The two chapters in Part 4 (eight–nine) will look more carefully than has heretofore been the case, at the roots of King's understanding of Christian love, from the teachings and example of his mother and maternal grandmother, to his formal study of love in seminary and during doctoral studies. This will be the primary emphasis in chapter eight. Although in numerous writings and speeches King discussed the difference between *eros*, *philia*, and *agape*, we will see that he at times spoke also of three other levels of love: motherly love, humanitarian love, and utilitarian love. In every case, however, he was clear that agape is the highest form of love and is applicable not only to individuals, but to groups and nations as well. In this regard, he rejected Reinhold Niebuhr's view that agape is not applicable to groups such as nations, arguably the largest, most complex of groups. He also rejected what he saw as Niebuhr's ethical dualism. In addition, the chapter examines the question of whether King actually read and pondered the most definitive study on eros and agape, written by Anders Nygren (*Agape and Eros*), a classic book that was included in the collateral reading list of one of his courses in seminary. More than previous books on King, chapter eight will provide a deeper discussion on Nygren's view of agape and what King, in light of his personalistic stance and his experience as a black

5. See Cheryl A. Kirk-Duggan, *Refiner's Fire: A Religious Engagement with Violence* (Minneapolis: Augsburg Fortress Press, 2001), ch. 5, "Ballads, Not Bullets: The Nonviolent Protest Ministry of Martin Luther King, Jr." Kirk-Duggan has given attention to King in the context of other writings as well, although not as extensively as in the aforementioned book. See her *Exorcizing Evil: A Womanist Perspective on the Spirituals* (Maryknoll, NY: Orbis, 1997), especially ch. 9, "Mass Meeting"; and *Misbegotten Anguish: A Theology and Ethics of Violence* (St. Louis: Chalice, 2001), 87, 179, 180. Traci C. West, "Gendered Legacies of Martin Luther King, Jr.'s Leadership," *Theology Today* 65 (2008): 41–56. In addition, Kirk-Duggan and West each contributed a creative and instructive chapter to Lewis V. Baldwin and Rufus Burrow Jr., eds., *The Domestication of Martin Luther King, Jr.: Clarence B. Jones, Right-Wing Conservatism, and the Manipulation of the King Legacy* (Eugene, OR: Cascade, 2013), chapters 5 ("Drum Major for Justice or Dilettante of Dishonesty"), and 7 ("Gay Rights and the Misuse of Martin"), respectively.

6. Katie G. Cannon, *Black Womanist Ethics* (Atlanta: Scholars, 1988), ch. 6, "Resources for a Constructive Ethic in the Theology of Howard Thurman and Martin Luther King, Jr."

person in a racist society, considered to be a major flaw in his position. The chapter also examines the influence of Gandhian nonviolence, and how King's doctrine of nonviolence began to take shape once agape and black cultural and religious ideas and practices were combined with Gandhian ideas. It will also be seen that contrary to what many believed, King did not begin his leadership of the Montgomery bus boycott by focusing on explicitly Gandhian principles and techniques of nonviolence. He had not, by this time, had any experience applying relevant aspects of Gandhi's philosophy of nonviolence and its techniques, and thus did not know how to apply them. Moreover, consistent with much southern culture, he was initially committed to an ethic of self-defense, owned a pistol, and had armed bodyguards around him as well as around his house. A key question to be addressed in this chapter is: When did King actually begin to commit to the Gandhian type of nonviolence and what led him to do so? Whether King's mature doctrine of nonviolence differed from Gandhi's and was more relevant to the United States context will also be explored.

Chapter eight aims to do something else as well, namely, to clarify some misleading statements that King made in various places regarding his evolution toward his stance of nonviolence as a way of life. For example, when we read either of the two versions of King's brief intellectual autobiography, "Pilgrimage to Nonviolence,"[7] we are given the impression that he was first introduced to Gandhi's concept of nonviolence while he was in seminary, that he heard a lecture on Gandhi given by Howard University president Mordecai Johnson during his senior year, and that he was forever after a committed Gandhian. In truth, all of this, except the fact that he heard Johnson's lecture on Gandhi, is misleading. We will see that Bayard Rustin of the War Resisters League and Glenn Smiley of the Fellowship of Reconciliation did much to help King to move from an ethic of self-defense to the type of nonviolence that was advocated by Gandhi. King was not a Gandhian when he arrived in Montgomery, but having met and been advised by these two men he quickly evolved as a proponent of Gandhi's ideas as he worked to devise a type of nonviolence that was more relevant to the Deep South context.

Chapter nine probes the process of actual training in nonviolence and how it evolved in King's practice, beginning with the very first informal training session near the end of the Montgomery bus boycott. We will also get a clearer sense of how important Richard Gregg's concept of *moral jiu-jitsu* was for King's doctrine and practice of nonviolence. Indeed, it may be reasonably

7. See Martin Luther King Jr., *Stride Toward Freedom* (New York: Harper & Row, 1958), ch. 6, and *Strength to Love* (New York: Harper & Row, 1963), ch. 17.

argued that what "success" there was in places like Birmingham and Selma was a result of applying moral jiu-jitsu, thus effectively knocking and keeping the likes of Police Commissioner Bull Connor and Sheriff Jim Clark off balance morally.

The final section of this book, Part 5, is comprised of one chapter (ten). It examines the question of where we go from here. By his own admission, Martin Luther King was wedded to nonviolence as the only way of living in the type of world created by the God of his faith. This God, he believed, infused the world with morality and intends that human beings live in ways that are consistent with this. For King, a world that hinges on morality works best when people behave and live nonviolently. And yet, as committed as King was to nonviolence as a way of life, one wonders why the trilogy of social problems he was so devoted to eradicating (meaning racism, militarism, and economic injustice) continue to exist long after he was assassinated. What, if any, forces did King believe created openings for hope that the United States could—indeed would—more nearly approximate the beloved community? This final chapter explores five such forces. Just how relevant is the Kingian model of nonviolent direct action in the twenty-first century? These and related questions are explored in chapter ten.

PART 1

Roots of Protest and Nonviolence in the King Family

Coretta Scott King once recalled the story that Martin Luther King Sr. (Daddy King) told her about his mother's physical retaliation against the white mill owner who beat him one day when she sent him on an errand. When he returned home in bloodied condition, Delia King commanded her son to tell her what happened. Afterward, he was instructed to not tell his father about the incident. Mrs. King knew that her husband would go after the man with his gun.

Delia King made a dangerous and potentially life-threatening decision, especially in a place like Stockbridge, Georgia during the first two decades of the twentieth century. She took her son and confronted the white man who beat him. A scuffle ensued, and according to Daddy King's account she physically took the man down to the ground, and commenced pounding him in the facial area with her fists, all the while lecturing him on what would happen if he ever put his hands on one of her children again. During the scuffle, she gave no thought to the possible consequences of her actions for she and/or members of her family. For during that period in the Deep South it was not uncommon for whites who believed they were in one way or another insulted by a black person—whether intended or not—to retaliate not only against the perceived offender, but against family members as well, including children. Delia King was not by nature a violent person. She, pure and simple, was a mother who loved her children and would go to great lengths to protect them, even if it meant risking her life and that of other family members. In such cases Delia King was not disposed to nonviolence.

As it turned out, James King did hear about the incident, and as Delia King predicted, he went after the white man with his gun. The mill owner could not be found, so King left. He later heard that a mob of white men was forming and that he was the target. Rather than return home, he went into hiding deep in the woods for about six weeks.[1]

Based on what Daddy King told her about the beating incident, Coretta King concluded that "the spirit of nonviolence was not inherited from Martin's family."[2] However, this was only a partial truth. It would have been more accurate to say that while King Jr. did not inherit the spirit of nonviolence from either his father or his paternal grandparents,[3] his mother and maternal grandparents most certainly provided a significant example of nonviolent direct action.

The three chapters in Part 1 uncover and examine some of the roots of the protest and nonviolence traditions in Martin Luther King Jr.'s family history. While nonviolence implies protest, protest does not necessarily allude to nonviolence. For protest can be of the nonviolent or violent type. Taking "protest tradition" as an umbrella term, it would be true to say that it roots deep in the family lineage of King. But as we saw above, the nonviolence tradition does not apply to both sides of his family. Historically, both sides unhesitatingly protested injustice and violations to their personhood. Without doubt, King inherited the spirit of protest from both sides of his family. However, as we will see, only the maternal side can be credited with influencing him to be nonviolent.

Like most things, it can generally be said that violence and nonviolence are learned behaviors, such that it cannot be said that John Doe was born violent, or that Jane Doe was born nonviolent. (I don't know if it's possible to have a violent or nonviolent gene or to have either in one's DNA, but in King's day this was not thought to be the case.) Martin Luther King was not

---

1. Martin Luther King Sr. with Clayton Riley, *Daddy King: An Autobiography* (New York: William Morrow, 1980), 35.

2. Coretta Scott King, *My Life with Martin Luther King, Jr.* (New York: Holt, Rinehart & Winston, 1969), 77.

3. Lewis V. Baldwin, *There Is a Balm in Gilead: The Cultural Roots of Martin Luther King, Jr.* (Minneapolis: Fortress Press, 1991), 124. Baldwin rightly calls into question Coretta King's claim that her husband inherited nothing of the nonviolent spirit from his family.

born with the propensity for one or the other of these tendencies. However, his family upbringing, church attendance, schooling, and other environmental factors were potential contributors to whether he inclined toward violence or toward nonviolence.

King's mother had a very gentle personality in comparison to the volatile temper of her husband. Having grown up in the same house with both parents, King seems to have been more influenced by his mother's temperament. She was thought to have a loving and gentle spirit and King seems to have taken after her. This is not to say that either King or his mother never got angry and blew their stack. It is to say, however, that this would have been exceptional, uncommon behavior for either of them.

The ethics of nonviolence and the determination to resist or protest injustice is central to King's theological social ethics, and to a large extent it set him apart from virtually everyone else in the United States. King did not merely write about protest and nonviolence, he lived, practiced, and baptized them in the white-hot heat of the civil rights movement. I think we learn much about Martin Luther King the human being and "drum major for justice" when we look seriously at the protest and nonviolence traditions in his family background. By so doing, we learn much about his character, that is, his capacity and will to discipline himself to work toward the achievement of a specific set of values and to stay the course, no matter what. We will see that King certainly did this as he sought the attainment of the beloved community. He made personal moral slip-ups along the way, but by and large he was totally focused on the achievement of justice for those counted among the least of these.

Martin Luther King was a human being, no more or less so than any member of his family tree, or any other human being. I happen to think that it is important to acknowledge this at the outset of any discussion on King, because failure to do so might well lead to the troublesome tendency to dismiss his many contributions toward making better persons, a better nation, and a better world when it is discovered that he made egregious moral mistakes. Many people on the religious and secular far right have a strong track record of denouncing and dismissing King's many contributions because of his perceived moral weaknesses. Failure to acknowledge King's humanity may also cause some people to claim that while they still respect his sense of commitment and his courage to do all in his power to achieve the beloved community, they have lost respect for him as a human being because of the charge of moral wrongdoing, namely, plagiarism and womanizing.

Although this is the tendency of many on the religious and secular right, curiously it is also the stance exhibited by one of the best-known, most competent King scholars, David J. Garrow, who had the equivalent of a meltdown when Clayborne Carson, Director of the King Papers Project at Stanford University, and his collaborators broke the plagiarism story in 1990. A member of the Board of Directors of the King Papers Project, Garrow claimed to have been so troubled and distraught by the discovery that King plagiarized on a persistent basis during his seminary and doctoral studies that he could no longer hold him in as high regard as he previously had, even though he claimed to have retained great appreciation and respect for his courage, commitment, and contributions to the civil and human rights struggle.[4]

Every person develops in and emerges from a specific sociocultural and family context. Martin Luther King was no different. As King's sister has written, contrary to what many seem to believe, he did not just appear. "They think that he simply happened, that he appeared fully formed, without context, ready to change the world. Take it from his big sister, that's simply not the case."[5] It stands to reason that people like King, who pursue formal intellectual studies, necessarily bring much to the classroom. Depending on the nature of one's formative influences, it might well be that he will easily resonate to certain formal intellectual ideas. I have tried to show in my previous writings on King that this is precisely what happened to him—that because of his family upbringing; because of the love and affection of his parents and maternal grandparents for each other and for the King children; because of his father's and maternal grandfather's outlook on ministry and their insistence that a minister is obligated to address the needs of the whole person; because of the liberal theological and social gospel influence of Benjamin Mays and George Kelsey at Morehouse College, in addition to the Christian realist ideas of Kelsey along with those of Walter Chivers and Samuel Williams, King was easily influenced by the social gospel teachings of Walter Rauschenbusch, the Christian realism of Reinhold Niebuhr, and the personalism of Borden P. Bowne, Edgar S. Brightman, and L. Harold DeWolf. And yet, King himself brought a lot to the table, such that we should not presume that he took everything from others, and had nothing of his own to give. He worked

4. See Rufus Burrow Jr., *God and Human Dignity: The Personalism, Theology, and Ethics of Martin Luther King, Jr.* (Notre Dame: University of Notre Dame Press, 2006), 9. See Peter Waldman, "To Their Dismay, Scholars of Martin Luther King Find Troubling Citation Pattern in Academic Papers," *Wall Street Journal*, November 9, 1990, 1.

5. Christine King Farris, *Through It All: Reflections on My Life, My Family, and My Faith* (New York: Atria, 2009), 3.

hard and diligently with others' ideas, but these were filtered through his own sociocultural, religious, and family context.

Other than in my courses on Martin Luther King, I have not—before now—written much about the protest and nonviolence roots of King's thought and practice. This first section of the book seeks, in part, to show that even though there was a period when the boy King—like many young boys—did not hesitate to settle disputes with his fists or wrestling skills, he soon grew out of this and was much more inclined to use his intellect to resolve conflicts, which also made him amenable to nonviolence. In part, this appears to have been the result of the guidance and tender care of his mother and maternal grandmother. Just as King was counseled by his mother when he was a boy, that the Christian faith required that he love the racist parents of his white friend who forbade them to play together because of their racial difference, we can be sure that Mama King, a Christian and First Lady of Ebenezer Baptist Church, continued to remind him periodically of this requirement. Indeed, Lewis Baldwin, reflecting on an interview with Philip Lenud, a boyhood friend of King, reports that King's first direct and real contact with nonviolence was through his mother who, according to Lenud, "was the strong pacifist in the family, and [King] took that from her."[6] Baldwin contends that Mama King's pacifism derived from her deep emotional and spiritual security, on which King Jr. apparently drew heavily.[7]

We will see that in one form or another Martin Luther King was exposed at home and in church to some of the basic ideas of personalism, Christian realism, the social gospel, and liberal theology. But this was not all. He also gained rudimentary knowledge about nonviolence during his formative upbringing. Moreover, he would not learn the formal names of most of the aforementioned schools of thought until he entered Crozer Theological Seminary in the fall of 1948. King's father, maternal grandfather, and teacher-mentors at Morehouse College taught and lived social gospel Christianity, took seriously the prevalence and power of sin (as stressed in Christian realism), and emphasized the idea of a personal God and the dignity of persons, as stressed in personalism and liberal theology. Thus, King could declare in his first term at Crozer, and even before he read Walter Rauschenbusch(!), that he was "a profound advocator of the social gospel."[8] After all, this was the type of ministry done by his father and maternal grandfather, as well as other black Atlanta

6. Baldwin, *There Is a Balm*, 123.

7. Ibid.

8. Clayborne Carson, ed., *The Autobiography of Martin Luther King, Jr.* (New York: Warner Books, 1998), 19.

ministers with whom King was acquainted when he was a boy, such as William Holmes Borders. In addition, we will see that King likely got his first formal introduction to Gandhian nonviolence not at the predominantly white Crozer Theological Seminary, but through Benjamin E. Mays's Tuesday chapel talks at Morehouse College. The idea of nonviolence as the most reasonable and Christian way to resolve conflicts was instilled in King by his mother, with the support of his maternal grandmother. This we may refer to as his *homespun* sense of nonviolence.

In my work and teaching on King I assume his humanity, with all of the strengths and weaknesses thereto pertaining. King was a human being, pure and simple. By his own admission, he was, in this sense, as much a sinner as anybody else. His aim was not to be perfect, nor to be a saint—for these were impossible in any case—and nothing I shall say will in any way be aimed at making him out to be otherwise. Perhaps like Gandhi, King also believed that the word *saint* should not even be part of the human vocabulary. The limitations and weaknesses of human beings are such that the word "is too sacred . . . to be lightly applied" to human beings, said Gandhi.[9] Martin Luther King sought only "to be a good man,"[10] to be faithful to his God, and to be a drum major for justice and righteousness.[11] When it is remembered that he was first and last a human being, it should not be difficult for the thinking person to concur with those who conclude that notwithstanding his moral shortcomings, Martin Luther King was indeed faithful to his people and to his God to the very end.

What do we learn about Martin Luther King Jr.'s commitment to protesting injustice, and doing so nonviolently, when we examine his family roots? When we look at the contributions of some of the key members of King's family tree he comes alive to us in new ways. We get a better sense of why he was the person he was, and why, despite his shortcomings and limitations, he remained faithful right up to the moment that a 30.06 slug from a high-powered rifle ended his life. Were there attributes of his grandfathers, grandmothers, and parents that made him more susceptible to being influenced by certain of the formal intellectual ideas he was exposed to at Morehouse College, Crozer Theological Seminary, and Boston University? Do we at least see evidence of some of these ideas in members of his family tree? Are there

9. M. K. Gandhi, "Neither a Saint Nor a Politician," in *In Search of the Supreme* in three volumes compiled and edited by V. B. Kher (Ahmedabad: Navajivan, 1961), II:241.

10. Martin Luther King Jr., "Unfulfilled Dreams," in *A Knock at Midnight*, ed. Clayborne Carson and Peter Holloran (New York: Warner Books, 1998), 198.

11. See David Garrow, *Bearing the Cross: Martin Luther King, Jr., and the Southern Christian Leadership Conference* (New York: William Morrow, 1986), 555.

particular attributes of King's grandparents and parents that are revealed in his own personhood and public work? Do we find roots of his personalism, social gospel Christianity, and Christian realism in his grandparents and parents? Do we find evidence of these in his teachers at Morehouse? Or is it the case that he was first introduced to the ideas represented in these doctrines by his white seminary and graduate school professors?

Indeed, can it be reasonably argued that King was not influenced by the philosophy of personalism to any significant degree, as Garrow, David Chappell, and Keith D. Miller[12] seem to imply, or that it is the influence of Reinhold Niebuhr's Christian realism that stands out most in King's theology and social activism,[13] and not personalism, as Chappell contends? Or is it more plausible to say that King was much influenced by aspects of both schools of thought as well as others, although his basic philosophical stance was personal idealism or personalism? In any case, a consideration of some of the key personalities in King's family tree will shed some light on these and related questions, as well as the spirit and practice of protest and nonviolence that were at the center of King's adult life. What do we learn about such matters through an examination of contributions of his grandparents and parents? This is the focus of the three chapters in Part 1.

12. See David Garrow, *Martin Luther King, Jr., and the Civil Rights Movement* (New York: Carlson, 1989), I:xiv; David L. Chappell, *A Stone of Hope: Prophetic Religion and the Death of Jim Crow* (Chapel Hill/London: University of North Carolina Press, 2004), 53, 54, 222n32; and Keith D. Miller, *Voice of Deliverance: The Language of Martin Luther King, Jr. and Its Sources* (New York: Free Press, 1992), 7, 17.

13. This is a position advocated by David L. Chappell in his *A Stone of Hope: Prophetic Religion and the Death of Jim Crow* (Chapel Hill and London: University of North Carolina Press, 2004).

1

———

Paternal Grandparents

JAMES ALBERT KING

Martin Luther King Jr.'s paternal grandfather, James Albert King (1864–1933), was the son of an enslaved Afrikan, and was himself a sharecropper in Stockbridge, Georgia. The white plantation owner and landlord, whose name was Graves, provided James King's family with many of the necessities for survival, although those provisions came at a very high price. That is, they were supplied in a way that King would always be financially indebted to the plantation owner. Indeed, he would find himself deeper in debt at the end of each year. Graves did not hesitate to take advantage of the illiterate sharecropper. In theory, James King was to receive 50 percent of the earnings when all of his crops were harvested. However, he had no mathematical skills and could not read and write. Because the landlord was dishonest and racist, King slipped deeper and deeper into indebtedness to him and was simply not able to see his way to financial freedom. After all, it was Graves who did all of the computations and kept the records. What the owner said was owed at the end of the year, then, could not be disputed by King.

James King was likely born in Ohio according to the 1900 census. His father was of Irish Afrikan descent, and his mother was born in Pennsylvania. Historian and Director of the King Papers Project Clayborne Carson, at Stanford University, cautions us that much of the available information regarding the lineage of James Albert King is contradictory.[1] This is not unusual for the period of time in question, since public officials made little effort to retain accurate records of birth, marriage, and death dates, as well as other pertinent information about Afrikan Americans.

Christine King Farris described her paternal grandfather as "a lean, tough man . . ."[2] In his younger years, James King was a relentless and hard worker

---

1. Clayborne Carson et al., eds., *The Papers of Martin Luther King, Jr.* (Berkeley: University of California Press, 1992), 1:19n61.

who dreamed of buying a house and some land for his family. He initially worked in a Stockbridge rock quarry, until he lost part of his right hand in an explosion.[3] This led him, like so many blacks, to seek work as a sharecropper on a plantation. It did not take him long to realize, however, that the racism and dishonesty of the plantation owner made his an impossible dream at best. It was not long before he began to feel a sense of helplessness and hopelessness, the likes of which poor whites of his day could not begin to imagine. Many of them suffered the same sense of helplessness and hopelessness as blacks, but they did not have to contend with the devastatingly destructive force of racism and racial discrimination. James King's sense of worth as a human being slowly faded as he did what so many black men of his day did, in his predicament. He slowly turned to heavy, almost continuous drinking, as if this would somehow wipe away all his troubles and make possible the realization of his dreams. He was in a rut, and his drinking only made it more difficult for him to extricate himself. Unlike his wife, Delia, James King found no comfort, no solace in religion. Rather, whiskey was his opiate.

King Jr.'s paternal grandfather was but one of hundreds of poor southern blacks who worked from sunup to sundown almost every single day of their lives, but had absolutely nothing to show for their labors except hard times, increasing indebtedness to the plantation owner, internalized rage, depression, and alcohol abuse that inevitably led to spousal and child abuse. There seemingly was no other outlet for the internalized rage and self-hatred, since to act out against the true cause of this would be met with maximum violence, terror, and retribution by white racists and the racist system that benefited and was controlled by whites. Unable to lash out against the real perpetrators who caused his rage, James King turned his violence on himself (through the misuse of alcohol), his wife, and his children.

There is no question that King Jr. was aware of the dilemma faced by his grandfather and countless blacks like him. The "natural" thing for one to do when verbally, physically, psychologically, emotionally, or otherwise assaulted is to retaliate in some way against the perpetrator. However, when the perpetrator has put into place an entire system that is undergirded by acts of terrorism and a legal system that defends against such retaliation, it would seem that the "sensible" thing is to internalize one's anger, frustration, and rage and lash out against safe targets, that is, those less likely to retaliate, such as one's spouse and/or children. Farris comments on this aspect of her grandfather's life:

2. Christine King Farris, *Through It All: Reflections on My Life, My Family, and My Faith* (New York: Atria, 2009), 13.

3. Ibid.

There were nights when, returning home after being marginalized and exploited all day, he would pick fights with his oldest son, my father. Some of these confrontations lasted until well into the night. He'd often fall asleep on the kitchen floor with a bottle inside his hat near his head. Incredibly, the mornings following these tirades were often filled with the jokes and laughter of a conflicted father trying to love and provide for his family. The family, in turn, naturally lived on edge. They knew nightfall was likely to bring more of the violence and the unknown to which they had grown accustomed.[4]

Although clearly against the idea of blacks retaliating violently against whites, many years later King Jr. expressed strong concern about black-against-black violence and a major cause of it: "By turning his hostility and frustration with the larger society inward, the Negro often inflicts terrible acts of violence on his own black brother."[5] In a more extended comment about this tragic phenomenon, focusing primarily on the black male, King said:

> The rage and torment of the Negro male were frequently turned inward because if it gained outward expression its consequences would have been fatal. He became resigned to hopelessness and he communicated this to his children. Some, unable to contain the emotional storms, struck out at those who would be less likely to destroy them. He beat his wife and his children in order to protest a social injustice, and the tragedy was that none of them understood why the violence exploded.[6]

Were King alive today, and adhered to the same ideas and ideals, he most surely would acknowledge that this internalized rage is a driving force in the tragic phenomenon of intracommunity violence and homicide among large numbers of young black males, a phenomenon that I discuss more fully in chapter ten. What is important for our purpose, however, is that King Jr. was aware of the tragic dilemma experienced by his grandfather and vast numbers of black men. However, we will see momentarily that there was one situation in which both James King and his wife did not hesitate to give violent response to white people.

4. Ibid.

5. Martin Luther King Jr., *Where Do We Go from Here: Chaos or Community?* (Boston: Beacon, 1967), 64.

6. Quoted in Lewis V. Baldwin, *There Is a Balm in Gilead: The Cultural Roots of Martin Luther King, Jr.* (Minneapolis: Fortress Press, 1991), 96–97.

James King was vigilant in his efforts to curtail his annual expenses. He and his wife were constantly cutting back, and still they would end up owing the plantation owner hundreds of dollars at year's end. It actually seemed to James King that he was working merely for the "privilege" of having a low-paying, dead-end job. To be sure, King had a job, but it came nowhere close to providing a living wage, and thus was not meaningful employment. It was very hard to see or feel a sense of dignity about such labor.

It is quite likely that James King's famous grandson was later influenced by what Daddy King most certainly told him about his father's experience as a sharecropper, for as a civil rights activist King Jr. was a strong supporter of labor, and on numerous occasions insisted on the dignity of all labor. In a speech to Local 199 National Union of Hospital and Health Care Employees in New York City in March 1968, King said that "no labor is really menial unless you're not getting adequate wages. . . . if you're getting a good wage . . . that isn't menial labor. What makes it menial is the income, the wages."[7] A week later, he told the American Federation of State, County and Municipal Employees (AFSCME) in Memphis, that "whenever you are engaged in work that serves humanity and is for the building of humanity, it has dignity, and it has worth."[8] By this definition it can be said that the dignity of James King's labor was held hostage by the plantation owner. King got little to no satisfaction from his labor, in part because much of its value was systematically stolen by the white plantation owner, thus making it impossible for him to adequately provide for his family. He had no sense of pride in his job, and therefore possessed no sense of dignity toward it. Nor did the job enable him to feel a sense of worth.

Although poverty was not Martin Luther King Jr.'s personal experience, it was the experience of his father and paternal grandparents on the plantation that gave him his first sense of the depth and impact of both poverty and economic injustice. There must have been times when King Jr. thought about this, for years later he devoted his adult life to fighting for decent jobs and a living wage for blacks and other poor people. Moreover, it is quite likely that knowledge of his father's and grandfather's poverty helped him to avoid classism, and to be critical of the classism he witnessed within the black community and church.[9]

King Jr. insisted that dignity should be inherent in work, and that a job should serve to lift one's sense of dignity to a respectable level. The problem,

7. King, "The Other America," in *All Labor Has Dignity*, ed. Michael K. Honey (Boston: Beacon, 2011), 158, 159.

8. King, "All Labor Has Dignity," in *All Labor Has Dignity*, ed. Honey, 171.

9. King, "The American Dream," in *A Knock at Midnight*, ed. Clayborne Carson and Peter Holloran (New York: Warner Books, 1998), 92–93.

as King Jr. saw it, was that far too many people were being forced to work dead-end jobs. Such jobs did not provide a living wage. To this extent they were jobs that were unable to lift or enhance the worker's sense of dignity. This was the experience of his paternal grandfather, an experience that was not lost on King Jr. as he fought—especially in the last three years of his life—to eradicate economic injustice in this country and throughout the world. Furthermore, although the basic material needs of his own family were met, King Jr. witnessed deadening poverty and bread lines while growing up in Atlanta. His experience of this, as well as his awareness of the poverty of James King's family, might well have had something to do with his early conviction in seminary that one of the three social problems he would address throughout his ministry would be economic injustice and poverty. This was an issue that remained close to King Jr. Nothing dramatized his concern about this problem like the impending Poor People's Campaign in 1968 that he did not live to lead.

King Jr. would have characterized his grandfather as one of the millions of "working poor" in this country. Such people work, often very hard every day, but for wages that do not come close to meeting their basic needs. This is what 2012 conservative presidential candidate Mitt Romney and others on the far right were so blindly and conveniently unaware of, and Romney actually pontificated about how hard he and his father worked to amass and secure their massive wealth. Romney implied that in a capitalistic economy virtually anyone can achieve such wealth and financial security if they would only work hard enough. Martin Luther King Jr. was very well aware that tens of millions of people in this country worked hard every day of their adult life but had nothing of a material nature to show for it when they retired or died. In this regard, he told members of AFSCME, in Memphis, Tennessee in 1968, that such people "are making wages so low that they cannot begin to function in the mainstream of the economic life of our nation."[10] Perhaps it was knowledge of his paternal grandparents' poverty that helped to sensitize King to the plight of the impoverished and those who worked full time but received poverty wages. King Jr. and his grandfather did not complain about labor as such. Labor, King argued, is menial only when the wages are inadequate.

James Albert King and Delia King were the parents of ten children, one of whom (Lucius) died in infancy. The others included five daughters, Woodie, Cleo, Lenora, Lucille, and Ruby, and four sons, Mike, James, Henry, and Joel. "Mike" (Daddy King) was born on December 19, 1899. Census records suggest, however, that he was more likely born two years earlier.[11] He was the second

10. King, "All Labor Has Dignity," 172.
11. *The Papers*, 1:21n63.

born, and the first son born to his parents. There was parental disagreement over what to name the child. Daddy King would say later that his mother wanted to name him Michael, after the archangel. His father, on the other hand, wanted to name him after his two brothers, Martin and Luther.[12] A compromise was reached, and he was called "Mike." Daddy King reported that his father made a deathbed request that he change his name officially to Martin Luther. This was in 1933. He wrote about the incident in his autobiography: "I'd never had a birth certificate. They weren't common around the turn of the century in places like Stockbridge, Georgia. During his last hours, Papa asked me to make my name officially what he said it was. . . . When he was gone I took out the necessary legal papers and was therefore called Martin Luther King Sr. And little Mike became M. L. to his family. . . ."[13] But there is some confusion around the renaming of Daddy King and King Jr.

According to Taylor Branch, the name change occurred when King Jr. was five years old, and after Daddy King returned from a trip to Europe and the Middle East in the summer of 1934.[14] Although Daddy King refers to this trip in his autobiography, he did not state whether the name change occurred before or after the trip abroad.[15] Branch reports that State Department records reveal that a birth certificate filed on April 12, 1934 for King Jr. listed his name as Martin Luther King Jr.[16] Were this the case, it means that Daddy King made the name changes prior to his trip abroad during the summer of 1934, or shortly after his return to the States. This is consistent with his claim that while his father was on his deathbed in 1933, he asked him to officially change his name to Martin Luther, which he did, not long after James King died.

Branch, however, is not quite comfortable with Daddy King's explanation. Recalling that there was a stormy relationship between James King and his son, Branch questions the plausibility of Daddy King's account of the name change, although he agrees that his story "has the advantage of eliminating the ten-year delay and the hospital mix-ups. . . ."[17] Since Daddy King was much closer to his mother, who preferred "Michael," Branch argues that it is more reasonable

12. Martin Luther King Sr. with Clayton Riley, *Daddy King: An Autobiography* (New York: William Morrow, 1980), 26. Christine King Farris contends that at birth her father was actually "named Martin after one uncle and Luther after another." Daddy King reportedly told her that this is what James King told him. See Farris, *Through It All*, 21.

13. King Sr., *Daddy King*, 88.

14. Taylor Branch, *Parting the Waters: America in the King Years, 1954-63* (New York: Simon & Schuster, 1988), 44–47.

15. King Sr., *Daddy King*, 97–98.

16. Branch, *Parting the Waters*, 47.

17. Ibid., 46.

that he would not have favored his father's deathbed request. After all, there had been a turbulent relationship between father and son, a point I return to momentarily.

I am inclined to challenge Branch's conclusion regarding the name change. Branch, it seems to me, overlooks one very important point here. Although it is true that Daddy King got angry over his father's heavy drinking, and once fought physically with his father in an attempt to keep him from beating his mother while he was in a drunken state, he never forgave himself for wrestling with his father and literally taking him down to the floor and holding him there. It was the only way to keep his father from hurting his mother, and yet for having done this his conscience nearly ate him alive. For through his mother he had been reared in the southern black Baptist church tradition, which required that children always honor, obey, and respect their parents. Indeed, Daddy King himself recalled how he agonized over having fought with his father,[18] for he was tormented by the verse: "Honor thy father and thy mother" (Exod. 20:12).

It is reasonable to surmise that as Daddy King matured, he understood more clearly that his father was simply trapped and defeated by racism and racial discrimination, and that he was really a much better man than he was able to exhibit under the constant violent force of racism, dehumanizing poverty, and whites' denial of his personhood. Racism destroyed both of his parents—his father more so in some ways, since he was not, like Delia King, anchored in the church. In any event, knowing how his father suffered, and having felt that he took something from James King when he fought with him to keep him from beating his mother, it is not unreasonable that Daddy King would seriously consider honoring his father's deathbed request that he change his name to Martin Luther. For in the end, Daddy King's problem was less with his father, than with the racism that took its toll on both of his parents and made theirs a miserable life.[19] Without question, there was a stormy relationship between father and son, which might suggest to one outside the black community (such as Branch) that the son did not possess enough love and respect for his alcoholic, abusive father to honor his deathbed request to change his name to Martin Luther. Nevertheless, it is reasonable to suggest that Daddy King came to understand that James King's drinking and abusiveness had less to do with him than with the racism that demeaned and crushed, and indeed killed his dreams. Moreover, by his own admission, Daddy King loved his father, a point that he made nearly fifty years after his death in 1933. Acknowledging the difficulties

18. King Sr., *Daddy King*, 47, 49.

19. Ibid., 74–75.

he and his father had that "far outweighed the things that made us father and son," Daddy King went on to say:

> *Still, I loved him.* Not in the demonstrative way some sons can show their fathers, with a lot of attention, a lot of time spent together. That is the way some people can express affection. I knew that James King was a man who wanted more than he could ever have. And what he wanted wasn't really that much—a decent home for his family, a day's pay for a day's work, the freedom to be judged as a human being and not a beast, a nigger, a nightmare in the white mind. But for him, these things were never to happen. *Maybe tomorrow, just maybe*—Papa must have thought that so many, many times. And every time he did, it had to cut through his soul—the fact that, for no reason that could ever make sense, he would not live to see, to feel, to *be* a part of that new day.[20]

I think that Daddy King's explanation is difficult for most whites to grasp and understand, but in the end they don't have to—blacks do. Branch drew the easy conclusion that because of the strained relationship between Daddy King and his father, it is unreasonable to conclude that he honored his father's deathbed request. Unlike whites, Daddy King, like his father, carried the heavy weight of the consequences and burden of racism on his shoulders every moment of his life, and he knew how destructive this was to black lives. Moreover, he knew that much of his father's abusive behavior was derivative, the result of racism and a cruel sharecropping system. This is why he could say: "Still, I loved him." Daddy King respected his father for the man he knew he could be in a racism-free society where the playing field was level.

I grew up in an abusive household where alcohol dependency and abuse ultimately killed my father, but not before long years of spousal abuse and family neglect had occurred. Although I never fought physically with my father, there came a time when he understood—as I suspect all men do who have sons—that he and his oldest of five sons would indeed fight if he continued to physically abuse my mother. Naturally I would get angry with and disappointed in my father when he drank heavily and behaved in an abusive manner. And yet, I never hated, disrespected, or dishonored him to the extent that I would not have given him the world on a silver platter if I had it to give. For like Daddy King, I knew the giant of a man that was my father during his sober moments when he could be witty, and playful, and concerned about the well-

20. Ibid., 58–59 (my italics).

being of his family. I knew of his dreams of a better life. Indeed, I understood that racism and racial discrimination drove him to drink as he did, and once he became dependent on the alcohol drug he was not able to liberate himself from it. Just as racism ultimately killed James Albert King—and Daddy King knew it—I have no doubt that racism was also a key factor in my father's death at the tender age of forty-seven. No matter how turbulent my relationship with my father, I would have honored any reasonable deathbed request had he made one. Knowing what I know about dozens of black males' stormy relationship with their fathers and their deep love and respect for the person they believed their fathers could be given a real chance in this country, I am confident that Daddy King did indeed honor his father's deathbed request to change his name to Martin Luther. I therefore part company with Taylor Branch on this matter.

James King may have been a drunk who abused his family, but on "good" days when he was sober he exhibited his deep love for his family and would do everything in his power to provide for and protect them. Daddy King recalled a case in point. There was an incident involving an encounter between James King and the plantation owner for whom he sharecropped. When it was time for King to be paid for his crop, his son spoke up and said that his father was being cheated. This was against the senior King's earlier directive that he be silent during the transaction. But when the owner threatened to do bodily harm to the boy, James King looked him in the eyes and without flinching said: "Don't nobody touch my boy, Mr. Graves. Anything need to be done to him, I'll take care of it."[21] Daddy King recalled that his father did not back down. What this tells us—in addition to the fact that James King loved his son—is that King Jr.'s paternal grandfather was steeped in the resistance or social protest tradition. Later, we will see that James King was not averse to resisting violently if whites harmed his children.

DELIA LINDSAY KING

Because of Daddy King's close relationship with his mother, it is surprising that Christine King Farris says very little about her in her memoir. Farris tells us who her paternal grandmother was, where and when she was born, who her paternal great-grandparents were, where and when her grandmother was married, and the names of her children.[22] She tells us nothing of her grandmother's trials, hopes, faith, how she and her children related (especially Daddy King), and what type of relationship she had with her husband. This omission is odd

21. Ibid., 41.
22. Farris, *Through It All*, 12–13.

considering the very close relationship that Daddy King had with his mother, in comparison to his father. Surely Daddy King told his children about their paternal grandmother, the woman he knew to possess such deep religious faith, and who taught her children not to hate, even the white people who went out of their way to make life miserable for them.

Delia King's father, Jim Long (c. 1842–?), was forced by the white enslaver to be a breeder of children. He was what was known as a stud. He found himself the father of two sets of children. Long's relationship with Jane Lindsay (1855–?) led to the birth of Delia Lindsay (1875–1924) in Henry County, Georgia, who would marry James Albert King in Stockbridge, Georgia on August 20, 1895. Having been raised in a farm family, she was a very hard worker before and after her marriage. After setting up housekeeping, the couple sharecropped cotton. However, we have seen that they were always cheated out of a large percentage of their wages by the owner. This made it virtually impossible for them to get out of their financial indebtedness to him. In addition, Delia King's earnings as a domestic worker were grossly inadequate.

The paternal grandmother of Martin Luther King Jr., Delia King was a woman of deep religious faith who lived by the conviction that God would provide; indeed, would make a way out of no way. Hers was the God who is able, the God that her famous grandson would preach about many years later. When King Jr. preached the sermon, "Our God Is Able," one wonders whether he might have thought about, even been influenced in some way, by the knowledge that this was a staunch belief of his paternal grandmother.[23] Come what may, God is able.

At any rate, Delia King's religious faith offered her and her children at least a modicum of relief amid the hardships of racism, sharecropping, domestic work, and spousal abuse. "Although the family occasionally attended a local Methodist as well as the Baptist church, they established enduring ties with Floyd Chapel Baptist Church in Stockbridge. Its Sunday services, Wednesday prayer meetings, baptisms, weddings, funerals, and special Christmas and Easter services offered welcome diversions."[24] Delia King's faith in God enabled her to be "at peace with herself," said Daddy King. In this, she possessed a kind of spiritual and emotional security and peace of mind that eluded James King. "God's wisdom was the guide in Mama's life," Daddy King said, "and even in her times of great suffering, which came so many times in her life, she never lost sight of the Lord. No tears could blind her to His presence, and she could

---

23. See Martin Luther King Jr., "Our God Is Able," in his *Strength to Love* (New York: Harper & Row, 1963), ch. 13. King preached an earlier version of this sermon during the Montgomery bus boycott.

24. *The Papers*, 1:21.

not close her eyes so tight in sorrow or in rage that she did not see God's hand reaching out to her. In the worst years, she never surrendered to self-pity or doubt."[25] Daddy King loved his mother and wanted a much better life for her, materially, as well as a life without the hardships of racial hatred and segregation.

It was truly a marvel to Daddy King that his mother managed to retain her dignity and sanity while raising her nine surviving children, working the cotton fields for a pittance, and doing domestic work in the homes of white people who persistently underpaid her. Delia King always assured her son that God gave her the strength and the will to do the things she needed to do. Her God was able. Indeed, even she was "so able, so strong," said Daddy King, because God made her so. What angered young King was that his mother worked as hard as she did, for as long as she did, but without reaping any of the material benefits of all her labors and sacrifices. "Something was wrong, I knew," said Daddy King, "when someone who tried so hard, who kept her faith, and who provided so much of a sense of the righteous path for all her children, come away, finally, with so little for herself."[26] This memory and the anger that arose from it likely contributed to his later determination to acquire a piece of the American pie for his own family. So incensed was Daddy King about how his mother suffered, and other manifestations of racism when he was a teenager, that he vowed to hate all white people, just as King Jr. would vow to do when he was a young boy of about six years of age.[27]

Since blacks were thought by most whites to be less than human, and according to Chief Justice Roger B. Taney's majority opinion in *Dred Scott v. Sanford* (1857), were thought to have no rights that the white man was legally bound to respect,[28] James King became increasingly bitter and enraged, frequently taking it out on his undeserving wife and children. This scenario obviously weighed heavily on Delia King, who essentially had to shoulder

25. King Sr., *Daddy King*, 25.

26. Ibid., 26.

27. See ibid., 74, and King Jr., *Stride Toward Freedom* (New York: Harper & Row, 1958), 90.

28. In a most provocative statement, Taney wrote of enslaved blacks: "They had for more than a century before been regarded as beings of an inferior order; and altogether unfit to associate with the white race, either in social or political relations; and so far inferior that they had no rights which the white man was bound to respect; and that the negro might justly and lawfully be reduced to slavery for his benefit. . . . This opinion was at that time fixed and universal in the civilized portion of the white race" (*Documenting Our Past 1492-1974*, ed. Robert C. Baron [Golden, CO: Fulcrum, 1989], 239). Martin Luther King observed that the Court's ruling made clear how it viewed blacks and their status. Essentially the Court declared "that the Negro was not a citizen of the United States, but that he was properly subject to the dictates of his owner" (*The Papers* [2007], 6:509).

much of the responsibility for keeping the family together and making a way out of no way. Although she loved her children dearly, Delia King was a strict disciplinarian as well. She expected her children to be mindful at all times of the values instilled in them and to obey her whether they were in her presence or not. There would be consequences for being deceitful or otherwise misbehaving. Daddy King recalled an incident that reminded him in no uncertain terms that his mother meant business.

At the age of fourteen, Daddy King's physical stature was such that he was able to lie about his age in order to obtain employment at the local rail yard. He knew how desperately poor the family was, especially how difficult it was for his mother to make ends meet. He saw an opportunity to make a large sum of money that would ease his mother's burden. He worked the job for only a few days before his mother found out. When she did she marched down to the rail yard, terminated his employment on the spot, refused to allow him to be paid the considerable sum of money he had already earned, scolded him in the presence of the other workers and the supervisor, and then marched him home.[29] Although thoroughly embarrassed and humiliated, Daddy King said that he realized there was nothing he could do about it, "because it was Mama, and I'd been raised to respect anything she said to me or asked me to do."[30] His mother had instilled in him and his siblings the value of honesty, as well as the sense that children should obey their parents and seek their permission to engage in activities (such as employment) outside the home.

Although Daddy King recalled that it rarely manifested itself, Delia King did in fact possess a temper. Unlike her husband, it was usually deep within her and generally kept at bay. It really took a major event of some sort to upset his mother enough to cause her to lose her temper. Whenever this happened, Daddy King recalled, it usually meant big trouble for the one who caused her to lose control.

By all accounts Delia King, not unlike her husband, was very protective of her children and did not hesitate to let this be known, even to white people in rural Stockbridge. This is a crucial point inasmuch as it reveals the importance on both sides of King Jr.'s family of fighting to preserve and enhance one's dignity, even though James and Delia King were at best only pragmatic nonviolent resisters of social evil. That is, they were nonviolent as long as the desired results were achieved. However, when it came to her children Delia King's response was not always of the nonviolent type. She was not only in touch with her own sense of self and dignity, but was willing to

29. King Sr., *Daddy King*, 52–53.
30. Ibid., 53.

do whatever she believed was necessary to defend it. In addition, she strove to instill in her children this same sense of self and dignity, as well as the determination and courage to stand up for themselves when being disrespected and otherwise violated by others. We will see later that Daddy King would instill this same attribute in his children.

Much has been written about the spirit of racial uplift and protest that was exhibited by the father and maternal grandfather of King Jr. and the fact that he was heir to this tradition. We now know that this same spirit of protest was exhibited in Delia and James King, even if there was no obvious religious foundation as in the case of A. D. Williams, and later, Daddy King. Delia and James King were not opposed to violence if they believed their children to be in harm's way. As we saw in the case of James King, it did not matter that white people were the culprits, which means that he was willing, just as his wife, to risk life and limb to protect his children, which was also a means of asserting his own humanity and manhood.

This chapter opened with the reference to Coretta Scott King's recollection of the story Daddy King told her about his mother's fight with the white man who beat him. When he was around twelve years of age, he was severely beaten by the local sawmill owner when he was returning from an errand for his mother. When he arrived home, bloodied and disheveled, and told his mother what had happened, Delia King was furious. Apparently, the mill owner ordered him to fetch a bucket of water for his workers, and when he said that he could not do so because he was on an errand for his mother, the man grabbed him and began beating him. His refusal to do what the white man commanded was a violation of Deep South racial etiquette. According to the custom of that period, blacks were, at the command of whites, to stop immediately what they were doing in order to comply with whatever was being commanded of them. Delia King took her son and confronted the mill owner. His attempt to intimidate her failed. Daddy King recounted the incident in his Autobiography.

> I had never seen my mother move so quickly. She leaped at this man, dug her shoulder into his middle and knocked him back against the side of the mill shed. My mother had worked all of her life, she was powerfully built and had the strength of any man. The mill owner was shocked. He tried to grab hold of her, but she tripped him up and he fell to the ground. Oh, Lord, what did he do that for? Mama jumped down on him, pounding away at his face. Some of the mill hands tried to get her off the man, but she punched one of them right

in his mouth so hard he spun around and stumbled back, looking as if he'd never been hit that hard in his life. The mill owner pushed and turned, but he couldn't get Mama off him. She raised up and brought both her fists down across his nose, and blood spurted out of his face all over the ground. Then she got up. The other men had moved back a little. She stared at them. Her eyes were like coals blazing out of their sockets.

"You can kill me!" she shouted. "But if you put a hand on a child of mine, you'll answer."[31]

This was a very dangerous act on the part of Delia King, for in those days blacks were beaten and/or lynched for much less than an act of retaliation against a white person, whether in defense of self or one's child. Delia King's action should dispel any tendency to think that the spirit of nonviolence was pervasive in King Jr.'s family background. This is the incident that Coretta King was remembering when she said that King Jr.'s nonviolent spirit was not inherited from his family. However, we must be precise, for the nonviolent spirit was indeed present in his family history, but on the maternal side, a point that Coretta King did not know at the time. King Jr.'s maternal grandfather, for example, was always ready to protest and resist social injustices, although he did so nonviolently through church efforts, the NAACP, other organized groups such as the Georgia Equal Rights League, and through nonviolent direct action. I return to this in the next chapter.

In addition to standing up for her own humanity and dignity, and that of her children when they were mistreated by whites, Delia King also exhibited in her own home what present-day *womanist* thinkers and activists characterize as "sass," that is, the spirit of self-determination; of being in charge; of being responsible, thinking her own thoughts, and speaking in her own voice.[32] This is easily illustrated in the case of Delia King. On one occasion James King had been out drinking heavily and returned home intoxicated and with a large fish. Mrs. King was already preparing dinner when he demanded that she cook the fish for him "right now." Continuing her work over the stove, she looked him square in the eyes and said with authority that she was already preparing dinner. He could see in her eyes that she was not going to cook the fish that evening.[33]

31. Ibid., 34.

32. See Alice Walker's characterization of *womanist* in her *In Search of Our Mothers' Gardens* (New York: Harcourt Brace Jovanovich, 1983), xi–xii. The entire book is a collection of womanist prose, and fleshes out the meaning of "womanist," 3–393.

33. King Sr., *Daddy King*, 46.

She had behaved in a very *womanish, grown-up, self-determined* fashion. The consequence of her action that evening was the fight that ensued, with Daddy King overpowering his father, wrestling him to the floor, and telling him that he would not allow him to beat his mother.[34]

Not unlike her husband, Delia King was unable to read and write, but like many black parents in the Deep South she had a strong sense of the value of education for her children. James King did not share this sense of the importance of education, but he had a strong sense of the importance of economic security and frugality, even though he had no money. However, these were traits that would be influential to his oldest son, who, by example and verbal instruction, would instill them in his own children.

Daddy King remained on the Stockbridge plantation until the age of sixteen before he finally reached the point that he simply could no longer live with sharecropping and the dehumanizing practices that came with it. He despised the fact that his father was daily being cheated and used by the plantation owner and being driven ever deeper into indebtedness to him. He loathed the idea of his mother having to pick cotton and then go to work as a domestic in the home of a racist white family. He wanted a better life for himself. Furthermore, his relationship with his father was strained to the point that he saw no way that he could remain in his house and continue to respect him, even though he continued to love him. He understood that much that happened to his father and so many others like him was not entirely his fault; that racism and racial discrimination were the chief culprits. The young man therefore packed his meager belongings and headed for Atlanta, Georgia.

I now turn to a consideration of Adam Daniel and Jennie Celeste Williams, King's maternal grandparents. What were their contributions to the protest and nonviolence traditions in their grandson's family history?

---

34. Ibid., 46–47.

2

Maternal Grandparents

ADAM DANIEL WILLIAMS

Adam Daniel Williams (1863–1931) was King Jr.'s maternal grandfather.[1] A. D.'s father, Willis Williams (1810–1874), was an old-time enslaved preacher (or "exhorter" as they were called in those days) who joined Shiloh Baptist Church (1846) in Penfield, Georgia nearly 100 miles east of Atlanta. This means that King Jr. was the son, grandson, and great-grandson of Baptist preachers. A. D.'s mother was Lucrecia Daniel, who was called Creecy (1840–?). Her husband was thirty years her senior.[2] The couple gave birth to five children. Their granddaughter, Christine King Farris, observes that prior to the Civil War her paternal great grandparents attended Shiloh Baptist Church together. Willis,

---

1. Lewis V. Baldwin mistakenly refers to Williams as Alfred D., and states that King's brother was named Alfred D. after him. See Baldwin, *There Is a Balm in Gilead: The Cultural Roots of Martin Luther King, Jr.* (Minneapolis: Fortress Press, 1991), 94, 102, 160. James Cone errs similarly in *Martin & Malcolm & America* (Maryknoll, NY: Orbis, 1991), 20. Coretta Scott King names the maternal grandfather Adam Daniel in *My Life with Martin Luther King, Jr.* (New York: Holt, Rinehart & Winston, 1969), 78. Volume one of *The Papers of Martin Luther King, Jr.* agrees (1:3), as does David Collins in *Not Only Dreamers* (Elgin, IL: Brethren, 1986), 45; L. D. Reddick, *Crusader without Violence* (New York: Harper, 1959), 49; David L. Lewis, *King: A Biography* (Urbana: University of Illinois Press, 1970), 4–5. Stephen B. Oates concurs, and rightly states that King's brother was only "partly" named after his maternal grandfather (*Let the Trumpet Sound: A Life of Martin Luther King, Jr.* [New York: Harper, 1994], 7). In my query about the discrepancy in King's maternal grandfather's name on September 30, 2009, Baldwin responded in an email on October 1: "I must admit that you are right and we (Cone and I) are wrong. I discovered the mistake some time ago, and said I would correct it when I revise *There Is a Balm*. Although both were called A. D., the grandfather was Adam and the grandson Alfred." Also of note, Clayborne Carson reminds us that A. D. Williams never knew his exact date of birth, "but he chose to celebrate it as January 2, 1863, the day after the Emancipation Proclamation became effective" (Carson, *Martin's Dream: My Journey and the Legacy of Martin Luther King, Jr.* [New York: Palgrave Macmillan, 2013], 141).

2. Christine King Farris, *Through It All: Reflections on My Life, My Family, and My Faith* (New York: Atria, 2009), 4.

along with his wife, actually joined that church before his "owner," William N. Williams. Farris notes the irony of this latter reference: "concurrent Christian church membership and simultaneous slave ownership."[3] In any event, for its time and location in the Deep South, Shiloh Baptist Church was fairly progressive in the sense that the enslaved blacks were full members just as the whites.[4] Unlike King Jr.'s paternal grandmother, who sometimes attended the local Methodist church but finally settled for Floyd Chapel Baptist Church in Stockbridge, Georgia,[5] his maternal grandparents worshiped only in the Baptist church. This means that King Jr.'s Baptist roots extended deep in his family lineage.

A. D. Williams had a twin sister named Eve, who died quite early.[6] During his childhood, there was strong evidence that Williams desired to follow in his father's footsteps by becoming a preacher. After the death of his father, Williams's mother moved the family from the Williams plantation to nearby Scull Shoals where they became sharecroppers.[7] Williams early gained a reputation among neighborhood children for preaching the funeral of any animal that died. When young Williams would receive word of the death of an animal, he and some of the children would congregate as he preached the last rites. Because of the sharecropping system, it was not possible for Williams to attend school. However, he displayed a strong ability to count, which made a huge impression on people for miles around.[8]

Having undergone a religious conversion experience and then baptism in the summer of 1884, Williams was then aided by his pastor in preparing for ministry. He was licensed to preach in 1888. In the rural area of Greene County's Oconee River Valley in Georgia, where he lived, Williams found it difficult and frustrating to earn a living as an itinerant preacher, even when he supplemented his income with various types of labor. He finally came to see what so many other blacks in rural areas in the Deep South had seen: namely, that one with vision and who sought real opportunities to make a life worth living had to leave Greene County. Therefore, in January 1893 he migrated to Atlanta where he lived out the remainder of his life.

3. Ibid.

4. Ibid.

5. Clayborne Carson et al., eds., *The Papers of Martin Luther King, Jr.* (Berkeley: University of California Press, 1992), 1:21.

6. Farris, *Through It All*, 5.

7. Clayborne Carson, *Martin's Dream: My Journey and the Legacy of Martin Luther King, Jr.* (New York: Palgrave Macmillan, 2013), 141.

8. *The Papers*, 1:4.

A. D. Williams worked in a machine shop for a few months after arriving in Atlanta, and then he became pastor of two small Baptist churches. Not long thereafter, in March 1894, he was called to pastor Ebenezer Baptist Church. Ebenezer was founded by the Rev. John Andrew Parker, who had recently died. The church had a membership of thirteen and no building, so worship services were initially held in a private home.[9] However, the energetic, enterprising, committed, and creative Williams was not to be outdone or defeated. By the end of the first year of his tenure as pastor, sixty-five new members had joined. Although he considered leaving Ebenezer after a couple of years, it became increasingly evident to him that he and that church were a very good match.

It was not long before both Williams and the church were prospering, especially after he stopped supply-preaching at other churches to supplement his income, and decided to focus solely on the work at Ebenezer. When this decision was made, things really began to turn around, for he was now devoting his full attention and energy to one church only. His recipe for building a strong congregation and ministry included "forceful preaching" that *stressed the humanity and everyday needs and struggles of the members.*[10] Therefore, early in his tenure as pastor of Ebenezer, there was evidence that A. D. Williams was committed to good preaching *and* social gospel Christianity.

Farris recalls being told that her grandfather "was quite a man," "was tall and quite handsome," "had a powerful, billowing voice," "was a great speaker and a superb organizer," and "a freedom fighter."[11] And more, he stressed both the social and political dimensions and requirements of the gospel. "He believed not only that the church should be involved in the lives of its members, but that it should be equally politically active in the community."[12] In short, Williams was a model *social gospel* minister, even if he was not aware of that term or the social gospel movement. He did not learn about social gospel preaching and ministry from white ministers and social gospel advocates. He read and mastered the contents of the Bible and knew that the biblical message was a social gospel that was concerned about the well-being of the entire human being—mind, soul, and body. The gospel was social for Williams, or it was nothing. Ministers and would-be ministers who could not comprehend this needed to be doing something else, a stance not at all different from Daddy King and his famous son. The gospel that A. D. Williams preached, taught, and witnessed to addressed the spiritual as well as the material needs of people. If

9. Carson, *Martin's Dream*, 142.

10. *The Papers*, 1:7.

11. Farris, *Through It All*, 6, 8.

12. Ibid., 6.

the humanity and dignity of people were undermined by laws that would not permit blacks to vote, or that made it impossible for them to get an education worth having, decent housing, medical care, and so forth, it is the Christian minister's religious and moral obligation to preach and protest against such things. This was how Williams saw and understood Christianity and ministry, which also meant being willing to take on the Ku Klux Klan. Farris describes her grandfather as social gospel minister and what this entailed.

> Granddaddy Williams saw it as his duty and responsibility, as both pastor and community activist, to combat these laws, which sanctioned and codified the systemic mistreatment and oppression of those of God's children who happened to be black citizens of southern states.
>
> In this horrible period in American history, his primary targets became segregation, disparities in public education, unfair wages, discriminatory employment practices, and the general campaign of terror so expertly employed by the Ku Klux Klan, among whose tactics were church and home arson, lynching, castration, murder, intimidation, and other forms of torture.[13]

Through sermons and other public speeches, Williams opposed the atrocities that the Klan and other racist groups committed against black people. Moreover, he refused to dignify the Klan's form of religion as anything remotely Christian, no matter how many men, women, and children in the Klan kingdom attended church on a regular basis. As we will see in subsequent chapters, King Jr. was certain that such people worship the God of the Hebrew prophets and Jesus Christ aesthetically only, not morally.

Clayborne Carson rightly contends that Williams was one of the black ministers in Atlanta "who connected biblical teachings with civil rights advocacy, creating a black variant of the social gospel movement that also attracted widespread support among white clergymen during the early twentieth century."[14] The church, according to Williams, was responsible for not only addressing the spiritual needs of members, but their material needs as well. It was a both/and enterprise. *This* was social gospel ministry. Williams also knew the value of education and, therefore, sought to overcome some of his own educational deficiencies by enrolling in the Atlanta Baptist College, later Morehouse College, where he earned his ministerial certificate. Even so,

13. Ibid., 7.
14. Carson, *Martin's Dream*, 142.

he continued to struggle with English grammar in his speaking and writing.[15] Indeed, in his autobiography Daddy King shares a fond memory about his father-in-law as he and Mrs. King drove home from the cemetery after his burial.

> And while driving back from the cemetery after we'd buried the Reverend, I recalled a priceless Sunday morning at Ebenezer when he'd been the subject of some whispers along the front pews as several schoolteachers attending services began snickering and exchanging cutting remarks about the pastor's grammar. He'd responded by saying to one of them that during the time the church was raising its building fund several years back, "I have give a hundred dollars while the man with the good speech have give nothin'!"[16]

Before long, Williams met and became engaged to Jennie Celeste Parks (1873–1941), daughter of William and Fannie Parks. She was one of thirteen children. Her father was a carpenter. Jennie Parks attended Spelman Seminary, later Spelman College. Considered a deeply pious and spiritual woman, she and Williams eventually married. She was considered by many of that period to be the quintessential minister's wife. On September 13, 1903, the couple gave birth to their sole surviving child, Alberta Christine Williams, the mother of Martin Luther King Jr.

By virtue of his "experience and profound thought and his intensive practical ways in expounding the gospel,"[17] A. D. Williams earned the reputation of being one of the leading ministers among his peers. By the end of 1903, Ebenezer's membership had grown to approximately four hundred, although this was nowhere near the membership of Wheat Street Baptist Church, where the Rev. Peter James Bryant was pastor. Williams and Bryant would become close friends and colleagues in ministry. They frequently supported each other's initiatives and efforts to apply the gospel to eliminating social problems that demeaned and crushed their people. In fact, Clayborne Carson rightly maintains that Williams, along with other black religious leaders

---

15. Martin Luther King Sr. with Clayton Riley, *Daddy King: An Autobiography* (New York: William Morrow, 1980), 85. From my reading of A. D. Williams's NAACP address in Cleveland, Ohio in 1917, I can confirm that English grammar was a challenge for him. The speech is in the Martin Luther King, Jr. Papers Project at Stanford University.

16. King Sr., *Daddy King*, 90.

17. Quoted in *The Papers*, 1:9.

of the period, served as a pioneer in advocating "a distinctive African-American version of the social gospel, endorsing a strategy that combined elements of [Booker T.] Washington's emphasis on black business development and W. E. B. Du Bois's call for civil rights activism."[18]

There is no question that Daddy King was influenced by this brand of social gospel ministry after he became closely associated with A. D. Williams. Both men preached a social gospel Christianity that combined an emphasis on personal salvation with "the need to apply the teachings of Jesus to the daily problems of their black congregations."[19] Since neither man attended seminary, it is quite likely that they knew little if anything about the writings and work of white social gospel leaders such as Walter Rauschenbusch, Washington Gladden, and Josiah Strong. Instead, their own understanding and interpretation of the Christian message and their recognition of the material and social justice needs of their people was enough to convince them that the gospel was social; that the gospel had more to do with what one did, than with what one claimed to believe. They did not need the familiarity of white proponents of the social gospel in order to know that their own ministry must address both the spiritual and material needs of their people. Daddy King, reflecting on Williams's understanding of the role of the minister, said that "[a] minister, in his calling, chose to lead the people of his church not only in the spiritual sense, but also in the practical world in which they found themselves struggling."[20] Williams, according to King, was unswervingly committed to "his vision of a better day for his people. . . ."[21] Daddy King's involvement with social reform and his initiative to apply Christian principles to solving social problems is one of the reasons that King Jr. admired him as minister, even though he strongly disagreed with some of his father's fundamentalist teachings, namely, the inerrancy of the Scriptures, the virgin birth, and the bodily resurrection of Jesus.

The social gospel heritage in King Jr.'s family history contributed much to his own burning desire to fight against racial discrimination and other vexing social problems.[22] This is an important point for us to remember, inasmuch as it goes to the issue of young King's sense of the need for a sound theological grounding for his developing social conscience even before his matriculation at Crozer Theological Seminary. For King himself said that

18. *The Papers*, 1:10.

19. Ibid., 1:26.

20. *Daddy King*, 82.

21. Ibid., 86.

22. Carson, ed., *The Autobiography of Martin Luther King, Jr.* (New York: Warner Books, 1998), 5.

while his social conscience was already well established by the time he arrived at Crozer, his hope was that his seminary training would provide for him a theological rationale on which to ground his already strong and expanding social conscience. However, increasingly, it appears that this point needs to be qualified. That is, since social gospel Christianity was a chief characteristic of his father's and grandfather's ministries and that of other southern black ministers with whom King was familiar, it must be the case that he gained through them at least a biblical or homegrown theological rationale for doing social gospel ministry. Therefore, it seems reasonable to say that it is not so much that King discovered a theological rationale for his social conscience at Crozer. Rather, he discovered in the work of social gospel advocates such as Walter Rauschenbusch a more *formal, academic rationale* to supplement the biblical foundation for social ministry that accompanied him to seminary. This biblical foundation was shaped by the sermons, social witness, and practice of his father, grandfather, and other black preachers such as William Holmes Borders. Indeed, it was enhanced by the more refined theological views of his pastor-scholar teachers at Morehouse College such as George Kelsey, Benjamin Mays, Samuel Williams, and Walter Chivers. Each of these men also expressed a profound realism regarding their understanding of racism and class issues in the South and the need to resist them. Each saw both the relevance and imperative of the Christian gospel to addressing such issues; to protesting injustice and establishing justice.

As part of his thrust to address social issues that adversely affected his people, A. D. Williams joined over five hundred black Georgians, many of whom were religious, civic, and educational leaders, to form the Georgia Equal Rights League in February 1906. There were at least two reasons that the League was established. One was "to mobilize resistance to lynching and the Jim Crow laws that had been passed in Southern states to reverse Reconstruction-era racial gains."[23] A second reason for the formation of the League was in response to blacks' being barred from participation in the democratic primary. These white primaries in the South would be made illegal by the Supreme Court's decision in *Smith v. Allwright* in 1944. (Lonnie Smith, a black resident of Harris County, Texas, was not allowed to vote in the Democratic Party's primary election, even though he met all legal requirements. With the help of the NAACP legal defense team led by Thurgood Marshall, Smith sued S. S. Allwright, the election official.) The Georgia Equal Rights League sought to challenge this racist, exclusionary practice. The militant

23. Carson, *Martin's Dream*, 142.

Bishop Henry McNeal Turner (1834–1915) of the A.M.E. Church was voted one of the vice presidents of the League, and was a strong and outspoken advocate of black consciousness and racial pride. He lambasted the white primary system and the exclusion of blacks from participation. Clayborne Carson summarizes the complaint of the League, noting that A. D. Williams signed the address along with Turner, Peter James Bryant, W. E. B. Du Bois, and over a dozen other black leaders. The convention "protested lynching, peonage, the convict lease system, inequitable treatment in the courts, inferior segregated public transportation, unequal distribution of funds for public education, and exclusion of black men from the electorate, juries, and the state militia."[24]

Tragically, in September of the same year (1906) race rioting was precipitated by whites' allegations of black male assaults on white women. A. D. Williams responded by organizing the Atlanta Civic League to meet with white civic leaders in an attempt to ease racial tensions in the city. In addition, when the white newspaper editor of the *Georgian* characterized Atlanta black residents as "dirty and ignorant," and defamed the character of blacks in other ways, this understandably elicited the outrage of the black community. Some wanted to burn down the building that housed the newspaper. Rev. Williams counseled otherwise, saying to an angry growing mob of blacks: "Violence begets violence,"[25] a mantra that would be frequently uttered by his famous grandson many years later. Williams first went to see the publisher to lodge his protest. When it became clear why he had come, the publisher ordered him off the premises, "yelling that no nigger was going to dictate editorial policy for white folks, not ever!"[26] Within hours after that exchange, Williams had called a number of pastors and others to a meeting at Ebenezer, where they came up with the idea of organizing a boycott of the newspaper. Black pastors agreed to announce from their pulpits the following Sunday the local businesses their members were to boycott, including the *Georgian*. Within a few months the boycott led to the downfall of the newspaper.[27] This was not the aim of Williams and his supporters. They wanted justice. The publisher, on the other hand, preferred to go out of business rather than right his wrong by apologizing to black residents.

What is most important for our purpose is the intentional involvement of A. D. Williams in such organized social protests as that sponsored by the

24. *The Papers*, 1:10.

25. Quoted in Collins, *Not Only Dreamers*, 70.

26. *Daddy King*, 86.

27. See the discussion in ibid., 85–87.

Georgia Equal Rights League, and the organized boycott of the *Georgian*. For this goes to the matter of the deep roots of Christian social concern and protest, or social gospel Christianity in King's family lineage. Just as I have written elsewhere of King's homegrown or *homespun personalism*,[28] it is just as plausible to say that he was the recipient of a *homespun social gospel religion* as well. This idea is supported by the fact that during his very first term in seminary, King acknowledged in Robert E. Keighton's course on Preaching Ministry of the Church that he was an advocate of the social gospel.[29] This acknowledgment was made even *before* he read and studied social Christianity and key social gospel advocates such as Walter Rauschenbusch. He had witnessed social gospel Christianity in action in the ministry of his father and other southern black ministers, and therefore arrived at seminary already committed to it.

Similarly, we can also argue for the idea of King's *homespun Christian realism*, a point to be developed in chapter five. For now, suffice it to say that although he studied the Christian realism of Reinhold Niebuhr in seminary and later during doctoral studies, there is absolutely no question that King was already rooted in Christian realist ideas, for example, human beings' propensity to sin, prior to his introduction to and formal study of Niebuhr. Although he does not use my nomenclature, Michael G. Long has done an admirable job of substantiating this important point. In *Against Us, but for Us: Martin Luther King, Jr. and the State* (2002), Long argues convincingly that King received strong dosages of Christian realism through witnessing his father's ministry and hearing about that of his maternal grandfather. King was also quite aware of the realism of William Holmes Borders, who succeeded Peter James Bryant as pastor of Wheat Street Baptist Church,[30] for during a period of his adolescent years King was a regular visitor at Wheat Street. In addition, Long skillfully shows that on the formal academic side, King was exposed to the Christian realist influences of his Morehouse teachers—Kelsey, Chivers, Mays, and Williams.[31] The point of this is not to disparage the role and contributions of the white academy to King's intellectual development, but only to fill the void left by an earlier generation of King scholars who failed to acknowledge and account for the informal family, black church, and black southern cultural influences on the development of his most important intellectual ideas. It is

28. See Rufus Burrow Jr., *God and Human Dignity: The Personalism, Theology, and Ethics of Martin Luther King, Jr.* (Notre Dame: University of Notre Dame Press, 2006).

29. *The Papers* (2006), 6:72.

30. See Michael G. Long, *Against Us, but for Us: Martin Luther King, Jr. and the State* (Macon, GA: Mercer University Press, 2002), ch. 1, "Black Church, White State."

31. Ibid., ch. 2, "Morehouse and More Democracy 1944-1948."

high time that King scholars acknowledge the only real truth in this matter: namely, that King was most assuredly influenced by *both* sets of factors, that is, informal and formal; informal family, church, and cultural, as well as the formal academic influences. It was both/and, not either/or. There is no question of the home, church, and cultural influences on King's personalism, social gospel Christianity, and realism. On the other hand, King himself acknowledged the influence of the academy regarding the formal grounding of these ideas. Only by attesting to and taking both sets of facts seriously can one hope to develop the most complete and fullest understanding of Martin Luther King Jr. as man of ideas and of Christian nonviolent social activism.

It is important that we not make the mistake of early King scholars, namely, Ira Zepp Jr. and Kenneth Smith, David L. Lewis, and John Ansbro, who tended to undermine the importance of the homespun and southern black cultural influences on his intellectual maturation—and undermined them through their silence about those influences. However, we should also avoid the mistake of more recent King scholars, namely, David Garrow and David L. Chappell, who tend to either undermine or overemphasize some of the more formal intellectual influences, for example, personalism, and Niebuhrian realism, on King's thought and social activism. Both Garrow and Chappell downplay the influence of personalism on King.[32] In addition, Chappell overemphasizes the Niebuhrian influence.[33] Such tendencies can only lead to a truncated understanding of King's formal intellectual development, especially since he himself affirmed the centrality of the importance of personalism for his thought. Moreover, although he also named Niebuhr as the one who essentially saved him from his tendency in seminary to accept uncritically virtually the entire liberal theology platform, I have yet to see evidence that Niebuhr's realism affected King quite like personalism's emphasis on a personal God and the absolute dignity of human beings. We are on more solid ground when we simply say that King was very much influenced by both personalism *and* the realism of Niebuhr.

A. D. Williams and approximately fifty other prominent black men in Atlanta organized the local chapter of the NAACP. Williams was appointed its president in 1917. He injected the local membership with new energy and life and was instrumental in spearheading significant membership growth and

32. See David J. Garrow, "Intellectual Development of Martin Luther King, Jr.: Influences and Commentaries," in *Martin Luther King, Jr., and the Civil Rights Movement*, ed. David Garrow (New York: Carlson, 1989), 2:451n23; and David Chappell, *A Stone of Hope: Prophetic Religion and the Death of Jim Crow* (Chapel Hill/London: University of North Carolina Press, 2004), 53, 308–9.

33. See Chappell, *A Stone of Hope*, 53–54.

black voter registration. He led an Atlanta delegation to the NAACP national convention in Cleveland, Ohio during his first year with the organization. It is significant that he publicly praised the work and efforts of black women in getting large numbers of blacks to register to vote. "That was done largely because the women were allowed to make speeches," Williams said. "They made such speeches you would be surprised."[34] He said further that "the great success of the membership and registration and the campaigning was largely due to the activity of the women."[35] This is noteworthy because it is at least one clear instance in which a southern black Baptist pastor of the period was in clear support of black women's leadership in the public sphere. What is not evident, however, is how consistent Williams was in this regard, and whether women held significant pastoral leadership positions at Ebenezer Baptist Church during his tenure as pastor.

It was largely due to the leadership of Williams that bond issues were passed that ultimately led to the construction of two black schools in Atlanta that King Jr. would later attend: David T. Howard Elementary School and Booker T. Washington High School. A. D. Williams was a model black social gospel minister who had a strong influence on Daddy King. This legacy of Christian social responsibility and protest against injustice was without question passed on to King Jr., who was without peer as an activist social gospel minister.

Farris recalls the exact spring day when her grandfather collapsed and died at home. She was in the kitchen helping her grandmother prepare breakfast when they heard a loud thump upstairs. Instructed by her grandmother to go up to see what the noise was, the nearly four-year-old Christine returned to say that her grandfather was sleeping on the floor.[36] He died of a stroke.

When Williams died that early Saturday morning, March 21, 1931, he was remembered as "a sign post among his neighbors, and a mighty oak in the Baptist forest of the nation. He was a philanthropist who lived to serve his church, race, and country."[37] Moreover, we are told that he was "not educated below or above his people, but among them. . . . He was a commoner and touched all classes of people."[38]

34. Quoted in *The Papers*, 1:16.
35. See A. D. Williams's NAACP address in Cleveland, Ohio, in 1917, 2.
36. Farris, *Through It All*, 5.
37. As reported in *The Georgia Baptist* 50, no. 47: 1.
38. Ibid.

JENNIE CELESTE WILLIAMS

Jennie Celeste Parks (1873–1941) was one of thirteen children born to William and Fannie Parks, both born in Georgia in 1825 and 1830, respectively. William Parks was a carpenter and Fannie Parks was a traditional housewife. Jennie Parks began the educational tradition for her own daughter, granddaughters, and other women in the family. She attended Spelman Seminary, later Spelman College, but did not complete all degree requirements to graduate.[39] Parks married A. D. Williams on October 29, 1899. Farris remembers her as a strong, independent-minded woman who was her own person, in addition to being the ideal loving grandmother. The tradition was that women worked in the home. "They were expected to tend to their families, raise the children, cook, clean, sew, and make few waves. My grandmother was a bold exception to this formula," said Farris. "She had her own unique trajectory, one that was created and not dictated."[40] One example of this was her recognition of the importance of education at a time when whites did all they could to make it impossible for blacks to attain it. Rather than passively accept this, she sought and gained admission to Spelman. Her strong sense of self, her self-determination, and her unwillingness to be typecast in a specific role as woman is evidence that she possessed *womanist* traits.

Like Delia King (the grandmother that King Jr. and his siblings did not get to know because she died before any of them were born), Jennie Celeste (Parks) Williams, the maternal grandmother of Martin Luther King Jr., was a devoutly religious person. She was affectionately known to her grandchildren as "Mama," "Big Mama," and "Grandmother Jennie."[41] Of a different spirit, personality, and social class than Delia King, Jennie Williams was more inclined to the nonviolent spirit of protest, as was her husband.

King was about two years old when his grandfather, A. D. Williams, died. His grandmother lived with his family until her death about ten years later. What King learned of his grandfather he learned from her, his mother, and Daddy King. The relationship between Jennie Williams and her grandson was an especially close one. In addition, she contributed much to teaching King

---

39. It is of interest to note that Farris contends that her grandmother attended Spelman but does not say whether she actually completed the degree requirements. "My grandmother's admission to Spelman marked the beginning of a rich and proud tradition for the women of our family," Farris writes. "Her matriculation set an example of achievement and high standards for all the women of the King family who followed" (Farris, *Through It All*, 11). The implication seems to be that she graduated, but there is no record that she did.

40. Farris, *Through It All*, 10

41. See Baldwin, *There Is a Balm in Gilead*, 107.

and his two siblings important values. She particularly impressed on them the importance of family, religious, and cultural values, frequently using biblical storytelling as the teaching medium. By all accounts she was a superb storyteller, frequently holding her grandchildren in a trance-like state as she told them stories from the Bible.

Besides being "a saintly grandmother," King said that "[s]he was very dear to each of us, but especially to me."[42] He believed himself to be his grandmother's favorite grandchild. This helps to explain in part, at least, why he reportedly attempted suicide on two occasions when as a youngster he thought in one instance she had been accidentally killed by one of his brother's boyish pranks, and then when the news came a few years later that she had in fact died during a church engagement.[43] King's first biographer characterized Jennie Williams as "[a] woman of health and spirits," who "radiated cheerfulness wherever she went."[44] She felt particularly close to King, and frequently "did little things especially for him. . . ."[45] King essentially thought of his grandmother as his second mother.

Recalling E. Franklin Frazier's discussion on the central role and place of the black grandmother during the time of slavery, Lewis Baldwin rightly maintains that the role of Jennie Williams in the King household was every bit as important as that of the black grandmother during slavery.[46] In her was a deep repository of black folk wisdom, cultural and other values, as well as the memory of bygone generations of her people that provides continuity to the generations. In addition, she was a tremendous source of experience and wisdom that was passed on to King and his siblings. Baldwin writes about the significance of Jennie Williams's role and place in the King family: "She was a strong spiritual force, a bearer of culture, and a pillar of strength. She was held in high regard, even reverence, as a pillar in the family, church, and larger black community of Atlanta. She was a wise teacher whose advice the young and elderly alike took seriously."[47] So significant was the black grandmother's role during and beyond the enslavement period that Frazier wrote: "Even grown men and women refer to her as a second mother and sometimes show the same

---

42. King, "An Autobiography of Religious Development," in *The Papers*, 1:359.

43. See L. D. Reddick, *Crusader without Violence*, 60–61.

44. Ibid., 51.

45. Ibid.

46. Baldwin, *There Is a Balm in Gilead*, 108. See E. Franklin Frazier's instructive chapter in *The Negro Family in the United States*, revised and abridged edition (Chicago: University of Chicago Press, 1967; original edition 1939, University of Chicago Press), ch. 8, "Granny: The Guardian of the Generations."

47. Baldwin, *There Is a Balm in Gilead*, 109.

deference and respect for her that they accord their own mothers."[48] Jennie Williams was held in similar high regard.

Farris recalls that in addition to being a strong, devoted churchwoman who served as president of the Women's Missionary Society at Ebenezer, and helped to organize and lead a number of fundraising drives, her grandmother was also noted for her love of cooking, and her strong sense of fashion. It was not simply the love of cooking that was outstanding about Grandmother Williams, but the tender love she always displayed when preparing the family meals that came to be so important in the King family. "Wonderful food was always plentiful, but never more so than on Sundays," according to Farris. "I can remember the table overflowing with fresh greens from the garden, baked macaroni and cheese, fried chicken, glazed ham, smothered pork chops, and corn on the cob. Desserts included cakes and pies, bread pudding, and various cobblers."[49] Family meals at the King home were truly something special. Moreover, they were mandatory and not optional. There was a permanent seating arrangement at the dinner table, with Daddy King at the head and Mama King at the other end. Truly, family meals were a time for continuing education and moral-ethical instruction, among other important matters. In all of this, Grandmother Jennie was the abiding influence.

There were many important lessons taught during family meals that shaped the lives of the King children. Grandma Jennie's role went well beyond preparing the inviting and delicious meals. She told her grandchildren stories from the Bible and the moral of each. She also told them about their maternal family history. But the children learned many lessons from their parents during family meals as well. "These meals were filled with laughter and joy, good eating, and most important," Farris writes, "lessons from Mother and Daddy. . . . They reinforced in us that we were as good as anybody, and that the segregation we saw all about us was mandated by law, that it was not proper, nor was it in keeping with our social and religious beliefs."[50]

During family meals the King children learned about the deeply entrenched racism and segregation that was put in place to deny the humanity and dignity of black people—in effect, "to hold black people back and 'in our place.'"[51] Right there during the family meal they were taught the raw, honest version of race relations. "It was a world in which our progress and achievement were frustrated and denied. They taught us that our existence in

48. Frazier, *The Negro Family in the United States*, 119.

49. Farris, *Through It All*, 11.

50. Ibid., 16.

51. Ibid.

such a world was the residual result of our being descendants of African slaves. They went on to explain that it was the present-day, tangible consequence of the fact that our skin was darker than that of our white contemporaries."[52] The King children were taught the importance of raising their voice in protest against bigotry and hatred of all kinds, as well as "how to stand up for what was right." When one does this, they were assured by their father, they could be confident that God was on their side. They were also taught during those delicious family meals the importance of respecting their elders, a long-lost value in most communities today, regardless of race or ethnicity. Another frequent topic for discussion at meal time was the children's school day, what they learned, and what homework assignments they had. Indeed, so very much of what contributed to the shaping of the character and moral outlook of King Jr. and his siblings happened over the mouthwatering family meals prepared by a loving grandmother.

In addition to having a deep love for preparing family meals, Jennie Williams also possessed a strong sense of fashion, which she always kept under control. "She loved shoes, gloves, hats, and her black purse. She was understated and never chose anything outlandish."[53] In this she was much more influential to her granddaughter, who prayed often that she would grow up to be like her.

As implied earlier, King would have learned much from his grandmother about his grandfather's ministry and social activism, much of which talk undoubtedly occurred during family meals. Coretta Scott King recalls that he told her "of his grandmother's wonderful spiritual qualities and also of her soft heart,"[54] especially regarding him. She frequently cried and left the room, for example, when Daddy King, the strict disciplinarian, felt it necessary to subject him to corporal punishment. Daddy King was a staunch adherent of the biblical text: "Those who spare the rod hate their children, but those who love them are diligent to discipline them" (Prov. 13:24). In this regard, we can say that he was strictly "Old Testament" when it came to childrearing. He therefore took the task of disciplining and punishing his children seriously, but neither King's grandmother nor his mother had a stomach for it—either as witness or participant. Generally King, small of stature, refused to cry when subjected to corporal punishment by his father.[55] In any event, King loved his grandmother.

52. Ibid.

53. Ibid., 11.

54. Coretta Scott King, *My Life with Martin Luther King, Jr.* (New York: Holt, Rinehart & Winston, 1969), 78.

55. Frederick L. Downing, *To See the Promised Land: The Faith Pilgrimage of Martin Luther King, Jr.* (Macon, GA: Mercer University Press, 1986), 115.

Indeed, as we saw before, he referred to her as "saintly," and as having a powerful impact on his formative development. There are also a number of things to be gleaned from King's parents as we think about the protest and nonviolence traditions in his family lineage, and that is the subject of the next chapter.

3

Parents

MICHAEL KING

An industrious, hardworking, eager youth who was steeped in fundamentalist Christian faith and ideas, Michael King worked long, hard hours once he settled in Atlanta. He saved most of his money, attended school at night, and studied assiduously. After graduating from high school he tried unsuccessfully—at first—to enroll in Morehouse College. The registrar told him that he did not have the academic foundation and thus did not meet the admissions requirements. Therefore he could not be admitted. But young King was as stubborn and determined as they came and refused to be denied the chance to try. He therefore left the registrar's office and pushed his way past the secretary to the office of then president, John Hope. Once there, his importunity resulted in his finally being granted special permission to begin studies at Morehouse.[1] He was not a stellar student, but, arguably, none worked harder. He himself admitted years later that his studies at Morehouse "were the toughest of my life."[2] Having failed freshman English twice, the professor finally gave him the passing grade of D when he took the course a third time during summer school. Fortunately, he did not have a similar experience with other courses.

While attending Morehouse, Mike King was pastor of two small churches in Atlanta. It was not long before he met Alberta Williams, the daughter of

1. Taylor Branch, *Parting the Waters: America in the King Years 1954-63* (New York: Simon & Schuster, 1988), 37. Clayborne Carson tells us that King actually was aided by A. D. Williams in his attempt to gain admission. "Williams interceded with Morehouse president John Hope to gain admission for his future son-in-law" (Clayborne Carson, *Martin's Dream: My Journey and the Legacy of Martin Luther King, Jr.* [New York: Palgrave Macmillan, 2013], 143). Considering Williams's stature in the Atlanta black community by this time and his close relationship with John Hope, I would say that Carson's claim is more than plausible.

2. Martin Luther King Sr. with Clayton Riley, *Daddy King: An Autobiography* (New York: William Morrow, 1980), 87.

one of the leading ministers in the city, Rev. Adam Daniel Williams. Williams, we have seen, had a reputation for always courageously standing up to white people.[3] Daddy King recalled that the idea of justice for his people burned in Williams's soul. These are significant points inasmuch as they reveal his conviction that the gospel, rightly understood, is social. The gospel is relevant to the problems that demean and dehumanize human beings. Williams's was social gospel Christianity at its best. Daddy King gave expression to what Williams taught him about what it means to be called to ministry: "Church wasn't simply Sunday morning and a few evenings during the week. It was more than a full-time job. In the act of faith, every minister became an advocate for justice. In the South this meant an active involvement in changing the social order all around us."[4] In addition to his profound commitment to applying the gospel to social problems that adversely affected his people, Williams had a propensity and reputation for being able to accumulate material valuables. He was unquestionably one of black Atlanta's elites.

Although Mike King was much influenced by Williams's style of ministry and his concern for the least of these, it should be noted that even before King was ordained he already understood and took as his own the idea that it is the pastor's obligation and responsibility to address the everyday needs of parishioners.[5] In addition, as a youngster he had much respect for those black preachers who stood up to whites and did not soften their prophetic critique against racism and injustice. From early in his ministry, then, Mike King's social gospel Christianity included preaching sermons that appealed both to the mind and the emotions of the people while also addressing their material condition.[6] By his own admission, he became a "chronic complainer" regarding the plight of his people. Looking back, he recalled that when he complained about segregation on buses and in other areas of the Atlanta community he "was told by more than a few Negroes to stop grandstanding about the racial situation in Atlanta because it was pretty darn good compared to a lot of places, and we should just be satisfied with it until whites could see their way clear to work with us on some changes."[7] Of course, such comments always infuriated him, and his wife would be so kind as to calm him down, thus helping his

3. Stephen B. Oates, *Let the Trumpet Sound: The Life of Martin Luther King, Jr.* (New York: Harper & Row, 1982), 6–7.

4. King Sr., *Daddy King*, 82.

5. Clayborne Carson et al. eds., *The Papers of Martin Luther King, Jr.* (Berkeley: University of California Press, 1992), 1:24.

6. King Sr., *Daddy King*, 60.

7. Ibid., 96.

blood pressure to return to near normalcy. Even so, he still believed that he was right to protest discrimination against his people; that this was the responsibility of the minister. Moreover, he rejected the stance of those blacks who thought it prudent to sit around waiting for white people to decide when, or even whether, they would work with blacks to change things. He had only one response to this: "*We* would have to change things."[8] He was more certain of this than most things: "No initiative to end segregation and the bigotry it helped maintain would emerge from the white community. Any actions that produced change would have to come from the Negro community. And then only if leadership was developed on a larger scale and respected and followed as well."[9] He would not hold his peace, or his tongue, since he was not satisfied with his people's situation.

Mike King and Alberta Williams fell in love and were eventually married on November 25, 1926. As was often the practice in those days, they moved in with Alberta's parents until they could afford their own house. Although it took some doing, Rev. Williams persuaded young King to be his associate pastor at Ebenezer. He remained in that capacity until Williams died five years later in 1931. Shortly thereafter, King, strongly supported by Jennie Celeste Williams,[10] was appointed senior minister.

Like A. D. Williams, Mike King became a member of the black elite and ruling class of Atlanta. Nowhere is this clearer than his reflection about being "a prosperous young pastor, a husband and father whose family had never lived in a rented home or driven a car on which a payment was ever made late. We dressed well, we ate well, we enjoyed great respect among the people of our community."[11] But he added that although for many this would have been more than enough, he could not be at peace because his people were subjected to injustice and the force of racism and discrimination. Consequently, he was also "among the pioneer leaders of the modern Negro resistance movement."[12] He had to take on not only white racists and their discriminatory practices, but black ministers and others in black Atlanta who did not want to rock the boat. This is why black pastors rejected his proposal that they use the black churches as voter registration stations, thus making it possible for massive numbers of blacks to register to vote. "The idea fell on deaf ears."[13] But Daddy King did not

8. Ibid. (King's italics).

9. Ibid., 107.

10. Ibid., 92.

11. Ibid., 98.

12. Lerone Bennett Jr., *What Manner of Man*, abridged edition (New York: Johnson, 1968), 17.

13. King Sr., *Daddy King*, 99.

allow such rejections to silence him or cause him to cease protesting injustice. If other ministers would not get on board, he would focus on leading the Ebenezer congregation to protesting injustice. Although some members were slow to get on board, he successfully led members in a voting rights march to City Hall, anticipating the voter registration demonstrations led by his famous son in the 1960s. With participating members from Ebenezer and supporting members and a few pastors from other churches, "there were several hundred Negro Americans marching that afternoon in 1935, down to the Atlanta City Hall, in a demonstration such as no living soul in that city had ever seen."[14] Sometimes Daddy King was the lone protester, as when black ministers refused to go with him to city hall to protest its segregated water fountains and elevators. It was not an excuse to do nothing just because others would not lend their concrete support. Daddy King understood that there comes a time when a person desiring to do the right thing has to be a majority of one. In addition, he understood the Christian message as permitting no exception to protesting injustices of which one is aware. King Jr. surely took note of his father's stance in this regard.

Imagine! Daddy King—with volatile temper and all—led several hundred people in a *nonviolent* demonstration for voter registration in 1935. Martin Luther King Jr. was about six years old at the time. Indeed, when his maternal grandfather led such nonviolent demonstrations in the early 1920s, such as against a municipal bond issue because there was no provision in it for a high school for black students, King Jr. was not yet born. Although Daddy King engaged in a number of other nonviolent direct action measures during his son's boyhood, such as leading black teachers' fight for equal pay with their white peers, there is no indication during that period that he came to view nonviolence as a way of life. He seemed to think of it in more pragmatic terms as a technique that one appeals to as long as it works. What is important in this, however, is that there is clear evidence of not only the protest tradition in King Jr.'s family lineage, but also evidence of an early adherence to nonviolent direct action in his father. Nevertheless, indicators are that Daddy King was not, in earlier years, wedded to nonviolence in an absolute sense like his son. However, we will see later in the chapter that he did arrive at such a stance later in life.

King Jr. himself emerged from the soil of black Christian social gospel activism. Black preachers in that tradition did not—like Josiah Strong, Walter Rauschenbusch, Washington Gladden, and other white social gospel leaders—publish books on the subject. Most could not, even had they wanted to,

14. Ibid., 100.

given the social and racial climate of their day. However, they went one better than their white counterparts, inasmuch as they preached and *lived* social gospel Christianity in the way they did ministry. King Jr. was much influenced by this way of thinking about and doing ministry. Even as a boy he admired his father's courage and determination to protest injustices against his people, even if he did not appreciate his emotionalism and fundamentalist beliefs. It was Daddy King's social gospel ministry that earned King Jr.'s deepest respect and admiration for him as a man and a Christian minister. Indeed, King's sister reminds us that their father was "a profound influence" on her and her two brothers, but most especially, Martin.[15]

ALBERTA WILLIAMS KING

Martin Luther King Jr.'s mother was an only child who was reared in very comfortable home, neighborhood, and church surroundings. She attended what came to be Spelman College, and later matriculated at Hampton Normal and Industrial Institute where she earned her teaching certificate. Unfortunately, the local school board in Atlanta did not allow married women to teach during that period of U.S. history. Therefore, Alberta Williams taught only briefly before her marriage to Michael King on Thanksgiving Day in 1926.

Following in the footsteps of her mother, Alberta King attended Spelman College, and when married she slowly became a very influential presence at Ebenezer Baptist Church. She was founder of the church choir, and was one of its organists for nearly forty years, and was in fact killed while playing the organ in 1974. She was also active in the YWCA and NAACP, as well as the Women's International League for Peace and Freedom.

We have seen that the nonviolent spirit was most evident in King Jr.'s mother and maternal grandparents. We also saw earlier that while Daddy King did not seem to possess the nonviolent temperament, he successfully led a number of important nonviolent direct action marches. Lewis Baldwin contends that King's first direct contact with pacifism was through his mother. This is an important claim, since it was reported by early King scholars such as David Lewis that King read Henry David Thoreau's famous essay "On Civil Disobedience" in an introductory philosophy course at Morehouse College,[16]

---

15. Christine King Farris, *Through It All: Reflections on My Life, My Family, and My Faith* (New York: Atria, 2009), 17.

16. See David L. Lewis, *King: A Critical Biography* (New York: Praeger, 1970), 20. King's sister mistakenly writes that he read Thoreau's famous essay while a student at Crozer Theological Seminary. See her book, *Through It All*, 50.

implying that this was King's first real encounter with nonviolence. Indeed, King himself contributed—albeit unwittingly—to this misleading notion. For he said that it was through this essay that "I made my first contact with the theory of nonviolent resistance."[17] He said nothing about the nonviolent spirit of his mother and grandmother and how this affected him as he was growing up. King's reading of Thoreau's famous essay might well have been his first theoretical encounter with nonviolent resistance to evil, but this cannot be said of the actual practice of it. For his first contact with the *practice* of nonviolent resistance to social evil was through observing and/or hearing about his father's Christian social activism and his efforts to organize blacks to protest against instances of injustice, for example, the lack of parity in the salaries of black and white teachers in the Atlanta public school system.

The important point to be made here is that when we look for the family roots of King's ethic of nonviolence, we should not look to his paternal grandparents. Nor should we look to his father, if we expect to find one committed to nonviolence as a way of life. A pragmatic nonviolent resister might well possess a volatile temper, as Daddy King did. Indeed, it was reported that Daddy King once got physically violent with a ministerial colleague who failed to repay a debt to him.[18] However, we *do* find in these paternal family members a strong determination to resist injustice and white racism. The legacy of impassioned protest was indeed passed on to King by his paternal grandparents. His father was also a significant contributor in this regard. We saw in the previous chapter that the King children learned a great many lessons at the family dinner table about the history and practice of racism and deeply entrenched segregation. Many of these important lessons were taught by Daddy King, but Mama King and Grandma Jennie played roles that were just as important in this regard. Daddy King also contributed the spirit of direct action, although he was at best a nonviolent minimalist for much of his earlier life. In addition, King's mother and maternal grandparents not only passed on this legacy of protest, but a strong sense of mission and the importance of nonviolence.

King Jr. had a deep love and respect for his mother, acknowledging in an early paper written in seminary that while he and his siblings were growing up, she was "behind the scene setting forth those motherly cares, the lack of which

17. Clayborne Carson, ed., *The Autobiography of Martin Luther King, Jr.* (New York: Warner Books, 1998), 14.

18. See Lewis V. Baldwin, *There Is a Balm in Gilead: The Cultural Roots of Martin Luther King, Jr.* (Minneapolis: Fortress Press, 1991), 124. This was reported to Baldwin during his interview with Philip Lenud, April 7, 1987.

leaves a missing link in life."[19] King described his mother as "a very devout person with a deep commitment to the Christian faith," who, unlike his father, "is soft-spoken and easygoing."[20] One gets a sense of this from King's sister's recollection of her mother's talk with her the night before she was to leave for Columbia University in New York City to pursue a master's degree. While packing, she was summoned by her mother to come downstairs.

> I headed downstairs with absolutely no idea what she wanted. When we sat on the couch, she took my hands in her own and placed them gently on her lap.
>
> "Christine, you know, New York is a lot different from Atlanta. Northerners are different from southerners. They do things differently. Your father and I want you to be on your best behavior and we know that you will. Remember, well-brought-up young ladies are always supposed to act accordingly." . . . She reminded me yet again to be polite and to always say "thank-you."
>
> I listened intently, but remained mostly silent during our chat. When Mother Dear finished, we embraced and I returned upstairs to finish packing.[21]

Remember, by this time Christine, still living with her parents, had already graduated from Spelman College. And yet the parental relationship was such that the mother could gently counsel her daughter, who respectfully received the advice given. One gets the sense that this was Mama King's way with all three of her children. And of course, we remember the famous incident in which she gently placed a six-year-old King Jr. on her lap as she tried to help him understand why the parents of his white friend forbade them to play together.

Although Alberta King was materially comfortable most of her life, she did not complacently adjust to the system of segregation, and taught her children to adopt a similar stance. "She instilled a sense of self-respect in all of her children from the very beginning,"[22] said King. Moreover, writing to her from seminary during his first term, King told his mother that he often told his peers on campus that he had "the best mother in the world."[23]

19. *The Papers*, 1:360.
20. Carson, ed., *The Autobiography*, 3.
21. Farris, *Through It All*, 46.
22. Carson, ed., *The Autobiography*, 3.
23. *The Papers*, 1:161.

Alberta King was well respected and admired by the entire King family, as well as the members of Ebenezer. To her grandchildren and extended family at Ebenezer, she was "Big Mama." King Jr.'s youngest son, Dexter, has written: "Everybody in our family called her Big Mama, and she was clearly the one who was the behind-the-scenes mover and shaker of her family. She got us together as a family. She was Big Mama to everybody even beyond the King family—Big Mama of Ebenezer."[24] This characterization reminds us of the high regard in which blacks (historically at least) held the grandmother in the family. Tragically, this is a phenomenon that we seldom see today. The black grandmother was generally revered by family members, as well as people outside the home who considered her to be their mother away from home. Indeed, it was not unusual to hear black people who barely knew her address her respectfully as "Granny."

In any event, as she played the organ at Ebenezer one Sunday morning in 1974, Alberta King was shot to death by a madman, Marcus Wayne Chenault, a twenty-one-year-old black man from Dayton, Ohio. I remember that day well, since I was a recent college graduate working in Dayton as an adult probation officer. There was no motive for the shooting, other than Chenault's claim that "[a]ll Christians are my enemies."[25] His intention, apparently, was to kill a number of black ministers, beginning with Daddy King, who was sitting in a pew, hoping to leave service early to catch a flight. Mrs. King was seated at the organ playing the Lord's Prayer when she was shot, along with Deacon Edward Boykin (also mortally wounded) and Mrs. Jimmie Mitchel, who survived.

Derek King, a grandson and seminary student at the time, was in the pulpit area when his grandmother was shot. With no thought for his own safety, he instinctively leaped on the gunman and was one of those who sought to restrain him. In a private conversation in my office at Christian Theological Seminary in Indianapolis in 1999, King told me that he was out of his mind with rage and that he beat Chenault mercilessly. This account is confirmed by his cousin, Dexter Scott King, who was also in the sanctuary, but was being restrained by several deacons. In *Growing Up King: An Intimate Memoir* (2003), Dexter King wrote that the gunman tried to shoot Derek twice when he leaped on him from the pulpit, but Chenault's gun misfired both times. Dexter King recounts the horrific event and his cousin's actions:

24. Dexter Scott King, *Growing Up King: An Intimate Memoir* (New York: Warner Books, 2003), 79.

25. Quoted in *The Martin Luther King, Jr., Encyclopedia*, ed. Clayborne Carson et al. (Westport, CT: Greenwood, 2008), 173.

Chenault reached to get ammunition to reload. By then, Derek and some deacons were on top of him, Derek's fists hurtling into Chenault. Derek did a good job of subduing him, screaming at him at the same time. All the frustration and anger poured out of Derek then. His Uncle M. L., gone, his father, A. D., gone, now Big Mama, gone, shot right there in church. The remaining deacons who weren't holding my grandfather back on one side of the church and me and Isaac on the other, got to Derek, in the process of beating Chenault into submission. If the deacons hadn't pulled Derek off Chenault, there might have been another murder in the sanctuary.[26]

Although he remembered Daddy King being completely overwrought by grief, Dexter King also recalled being stunned when, rather than try to attack the gunman at the hospital, his grandfather asked him almost calmly: "Why did you shoot my wife, son?" The young King had no words for this reaction from Daddy King, who was "usually so stern,"[27] but who forgave Chenault.[28] The only thing that made sense to Dexter King in that moment was that his father's doctrine and practice of nonviolence had finally worked its magic on his grandfather. In this regard, King said: "I believe this moment was the culmination of the nonviolent influence of our father on Granddaddy's life, his conduct, his sensibility."[29] Indeed, Daddy King himself implied that this was precisely the case. He knew full well that the two people in the world that others expected him to hate were James Earl Ray (who murdered his son) and Marcus Wayne Chenault. Despite the pain and grief each man caused him, members of the King family, and countless others, he simply could not stoop low enough to hate them. "There is no time for that and no reason, either," he wrote in his autobiography. "Nothing that a man does takes him lower than when he allows himself to fall so far as to hate anyone."[30] At the end of the day love, not hatred, wins out and keeps open the door to any possible reconciliation. Further clarifying the point, he said: "If we achieved a victory in the South it was over inhumanity. When the evil heart of segregation could beat no more, it was because it had been stopped by people who did not counsel violence, who did not brutalize and bomb, who never sought to take away any part of anyone else's identity as a human being. These things triumphed over the exaggerated

26. D. King, *Growing Up King*, 81.

27. Ibid., 83.

28. Ibid., 86.

29. Ibid., 83.

30. King Sr., *Daddy King*, 208.

power of hatred."[31] Daddy King went on to express deep appreciation for the lesson his son taught him and countless others around the nation and the world "about the enormous personal power of nonviolence." So utterly touched was he about the lesson his son taught that he made the conscious decision to not allow room within himself for hatred and the desire to return violence for violence. Asked why he continued to be committed to nonviolence—especially after having lost his son and wife to senseless violence and hatred—he said in language not different from his son, "that it remains not one of the ways but the only way to victory over the forces of evil in this country. If we live for a sense of oneness, we will not have time for the violence of revenge or oppression."[32] This is a far cry from Daddy King's earlier pragmatic view of nonviolence.

Birth and Childhood of Michael King Jr.

While still residing with A. D. and Jennie Williams, Daddy King and wife Alberta became parents of their first child, Willie Christine (1927). Although few knew and rarely called her by "Willie," the name was chosen as a way to honor the maternal side of her family, particularly her grandfather, A. D. Williams.[33] After Christine came Michael King Jr. (1929), and then Alfred Daniel (A. D., 1930), who was partially named for his maternal grandfather. Upon being delivered, baby Michael appeared to have been stillborn, having failed to respond to the doctor's first slap to his bottom. It was therefore necessary to deliver several slaps before the baby finally gave the first sign that he would live.[34]

Daddy King wanted his first son to be named after him. Since Alberta King had always referred to her husband as "Mike," the doctor who delivered the child took this to mean that he was to be named Michael King Jr., so that is the way he signed the birth certificate. Not long after the boy joined the church at the age of five, his father "officially corrected both their names to Martin Luther King, Sr. and Jr."[35] We saw in chapter one that there is some disagreement as to when, and more especially why, the name change occurred in the first place. Daddy King said that in honor of his father's deathbed request he changed his name to Martin Luther (after James King's two brothers). Daddy King did so

---

31. Ibid.

32. Ibid., 214.

33. Farris, *Through It All*, 20.

34. Bennett, *What Manner of Man*, 6.

35. Oates, *Let the Trumpet Sound*, 4.

not long after his father's death. Clayborne Carson has also written about the confusion pertaining to the name change.

> After returning from Europe in 1934, he [Daddy King] rarely referred to himself as Michael Luther King and typically used either Martin Luther King or M. L. King. As for King, Jr., his birth certificate was filed on 2 April 1934, before the European tour, under the name Michael King, but was altered on 23 July 1957 to list King as Martin Luther King, Jr. Atlanta public school transcripts for King, Jr. obtained by the King Papers Project, initially listed him as M. L. King, although this record was altered, probably during the 1930s, to identify him as Martin Luther King, the name that is also on his elementary school "Test Scores and Ratings."[36]

Martin Luther King Jr. was born on January 15, 1929. In comparison to millions of other black babies across the country, he was born into a comfortable, privileged setting. He was shielded from the economic depression that would come crashing down less than a year after his birth. King was a normal child who grew up in a middle-class environment. Many of the basic values that he learned were not different from those of white children who grew up in middle-class households. There was, for example, an emphasis in the King home on hard work, thrift, saving, service to others, the desire to be upwardly mobile, the importance of education, responsibility, and sacrifice. However, and unlike many white children, King was not taught to despise or hate people merely because of their race. In addition, his childhood was marked by "order, balance, and restraint." Illustrating this pattern, Lerone Bennett observes: "Sunday School and Church on Sunday, playtime in or near the house on weekdays, an afternoon job throwing papers (not necessarily for money but for discipline and training), early to bed, early to rise. Days began and ended in the King home with family prayers, and King and his brother and sister were required to learn Bible verses for recitation at evening meals."[37]

Fundamentalist teachings regarding the Bible were basically conveyed to King and other Ebenezer youths by Sunday school teachers and through sermons preached by his father and guest preachers. They were taught to believe in the inerrancy and infallibility of the Bible,[38] the virgin birth, and the

36. *The Papers*, 1:31n98. Carson notes that the source of the elementary school information is Dulcie Shrider, Records Manager, Atlanta Public Schools.

37. Bennett, *What Manner of Man*, 14.

38. Oates, *Let the Trumpet Sound*, 3.

bodily resurrection of Jesus, for example. From all indications, they were not permitted to question these or any of the other orthodox Christian teachings. What they heard preached from the pulpit and what they were taught in Sunday school was, for all intents and purposes, the truth and nothing but the truth. How can one question the truth?

However, by age twelve or thirteen King was already beginning to question some of these teachings. For example, he reported that in a Sunday school class he voiced his doubt about the truth of the literal bodily resurrection of Jesus, which created a real stir among his classmates and teacher.[39] But for the young King, this was a significant period in his life, for it was evidence that he was beginning to subject some of his long-held beliefs and faith-claims to criticism. It was evidence that he was beginning to *think* about what he was being taught in Sunday school and hearing in sermons. This is an important point, because it suggests that by the time King entered Morehouse College, he was already poised to think about his faith-claims and the degree to which they made sense or not. All he needed was guidance and encouragement. He was aided considerably in this regard in his two Bible courses under George Kelsey at Morehouse. Therefore, by the time he matriculated at the liberal, predominantly white Crozer Theological Seminary he was not at all threatened (as many of his southern Baptist classmates were) by the emphasis placed on reason and subjecting all things to criticism. King was as successful as he was as a student at Crozer because he had already grown comfortable with the faith/reason tension before he arrived there, and because he had already learned the importance of being willing to subject all things to the court of reason.

Furthermore, after those early outbursts in Sunday school, all kinds of changes and questions began to arise in young King. He grew increasingly "skeptical of Sunday-school Christianity. . . . At the same time, he became disillusioned with the unbridled emotionalism."[40] King was also ill-at-ease about the whooping and emotionalism of his father's preaching.[41] Looking back, he recalled: "I revolted, too, against the emotionalism of much religion, the shouting and stamping. I didn't understand it, and it embarrassed me. I often say that if we, as a people, had as much religion in our hearts and souls as we have in our legs and feet, we could change the world."[42] In addition, King was ashamed of his father's practice of "walking the benches," as he told Ralph Abernathy many years later in Montgomery. This practice "referred to

39. *The Papers*, 1:361.
40. Oates, *Let the Trumpet Sound*, 14.
41. Ibid., 4.
42. Carson, ed., *The Autobiography*, 15.

ministers who leaped from the pulpit in mid-sermon to preach ecstatically as they danced up and down the pews, literally stepping over the swooning bodies in the congregation."[43] King considered this practice "the most vaudevillian, primitive aspect of his heritage."[44] This trait, as well as the fundamentalist beliefs of many black preachers, is what initially caused him to reject ministry as the best means of serving his people and working to eradicate the injustices that plagued their lives. Although he believed such practices were of no use to the black struggle to overcome racism and injustice, King would not have disagreed with those who held that whooping and walking the benches had more than mere entertainment value for many parishioners at Ebenezer and other black Baptist churches. It is highly likely that there were many parishioners for whom such practices had significant survival and therapeutic, as well as entertainment value, especially after having to deal with racism, racial discrimination, and other dehumanizing practices throughout the week on their jobs and in other areas of their lives.

King's sister recalls that when he was in high school he and a number of other students had the good fortune to sit for a special exam at Morehouse and Spelman that would allow outstanding juniors "to be admitted directly into college,"[45] thereby foregoing his senior year of high school. He therefore entered Morehouse College where he came under the influence, discipline, and preaching of Benjamin E. Mays and George Kelsey. According to Reddick, Kelsey was his favorite professor,[46] and it was under Kelsey that he earned his only A in college. Under the mentoring and example of Mays and Kelsey, King came to realize that not all black preaching was, or had to be, unduly emotional and border on theatrics and the absurd. It is therefore not surprising that he both heard and accepted the call to ministry in his junior year at Morehouse.[47]

King saw in Mays and Kelsey the quintessential minister-scholar who also loudly protested injustice and racism—who loudly and courageously told the powers what God said about injustice and the need to "[l]et justice roll down like waters, and righteousness like a mighty stream." Before he enrolled at Morehouse, however, he wondered whether "religion could ever be

---

43. Branch, *Parting the Waters*, 267.

44. Ibid.

45. Farris, *Through It All*, 38.

46. Lawrence D. Reddick, *Crusader Without Violence: A Biography of Martin Luther King, Jr.* (New York: Harper & Brothers, 1959), 74.

47. There was no call event as such for King. His experience was that of many. It was a process over time that finally led to his decision to enter ministry. However, we will see later that King's understanding of what it meant to be called by God was profoundly different from most ministers.

'emotionally satisfying' or 'intellectually respectable.'"[48] Once he was at Morehouse, it was mainly Kelsey who helped him to work through his issues with fundamentalist teachings, and pushed him on the need to apply reason to his faith-claims and his study of the Bible. For example, Kelsey challenged King to look behind the myths in the Bible stories for the deep abiding truths that many of them contained. He was encouraged to focus on the truths contained in the myths, not the myths themselves. Like young King, Kelsey had little use for, and patience with, theatrics and overly emotional preaching, and believed them to be obsolete in any case. Kelsey believed, moreover, that "the modern minister should be a philosopher with social as well as spiritual concerns." King reflected that thanks to Kelsey, "the shackles of fundamentalism were removed from my body. . . ."[49]

It was, of course, in Mays that King saw "what he wanted 'a real minister to be'—a rational man whose sermons were both spiritually and intellectually stimulating, a moral man who was socially involved."[50] In other words, his ideal of the minister was one who is intellectually astute and invigorating, as well as strives to live by and apply the ethical ideals of the Jewish and Christian faiths to the social struggle and people's everyday lives.

Although King believed that Mays exemplified the ideal minister, it would be far from true to say that he did not also admire much about Daddy King's style of ministry, particularly his deep sense of the need for individual Christians and the ecclesial community to engage social issues as a way of authenticating their faith. For example, he admired the fact that Daddy King never adjusted or bowed to racism and racial discrimination. King credited his father with doing much in the way of shaping his social conscience as a boy.[51] He reported on his father's social activist activities, which left a permanent mark on his own sense of what is important in ministry, and deeply influenced his ministry at the Dexter Avenue Baptist Church in Montgomery, Alabama. Without question, King patterned much of what he did at Dexter on what he witnessed his father do at Ebenezer. Daddy King's ministry focus was on the spiritual as well as the material needs of the members of Ebenezer, which meant that the pastor had to be willing and courageous enough to apply the principles of the Christian faith to the day-to-day needs of the people. Reflecting on his father's involvement in social issues, or social gospel ministry, King said:

48. Oates, *Let the Trumpet Sound*, 14.

49. Ibid., 19.

50. Ibid., 20.

51. Carson, ed., *The Autobiography*, 8.

My father has always had quite an interest in civil rights. He has been president of the NAACP in Atlanta, and he always stood out in social reform. From before I was born, he had refused to ride the city buses after witnessing a brutal attack on a load of Negro passengers. He led the fight in Atlanta to equalize teachers' salaries and was instrumental in the elimination of Jim Crow elevators in the courthouse.[52]

King admitted that his "admiration" for his father's social gospel ministry was an important factor in his decision to answer the call to ministry.[53]

In truth, it can be said that Martin Luther King Jr. resonated so much with the thought of Walter Rauschenbusch in seminary precisely because of the social gospel ministry of his maternal grandfather, Daddy King, William Holmes Borders, Mays, and Kelsey. It was the witness and practice of these men of faith that helped implant in him a strong sense of the social character of Christianity and the need to apply its basic principles to social evils. Walter Rauschenbusch supplied him with a *formal* theological rationale on which to base his deepening social conscience. Daddy King and others in the black church tradition supplied him with actual *models* for doing social gospel ministry based on their understanding of the Christian gospel. In these men, the boy King saw firsthand what it meant to be a social gospel minister who did not shy away from protesting injustice in the face of the powers.

All of this is to say, that we should not downplay the importance of Daddy King's influence on his son's ultimate decision to enter ministry, nor the way in which he sought to do ministry. Despite some of Daddy King's pulpit antics and his adherence to rigid fundamentalist beliefs, King had great respect for him as a man, father, and social justice advocate for his people. Although he praised Mays and Kelsey for their influence on him, King also expressed his admiration for the witness and example of his father, as well as contributions made to his own development and journey toward ministry.

CONCLUSION

Having examined some of the important and influential personalities in King's life and family tree as a means of determining what they may have contributed to his formative development and the spirit of protest and nonviolence, it may be helpful to list, without discussion or commentary, some of the more important ideas and contributions and who made them.

52. Ibid., 5.
53. Ibid., 16.

- Idea that God is able to make a way out of no way—Delia King
- Spirit of Nonviolence—A. D. Williams, Jennie Williams, Alberta Williams, Daddy King (pragmatic nonviolence)
- Spirit of Protest against injustice—Both sets of grandparents, parents, Benjamin Mays, George Kelsey, Samuel Williams
- Social Gospel Christianity—A. D. Williams, Daddy King, Jennie Williams, Benjamin Mays, George Kelsey
- Applying thinking to faith-claims—George Kelsey, Benjamin Mays, Samuel Williams
- Christian realism—George Kelsey, Benjamin Mays, Samuel Williams, Daddy King
- Sensitivity to poverty/economic injustice/issues of class—Both sets of grandparents, Daddy King, Walter Chivers, Kelsey, Mays, Williams
- Significance of organizing and boycotting—A. D. Williams, Daddy King
- Standing up to white people—A. D. Williams, Daddy King, James and Delia King, Benjamin Mays
- Faith in God—Paternal grandmother, maternal grandparents, and parents

We have seen that the social protest and nonviolence traditions root deep in King's family history, although one must be careful to distinguish which side of the family stressed one or the other or both of these. Both paternal and maternal sides of the family emphasized the protest tradition. The maternal side stressed nonviolence and the importance of a strong sense of mission. Daddy King led a nonviolent voter registration march, and engaged in other nonviolent direct action events.

Although the boy King was generally inclined to settle disputes rationally, or as his father recalled, "was always one to negotiate a dispute instead of losing his temper,"[54] one incident in particular should serve as a reminder that as a boy, King was nowhere close to his later stance of nonviolence as a way of life. Daddy King recalled the incident: "One summer afternoon when [the] three youngsters were playing around the house, A. D. was antagonizing his sister to the point where she was close to tears. It was all fun to him, but as Bunch and I sat out in the back yard we heard a yelp, and went inside to discover that the great little negotiator, M. L., had conked his battling brother over the head with a telephone, leaving him dazed and wobbly on his feet."[55] As a boy, then, King

54. King Sr., *Daddy King*, 126.
55. Ibid., 126–27.

was a long way from being "Alabama's Gandhi,"[56] but he was at least what we might call a nonviolent minimalist, or a pragmatic nonviolent resister.

Without question, Martin Luther King Jr. was the heir to a long tradition of protest against injustices of various kinds. It is little wonder that he knew from the time he was a boy that he would partake of this tradition to help emancipate his people from injustice, even if he did not know at the time what form the help would take. We should therefore not be surprised that when he forcefully spoke and acted against injustice he was merely keeping alive the chorus of voices and the ongoing spirit of resistance so deeply rooted in his family tree. Consequently, when King spoke and when he resisted injustice, his were also the voices and actions of his ancestors, a point made very well by Lewis Baldwin.

> When he spoke, he was speaking not only his own words but also the words of his parents and grandparents. Their dream became his dream, and their struggle, his struggle. Young Martin himself, referring specifically to his father's image as a civil rights leader, but certainly with a broader knowledge of the struggles of other family members who preceded him, insisted that "With this heritage, it is not surprising that I had also learned to abhor segregation, considering it both rationally inexplicable and morally unjustifiable." "I could never adjust to the separate waiting rooms, separate eating places, separate rest rooms," he continued, "partly because the very idea of separation did something to my sense of dignity and self-respect."[57]

Martin Luther King Jr. had already decided as a boy that he wanted to do something to help his people. Indeed, after his father stood up to a police officer who tried to insult him, and then had to explain to the young boy what was going on, the child promised to do all he could to help him eradicate racism.[58] He considered going to law school or medical school, but finally felt that God was calling him to ministry; that this would be the best way he could make his contribution to addressing the injustice and racism against his people. What were some of the ideas King studied in school that influenced how he would respond to racial injustice? To get at this and related issues, I next examine some

56. *The Papers* (1997), 3:20.

57. Baldwin, *There Is a Balm in Gilead*, 124.

58. King Sr., *Daddy King*, 109.

of the formal intellectual ideas that contributed much to King's preparation for the enormous challenges posed by ministry.

PART 2

Formal Intellectual Influences

In his seminal popular book *Martin & Malcolm & America: A Dream or a Nightmare* (1991), theologian James H. Cone helpfully declared that Martin Luther King was not an academic theologian, but "a theologian of action, a liberation theologian (in the best sense) whose thinking about God was developed in his efforts to achieve freedom and dignity for black people."[1] King was not only a man of ideas and ideals, but a man of lived or "practiced" ideas during nonviolent direct action demonstrations, primarily in the South, but also in the North.[2] Contrary to the claim of some scholars, King was truly a theologian in the best sense. Cone put it in a helpful way: "He did not develop his theology in the classroom, teaching graduate students, or in professional theological societies, reading learned papers to professors of theology. Rather King's theology was *embodied in his life*, that is, in what he did and said about justice and love between blacks and whites and about God's will to realize the American dream, reconciling, as brothers and sisters, the children of former slaves and former slaveholders."[3] And yet, there were formal elements of theology that influenced and were influenced by all that King brought to the theological enterprise. He was in the best sense an organic theologian.

After his father's ugly encounter with a traffic cop, the boy King told Daddy King that he would help him to fight racism. Whether as an adult King

---

1. James H. Cone, *Martin & Malcolm & America: A Dream or a Nightmare* (Maryknoll, NY: Orbis, 1991), 123.

2. I borrow the term *practiced* from Cone, ibid.

3. Cone, *Martin & Malcolm & America*, 123.

Jr. actually remembered saying this or not, it is known that he was sensitive to the issue of racism from around the age of six when the white parents of his best friend would no longer allow the two boys to play together because of race. Even at that early age King sensed that racism was wrong, and his parents taught him that it was not to be passively accepted, but resisted with all one's might.

We have seen that the spirit of social protest roots deep in King's family tree. While his paternal grandparents were known for their violent resistance to certain manifestations of racism, his maternal grandparents favored nonviolent resistance. The spirit of social protest was inherited from both sides of his family. Perhaps because he grew up in the South, King had a deep sense of appreciation for self-defense, a point to be examined in chapter eight. As a boy he was known to defend himself when a fight came to him. Although as he got older he learned to use his mind to avoid fights, we will see that as late as the startup of the Montgomery bus boycott he still adhered to an ethic of self-defense, even to the extent of having armed bodyguards and owning a pistol.

By the time King enrolled in seminary in the fall of 1948, he had set for himself two important goals, one of which was to find the most reasonable method for addressing and eradicating racism and related social evils that adversely affected his people. He hoped to do this through the study of theology, philosophy, social philosophy, and ethics. Through his formal study of these areas of thought, he was introduced to a number of ideas that would later be key elements in his theology, social ethics, and philosophy of nonviolent direct action.

The primary aim of the two chapters in Part 2 is to examine the relevant ideas of Walter Rauschenbusch and Reinhold Niebuhr that significantly influenced King's intellectual development and his commitment to applying the gospel to eradicating racism, economic injustice, and militarism. Rauschenbusch and Niebuhr aided King by providing a formal theological foundation for the social conscience he developed while growing up in the racist Deep South. We will see in chapter eight that Gandhi gave him the method he sought to address and attack racism and other social problems that threatened to destroy his people and the poor. Although King used ideas from each of these to forge his philosophy of nonviolence, what made his doctrine and practice distinct was his insistence on the absolute dignity of human beings as such, and his conviction that reality hinges on a moral foundation. These two convictions are foundational Christian as well as personalist principles. Each has deep roots in black religious tradition and thought.

Just as important, the following two chapters point out that King himself brought much to the table when he studied the ideas of each of the men under consideration. King's mind was not a passive blank screen when he was formally introduced to the ideas of Rauschenbusch and Niebuhr. In each case, he brought his own homegrown ideas to the table, which made it easy for him to resonate to what he was introduced to in the classroom. This was most especially the case regarding the personalism of Borden P. Bowne and Edgar S. Brightman, the social gospel of Rauschenbusch, and the Christian realism of Niebuhr. We will see later that the same holds true regarding Gandhi's philosophy of nonviolence.

King named *personalism* or *personal idealism* as his "basic philosophical position."[4] Therefore, there is no need for speculation about the influence of personalism on his thinking and practice. He primarily studied this philosophy under Edgar S. Brightman (1884–1953) and L. Harold DeWolf (1905–1986) at Boston University, at one time the most recognized center of personalistic studies in the United States.[5]

King defined personalism as "the theory that the clue to the meaning of ultimate reality is found in personality."[6] By his own admission, personalism gave him the philosophical grounding he needed for two of his long-held beliefs: 1) that God is personal, and 2) persons as such possess inherent and inalienable dignity. It is significant that these were convictions that King held long before he formally studied the philosophy of personalism. This supports the claim that these ideas root deep in his family upbringing and the black church. Although he knew these as Christian ideas, he would learn through his formal study that they were key personalist ideas as well.

In a nutshell, the type of personalism that influenced King and served as his basic philosophical point of departure not only maintains that *God is personal*, and that *human beings possess inviolable worth* by virtue of their relationship with God. This personalism is also *freedomistic* and considers God to be Creator. In addition, it contends that God is a relational Creator who has created a relational creation, meaning that all aspects of creation are to some degree interdependent. This personalism also stresses the centrality of freedom in its metaphysical, ethical, social, and political forms. Freedom, accordingly, is what it means to be a person.[7] This idea was reinforced and further solidified for King through his

4. Martin Luther King Jr., *Stride Toward Freedom* (New York: Harper & Row, 1958), 100.

5. The other major center of personalistic studies was at the University of Southern California, under the leadership of Ralph T. Flewelling, a former student of Bowne's. Flewelling also founded *The Personalist* in 1920.

6. King, *Stride*, 100.

study of existentialists such as Paul Tillich.[8] It is therefore reasonable to say that to be free is to be a person; to be a person is to be free. That is, the essence of being human is found in freedom. According to King's personalism, then, God is the source or creator of all things and freedom is basic to what it means to be a person. Indeed, King held that even though blacks were not free in the concrete sociopolitical sense, he was convinced that he and his people "are free in the sense that freedom is that inner power that drives us to achieve freedom."[9] He believed similarly about the beloved community. It is not yet here, and yet it *is* here in the sense that there are individuals in whom there is an inner power or drive that daily pushes them to seek its actualization.

In order to adequately introduce discussion on some of the chief formal intellectual influences on King's thought, it is important to at least give brief consideration to some of the family or informal influences. Already we have seen, and will see even more clearly subsequently, that a number of the formal intellectual influences have their foundation in ideas that were generated during King's family and church upbringing. This is the case of his personalism, for example. Although he did not have a name for it while he was growing up, King was an early proponent of the convictions that God is personal and that human beings are sacred beings, created in God's image. Although unknown to the boy King, these are two fundamental tenets of personalism. Consequently, even before King was introduced to the term *personalism* (quite possibly at Morehouse College), was introduced to some of its basic tenets in seminary, and studied it systematically at Boston University, he already subscribed to what I have called *homespun personalism*.[10] I also find this to be the case regarding the influence on him of nonviolence, the social gospel, and Christian realist teachings that engaged his thought from Morehouse College to Boston University, which is to say that one might also speak of his *homespun nonviolence*, *homespun social gospel*, and *homespun Christian realism*. In light of this, it makes sense to begin this discussion on formal intellectual influences on King's developing social ethics and philosophy of nonviolent direct action by first briefly considering contributions from home and church.

7. Borden P. Bowne, *Metaphysics*, rev. ed. (New York: Harper & Brothers, 1898), 406, 416.

8. Martin Luther King Jr., "How Should a Christian View Communism?" in his *Strength to Love* (New York: Harper & Row, 1963), 95.

9. King, "Why a Movement," address to SCLC Staff Retreat at Frogmore, SC, November 28, 1967, King Center Library and Archives, 6.

10. See Rufus Burrow Jr., *God and Human Dignity: The Personalism, Theology, and Ethics of Martin Luther King, Jr.* (Notre Dame: University of Notre Dame Press, 2006), 5, 6, 8, 77, 79.

IDEAS FROM HOME AND CHURCH

King's social passion and his desire to find solutions to his people's plight were kindled while he was still a teenager. King was allowed to enroll at Morehouse College at the age of fifteen for primarily two reasons: 1) He was allowed to skip two grades during his secondary education, and 2) admissions standards were lower as a result of low college enrollments throughout the country during the onset of World War II. By King's own admission, by the time he entered Morehouse in 1944, his "concern for racial and economic justice was already substantial."[11] Even before enrolling in college, his social conscience was more developed than that of many people in his generation.

It is important to remember that Martin Luther King was not born—anymore than anybody else—with a sense of wanting to serve his people by contributing to the eradication of the injustices that demeaned and crushed their lives. However, as a boy, he had significant examples of both ministerial and other professional blacks who were committed to giving something back to their community. Although as a teenager he rejected a number of his father's fundamentalist religious teachings, for example, the inerrancy of scripture and the doctrine of the literal bodily resurrection of Jesus, we have seen that King admired his father's determination to apply the teachings of the gospel to the predicament of his people and the everyday affairs of their lives. The elder King held the view that God created human beings as psycho-physical or spiritual-bodily beings, and thus proponents of Christianity must address the needs of the whole person—mind, spirit, and body. He further believed that the whole world belongs to God, who is concerned about all that happens in it. The concern of Christians and the church, therefore, must be for the whole world rather than select or convenient segments of it. This way of thinking, correspondingly, rejects any tendencies toward *restrictionism*. As used here, this term refers to the idea that there are certain privileged areas of existence, for instance, politics, government, business, and academic institutions, including theological seminaries, where moral principles and divine expectations are suspended, and thus do not apply in decision making. Those in positions of power in these entities will argue to the contrary, but thirty years in the theological academy convinces me that they are only being disingenuous. People who work in these areas of life seem to believe they can do whatever they want to do, without fear of consequences. There are, of course, moral consequences, but these do not matter to them. Martin Luther King insisted that the whole world belongs to God, and because God established the world

11. King, *Stride*, 91.

on a moral foundation every area of existence must conform to moral law. Consequently, in Kingian ethics, at least, there is no place for restrictionism. Moral law, King held, applies to every area of human existence.

From his parents, grandparents, and the black Baptist church, King inherited a strong tradition of protest, the nonviolence tradition, a strong sense of the relevance of Christian principles to addressing social injustices, and the gospel mandate to do so. Both his father and maternal grandfather were steadfast in the conviction that the black preacher was obligated to stand up for and with the poor, weak, and disinherited of their community. Daddy King and A. D. Williams reasoned that the black preacher is often not in the employ of whites, and therefore need not worry about losing his job when he honors the prophetic tradition of the church and vigorously protests against injustices committed against his people. King's father and grandfather always related the gospel to the social crisis confronting their people. In this sense, we can say that they were merely being consistent with the long history of the social gospel from the inception of the universal church generally, and the black church in the United States, in particular. Both men believed wholeheartedly that in human relations, progress and growth come only through incessant struggle, an idea that was espoused by the philosopher Georg W. F. Hegel, as well as the nineteenth-century abolitionist-orator Frederick Douglass.[12] A. D. Williams and Daddy King both lived and did ministry in accordance with this very dictum, and we can be sure that this was a principle that influenced young King Jr. and remained a prominent idea throughout his civil rights ministry. King believed that progress in the social order generally does not happen willy-nilly—"does not roll in on the wheels of inevitability,"[13] as he liked to say. It must be *made* to happen, just as the privileged and powerful must be made to share privilege and power with the traditionally left out. They generally do not

12. Although the philosopher Hegel stressed the idea that there can be no progress without struggle, I have seen no evidence that Williams and/or King Sr. ever read Hegel. It is at least possible, however, that Williams read or was otherwise familiar with Frederick Douglass's quite similar statement in his 1857 speech on West India Emancipation: "The whole history of the progress of human liberty shows that all concessions yet made to her august claims, have been born of earnest struggle. . . . If there is no struggle there is no progress" (Frederick Douglass, "West India Emancipation," in *The Life and Writings of Frederick Douglass*, ed. Philip S. Foner [New York: International Publishers, 1975], 2:437). Or it might well be that Williams learned the concept from long experience of struggling against racism and injustice, and King Sr. learned it from him. See Martin Luther King Sr. with Clayton Riley, *Daddy King: An Autobiography* (New York: William Morrow, 1980), 82. King Jr. expressed his appreciation for Hegel's view that "growth comes through struggle" (*Stride*, 101).

13. King, "Remaining Awake Through a Great Revolution," in *A Testament of Hope: The Essential Writings of Martin Luther King, Jr.*, ed. James M. Washington (New York: Harper & Row, 1986), 270.

do so willingly or on the basis of some sense of morality. They must be made to share power and privilege, or be shown that it is more to their advantage to do so, than not.

Since Daddy King and A. D. Williams believed that the whole world belongs to God, the preacher and the church must be concerned about all that happens in the world, most especially the effects on the least of these. True Christians must be agents for social change, as well as concerned about the spiritual well-being of people. The church, Daddy King learned from Williams, must seek to influence every area of human life, a principle that King Jr. learned by observing his father do ministry, and that he would also read about in Rauschenbusch's *Christianity and the Social Crisis*. Daddy King and Williams would have agreed with historian Carter G. Woodson that the black church is to be an "all-comprehending institution."[14] Indeed, historically not only was the church "the greatest asset of the race," it was also "the clearing house for all other useful activities."[15]

Both Williams and Daddy King believed that the preacher should be proactive when confronted with injustice. Both men hoped that there would be some leadership forthcoming in this regard from white preachers of their day, but to their chagrin—but not surprise—this only occurred among a very small number. Daddy King lamented this fact many times.[16] He and Williams knew that blacks could not afford to wait for even otherwise good white Christians to take up their cause. Instead, they needed to be self-determined. The only thing that white preachers were adept at was urging Daddy King to not stir things up,[17] which is quite interesting, because King Jr. would compose his classic "Letter from Birmingham City Jail" in response to white clergymen who urged him neither to rush into nor stir things up in Birmingham in 1963.

In 1961 Gurdon Brewster, a white Episcopalian student at Union Theological Seminary in New York City, spent the summer living in the home of Daddy King and doing volunteer field education work at Ebenezer Baptist Church. The relationship between the two men evolved such that years later Daddy King told the chapel audience at Cornell University where Brewster was chaplain that he was like a son to him,[18] and Brewster said Daddy King

14. Quoted in Lewis V. Baldwin, *The Voice of Conscience: The Church in the Mind of Martin Luther King, Jr.* (New York: Oxford University Press, 2010), 25.

15. Carter G. Woodson and Charles H. Wesley, *The Negro in Our History*, 12th ed., revised and enlarged (Washington, DC: Associated Publishers, 1972 [1922]), 592.

16. Martin Luther King Sr. with Clayton Riley, *Daddy King: An Autobiography* (New York: William Morrow, 1980), 87, 103, 112.

17. Ibid., 105.

had been like a father to him.[19] Brewster recalled a sermon in which Daddy King characterized the preacher and Christian ministry and the very high stakes involved. He also talked about the legacy of A. D. Williams. Brewster quotes Daddy King as saying:

> Even the Negro ministers told me to keep quiet when I preached about equal rights and voter registration. They didn't want me rocking the boat in the pulpit, but I raised my voice for the downtrodden. I preached the Word, and I tried to live the Word.
>
> I got tired, but you can't get tired enough to stop. You've got to preach to the pain of the people, and getting tired is part of the sermon. But you can't stop. Because now you're making history. I'm talking about the history Reverend [A. D.] Williams made. He caused a lot of things to change. I continued his legacy. I wanted to see God working now, not after all the people died. I wanted to see God working here and not in some far-off place.[20]

In the tradition of the Hebrew prophets, Daddy King declared elsewhere, "I intended to keep on complaining."[21] He realized that unlike the few white sympathizers, black people did not have the luxury of not participating in the struggle for justice. "Only whites could quit,"[22] said Daddy King.

According to Williams and Daddy King, then, the church's responsibility did not stop at the end of worship services on Sunday. Indeed, as Lewis Baldwin rightly points out, "Largely because of the work of A. D. Williams and King, Sr., Ebenezer became literally a benchmark for congregational and ecclesiastical activism, and a congregation quite conscious of its traditions and its role in the struggle. It was here that the Christian life was understood in terms of unconditional love and service to others, and King, Jr., absorbed this lesson almost unconsciously."[23] Is it any wonder that King's social conscience was being shaped and honed even during his high school years? *This* is the legacy that King inherited from his family and the black church tradition (more specifically Ebenezer Baptist Church), even before he went to Morehouse

18. Gurdon Brewster, *No Turning Back: My Summer with Daddy King* (Maryknoll, NY: Orbis, 2007), 230.

19. Ibid., 232.

20. Ibid., 100–101.

21. King Sr., *Daddy King*, 97.

22. Ibid., 107.

23. Baldwin, *The Voice of Conscience*, 25.

College, and then to seminary and graduate school. All of this would only be reinforced once he entered seminary and began studying the social gospel ideas of Walter Rauschenbusch and others.

When King studied Rauschenbusch's emphasis on the unity between religion, ethics, and the world at Crozer, it was not a new idea for him. He had seen this very emphasis on the integral relation between religion, ethics, and the world at work in the ministerial witness of his father, of Rev. William Holmes Borders, and of other black ministers who were as concerned about life on earth as in heaven. Therefore, we should see this social gospel principle, which is actually based on the Hebrew prophets' emphasis on doing justice, as one of those homegrown ideas for King that received formal theological grounding when he read and studied Rauschenbusch primarily, but other social gospel advocates as well.

Through his upbringing in the black Baptist church and the influence of his father and maternal grandfather, King already possessed a strong biblical foundation for Christianity's relevance to the social crisis (that affected his people) before he was introduced to the writings of Rauschenbusch in seminary. His formal studies provided what he considered an adequate theological and philosophical framework through which to articulate the relevance of Christianity to the social crisis of his day. These formal academic studies built on and supplemented what he had already learned and internalized as the son and grandson of black Baptist social gospel preachers.

Martin Luther King began to consciously think about best possible means to address the social injustices that dehumanized and emasculated his people, even before he arrived at Morehouse. Still essentially a child at the time, he did not give it the serious attention he would later, but it was on his mind. He very likely had this in mind when he read Henry David Thoreau's "Essay on Civil Disobedience" at Morehouse. He was so impressed with Thoreau's essay that he claims to have read it multiple times. Looking back on that experience, King wrote: "Fascinated by the idea of refusing to cooperate with an evil system, I was so deeply moved that I reread the work several times. This was *my first intellectual contact with the theory of nonviolent resistance.*"[24] But as we saw previously, even before reading that famous essay, King was already the heir to a legacy of ethical prophecy, social protest, and nonviolent direct action, courtesy of his parents, grandparents, and teacher-mentors at Morehouse. His mother and maternal grandparents were models of the nonviolent spirit for young King. Daddy King did not model the spirit of nonviolence as much

---

24. King, *Stride*, 91 (my emphasis).

as the importance of organized nonviolent resistance as a strategy for social change.

We have seen that through his academic studies, King hoped to find a sound theological rationale on which to formally ground his social conscience, and a method for addressing and eradicating racism and other social injustices that constantly made life miserable for him and his people. King's study of Rauschenbusch provided the formal theological validation and foundation for his strong social conscience. In addition, he heard Mordecai Johnson lecture on Gandhi during his senior year in seminary. This convinced him of the viability of nonviolent resistance to evil, although at the time he had no way of knowing the extent to which it might be effective in the Deep South. Furthermore, questions remained in his mind about the adaptability of such a method in the United States, and particularly in the South. Indeed, we will see that strangely, when the Montgomery bus boycott got under way, at least eight weeks passed before King explicitly introduced Gandhian principles and techniques into the movement, and this only *after* being urged and coached to do so. I discuss this more fully in Part 4, and chapter eight. In chapters four and five, respectively, systematic discussions occur on the contributions of Rauschenbusch and Niebuhr to King's intellectual development and his commitment to nonviolence as the best means of addressing injustice.

4

The Walter Rauschenbusch Factor

While in seminary, Martin Luther King read and pondered the work of many of the great Western theologians and social philosophers in an effort to satisfy his quest for a sound theological foundation for his deepening social conscience. Of all the thinkers he read during his seminary and doctoral studies, King was greatly impressed with the philosopher Hegel, and the church historian and ethicist, Walter Rauschenbusch. He was enamored with Hegel's dialectical method of thesis, antithesis, and synthesis as the best means to truth, and was fascinated with the Hegelian idea that growth comes through suffering and struggle.[1] At Boston University, King studied Hegel in depth in a yearlong seminar taught by his academic advisor, leading personalist philosopher Edgar S. Brightman. When Brightman died unexpectedly in 1953, his protégé, third-generation personalist Peter Anthony Bertocci (1910–1989), became the instructor. Bertocci reported on "how King in the seminar on Hegel 'almost took over the class' in his enthusiasm for Hegel's insight that the master is dependent on the slave for his consciousness of himself as master."[2]

As a civil rights leader, King was often criticized for taking too long in the decision-making process. However, it is quite possible that this was often a result of his desire to examine and weigh all sides of an argument before coming to decision. This was due, at least in part, to the influence of Hegel's method of arriving at truth; of examining both thesis and antithesis in order to arrive at a synthesis or higher truth. Add to this King's commitment to democratic process and coalition building and we are left with the image of one for whom important decision making in something as big as the civil rights movement is often a slow process. Even so, this practice was surely seen as questionable in the minds of detractors in the movement, for King strove to abide by certain ethical principles and to apply them to decision making regarding the civil

---

1. Martin Luther King Jr., *Stride Toward Freedom* (New York: Harper & Row, 1958), 101.

2. John J. Ansbro, *Martin Luther King, Jr.: The Making of a Mind* (Maryknoll, NY: Orbis, 1982), 298n63.

rights struggle. *He* knew that in highly charged sociopolitical and economic matters, there could be no perfect application of these principles, especially if one were making such decisions in conversation with others. King knew that his approach to decision making was always a matter of negotiating and seeking to arrive at the best possible decision or outcome. Inevitably, such decisions would be based on compromise. To the critics this had the appearance of selling out. This was precisely the criticism made by the youthful SNCC activists and others when King made the decision (without informing them ahead of time) to turn the marchers around during the second march after the devastating "Bloody Sunday" tragedy on March 7, 1965 in Selma, Alabama. King had initially said that he would violate the federal injunction against marching to Montgomery, but during closed-door conversations with federal officials a compromise was struck that led to King's decision (which stunned virtually all of the demonstrators) to march only to the place where the marchers were previously brutally attacked by police and deputized thugs (Sheriff Jim Clark's posse), to kneel and pray, and then turn around and return to Selma.

What the critics failed to understand and/or appreciate was that this approach to decision making was simply part of King's dialectical method—of considering all relevant facts and ideas, and trying to arrive at a synthesis that reconciled the respective truths of participating members. For King, the synthesis was often a mediating position at best, one that all parties could live with. It was a decision or solution that gave all contending parties—as far as possible—something they sought. Because concern for the least of these was one of King's operating principles, his aim was to always filter the contending claims and counterclaims through that lens in the hope that the outcome would favor the left-out more than others. And yet, the Kingian dialectic operated such that it was virtually impossible for any party to get all that was due them, or even most of what they desired. For King, the synthesis was generally a compromise between the contending parties. He was realistic enough to know that in the political arena this was the best that could be hoped for, and to that extent—at least in King's mind—this was not a betrayal of the left-outs. And yet, he knew that this is precisely what detractors, even within the SCLC family, believed. Indeed, who can forget SCLC board member Fred Shuttlesworth's angry outburst when King initially announced the need to call off the demonstrations during the Birmingham campaign in 1963, when it was believed that an agreement had been reached with business leaders—an agreement that Shuttlesworth rejected?

Shuttlesworth shot King a fierce look and promised, "I'll be damned if you'll have it like this. You may be Mr. Big now, but if you call it off, you'll be 'Mister Shit.' You're way up here, but you'll fall way down low, and you'll be Mr. Nothing. I'm sorry, but I will not compromise my principles and the principles we established." . . . The fiery leader continued to denounce King as a double-crosser who was squandering this perfect opportunity to put [Bull] Connor away.[3]

King was almost by nature a person who sought the advice of others when making important decisions. Indeed, Adam Fairclough makes this point very well: "Moral principles were only a rough guide to action: King had to adapt those principles to politics and practicality. A coalition builder by both instinct and philosophy, King regarded compromise as creative synthesis, not betrayal. His ethics were guided by realism."[4] It was never King's sense that he was compromising his principles. Rather, in light of his principles and the political exigencies and realities, he sought always to achieve the best possible outcome. Frequently, this meant that he did not get all that he hoped, which often—and I might add unfairly—gave the impression that he sold out.

REASONABLENESS OF KING'S CRITICISMS OF RAUSCHENBUSCH

At any rate, by King's own admission it was through the reading and study of Walter Rauschenbusch during his first year in seminary[5] that he discovered the formal theological foundation he sought.[6] Rauschenbusch, described by Reinhold Niebuhr as "the most brilliant and generally satisfying exponent" of social Christianity,[7] made a deep and lasting impression on King. (Niebuhr significantly influenced King, and had much to say about him, as we will see in the next chapter.) King did not agree with all that Rauschenbusch had

3. Andrew M. Manis, *A Fire You Can't Put Out: The Civil Rights Life of Birmingham's Reverend Fred Shuttlesworth* (Tuscaloosa: University of Alabama Press, 1999), 383.

4. Adam Fairclough, Foreword to *The Domestication of Martin Luther King, Jr.: Clarence B. Jones, Right-Wing Conservatism, and the Manipulation of the King Legacy*, ed. Lewis V. Baldwin and Rufus Burrow Jr. (Eugene, OR: Cascade Books, 2013), xv.

5. Taylor Branch, *Parting the Waters: America in the King Years 1954-63* (New York: Simon & Schuster, 1988), 73. See also King, *Stride*, where he writes that in seminary he "came early to Walter Rauschenbusch's *Christianity and the Social Crisis*," 91.

6. King, *Stride*, 91.

7. See Reinhold Niebuhr, *An Interpretation of Christian Ethics* (New York: Harper & Row, 1935), Preface.

written, however. For example, he believed that Rauschenbusch and many social gospel proponents had fallen victim to the nineteenth-century "'cult of inevitable progress,' which led to a superficial optimism concerning man's nature."[8] Believing in the principle of cooperative endeavor between persons and God, and in human self-determination, King rejected the idea of "inevitable progress," a doctrine he attributes to Herbert Spencer,[9] for the view that progress in the social order comes only when persons work intentionally and cooperatively with each other and God to bring it about. However, we must wonder whether King's criticism was justified. Is there evidence in the work of Rauschenbusch to suggest that while many social gospel advocates did indeed adhere to the doctrine of inevitable progress, the same cannot be said as definitively about him? Did Rauschenbusch advocate inevitable progress, or did he champion the idea that social progress depends on cooperative endeavor between human beings and God, much like King?

The kingdom of God was for Rauschenbusch the central "doctrinal basis for the social gospel."[10] When he wrote and talked about the kingdom of God, which he described as "humanity organized according to the will of God,"[11] and what would be needed to actualize it, he sounds little different from King's insistence that progress in the social order does not happen automatically and without the mutual cooperative efforts of human beings and God. Indeed, contrary to Reinhold Niebuhr's view that the kingdom of God is not achievable in history, Rauschenbusch declared on more than one occasion that the kingdom of God, "that perfect community of man," is achievable *if* persons cooperatively "work it out."[12] In addition, because *Christianity and the Social Crisis* was such an important book for King, he surely would have read Rauschenbusch's statement on the third page of the Introduction, "that the essential purpose of Christianity was to transform human society into the kingdom of God by regenerating all human relations and reconstituting them in accordance with the will of God."[13] This implies that Christians and the church would have to actually work to bring about such a transformation;

8. Clayborne Carson, ed., *The Autobiography of Martin Luther King, Jr.* (New York: Warner Books, 1998), 18.

9. See Clayborne Carson et al. eds., *The Papers of Martin Luther King, Jr.* (Berkeley: University of California Press, 2007), 6:498.

10. Walter Rauschenbusch, *A Theology for the Social Gospel* (New York: Macmillan, 1917), 131.

11. Ibid., 142.

12. Rauschenbusch, "The Kingdom of God," in *The Social Gospel in America*, ed. Robert T. Handy (New York: Oxford University Press, 1966), 267.

13. Rauschenbusch, *Christianity and the Social Crisis* (New York: Macmillan, 1907), xiii.

that it would not happen on its own without concerted and relentless human agency. Elsewhere Rauschenbusch declared: "We are most durably saved by putting in hard work for the Kingdom of God."[14] This did not mean that he believed in the possibility of a perfect manifestation of the kingdom of God on earth. After all, he concluded in *Christianity and the Social Crisis* that the most we can hope for are approximations of a perfect social order. "The Kingdom of God is always but coming."[15] Indeed, it is already here inasmuch as there is in some individuals the strength of will and the drive to work toward its actualization regardless of the cost. None of this sounds like one who advocated the doctrine of inevitable progress. Of this criticism, then, King actually missed the mark. It is a legitimate criticism of liberal social gospel proponents generally, to say that they put too much stock in the social Darwinist doctrine of inevitable progress. Nevertheless, the criticism does not apply to Rauschenbusch.

King also criticized Rauschenbusch for coming too close to identifying the kingdom of God with a particular social or economic theory and order.[16] But once again, we must wonder whether this is a justifiable criticism. Indeed, Rauschenbusch himself asserted: "The idea of the Kingdom of God is not identified with any special social theory. It means justice, freedom, fraternity, labor, joy."[17] Various social and/or economic theories might have something to offer, but Rauschenbusch insisted on sizing up the claims of each rather than uncritically identifying the kingdom ideal with any one of them. How may we account for what appears to be two unwarranted criticisms made by King?

Since exponents of the social gospel were more often adherents of liberal theology, a general criticism made by proponents of the neo-orthodox camp (such as Karl Barth and Niebuhr) was that many also possessed a too optimistic and sentimental view of human nature and human destiny. Most liberals believed in the fundamental goodness of human nature, but did not highlight the human propensity to sin. King shared this criticism, due in part to the influence of Niebuhr. King placed Rauschenbusch in this category, along with other liberal theologians, claiming that he exhibited an overly optimistic view of human nature. As legitimate as this criticism was of liberal theology in general, can the same be said—without qualification—of Rauschenbusch? I think it cannot. Instead, King's criticism at this point suggests that he did not read far enough into Rauschenbusch's writings.[18] We know, for example, that

14. Rauschenbusch, *The Social Principles of Jesus*, ed. Henry H. Meyer (New York: The Methodist Book Concern, 1916), 75.

15. Rauschenbusch, *Christianity and the Social Crisis*, 421.

16. King, *Stride*, 91.

17. Rauschenbusch, *The Social Principles of Jesus*, 75.

in the 1917 publication of *A Theology for the Social Gospel*, Rauschenbusch took sin much more seriously than most of his liberal counterparts.[19] When Rauschenbusch said in that text that "[d]epravity of will and corruption of nature are transmitted wherever life itself is transmitted,"[20] this was an attempt to show just how seriously he took evil and sin and his recognition of their prevalence in every generation, and on every level of human achievement.

Rauschenbusch also expressed a strong sense that orthodox Christianity was critical of social gospel advocates because of their failure "to show an adequate appreciation of the power and guilt of sin" in individuals.[21] For Rauschenbusch, however, the issue was not that the social gospel did not take sin seriously, for in his estimation it most certainly did. Unlike orthodox Christianity, the focus of social gospel Christianity was not on individual sins such as swearing, drinking, lying, pre- and extramarital sex, and so forth. Rather, the social gospel, under the influence of the Hebrew prophets, focused on the social or collective sins of groups, institutions, and nations. Rauschenbusch put it this way: "But on the whole the result consists chiefly in shifting the emphasis and assigning a new valuation to different classes of sins. Attention is concentrated [in the social gospel] on questions of public morality, on wrongs done by whole classes or professions of men, on sins which enervate and submerge entire mill towns or agricultural states. These sins have been sidestepped by the old theology. We now have to make up for a fatal failure in past teaching."[22] Indeed, Rauschenbusch made this very point in *Christianity and the Social Crisis*, the book that King praised so highly. In that

18. I came to this conclusion based on my own independent research into King's published and unpublished writings to determine whether he referenced *A Theology for the Social Gospel*. However, I am not prepared to take an absolutist stance on the matter, since I remain open to the possibility that at some point the King Papers Project under the leadership of Clayborne Carson may produce evidence that contradicts my present position that King did not refer to or cite ideas from that book. In addition, I should point out that I came to my conclusion independent of Lois Wasserman's. I only recently happened upon a footnote pointing to Wasserman's contention that King's charge that Rauschenbusch possessed an overly optimistic view of human nature was evidence he had not read Rauschenbusch's later writings. See Ansbro, *Martin Luther King, Jr.*, 313n66, where he references Wasserman, "Martin Luther King, Jr: The Molding of Nonviolence as a Philosophy and Strategy—1955-1963" (Ph. D. diss. in history, Boston University, 1972, 11).

19. See Rauschenbusch, *A Theology for the Social Gospel*, chapters 6–9. See also the fine article by Richard D. N. Dickinson, "Rauschenbusch and Niebuhr: Brothers Under the Skin?" *Religion in Life*, 27, no. 2 (Spring 1958): 163-71. Dickinson argues, among other things, that on the question of the prevalence, depth, and power of sin Rauschenbusch and Reinhold Niebuhr were in basic agreement.

20. Rauschenbusch, *A Theology for the Social Gospel*, 58.

21. Ibid., 32.

22. Ibid., 36.

text, Rauschenbusch made the strongest possible case that the Hebrew prophets were more concerned about social than individual morality. "They said less about the pure heart for the individual," he said, "than of just institutions for the nation. . . . The evils against which we contend in the churches are intemperance, unchastity, the sins of the tongue. The twin-evil against which the prophets launched the condemnation of Jehovah was injustice and oppression."[23] The prophets were essentially concerned about the everyday public affairs of human existence. They "demanded right moral conduct as the sole test and fruit of religion, and . . . the morality which they had in mind was not the private morality of detached pious souls but the social morality of the nation."[24] Indeed, King himself criticized the church for being harder on the use of profanity than for being racially prejudiced.[25] And yet, it is enigmatic that King either missed the emphasis on social sins when he read Rauschenbusch's book, or he simply failed somehow to make the connection. The social gospel, according to Rauschenbusch, was more concerned about the evils and sins of the "super-personal forces," that is, the powers and principalities. The aim of the social gospel, Rauschenbusch argued, was to transform the super-personal forces of evil by bringing them under the teachings and law of Jesus.[26] Of course, he did not mean this in a literal sense, declaring that "[a] state which deals with those who have erred in the way of teaching, discipline, and restoration, has come under the law of Christ and is to that extent a saved community."[27] Such is not a perfect community, but a better one than it was. In short, the Rauschenbusch of the pre- and post–World War II years took sin much more seriously than most liberals (and than King himself was aware), which also means that at the very least King should have mitigated his criticism that Rauschenbusch exhibited "a superficial optimism" regarding human nature.[28]

At this writing, I have found no concrete evidence that King read *A Theology for the Social Gospel*, despite the fantastic claim of Kenneth Smith (his ethics professor at Crozer) that in conversation with the student King he learned from him how important Rauschenbusch was to King and that he had in fact read all of his major books.[29] Without question, King was profoundly

23. Rauschenbusch, *Christianity and the Social Crisis*, 8.

24. Ibid., 11.

25. *The Papers*, 6:274.

26. See Rauschenbusch, *A Theology for the Social Gospel*, 111, 113.

27. Ibid., 113.

28. See Kenneth Smith and Ira Zepp Jr., *Search for the Beloved Community: The Thinking of Martin Luther King, Jr.* (Valley Forge, PA: Judson, 1974), 45; and Ansbro, *Martin Luther King, Jr.*, 172.

influenced by Rauschenbusch's classic text, *Christianity and the Social Crisis*, published ten years before *A Theology for the Social Gospel*. The former text did not focus on the human propensity to sin as did the latter.

THE KINGDOM OF GOD

Martin Luther King was much influenced by Rauschenbusch's view of the centrality of the kingdom of God in the teachings of Jesus. According to Rauschenbusch, the kingdom is a social rather than an individualistic ideal. This, despite the fact that Rauschenbusch himself sometimes implied that at bottom the concern was individualistic. In this regard, an early biographer, Dores Sharpe, quoted him as saying: "Remember the Kingdom of God can never come perfectly in the world until it comes perfectly in your own life."[30] On the surface, this seems to imply that at bottom the kingdom ideal has an individualistic emphasis. But the preponderance of the evidence suggests that for Rauschenbusch, Jesus frequently addressed individuals and worked through them, but his "real end was not individualistic, but social."[31] That is, Jesus aimed more at the creation of the new society, than the new individual.[32] The kingdom was "not a matter of getting individuals into heaven, but of transforming the life on earth into the harmony of heaven."[33] The kingdom ideal was based on the hope of a radical transformation of the world into the likeness of heaven, a place where love, justice, equality, and righteousness reign supreme.[34]

Rauschenbusch argued that since human beings are gregarious and social by nature, their morality consists in striving to be good citizens in their communities. It follows that love is the chief imperative of the Christian ethic,

29. Kenneth Smith, "Martin Luther King, Jr.: Reflections of a Former Teacher," *Bulletin of Crozer Theological Seminary* 57, no. 2 (April 1965): 3. Unfortunately, the King Papers Project has not yet uncovered any substantive evidence that corroborates the late Kenneth Smith's claim. In addition, Smith also claimed to have read a paper that King allegedly wrote on Gandhi in a course with his academic advisor and mentor at Crozer, George W. Davis, but he "does not remember anything about its contents. . . ." (See Smith and Zepp Jr., *Search for the Beloved Community*, 48.) Six volumes of *The Papers of Martin Luther King, Jr.* have been published at this writing, and none contains this paper, nor has my own search into the unpublished papers of King been fruitful in this regard. I would say that until there is corroborative evidence, both claims by Smith should be taken with a grain of salt.

30. Quoted in Dores Sharp, *Walter Rauschenbusch* (New York: Macmillan, 1942), 228.

31. Rauschenbusch, *Christianity and the Social Crisis*, 60.

32. Ibid., 61.

33. Ibid., 65.

34. Ibid., 77.

"because love is the society-making quality,"[35] the magnetic glue that draws and binds persons together in community.

Because Rauschenbusch was mindful of Jesus' attempt to work through individuals toward the social end of the kingdom, it would be reasonable to say that the kingdom ideal was for him both personal and social. There is no question that he frequently acknowledged the autonomy and value of the individual person. But as previously observed, he also stressed the social or relational character of human beings, who, by nature, are communal beings. Therefore, the truth is that Rauschenbusch's kingdom ideal emphasized the value and claims of both the individual and the community, just as Jesus did. Remember, Rauschenbusch himself maintained that Jesus essentially worked through the individual person, but for the social ends of the kingdom. We will see later that in a number of ways Rauschenbusch's doctrine of the kingdom of God is similar to King's concept of the beloved community (which was introduced into philosophical literature by the absolutistic personalist Josiah Royce [1855–1916]).[36]

Before considering the ideas in *Christianity and the Social Crisis* that so strongly impacted King's thinking, it may be of interest to note that he apparently was not aware of Rauschenbusch's tendency to stoop to what Gary Dorrien aptly calls "racist demagoguery."[37] Rauschenbusch did this a number of times in order to appeal to German donors who might contribute money to the German Department at Rochester Theological Seminary during the early part of his career as a member of that Department. Rauschenbusch scholar Christopher Evans has also written of his racism and paternalism, rightly declaring that like most white, liberal, middle-class reformers in the North, Rauschenbusch saw the race problem as essentially a southern problem.[38] Even though Rauschenbusch "frequently lectured at black colleges and vocational schools," Evans writes, "he shared much of white Progressive Era America's paternalistic view toward African-Americans. He embraced the view of many liberals of his generation who believed that in the eyes of God, social equality was inherent in all persons. Yet, he shared the social gospel's larger tendency to absorb African-Americans into other 'unregenerate' ethnic non-Protestant

35. Ibid., 67.

36. See Josiah Royce, *The Problem of Christianity* (Washington, DC: Catholic University of America Press, 2001 [originally published in two volumes by Macmillan, 1913]), 125, 129–31, 403–4.

37. Gary Dorrien, *Social Ethics in the Making: Interpreting an American Tradition* (Malden, MA: Wiley-Blackwell, 2009), 93.

38. Christopher H. Evans, *The Kingdom Is Always but Coming: A Life of Walter Rauschenbusch* (Grand Rapids: Eerdmans, 2004), 76.

groups that required Christianization."[39] Accordingly, the argument goes, in order for Afrikan Americans to become civilized and productive citizens they must be subjected to "the wisdom and example" of educated white middle-class people.[40] Furthermore, on occasion Rauschenbusch, in written correspondence, referred to rural black children he met in his travels as "pickaninnies."[41] Because Rauschenbusch's classic work, *Christianity and the Social Crisis*, made such a deep and lasting impression on King and provided the formal theological grounding for his social conscience and passion, I now turn to a consideration of some of the ideas in that book that impacted King most. What did Rauschenbusch seek to do in that text, and how did King react to it?

IMPORTANCE OF *CHRISTIANITY AND THE SOCIAL CRISIS* TO KING

The social gospel movement was a response to the new society that emerged as a result of the Industrial Revolution of the late nineteenth century. There were other liberal theologians and pastors, for instance, Josiah Strong and Washington Gladden, who were pioneers of that movement before Rauschenbusch's rise to fame. Anna Julia Cooper (1858–1964)[42] and Reverdy Ransom (1861–1959)[43] were Afrikan Americans who were influenced by, and contributed to that movement, although the argument is easily made that the adherents of black Christianity have always been proponents of their own version of the social gospel.[44]

39. Ibid., 255.

40. Ibid.

41. Ibid.

42. See Anna Julia Cooper, *A Voice from the South* (New York: Oxford University Press, 1988 [1892]).

43. See Reverdy C. Ransom, *The Negro: The Hope or the Despair of Christianity* (Boston: Ruth Hill, 1935); *The Pilgrimage of Harriet Ransom's Son* (Nashville: Sunday School Union, 1949); Anthony B. Pinn, ed., *Making the Gospel Plain: The Writings of Bishop Reverdy C. Ransom* (Harrisburg, PA: Trinity Press International, 1999); and Anne H. Pinn and Anthony B. Pinn, *Fortress Introduction to Black Church History* (Minneapolis: Fortress Press, 2002), 127–28, 153–58. Anthony Pinn contends that Ransom was interested in socialism and was influenced by the social gospelers ("Editors' Introduction" in *Making the Gospel Plain*, 3). Although he does not say specifically which social gospel leader(s) influenced Ransom, my own reading of a number of Ransom's books corroborates Pinn's claim. Indeed, a good brief statement of Ransom's social gospel ideas is found in his article, "The Institutional Church," in *Making the Gospel Plain*, 198–200, and "Duty and Destiny," in *Fortress Introduction to Black Church History*, 153–58. The Pinns are right to include Ida B. Wells-Barnett, Fannie Barrier Williams, and Fannie Lou Hamer as significant contributors to the black social gospel (ibid., 129–33).

44. See Ralph E. Luker, *The Social Gospel in Black and White* (Chapel Hill/London: University of North Carolina Press, 1991).

With the publication of his most famous book, *Christianity and the Social Crisis*, Walter Rauschenbusch was catapulted into the leadership of the social gospel movement. In fact, when he sent the manuscript to several large publishers and inquired about the possibility of publication, all expressed interest in publishing it. He chose the Macmillan Company, and the book was published in 1907. On reflection, Rauschenbusch wrote:

> I expected there would be a good deal of anger and resentment [apparently among faculty colleagues at Colgate Rochester Seminary where he taught, and also among more conservative pastors and laypersons]. I left for a year's study in Germany right after it appeared and I heard only the echoes of its reception. I eagerly watched the first newspaper comments on it and, to my great astonishment, everybody was kind to it. Only a few "damned" it.[45]

When he returned to the United States, Rauschenbusch found that the book's reception had made him a celebrity. He was famous. And for the first time in his career, he was a hotly pursued lecturer. But Rauschenbusch recalled that prior to writing the book, all evidence indicated that people (read "white" people) did not want to hear his message about the relevance of Christianity to the social crisis.[46] Indeed, some even thought that because of his interest in the poor and the welfare of workers he should not even be allowed to be a seminary professor.[47] This strong interest in the well-being of poor whites and of laborers developed during his ministry in New York City's "Hell's Kitchen."

However, it turned out that the time was ripe for the publication of *Christianity and the Social Crisis*. It was truly a book whose time had come, whose basic ideas had been tracked down by the Spirit of the times. Rauschenbusch's first biographer, Dores Sharpe, wrote about the events and changes in American society that paved the way for the fantastic reception the book received.

> Seldom has a great book ever appeared at so precisely the right moment. Like a confluence of rivers, separate streams of historical development converged. The author himself was just arriving at the high point of his intellectual maturity and the fullest command of his powers. In the religious world the results of the "historical method,"

---

45. Quoted in Sharpe, *Walter Rauschenbusch*, 233.

46. Sharpe, *Walter Rauschenbusch*, 232.

47. Rauschenbusch, "The Kingdom of God," in *The Social Gospel in America*, 266.

as applied to the Scripture and the development of Christian theology and the Christian Church, had become generally known and accepted by Christian thinkers. In American economic life, the changes caused by the closing of the frontier, by the rapid industrial expansion after the Civil War, and by the unexampled agglomeration of human beings in great cities, were beginning to be manifest even to the unthinking. A cyclic business depression was taking place, and there was widespread suffering and exceptional unemployment. The so-called "muck-raking" revelations of Lincoln Steffens, Ida Tarbell and others, had awakened the public mind to the fact that all was not well either in business or in politics. Yet the churches were numerous and influential and many of their people very earnest: religion was a dominant force. The public mind was patriotic and hopeful, even if shocked. Labor restlessness was evident, and socialism, though regarded as a radical and alien doctrine imported from Europe, was growing rapidly among the working classes. The great coal strike of 1905 was still in people's minds.[48]

INTEGRAL CONNECTION BETWEEN RELIGION AND ETHICS

Like the Hebrew prophets of the eighth century bce, who refused to separate religion from ethics, the focus of Rauschenbusch was on the affairs of this world and the relevance of religion to every sphere. This was an argument against restrictionism in decision making and behavior, that is, the popular practice among power holders in both the secular and religious arenas of suspending the highest ethical principles in their particular area of expertise, that is, business, politics, academic administration, and so forth. In any event, Rauschenbusch, like the Hebrew prophets, was concerned not about the hereafter, but about justice and righteousness in the here and now. Furthermore, he was convinced that the chief duty of the religious ethicist was "to stand for the rights of the helpless," a point to which King readily and easily assented.[49] Rauschenbusch espoused a Christianity that focused less on faith in a future life beyond the grave, and more on social justice in the present world, a prominent theme in the Hebrew prophets and to Martin Luther King. Contrary to the popular view that Christianity should involve itself only in spiritual matters, Rauschenbusch, echoing the stance of the eighth-century prophets, was convinced that the entire world belonged to God, and therefore insisted that "all the affairs of

48. Sharpe, *Walter Rauschenbusch*, 231.
49. Rauschenbusch, *Christianity and the Social Crisis*, 2.

the nation were the affairs of religion."[50] There was no area of human affairs in the world that was off limits or not relevant to the work of religion (and most especially Christianity), an emphasis that we saw in A. D. Williams and Daddy King. It stands to reason that King Jr. also saw religion as relevant to every area of society and insisted that it must be made effective in each. God is concerned about the whole world—sacred and secular, spiritual and mundane. In his sermon, "A Religion of Doing," King said:

> Religion must be effective in the political world, the economic world, and indeed the whole social situation. Religion should flow through the stream of the whole [of] life. The easygoing dichtymy [sic] between the sacred and the secular, the god of religion and the god of life, the god of Sunday and the god of Monday has wrought havoc in the portals of religion. We must come to see that the god of religion is the god of life and that the god of Sunday is the god of Monday.[51]

This is essentially what Rauschenbusch had in mind as he sought "a unity of life." "A real religion," he said, "always wanted unity. It wants to bring the whole world into one great conception that can inspire and fill the soul. It sees one God, it wants one world, and it wants one redemption."[52] He found the solution in the idea of the kingdom of God, a thoroughly social idea and an idea that readily appealed to Martin Luther King; appealed to him in large part because of his keen familiarity with the idea long before reading Rauschenbusch's explanation for it. Without question, King had seen this very idea of the unity of life, religion, and ethics at work in his father's ministry and had been made aware of the same focus in the way his maternal grandfather did ministry.

King was deeply influenced by the doctrine that the whole world belongs to God, and that not only is God concerned about all that happens in the world, the minister and Christians must be as well. Indeed, like Daddy King, he had little patience with those who counseled him on the role of the minister, saying that a minister's responsibility is to preach and attend only to the spiritual needs of human beings, and by all means to stay away from social issues. We get a good sense of King's stance in what he shared at a mass meeting at First Baptist Church in Montgomery on January 30, 1956.

50. Ibid., 27.
51. *The Papers*, 6:172.
52. Rauschenbusch, "The Kingdom of God," in *The Social Gospel in America*, 266.

This good white citizen I was talking to said that I should devote more time to preaching the gospel and leave other things alone. I told him that it's not enough to stand in the pulpit on Sunday and preach about honesty, to tell people to be honest and don't think about their economic conditions which may be conducive to their being dishonest. It's not enough to tell them to be truthful and forget about the social environment which may necessitate their telling untruths. All of these are a minister's job. You see God didn't make us with just soul alone so we could float about in space without care or worry. He made a body to put around a soul. When the body was made in flesh, there became a material connection between man and his environment and this connection means a material well being of the body as well as the spiritual well being of the soul is to be sought. And it is my job as a minister to aid in both of these.[53]

That King had already had these ideas modeled for him by his father and other southern black ministers devoted to social Christianity made it easy for him to accept Rauschenbusch's teaching.

King's Advocacy of the Unity of Religion and Ethics

In his own ministry, King unashamedly advocated for a social gospel, whether to white or black ministers. During the Birmingham campaign, for example, he reminded white Christians and their ministers (including the eight clergymen who prompted his writing of the famous "Letter from Birmingham Jail") of "the need for a social gospel to supplement the gospel of individual salvation. I suggested that only a 'dry as dust' religion prompts a minister to extol the glories of Heaven while ignoring the social conditions that cause men an earthly hell."[54] King also found himself periodically reminding black Christians and their ministers of the importance of ministering to the whole person—of being as concerned about one's social or bodily well-being as about one's spiritual well-being: "It's all right to talk about long white robes over yonder," King told the members of Mount Pisgah Missionary Baptist Church in Chicago in 1967, "but I want a suit and some shoes to wear down here. It's all right to talk about the streets flowing with milk and honey in heaven, but I want some food to eat down here. It's all right to talk about the new Jerusalem. But one day we must begin to talk about the new Chicago, the new Atlanta, the new New York, the

---

53. *The Papers* (1997), 3:114.
54. Martin Luther King Jr., *Why We Can't Wait* (New York: Harper & Row, 1964), 65.

new America."[55] At other times, King pleaded for strong leadership from black ministers. Reminiscent of both A. D. Williams and Daddy King, he reminded them that by virtue of being pastors of black churches they had more freedom and independence than others in the black community to be strong leaders and to stand up for justice.[56]

Earlier, I said that Rauschenbusch was much influenced by the Hebrew prophets' emphasis on the unity of religion and morality. King himself held that the Christian religion inherited from Jewish religion the profoundly important idea that there is no separation or dichotomy between religion and ethics. They are one.[57] This is an idea that repeatedly occurs in King's writings, speeches, and sermons. For example, King was highly critical of those people who give the outward appearance of being Christian, but who see no relation between their religion and their behavior in the social order. This is why so many white proponents of Christianity thought (and too many still think!) it acceptable to join terrorist groups such as the KKK and White Citizens Councils, and who actually committed heinous acts of violence and murder against blacks and Jews and expressed no regrets, no pangs of conscience, and felt no need for repentance and forgiveness. King was very much aware of this tendency to divorce religious faith from ethical behavior, as illustrated in the quote above. For him, it was not enough to attend church every Sunday, pay tithes, receive communion, and receive the benediction. He knew that such activities mean little if one behaves like the devil after worship service ends. One example of King's criticism of this tendency will have to suffice.

On October 9, 1966, King preached on the subject, "Pride versus Humility," using as his text the parable of the Pharisee and the tax collector (Luke 18:9-14). Here we have two men who went to the temple to pray. The Pharisee, in his arrogant and holier-than-thou attitude, thanked God that he was not like other people, including the tax collector. He went on to list things that he did, such as fasting multiple times each week, and regularly tithing. Standing some distance away, the tax collector, humbled and with head completely bowed, implored God to be merciful to him, "a sinner." Jesus reportedly responded: "I tell you, this man went down to his home justified rather than the other; for all who exalt themselves will be humbled, but all who humble themselves will be exalted" (18:14).

55. King, "Why Jesus Called a Man a Fool," in *A Knock at Midnight*, ed. Clayborne Carson and Peter Holloran (New York: Warner Books, 1998), 146–47.

56. King, *Why We Can't Wait*, 65. See also Martin Luther King Sr. with Clayton Riley, *Daddy King: An Autobiography* (New York: William Morrow, 1980), 99, 105, 125.

57. *The Papers*, 6:120.

King's commentary on this response provides a clear idea of his sense that the Jewish and Christian religions are profoundly and inextricably united with ethics; that frequency of church attendance, participation in the aesthetic aspects of worship such as the liturgy, or consistent tithing—these things alone—are not sufficient; are not ends in themselves. In King's estimation, Jesus condemned the Pharisee because he "confused ceremonial piety with genuine religious living."[58] The liturgical, offertory, and other formal aspects of religion are without question important, but these alone do not meet God's expectation of the truly faithful religious person as expressed by the prophet Micah, namely that such person do justice, love kindness, and walk humbly with God (Mic. 6:8). The Hebrew prophets did not condemn ceremonial acts of religion as such. Their condemnation was directed at those for whom these were the sole or most important acts of worshiping God. They wanted the people and the nation to understand that what God required was that they "[a]ct with justice and righteousness and deliver from the hand of the oppressor anyone who has been robbed" (Jer. 22:3). Moreover, as important as the ceremonial aspects of religion are, King interpreted Jesus' response to mean that "genuine religion is always followed up by the living of a meaningful life. The Pharisee was in danger of becoming so involved in the externals, in the outer parts of religion, that he had lost contact with the inner."[59] King added support to this stance by quoting the Apostle Paul's warning that in the last days many will be guilty of "holding to the outward form of godliness but denying its power" (2 Tim. 3:5). Those who succumb to such tendencies are not proponents of Christianity at its best. In this regard, King quoted approvingly a comment by E. Stanley Jones: ". . . so many people have been inoculated with a mild form of Christianity that they have become immune to the genuine article."[60]

Martin Luther King believed that the American practice of enslavement, with all of its attending evils and consequences that are still ongoing, as well as the system of apartheid in South Afrika, had the sanction and support of the church—of people who claimed to be Christians. He said that these were people who worshiped Jesus emotionally and aesthetically, but not morally.[61] King further strengthened the point by saying:

58. King, "Pride versus Humility," October 9, 1966, Library and Archives of the Martin Luther King, Jr. Center for Social Change, Inc., 1. It should be noted that this is an "incomplete transcript edited for broadcast." In addition, the transcriber gave as the title of this sermon, "Pharisee and Publican." However, in the opening sentence King named as the subject, "Pride versus Humility."

59. King, "Pride versus Humility," 2.

60. Quoted in King, ibid. King prefaces this quote by saying that Jones "says it something like this," signaling that this may not be a verbatim quote.

61. Ibid.

Go to your lynching mobs. So often Negros in Mississippi and Alabama and Georgia and other places have been taken to that tree that bears strange fruit. And do you know that folk [who] are lynching them are often big deacons in Baptist churches and stewards in Methodist churches, feeling that by killing and murdering and lynching another human being they were doing the will of the Almighty God? The most visious [*sic*] oppressors of the Negro today are probably in church. Ross Barnett [governor of Mississippi] teaches Sunday school in a Methodist church in Mississippi. Mr. Wallace of Alabama taught Sunday school for years. One white Sunday school teacher down in Mississippi said not long ago that God was a charter member of the White Citizens Council—using God to sanction their prejudice.[62]

Elsewhere, King made it crystal clear that the church had strayed far and wide from its mission regarding racial justice. American enslavement and ongoing systematic racial discrimination could never have been tolerated had the church taken a determined stand against it. Instead, in the area of race the church has failed its Christ miserably, said King. He went on to say:

This failure is due, not only to the fact that the church has been appallingly silent and disastrously indifferent in the realm of race relations, but even more to the fact that it has often been an active participant in shaping and crystallizing the patterns of the race-caste system. Colonialism could not have been perpetuated if the Christian Church had really taken a stand against it. . . . In America slavery could not have existed for almost two hundred and fifty years if the church had not sanctioned it, nor could segregation and discrimination exist today if the Christian Church were not a silent and often vocal partner.[63]

The church's record on race has been so persistently poor that King was convinced that it was subject to divine judgment. In the final analysis King held that too often Christians and the churches substitute aesthetic and emotional demands for moral and spiritual ones.

By the time Martin Luther King matriculated at Crozer Theological Seminary, he was already committed to the Hebrew and Christian principle

---

62. Ibid., 2–3.
63. King, *Strength to Love* (New York: Harper & Row, 1963), 97–98.

of the unity of religion and ethics. He had seen this principle at work in the ministry of his father and other southern black ministers and in his teacher-mentors at Morehouse. In addition, he knew the Bible well enough to know that this was a focus of the Hebrew prophets as well as Jesus. Consequently, his discovery of the same emphasis in Rauschenbusch was not new in itself. What was new, for King, was Rauschenbusch's systematic argument and theological grounding of the relevance of Christianity for social problems from the time of the Hebrew prophets, to the time of Jesus, the inception of the early church, and down to his own day.

Rauschenbusch's Call for Bold Proactive Faith

Rauschenbusch argued that although throughout its history Christianity had an impact on social issues at various times, such impact was often not a result of intentionality and conviction on the part of the churches and church leaders. Instead, Christianity's positive effects on controversial social issues and social reform often occurred as a result of minority protest voices within its ranks. Rauschenbusch illustrated this in an instructive passage when he wrote:

> For instance, the position of woman has doubtless been elevated through the influence of Christianity, but by its *indirect and diffused influences* rather than by any direct championship of the organized Church. It is probably fair to say that most of the great Churches through their teaching and organization have exerted a conservative and retarding influence on the rise of woman to equality with man. . . . It is this diffused spirit of Christianity rather than the conscious purpose of organized Christianity which has been the chief moral force in social changes. It has often taken its finest form in heretics and free-thinkers, and in non-Christian movements. The Church has often been indifferent or hostile to the effects which it had itself produced. The mother has refused to acknowledge her own children. *It is only when social movements have receded into past history so that they can be viewed in the larger perspective and without the irritation created by all contemporary disturbance of established conditions, that the Church with pride turns around to claim that it was she who abolished slavery, aroused the people to liberty, and emancipated woman.*[64]

---

64. Rauschenbusch, *Christianity and the Social Crisis*, 150 (emphasis added).

Rauschenbusch argued that Christianity and the church should be much more intentional about such matters. His own understanding of the prophets of Israel and the life and teachings of Jesus, for example, was that believers should consciously and vigilantly apply the principles of their faith to social questions. He was convinced that no one who claimed to be a Christian could be taken seriously if he was at peace with the status quo. "If a man wants to be a Christian," Rauschenbusch said, "he must stand over against things as they are and condemn them in the name of that higher conception of life which Jesus revealed. If a man is satisfied with things as they are, he belongs to the other side."[65] Although Rauschenbusch did not make the connection himself, on such a view, one simply cannot consistently be Christian and racist at the same time. King did make the connection, and did so in persuasive fashion.[66] Being a Christian requires that one live by the principles and teachings of Jesus and that one acknowledge and respect the image of God in every person, regardless of race, class, and gender.

This same idea was echoed in King's passionate criticism of white moderate pastors and their churches during the Birmingham, Alabama campaign in 1963. Writing from jail, in what came to be the famous "Letter from Birmingham Jail," King wrote of his deep disappointment in the failure of white churches and white pastors to be transformed nonconformists rather than conformists in the face of racial injustice. He had hoped that southern white ministers, priests, and rabbis would stand with the civil rights demonstrators as their strongest allies. "Instead," said King, "some have been outright opponents, refusing to understand the freedom movement and misrepresenting its leaders; all too many others have been more cautious than courageous and have remained silent behind the anesthetizing security of stained-glass windows."[67] These were too often otherwise good people who chose to remain silent in the face of social evil and injustice. King told the white clergymen that the people of his generation would have to repent "not merely for the hateful words and actions of the bad people but for the appalling silence of the good people."[68]

What Walter Rauschenbusch called for was a bold, proactive Christian faith in the face of existing social problems in the world. In addition, he was critical of earlier ascetic tendencies in Christianity, asserting that "[a]scetic Christianity called the world evil and left it. Humanity is waiting for a revolutionary Christianity which will call the world evil and change it."[69]

65. Ibid., 90.
66. *The Papers* (2000), 4:281.
67. King, *Why We Can't Wait*, 94.
68. Ibid., 89.

Rauschenbusch was not calling for the violent overthrow of existing institutions in this country, but only for their radical transformation, or the "Christianization" of the social order.

Unquestionably, the chief doctrine that served as the theological basis for Rauschenbusch's social concerns was the kingdom of God, or the idea of a radically transformed and regenerated society. He therefore became obsessed with the idea of Christianizing the entire social order, and wrote a book by that title.[70] Right or wrong, he argued that all of the basic institutions in the United States had been Christianized, except the economic and business orders.[71]

CHRISTIANIZING THE SOCIAL ORDER

The concept of Christianizing the entire social order is important as we try to understand King's later thought. Rauschenbusch did not mean that any area of society was or could be perfect, recognizing as he did that as long as human beings are human beings sin will be prevalent in the world, and as long as there is sin there can be no perfect society or given area of society.[72] To Christianize the social order only means that it has been humanized in the best sense, or formally brought into harmony with the ethical principles of Jesus. Rauschenbusch maintained, for example, that the church became Christianized when it let go of despotism and exploitation and came under the law of love and service,[73] just as the political arena in the United States was Christianized "when special privilege was thrust out of the constitution and theory of our government and it was based on the principle of personal liberty and equal rights."[74] This does not mean that in practice this is perfectly upheld in every case, but the basic structure is in line with the higher ethical principles. What Rauschenbusch said about the Christianized political community is important as we think about King's ideal of the beloved community and his efforts to establish it.

> Instead of legalizing class inequality, they at least try to be an organized expression of the equal rights of all. Instead of being a firmly wrought system for holding down the weak and depriving them of the natural means of self-help and even of a voice to utter

69. Rauschenbusch, *Christianity and the Social Crisis*, 91.

70. See Rauschenbusch, *Christianizing the Social Order* (New York: Macmillan, 1926 [1912]).

71. Ibid., ch. 3.

72. Ibid., 126.

73. Ibid., 141.

74. Ibid., 148.

their wrongs, our government tries to be a guarantee of freedom and a protection to the helpless. Instead of being constitutionally an organization of a clique for their private advantage, it is planned as an organization of all for the common good, and only falls into the hands of marauding interests through the ignorance and laziness of the citizens. Democracy is not equivalent to Christianity, but in politics democracy is the expression and method of the Christian spirit.[75]

As King developed the ethics of the beloved community (not viewed as a perfect community but as one that is humanized by principles such as the inviolable sacredness of persons where the dignity of every person is acknowledged and respected), he brought together in a coherent mosaic basic ideas of Rauschenbusch's kingdom ideal: basic elements of the philosophy of personalism, such as the autonomy and communal nature of persons, and the existence of an objective moral order. In addition, he integrated ideas about the role of religion in the world that he learned from his parents, maternal grandmother, and teachers at Morehouse. He also incorporated two other things: the longstanding tradition of protest that root so deep in his family lineage, and Reinhold Niebuhr's insistence that because of the prevalence, depth, and persistence of sin and the tragic aspects of human existence, it is necessary to persist in resisting the super-personal forces of evil.

We should not be surprised that King, the seminarian, was enamored with Rauschenbusch's ideas. There was no pretense in King about Rauschenbusch's influence on his thinking. He concluded that "Rauschenbusch had done great service for the Christian Church by insisting that the gospel deals with the whole man, not only his soul but his body; not only his spiritual well-being but his material well-being."[76] This left a deep and lasting impression on how King understood religion. In this regard he concluded:

It has been my conviction ever since reading Rauschenbusch that any religion which professes to be concerned about the souls of men and is not concerned about the social and economic conditions that scar the soul, is a spiritually moribund religion only waiting for the day to be buried. It well has been said: "A religion that ends with the individual, ends."[77]

75. Ibid., 153.
76. King, *Stride*, 91.
77. Ibid. See also *The Papers*, 6:451.

Rauschenbusch's Influence on King

Despite King's failure to read Rauschenbusch's later books that would have obviated, or at least caused him to soften some of his criticisms, there is no question that he found in Rauschenbusch some of the formal or intellectual answers he so desperately sought. These include:

- the idea of Christianity's relevance to the social question, and the obligation of Christians to be intentional about applying the principles of Christianity to social maladies that undermine the humanity and dignity of persons
- a clear preference for siding with the weak and the poor
- a predilection for the centrality of the eighth-century prophets and their emphasis on justice and righteousness
- an emphasis on the applicability of Christian principles to *every* area of life, since the whole world belongs to God
- the inseparability of religion and ethics
- emphasis on ethical conduct as the supreme and sufficient religious act
- emphasis on the public morality of society more than the private morality of individuals, that is, less focus on the saving of souls, and more emphasis on bringing the super-personal forces of evils under the law of Jesus

Each of these emphases in Rauschenbusch's work is consistent with King's upbringing in the black church, and how he essentially understood Christianity and ministry prior to enrolling in seminary. These would become important points for his leadership in his civil rights ministry, and would enhance the theological grounding of his social activism. King rejected what he called a "lopsided Reformation theology [that] has often led to a purely other-worldly religion. It has caused many churches to ignore the 'here' and emphasize the 'yonder.' By stressing the utter hopelessness of this world and emphasizing the need for the individual to concentrate his efforts on getting his soul prepared for the world to come, it has ignored the need for social reform, and divorced religion from life. It sees the Christian gospel as only concerned with the individual soul."[78] King went on to tell how the pulpit committee of a church seeking a new pastor listed as the first of several qualifications that a candidate "must be able to preach the true gospel and not talk about social issues."[79] King saw that such a thing could lead only to a "dangerously irrelevant church"

78. *The Papers*, 6:549.
79. Ibid.

where people assemble in a country-club atmosphere "to hear and speak pious platitudes."[80] As important as these ideas were for the maturing King, something else needed to happen in his theological pilgrimage.

Reinhold Niebuhr (1892–1971) began his ministry in Detroit, Michigan as a social gospel liberal in 1915, having been much influenced by the ideas of Walter Rauschenbusch and other social gospel theologians and pastors. Although Niebuhr had high regard for Rauschenbusch and social gospel liberalism, he had not long been the minister at Bethel Evangelical Church before he was convinced that the theology he learned at the Yale Divinity School was not appropriate for the problems of labor and race relations that confronted him in Detroit. Liberal social gospel theology was neither tough enough nor realistic enough to make sense of the outrageous practices and antics of industrial giants such as Henry Ford and the Ford Motor Company. Much of liberal theology was too soft, and even completely quiet, on sin, especially in its communal forms. In addition, liberal theology generally had what Niebuhr believed to be a much too optimistic view of human nature and human destiny. We learn from King that it was through his reading and study of Niebuhr's theological social ethics that he arrived at a more balanced view of social gospel liberalism. In the next chapter, I discuss at length some of Niebuhr's basic ideas, their influence on King, his reaction to them, and how he appropriated them in his thinking and practice.

80. Ibid., 6:549, 550.

5

The Christian Realism of Reinhold Niebuhr

As a doctoral student, Martin Luther King was formally trained in systematic theology or what he sometimes characterized as philosophical theology. Because of his early interest as a teenager to solve the social problems that nagged and hounded his people, he became progressively more interested in social ethics after he completed his doctoral work and began doing ministry in Montgomery.[1] Any astute theological student with King's interests in social philosophy and addressing social problems in the 1940s and 1950s inevitably encountered the work of Reinhold Niebuhr (1892–1971).

King was first introduced to Niebuhr's work while in seminary, where he read and was much impacted by *Moral Man and Immoral Society* (1932). During this period, he also familiarized himself with portions of volume one of Niebuhr's magnum opus, *The Nature and Destiny of Man*.[2] During doctoral studies under L. Harold DeWolf at Boston University he familiarized himself with most of Niebuhr's major books, including a lesser-known but important text, *The Contributions of Religion to Social Work* (1930).[3] However, I find it interesting that King's seminary and doctoral papers do not reference Niebuhr's first book, *Leaves from the Notebook of a Tamed Cynic* (1929), which consists of selections from the journal he kept during his thirteen-year ministry in Detroit. Many of the themes that made Niebuhr famous appeared in rudimentary form in that book. For example, we see evidence of Niebuhr's early grappling

1. Martin Luther King Jr., "Pilgrimage to Nonviolence," in his *Strength to Love* (New York: Harper & Row, 1963), 137.

2. See Clayborne Carson et al., eds., *The Papers of Martin Luther King, Jr.* (Berkeley: University of California Press, 1992), 1:277, 279. On page 195 King cites a passage from Niebuhr's text, but does not mention his name or provide a footnote. He includes the book in the bibliography.

3. See the bibliography for his essay, "Reinhold Niebuhr's Ethical Dualism," in *The Papers* (1994), 2:151–52. The essay was written for DeWolf's Seminar in Systematic Theology.

with the theme—later fully developed in *Moral Man and Immoral Society*—that individuals are not very lovely in the mass (or groups).[4] We also see the beginnings of his Christian realism, that is, his insistence on the need to see social realities as they are rather than as they ought to be, and to take sin generally much more seriously than most liberals, and social sins such as injustice much more seriously than orthodox Christians were inclined to do. Much of Niebuhr's critique of religious and secular liberalism occurred during the Detroit years (1915–28), and he wrote about it in his journal. In addition, in his oral history memoir, *The Reminiscences*, Niebuhr focused heavily on his experiences and thought formation, as well as the strong influence of Henry Ford and the Ford Motor Company, during the Detroit years.[5] Niebuhr told his biographer that he "cut [his] eyeteeth fighting Ford."[6] The thesis of his socio-ethical bombshell, *Moral Man and Immoral Society* (1932), that groups tend to be more immoral than individuals, had its early beginnings in *Leaves*. Without question, the latter text is a very important one in the Niebuhr corpus, and this writer wonders why it was not at least cited by King when he was a student, or whether he was even aware of it.

Looking back, Reinhold Niebuhr admitted that he had no use for metaphysics and epistemology. While a student at what was then Yale School of Religion, Niebuhr enrolled in no fewer than four courses in the college's philosophy department, but his grades were at best average, causing him to lose any interest in philosophy he might have had.[7] Niebuhr later reflected that such courses simply bored him, no matter how much he studied in preparation for them. "The more I threw myself into these philosophical studies, the more I got bored with all the schools of epistemology that had to be charted. . . . Frankly, the other side of me came out in the desire for relevance rather than scholarship."[8] Niebuhr felt that such courses in metaphysics and epistemology had little or nothing to do with the day-to-day struggles of "people with their backs pressed against the wall," to use a popular phrase of Howard Thurman.[9]

4. See Reinhold Niebuhr, *Leaves from the Notebook of a Tamed Cynic* (Chicago: Willett, Clark & Colby, 1929), 95.

5. Reinhold Niebuhr, *The Reminiscences of Reinhold Niebuhr* (New York: Oral History Research Office, Columbia University, 1957). Niebuhr was interviewed by Harlan B. Phillips. The first recorded interview occurred on February 14, 1953.

6. Quoted in June Bingham, *Courage to Change: An Introduction to the Life and Thought of Reinhold Niebuhr* (New York: Scribner's, 1961), 129.

7. Gary Dorrien, *Social Ethics in the Making: Interpreting an American Tradition* (Malden, MA: Wiley-Blackwell, 2009), 229.

8. Quoted in ibid. From Niebuhr, *The Reminiscences*, 16.

He therefore chose not to seek admission to a doctoral program after earning a master's degree in religious studies at Yale (although Gary Dorrien rightly observes that his performance in the philosophy courses was such that he did not meet the criteria for admission to a doctoral program[10]). This is amazing, considering that Niebuhr would later be the recipient of numerous honorary doctorates, and have numerous doctoral dissertations written on various aspects of his thought. In addition, his work in social ethics has been influential for most people who earned doctoral degrees in religious and theological studies up to and throughout the 1970s. For example, a course on Reinhold and H. Richard Niebuhr (co-taught by Paul Deats Jr. and Leroy S. Rouner) was required when I was a doctoral candidate in social ethics at Boston University in the late 1970s.

Although Martin Luther King was much influenced by some of Niebuhr's ideas, he was also quite critical of a number of them. In the discussion that follows, I offer a brief general overview of Niebuhr and some of his basic ideas, followed by a more in-depth examination of three areas of his thought that both influenced and caused problems for King. The primary focus of the discussion will be Niebuhr's *doctrine of sin*; his view of the *relation between love and justice* (or his ethical dualism); and his *critique of Gandhian nonviolence*.

OVERVIEW OF NIEBUHR AND HIS IDEAS

Without question, Reinhold Niebuhr was one of the most important theological social ethicists of the first half of the twentieth century. He always thought of himself as fundamentally a preacher and pastor, a point also acknowledged by his wife, Ursula M. Niebuhr.[11] In 1959, he said: "I am a preacher and I like to preach, but I don't think many people are influenced by admonition. Admonitions to be more loving are on the whole irrelevant. What is relevant are analyses of the human situation that discuss the levels of human possibilities of sin."[12] Niebuhr became a pretty good preacher and public speaker in his own right, making the rounds on numerous college campuses throughout the country even during his years as a pastor.[13]

Niebuhr reluctantly began his career as the senior pastor of the Bethel Evangelical Church in Detroit, Michigan right after earning his master's degree

9. See Howard Thurman, *Jesus and the Disinherited* (New York: Abingdon-Cokesbury, 1949), 13.

10. Dorrien, *Social Ethics in the Making*, 229.

11. See Ursula M. Niebuhr, "Introduction," in *Reinhold Niebuhr: Justice and Mercy*, ed. Ursula M. Niebuhr (New York: Harper & Row, 1974), 1.

12. Quoted in ibid.

13. Paul Merkley, *Reinhold Niebuhr: A Political Account* (Montreal: McGill-Queen's University Press, 1975), 9. See also Dorrien, *Social Ethics in the Making*, 231–32.

in religion at Yale in 1915. Dorrien contends that because of family financial issues Niebuhr had hoped that his first church would be able to provide a good salary, but "instead he was sent by synod President-General John Baltzar to a Germanic mission parish on the northwest edge of Detroit, Bethel Evangelical Church. That was deflating and frustrating."[14] Niebuhr did ministry at Bethel for thirteen years. He was helped greatly by his mother's pastoral assistance, which enabled him to travel all over the country delivering speeches and sermons at colleges and churches of all denominations (which he greatly enjoyed). This, in addition to the rising population growth in Detroit, contributed to Bethel's membership growth, even though Niebuhr was frequently on the road.[15] It was in Detroit, in the face of racial injustice and Henry Ford's (and other industrial magnates') mistreatment of laborers—some of whom were members at Bethel—that Niebuhr began to fashion views on theological social ethics that would later launch his career as a seminary professor at Union Theological Seminary in New York City. During the Union years he was also advisor to U.S. presidents and other world leaders.

Niebuhr rejected the title of theologian, preferring to characterize himself as a social ethicist. "I cannot and do not claim to be a theologian," he said in an intellectual autobiographical statement. "I have taught Christian Social Ethics for a quarter of a century and have also dealt in the ancillary field of 'apologetics.'"[16] To further drive home the point, he said: "I have never been very competent in the nice points of pure theology; and I must confess that I have not been sufficiently interested heretofore to acquire the competence."[17]

Niebuhr did more than most of his American contemporaries to stress the prevalence, stubbornness, depth, and power of sin, especially in corporate or group relations. In his view, sin is always present, on every level of human achievement,[18] which is why he was also adamant about the necessity of resisting social evil. Human beings therefore ought never to boast of being permanently extricated from sin as long as they are on this side of the grave. In a famous exchange with his brother, H. Richard, he said: "A truly religious man ought to distinguish himself from the moral man by recognizing the fact that he is not moral, that he remains a sinner to the end. The sense of sin is more central

---

14. Dorrien, *Social Ethics in the Making*, 230.

15. Ibid., 232.

16. Niebuhr, "Intellectual Autobiography," in *Reinhold Niebuhr: His Religious, Social and Political Thought*, ed. Charles W. Kegley (New York: Pilgrim, 1984; first published by the Macmillan Company in 1956 with Robert W. Bretall as co-editor), 3.

17. Ibid.

18. Niebuhr, *An Interpretation of Christian Ethics* (New York: Seabury, 1979 [1935]), 55.

to religion than is any other attitude."[19] And groups, according to Niebuhr, are much more immoral than individuals. And the larger, more complex and powerful the group, the more immoral it is likely to be. In this regard Niebuhr wrote:

> There will never be a wholly disinterested nation [arguably the largest, most complex, and powerful of groups]. Pure disinterestedness is an ideal which even individuals cannot fully achieve, and human groups are bound always to express themselves in lower ethical forms than individuals. It follows that no nation can ever be good enough to save another nation purely by the power of love. . . . Justice is probably the highest ideal toward which human groups can aspire.[20]

Niebuhr had little patience with those moralists—religious and secular—who believed they could live in history without sinning. His response to such people was simple: "There is no such possibility in history."[21]

Niebuhr's theological ideas were influenced by current events in Detroit and those on the national and international levels. In addition, he was much influenced by the formal theological ideas of historic and contemporary thinkers such as Augustine and Luther, and neo-orthodox theologians such as Karl Barth and Emil Brunner. More than anything else, it was current events—and a willingness to take them seriously—that led Niebuhr to take human sin in its corporate and social forms much more seriously than most liberal and social gospel theologians. I now turn to a consideration of how Niebuhr's conception of sin both influenced Martin Luther King and elicited criticism from him.

THE DEPTH AND PREVALENCE OF SIN

Reinhold Niebuhr argued that as long as there are human beings there will be sin, selfishness, and pride in the world, and that these will be present on every level of human progress in both interpersonal and group relations. For Niebuhr, there is *an equality of sin* where human beings are concerned, but *an inequality of guilt*. That is, all are sinners before God, but all are not necessarily guilty of

19. Niebuhr, "Must We Do Nothing," in *The Christian Century Reader*, ed. Harold Fey and Margaret Frakes (New York: Association Press, 1962), 224.

20. Ibid.

21. Niebuhr, "An Open Letter (to Richard Roberts)," in *Love and Justice*, ed. D. B. Robertson (Gloucester, MA: Peter Smith, 1976 [1957]), 270.

committing specific acts of sin, for instance, injustice and racism. Niebuhr held that "men who are equally sinners in the sight of God need not be equally guilty of a specific act of wrong-doing in which they are involved."[22] Nevertheless, according to Niebuhr not even divine grace can completely extricate persons from their sinful condition.

Martin Luther King expressed appreciation for Niebuhr's view, although at one time, while still a doctoral student, he implied that grace could in fact remove sin.[23] Nevertheless, in his sermon, "Man's Sin and God's Grace," he clearly reveals the influence of Niebuhr's doctrine of sin. In that sermon, King declares that there is a "gone-wrongness of human nature" that is "one of the basic assumptions of our Christian faith."[24] He believed this to be the basic human predicament: that on every level of human attainment we seem to be trapped in sin. In this regard, Niebuhr agreed with the reformer Martin Luther that persons are justified by faith alone, but the sin remains even in the justified state. In "Man's Sin and God's Grace," King concurred with Niebuhr's stance:

> Man can never escape evil in his life. He is part of the structure of society and so he must be a part of all the greed of society; he's a part of all the wars of society; and even if he's a pacifist, he's still contributing to the very thing that he's revolting against. This is the tragedy of collective and social life—that man *never* gets out of sin because he's caught up in society, and he can't get out of society because if he got out of that he wouldn't be man.[25]

However, King tried to avoid what he perceived as overly pessimistic tendencies in Niebuhr's doctrines of sin and human nature.[26] King argued that Christianity "sees over against man's sinfulness, man's tragic state, the graciousness of God's mercy, and His love and His forgiving power."[27] He therefore concluded that human beings are always sinners in need of God's grace. This was St. Augustine's stance, but King argued in a doctoral qualifying examination in History of Doctrine that Niebuhr, Karl Barth, and Emil Brunner had been influenced by the view that after the fall human beings were

22. Niebuhr, *The Nature and Destiny of Man*, two volumes in one (New York: Scribner's, 1941, 1943), 1:222.

23. *The Papers* (2007), 6:125.

24. Ibid., 6:382, 381.

25. Ibid., 6:387.

26. King, "Pilgrimage to Nonviolence," in *Strength to Love*, 136.

27. *The Papers*, 6:387.

corrupted to the point that they could do no real good without grace.[28] Human beings were, to the end of history, sinners in need of grace. Sin, according to these so-called neo-orthodox thinkers, occurs when human beings revolt against or turn away from God, and refuse to admit to their creatureliness. Instead, they desire to occupy God's throne—indeed to become God, a point that Niebuhr famously made.[29]

Although King believed that Niebuhr was much too soft on divine grace, he must also have known that Niebuhr acknowledged the power of divine grace when one stands repentant before God. As a doctoral student King appropriated ideas from volume two of Niebuhr's *Nature and Destiny of Man* as well as his *Faith and History*.[30] In these books, Niebuhr sets forth his views on divine grace. However, from King's perspective Niebuhr did not put enough emphasis on grace in his social ethics. After all, according to Niebuhr not even divine grace delivers one from sin once and for all.

On a more positive note, King claimed that reading Niebuhr during his senior year in seminary helped to snap him out of his uncritical liberal-social gospel stance. This was a revelatory and watershed event that changed a number of things for King, "including his fundamental outlook on religion." Reading Niebuhr also compelled him to reassess the place and power of reason and the uncritical emphasis placed on it by liberal theology. King said that Niebuhr helped him to see more clearly that the human propensity to sin "encourages us to rationalize our actions. Liberalism failed to show that reason by itself is little more than an instrument to justify man's defensive ways of thinking. Reason, devoid of purifying power of faith, can never free itself from distortions and rationalizations."[31] Without faith we can use reason to defend or justify our immoral acts. Of course, Niebuhr argued that even with faith, even with divine grace, the human inclination to sin means that to some degree reason must be held suspect. In his commentary on the point, Niebuhr wrote: "Rationalism [reason] in morals may persuade men in one moment that their selfishness is a peril to society and in the next moment it may condone their egoism as a necessary and inevitable element in the total social harmony. The egoistic impulses are so powerful and insistent that they will be quick to take advantage

28. *The Papers* (1994), 2:213.

29. See Niebuhr, *The Nature and Destiny of Man*, 1:200. Anders Nygren makes this same point in his classic work, *Agape and Eros*, trans. Philip S. Watson [one-volume edition] (Philadelphia: Westminster, 1953), 676.

30. See *The Papers* (1994), 2:141–52.

31. King, "Pilgrimage to Nonviolence," in his *Strength to Love*, 136.

of any such justifications."[32] King was profoundly impacted by this stance, although he had questions about Niebuhr's interpretation of love.

In 1945, while King was a student at Morehouse College, Dean Walter G. Muelder of Boston University wrote an article titled "Reinhold Niebuhr's Conception of Man." When King read the article as a doctoral student, it helped to deepen his understanding of agape. But it also led him to take issue with Niebuhr's interpretation of love.

Muelder applauded Niebuhr's criticism of sentimental and naïve interpretations of Christian love, but he found some aspects of the doctrine objectionable. He believed, for example, that the weakness of Niebuhr's position "resides in its inability to deal adequately with the relative perfection which is the fact of the Christian life."[33] Muelder argued, and King agreed, that there were historical, empirical evidences of Christian perfectionism such as that found in some of the perfectionistic Christian sects, for example, the Amish, which Niebuhr did not acknowledge. King quoted Muelder approvingly:

> There is a Christian perfectionism which may be called a prophetic meliorism, which, while it does not presume to guarantee future willing, does not bog down in pessimistic imperfectionism. Niebuhr's treatment of much historical perfectionism is well-founded criticism from an abstract ethical viewpoint, but it hardly does justice to the constructive historical contributions of the perfectionist sects within the Christian fellowship and even within the secular order. There is a kind of Christian assurance which releases creative energy into the world and which in actual fellowship rises above the conflicts of individual or collective egoism.[34]

John Ansbro has argued that Muelder's personalistic corrective of Niebuhr's view of agape is critical for King's adoption of nonviolent resistance as the chief means to the beloved community. King therefore gave more prominence to the power of agape in the social struggle than Niebuhr did. He was able to "combine an emphasis on the power of *agape* to create genuine community

32. Reinhold Niebuhr, *Moral Man and Immoral Society* (New York: Scribner's, 1932), 41. See his discussion of "The Rational Resources of the Individual for Social Living" in ch. 2.

33. Walter G. Muelder, "Reinhold Niebuhr's Conception of Man," in his *The Ethical Edge of Christian Theology: Forty Years of Communitarian Personalism* (Lewiston, NY: Edwin Mellen, 1983), 112.

34. Quoted in John Ansbro, *Martin Luther King, Jr.: The Making of a Mind* (Maryknoll, NY: Orbis, 1982), 158. Walter Muelder's article is found in his book, *The Ethical Edge of Christian Theology*, 103–14.

with a reliance on nonviolent methods of protest for active resistance to recalcitrant forces of evil in society, industry, and government."[35]

In addition to giving more credence to the transforming power of agape in the social struggle than Niebuhr, King, in his own mind, and following Muelder, also took more seriously the power of divine grace. He criticized Niebuhr for what he perceived to be a failure to take divine grace seriously enough in his theological social ethics.

Although Niebuhr was at one time a staunch proponent of the social gospel, he became its sharpest critic, as illustrated in *Leaves from the Notebook of a Tamed Cynic*, and in a much more systematic and poignant way in *Moral Man*. Niebuhr rejected all suggestions that there could be a perfect realization of the kingdom of God on earth. Because of his understanding of sin and how he viewed human nature and human destiny, he argued that it is virtually impossible for a perfect society to be realized as long as human beings exist.[36] For as long as human beings exist as they are, there will be the propensity and inevitability of sin and strife.

Niebuhr was at a loss as to how one could develop a reasonable social ethic out of a pure love ethic. "I cannot abandon the pure love ideal," he said in the famous exchange with his brother, "because anything which falls short of it is less than the ideal. But I cannot use it fully if I want to assume a responsible attitude toward the problems of society."[37] We saw in the previous chapter that King had a similar issue when trying to apply his ethical principles to political and economic matters. If he wanted to be both morally and politically responsible regarding societal problems he understood, as did Niebuhr, then he could not be as heavy-handed in applying those principles as he might like. In any case, human nature being what it is, along with the prevalence and power of sin in history, Niebuhr was certain that a perfectionist ethic such as agape could not win the day in the face of the misuse of massive unearned privilege, wealth, and power, which invariably leads to cruel injustice and oppression. Indeed, Niebuhr saw with greater clarity than most, particularly in the white community, that the prophetic tradition of the Jewish and Christian faiths reserved some of its sharpest judgments against the powerful, privileged, and wealthy, "accusing them of pride and injustice," as well as "the religious and

35. Ansbro, *Martin Luther King, Jr.*, 158.

36. See Niebuhr, "Must We Do Nothing," 226, and Walter Rauschenbusch, *Christianizing the Social Order* (New York: Macmillan, 1926 [1912]), 126. Here Rauschenbusch wrote: "Even a Christian social order cannot mean perfection. As long as men are flesh and blood the world can be neither sinless nor painless."

37. Niebuhr, "Must We Do Nothing," 226–27.

0 | Extremist for Love

social dimensions of sin. . . ."[38] The most cursory reading of the book of Amos, Isaiah, Micah, or Jeremiah substantiates this claim. Indeed, the prophets saw much more clearly than their contemporaries that "an inevitable concomitant of pride is injustice. The pride which makes itself the source and end of existence subordinates other life to its will and despoils it of its rightful inheritance."[39] Niebuhr had learned during the Detroit years that those individuals like Henry Ford who possess unchecked and enormous privilege, power, wealth, and other resources will use every conceivable means to protect their position, and thus are seldom if ever persuaded through preaching and moral suasion to do what love and justice require. None of this should be taken to mean that Niebuhr naïvely believed any one group of people, such as the privileged and powerful, to be naturally more sinful or depraved than another. And yet, his understanding of the long sweep of history and his close observation of local, national, and international current events convinced him that the wealthy and powerful tend to behave this way by virtue of their heightened sense of pride which invariably leads to injustice. Niebuhr put it this way in *The Nature and Destiny of Man*:

> This Biblical analysis agrees with the known facts of history. Capitalists are not greater sinners than poor labourers by any natural depravity. But it is a fact that those who hold great economic and political power are more guilty of pride against God and of injustice against the weak than those who lack power and prestige. Gentiles are not naturally more sinful than Jews. But Gentiles, holding the dominant power in their several nations, sin against Semitic minority groups more than the latter sin against them. White men sin against Negroes in Africa and America more than Negroes sin against white men. Whenever the fortunes of nature, the accidents of history or even the virtues of the possessors of power, endow an individual or a group with power, social prestige, intellectual eminence or moral approval above their fellows, there an ego is allowed to expand.[40]

Indeed, even the social gospel exponent Rauschenbusch observed that "when fed with money, sin grows wings and claws";[41] that "evils become bold and permanent when there is money in them."[42] At any rate, Niebuhr based all this

---

8. Niebuhr, *The Nature and Destiny of Man*, 1:223.

39. Ibid.

40. Ibid., 1:225–26.

41. Walter Rauschenbusch, *A Theology for the Social Gospel* (New York: Macmillan, 1917), 66.

on his honest appraisal of history and his own observations of the behavior and practices of privileged and wealthy people, and of white people's treatment of blacks. Needless to say, Niebuhr presented a real challenge to the essentially liberal theological perspective that King held during his first two years in seminary.

Some Niebuhr scholars contend that the permanent structure of his theological social ethics formed during a highly active period of writing, lecturing, and teaching in the 1930s and the early 1940s. In fact, a strong case could be made that the best outline of Niebuhr's social ethics is contained in volume two of his Gifford Lectures, *The Nature and Destiny of Man* (1941, 1943).[43] King said that he began reading Niebuhr's works in his last year of seminary.[44] Prior to this, in February 1950, he cited ideas from volume one of the *Nature and Destiny of Man* in a paper for George W. Davis's class, Christian Theology for Today.[45] Later, as a doctoral student at Boston University, he grappled with Niebuhr's ideas in a long paper written for the Dialectical Society (of which King was a founding member) titled "The Theology of Reinhold Niebuhr."[46]

INFLUENCE OF *MORAL MAN* ON KING

Although Niebuhr might well have set up a too sharp antithesis between personal and social ethics in *Moral Man and Immoral Society*, there is no question that King was much influenced by that book's basic thesis that groups tend to be more immoral than individuals. Niebuhr argued that "a sharp distinction must be drawn between the moral and social behavior of individuals and of social groups . . . ; and . . . this distinction justifies and necessitates political policies which a purely individualistic ethic must always find embarrassing."[47] King cited ideas from *Moral Man* in many of his writings and sermons.[48]

According to Niebuhr, human beings tend to be more moral as individuals, and considerably less so when they come together in groups of varying types

---

42. Ibid., 114.

43. This point was made by the late John C. Bennett, a close friend and colleague of Niebuhr's. See Bennett, "Reinhold Niebuhr's Social Ethics," in *Reinhold Niebuhr: His Religious, Social and Political Thought*, 101. See Niebuhr, *The Nature and Destiny of Man*, 2: ch. 9, "The Kingdom of God and the Struggle for Justice."

44. Martin Luther King Jr., *Stride Toward Freedom* (New York: Harper & Row, 1958), 97.

45. *The Papers* (1992), 1:277, 278,

46. *The Papers* (1994), 2:269–79.

47. Niebuhr, *Moral Man*, xi.

48. *The Papers* (2007), 6:386–87.

and sizes. However, he did not intend to convey the idea that individuals as such are not often quite immoral in their treatment of other human beings and groups. It was not his contention that individuals are necessarily and always moral in their outlook and behavior, while groups are always immoral. Instead, Niebuhr's point was that generally the behavior of groups is less moral than that of individuals because of the special qualities or character of groups and their inherent power, greed, and pride. Indeed, Niebuhr himself recognized the controversy prompted by the title of his provocative book: *Moral Man and Immoral Society*. Privately, he said that a more accurate title would be something like "*Immoral Man and Even More Immoral Society*,"[49] which more clearly acknowledges his awareness that individuals are often immoral as well.

King found many prophetic and realistic elements in Niebuhr's writings that deepened his understanding. He thought Niebuhr's emphasis on sin in both its individual and collective forms to be quite reasonable. In addition, he appreciated Niebuhr's observation that human nature is such that persons often find it difficult to place the interests of others before their own. He was also greatly helped by Niebuhr's realism about what one could expect of men who possess massive, unchecked power and privilege. In a nutshell, they could expect the abuse and misuse of power and privilege, and a refusal to willingly share their advantages (no matter how they came to possess them). In a related sense, King was influenced by Niebuhr's stance that the powerful and privileged rarely if ever share or give up their power and privileges without a brutal struggle, frequently to the death. Indeed, in 1957, King said, "[I]t is both historically and sociologically true that privileged classes do not give up their privileges voluntarily. And they do not give them up without strong resistance."[50] It is very rare that they share or give these up solely on the basis of rational and even moral considerations. Instead, they more often must be forced to do so; thus the need for organized resistance by the oppressed.

Furthermore, according to Niebuhr, just because the injustices and exorbitant greed of an institution, mega-corporation, or even mega-church have been exposed for all to see does not mean they will automatically begin to act justly, a point that was brought home in the most dramatic of ways during the economic meltdown that began in the United States and other nations in 2008 and continues to wreak havoc at this writing. Indeed, Niebuhr was nothing short of prophetic when he wrote in *Moral Man* (in 1932!): "Men will not cease to be dishonest, merely because their dishonesties have been revealed

49. Merkley, *Reinhold Niebuhr*, 83. See also Bob E. Patterson, *Reinhold Niebuhr* (Waco, TX: Word, 1977), 33.

50. *The Papers*, 4:127.

or because they have discovered their own deceptions. Wherever men hold unequal power in society, they will strive to maintain it. They will use whatever means are most convenient to that end and will seek to justify them by the most plausible arguments they are able to devise."[51] This statement is quite relevant in light of the attitude and behavior of executives of major financial institutions in the United States who were recipients of huge financial bailouts by the federal government (read "the American people") after their own greedy, cutthroat, deceptive practices led to the severe downturn of the economy. Even after these people's deceptions and greed were exposed to the entire nation, and though the entire country was on the brink of economic collapse because of what they did, the vast majority of them continued with business as usual, even to the point of paying out huge bonuses to top executives after receiving the bailouts, and then unashamedly tried to justify their actions. Niebuhr was right: "When power is robbed of the shining armor of political, moral and philosophical theories, by which it defends itself, it will fight on without armor. . . ."[52] This is precisely what many corporate executives who benefited from the bailouts did. Even when they and their politician friends could not produce plausible arguments for their behavior, they held their ground and pocketed the money.

Already a staunch believer in liberalism's idea of the goodness of human nature and the inherent worth of every person, Martin Luther King was helped by Niebuhr's insistence that sin exists on every level of human progress,[53] and that because of both selfishness and sinful pride, persons exhibit the inclination to evil as much as to good. He also applauded Niebuhr's keen awareness "of the complexity of human motives and of the relation between morality and power."[54] He saw each of these as significant contributions to theology. King could see the implications of this for social strategy. Niebuhr's stance also suggested to him why the oppressed generally have to struggle so hard and relentlessly against their oppressors to obtain even minimal justice and fair treatment.

We have seen that Martin Luther King was both helped and troubled by some aspects of Niebuhr's thought regarding sin and what may be achieved in history. Although he believed that Niebuhr was right to focus on the presence and power of human sin, King also concluded that Niebuhr overemphasized the place of sin to the extent that he could only end in pessimism regarding

51. Niebuhr, *Moral Man*, 34.

52. Ibid., 33.

53. Clayborne Carson, ed., *The Autobiography of Martin Luther King, Jr.* (New York: Warner Books, 1998), 27.

54. Ibid.

human nature and the possibilities of human social achievements in the world. He believed that Niebuhr was so preoccupied with the sinfulness of human nature that he did not place enough emphasis on divine grace and forgiveness.[55] King's critique of Niebuhr in this regard might well be a key reason that to the very end he remained hopeful about the achievement of equality of opportunity between blacks and whites, as well as a sense that despite the deeply embedded racism in the structures of this country, racial discrimination will be radically reduced, if not entirely eliminated. I will argue subsequently that on this very important point King's level of hopefulness should have been tempered with more Niebuhr, as well as lessons from black history and his own time. Nevertheless, King was challenged by Niebuhr's arguments regarding love and justice and his tendency toward ethical dualism, the subject of the next section.

Niebuhr's Ethical Dualism

As a doctoral student, Martin Luther King wrote a paper for L. Harold DeWolf's Seminar in Systematic Theology titled "Reinhold Niebuhr's Ethical Dualism." The essay was informed by a half-dozen of Niebuhr's most popular books. King discussed several elements of Niebuhr's ethics that appealed to him. This indicated his development beyond his previously uncritical acceptance of liberal theology's optimistic anthropology and confidence in the inevitability of human progress. Although King resigned himself to being a liberal, his would be a liberalism tempered both by his own experience of the sin of racism and injustice in the Deep South, and a good dose of Niebuhr's realism. Indeed, Michael Long is not wrong to say that in the end, King was a "tempered realist."[56]

Lest we mistakenly believe that had King not read Niebuhr he would have had no sense of the realistic aspects of Christianity and human experience, we should remember that he had on numerous occasions seen the uglier side of human nature as a boy in the segregated South and was much affected by it. He alluded to this in a paper written for George W. Davis in seminary, titled "How Modern Christians Should Think of Man." In the paper, King said that his inclination toward the neo-orthodox (i.e., realistic) conception of human beings "was quite likely linked to certain experiences that I had in the south with a vicious race problem."[57] For example, as noted before, when he was

---

55. Ibid., 31.

56. Michael G. Long, "Transforming Death: Life's Ultimate Tragedy and Hope for the Dawn," in *The Domestication of Martin Luther King, Jr.: Clarence B. Jones, Right-Wing Conservatism, and the Manipulation of the King Legacy*, ed. Lewis V. Baldwin and Rufus Burrow Jr. (Eugene, OR: Cascade Books, 2013), 233.

about six years old he was told by the parents of his white playmate that because he was a "Negro" he could no longer play with their son.[58] A couple of years later he was slapped and called a "nigger" by a white woman in a downtown Atlanta department store.[59] He witnessed the disrespectful behavior of the white police officer who tried to insult his father.[60] He had also been insulted by a white bus driver and forced to give up his seat to a white passenger during the return trip from a high school oratorical contest in Dublin, Georgia.[61] At the age of fifteen, he was forced to sit behind a curtain in a Jim Crow dining car on a train, and felt as if a curtain had been dropped on his personhood.[62] In addition, he was aware of the lynching of blacks by white racists, and had seen carloads of Ku Klux Klansmen riding through black neighborhoods in attempts to terrorize and intimidate residents.[63] It was this side of human nature that caused a six-year-old Martin Luther King, like his father before him, to promise to hate all white people.[64] Experiences such as these awakened his sense of realism and awareness of the prevalence of sin long before he heard Niebuhr's name. Unless King was completely naïve and undiscriminating in his thinking, these experiences would not have allowed him to be as optimistic about human nature as he claimed to be after his study of liberal theology in seminary. I return to this point momentarily.

John Ansbro provides a helpful discussion on King's struggle with Niebuhr during his student days at Boston University. Without question, King rejected Niebuhr's ethical dualism, that is, the idea that while individuals may periodically transcend self-interest and abide by the dictates of agape, groups never sacrifice their interests without being coerced into doing so. Individuals are more capable of abiding by the love principle than groups. Because the latter do not willingly sacrifice their interests, the most they are able to manage is the justice principle of balancing their interests against those of a competing group. Implied in this is the idea that love is more relevant to the actions of individuals than those of groups, which seem unable to overcome their self-interest and exorbitant egoism. Nothing was clearer to Niebuhr than the fact that religious and secular moralists lacked "an understanding of the brutal character of the

57. *The Papers* (1992), 1:274.
58. Carson, ed., *The Autobiography*, 7.
59. Ibid., 8–9.
60. Ibid., 8.
61. Ibid., 9–10.
62. Ibid., 11.
63. Ibid., 10.
64. See King, *Stride*, 18–19; Carson, ed., *The Autobiography*, 8–9, 10, 11–12.

behavior of all human collectives, and the power of self-interest and collective egoism in all intergroup relations."[65] Niebuhr concluded that "the best that can be expected of human groups is a wise rather than stupid self-interest."[66]

King believed that the crux of Niebuhr's ethical dualism lay in his sense of the relevance of love for individual and group spheres of action. According to Niebuhr, the inability of groups to willingly divest themselves of their self-interest means that love is less relevant for them. King said that Niebuhr arrived at this stance because he "noticed a terrible contrast between 'moral man and immoral society.' He observed a great distinction between the relatively decent, good behavior of man as an individual and man as society."[67] Niebuhr argues that the perfectionist nature of agape makes it almost irrelevant in the social struggle, since exorbitant and stubborn group interests and pride make it virtually impossible for groups to willingly relinquish their self-interests and respond in ways that are consistent with the demands of love.

According to Niebuhr, agape is a purely spontaneous, self-giving, other-regarding love that is concerned about the well-being of the neighbor. In addition, he believed it to be an ethic that does not resist evil. In this regard, he was similar to Leo Tolstoy. Unlike Tolstoy, however, Niebuhr argued that such an ethic is irrelevant to the sociopolitical struggle, at least from the standpoint of sociopolitical strategy. Agape is quite relevant in intimate interpersonal relations, he held, but not to the same extent and same way as in group or corporate relations involving complex power issues and group interests. Niebuhr therefore argued that in the social struggle, the best that one can hope to achieve is degrees of justice, which always fall short of what love requires. Niebuhr essentially argued that it is only the naïve or sentimental person who believes that in group or collective relations what is required by the love perfectionism of Jesus and the *resist not evil* ethic of the Sermon on the Mount is actually achievable.

The most that one should expect on any level of group achievement, according to Niebuhr, is a balance of interests and power, which is a rough equivalent of justice. But Niebuhr was aware that love requires more than the mere equilibrium of power, which is made necessary by love, but is not sufficient. And yet, this is the most that we can expect to achieve in conflicts between groups both in and out of the churches. Such achievement amounts to

65. Niebuhr, *Moral Man*, xx.

66. Niebuhr, "Can the Church Give a Moral Lead?" in *Essays in Applied Christianity*, ed. D. B. Robertson (New York: Meridian/Living Age Books, 1959), 83.

67. *The Papers*, 2:142–43.

justice, not love. For Niebuhr, only in the most intimate interpersonal relations is it possible to more nearly approximate what agape requires.

Therefore, in Niebuhr's ethics we find an irresolvable dualism between love and justice, where love is more relevant in individual relations, and justice in group relations. Consider what Niebuhr said about this in *Moral Man*. One cannot miss the tension and dualism between morality for the individual (roughly love) and morality for the group (roughly justice). More specifically, Niebuhr said: "This conflict, which could be most briefly defined as the conflict between ethics and politics, is made inevitable by the double focus of the moral life. One focus is in the inner life of the individual, and the other in the necessities of man's social life. From the perspective of society, the highest moral ideal is justice. From the perspective of the individual, the highest ideal is unselfishness."[68]

Although justice falls short of what love requires, Niebuhr argued that it is the most that can be achieved in the necessities of sociopolitical life. Therefore, everything possible should be done to achieve ever-higher degrees of justice, even if society "is forced to use means, such as self-assertion, resistance, coercion, and perhaps resentment, which cannot gain the moral sanction of the most sensitive moral spirit."[69] That we cannot achieve all that love requires is not a reason to cease efforts to approximate it, however. Indeed, for Niebuhr, that we inevitably fall short of love's expectations is among the chief reasons to keep trying and never give up if there is to be any semblance of civilized existence.

However, Niebuhr in no way maintained that there is mutual exclusiveness between these two moral perspectives, that is, between the ethics of the individual, and the ethics of society or the group. Nor did he see an absolute contradiction between the two. The moral imagination, ethical insights, and achievements of the individual are indeed relevant to societal living. Niebuhr makes the point: "The most perfect justice cannot be established if the moral imagination of the individual does not seek to comprehend the needs and interests of his fellows."[70] Niebuhr's claim that even in the sociopolitical arena justice is never enough by itself; that the continued existence of justice is dependent on something greater than justice; and that justice must be grounded in a higher ethic is strengthened by his conviction that "[a]ny justice which is only justice soon degenerates into something less than justice. It must be saved by something which is more than justice. The realistic wisdom of the statesman

68. Niebuhr, *Moral Man*, 257.

69. Ibid.

70. Ibid., 257–58.

is reduced to foolishness if it is not under the influence of the foolishness of the moral seer."[71] The political leader may be committed to achieving justice by any means, but may not be as careful about the way it is implemented and enforced. The moral seer, the person who may be naïve about the realities of the viciousness of politics but who is committed to righteousness and the love ideal, will insist that justice be implemented, but in ways that respect the dignity of persons. For such a person, justice is not just giving the oppressed their due, but doing so in a way that allows them to hold their heads high and retain their sense of dignity.

Although Reinhold Niebuhr believed that because of the stubborn persistence of group egoism and self-interest it is not possible to achieve all that love requires in collective relations, he maintained that love is always relevant in such relations to the degree that it serves to at least fine-tune the levels of justice that are achieved. It is also a constant reminder that higher levels of justice may be attainable. In this regard, Niebuhr wrote: "Every genuine passion for social justice will always contain a religious element within it. Religion will always leaven the idea of justice with the ideal of love. It will prevent the idea of justice, which is a politico-ethical ideal, from becoming a purely political one, with the ethical element washed out."[72]

Love is always the guiding ideal in Niebuhr's ethics, even though he insisted on the impossibility of achieving all that it requires as long as human beings are human beings. Love, for Niebuhr, is what he once characterized as the "impossible possibility."[73] By this he seems to have meant that love is impossible because we can never expect to achieve all that it requires in group relations. And yet, love is possible to the extent that there is always more that we can do to approximate what it requires, interpersonally and collectively. Therefore, in the social struggle, for example, we can never be quite satisfied that we have achieved all that can be achieved in the struggle for social justice and fairness. Love always requires more. Moreover, because sin is thought to be present on every level of human progress, this itself suggests that more must be done and that we must make the effort, rather than resign ourselves to doing nothing. There is no set level of justice beyond which a greater justice is not needed, or is not achievable in the world. More can always be done to more nearly approximate what the love ideal requires.

Niebuhr's ethical dualism is one of the issues that King struggled with in the paper he wrote for DeWolf. Ansbro provides a helpful comment.

71. Ibid., 258.
72. Ibid., 80–81.
73. See Niebuhr's discussion of this concept in *An Interpretation of Christian Ethics*, ch. 4.

[King] came to accept Niebuhr's critique of the naive optimism of liberalism, and to value his vision of the force of evil in the decisions of collectivities and of the need for active resistance to collectivities that use their concentrations of wealth to exploit the masses. However, despite his attraction to Niebuhr's theory on these points, in this paper King again assumed his usual dialectical approach and rejected Niebuhr's restrictions on the potential of *agape* for the transformation of society. He claimed that Niebuhr "fails to see that the availability of the divine *agape* is an essential affirmation of the Christian religion." He rejected Niebuhr's ethical dualism which in the main limited *agape* to the individual life and which spoke of the goal of society in terms of degrees of justice, achieved by physical force, if necessary.[74]

By the time King read *Moral Man* in seminary, he had made the decision to apply for doctoral studies. He claims that Niebuhr rocked the very foundation of his theological perspective. In "Pilgrimage to Nonviolence," he said that prior to reading Niebuhr he had emphasized only the essential goodness of human nature, and persons' ability to escape or overcome sin and to usher in the kingdom of God. Before reading Niebuhr, he was sure of his theological and religious foundations, and was desirous of pursuing a doctoral degree "for reasons of pleasure, inertia, and prestige."[75] Interpreting Niebuhr's influence on King, Taylor Branch writes:

> After Niebuhr, King experienced for the first time a loss of confidence in his own chosen ideas rather than inherited ones. The Social Gospel lost a good deal of its glow for him almost overnight, and he never again fell so completely under the spell of any school of thought, including Niebuhr's. . . . [T]he Niebuhr influence went to the heart of the public and private King and affected him more deeply than did any modern figure, including Gandhi. . . .[76]

King easily sensed from reading *Moral Man* that Niebuhr was a hardheaded, tough Christian realist who understood a good deal about the power, greed, and pride inherent in groups, and powerful individuals such as Henry Ford,

74. Ansbro, *Martin Luther King, Jr.*, 157.

75. Taylor Branch, *Parting the Waters: America in the King Years 1954–63* (New York: Simon & Schuster, 1988), 81.

76. Ibid.

and what it would take strategically to get them to share power and privilege. Niebuhr was convinced that because of human selfishness and pride and the way this gets acted out on the collective level, it is necessary to actively resist injustice, even to the point of taking coercive violent action. King was not sympathetic with Niebuhr's openness to the use of violence in the social struggle, but he fully agreed that it is necessary to be self-determined and to aggressively engage in the struggle against the forces of injustice. He agreed with Niebuhr's contention that it is naïve to think that the privileged and powerful will share their privileges and power without a struggle; without being made to do so. The difference is that for King, the means of resistance had to be nonviolent.

INFLUENCE OF NIEBUHR'S REALISM ON KING

Essentially, what Niebuhr did for King was to provide a formal theological framework for thinking about and addressing social evil, but King's early experiences with racism and other forms of social evil as a youth made it easy for him to resonate with Niebuhr's doctrine of human nature and human destiny and to be influenced by them as much as he was. On the intellectual plane, then, King's sense of Christian realism was only reinforced by his reading and study of Niebuhr. And yet, although aware of human beings' propensity to sin individually and collectively, especially when they possess massive unchecked power and privilege, King tended, on balance, to be optimistic about what they are capable of achieving in history, including equality of opportunity between whites and blacks,[77] as well as a racism-free society. This is all quite interesting considering Niebuhr's stance on what blacks could hope to actually achieve through their struggle to be admitted to a state of equality with whites. Niebuhr believed that it would be naïve for blacks to think that they can achieve this by uncritically trusting in the sense of fairness and morality of the white man. Any amount of justice and equality that comes about will happen not because of belief and trust in white men, Niebuhr declared, but through some type of well-organized resistance. But even through coercive means Niebuhr—a privileged white man himself and thus well positioned to understand the mentality of white people—was not optimistic that blacks could achieve justice and *full*

77. I realize that the issue of equality in the United States goes well beyond the traditional white–black binary to include other groups. As an Afrikan American, however, I refuse to pretend that the issue of equality between blacks and whites is any closer to resolution than fifty or a hundred years ago. It is therefore important that I focus on racism in the hope that I can do something to help eradicate it. In the meantime I remain ready and willing to be supportive of others in their respective struggles against injustice.

equality. "Whatever increase in the sense of justice can be achieved will mitigate the struggle between the white man and the Negro," Niebuhr wrote, "but it will not abolish it."[78] This seems to be an admission that blacks' struggle for equality and the eradication of racism in the United States will be a permanent one; that they may, through struggle, achieve degrees of equality—though, never truly *full* equality. Indeed, in *Moral Man*, Niebuhr removed all doubt as to what he meant, declaring: "However large the number of individual white men who do and who will identify themselves completely with the Negro cause, the white race in America will not admit the Negro to equal rights if it is not forced to do so. Upon that point one may speak with a dogmatism which all history justifies."[79] Nor did Niebuhr seem at all optimistic that blacks could force whites to admit them to equality of opportunity. On this issue, Niebuhr seemed to imply that something quite diabolical is at work in the matter of racism in the United States that militates against its eradication. He does not say precisely what it is, but he does make it clear that the elements of unchecked massive privilege and power are factors; that those who possess these in inordinate amounts will do whatever they deem necessary—and more—to retain them rather than have to share with the have-nots. Indeed, Niebuhr was not the first white man of repute to be pessimistic about whether blacks will ever be admitted to equal rights and equality of opportunity. After his tour of the United States in the early 1830s, French political theorist Alexis de Tocqueville made a similar assessment: "I do not believe that the white and black races will ever live in any country upon an equal footing. But I believe the difficulty to be still greater in the United States than elsewhere."[80] Thomas Jefferson held similarly, declaring in his *Memoirs* that there was nothing more certain than the eventual emancipation of the enslaved blacks. Jefferson went on to say that "it is equally certain, that the two races will never live in a state of equal freedom under the same government, so insurmountable are the barriers which nature, habit, and opinion have established between them."[81]

We will see in the last chapter that legal scholar-activist Derrick Bell would include "whiteness as a property right," along with inordinate power and privilege, as leading factors that hinder blacks' being admitted to full equality and equal rights. That blacks apparently cannot achieve full equality in a racism-free society, is the occasion to examine whether King's hopefulness

78. Niebuhr, "Can the Church Give a 'Moral Lead,'" in *Essays in Applied Christianity*, 81.

79. Niebuhr, *Moral Man*, 253; see also 120.

80. Alexis de Tocqueville, *Democracy in America* (New York: Everyman's Library/Alfred A. Knopf, 1994), 373.

81. Quoted in ibid., 373n46.

regarding the eventual achievement of equality with whites was realistic, then and especially, now. In any case, although King tended to have an optimistic outlook regarding human nature and what human beings can accomplish in history, this should not be taken to mean that he was naïve enough to believe that whites would, as a race, voluntarily share power and privilege with Afrikan Americans and other oppressed groups. King believed that human beings could achieve more in history not because he had faith in white people—or black people for that matter—but because of his absolute faith in God and his sense of what was possible through relentless cooperative human-divine endeavor. Indeed, the lesson that King gained from his study and understanding of the Hebrew prophets led him to believe that God is unswervingly faithful and compassionate toward the oppressed of the world and is always willing to work cooperatively with committed, faithful people to break open the floodgates of justice.

This is why King's faith in what human beings can achieve in history must be understood in light of his much deeper faith and trust in God. His faith in God, not in human beings of any race, is what led to his strong sense that the beloved community would be a reality some day, despite privileged and powerful people's refusal to voluntarily share privilege and power. What was the basis of King's unflinching hopefulness in this regard? James Cone is most certainly right when he responds by saying: "The answer is found in his faith in the biblical God of justice, love, and hope. No idea or strategy that King advocated can be understood correctly apart from his deep faith in the Christian God as defined by the black Baptist and liberal Protestant traditions. The new age is coming and cannot be stopped, because God, who is just and loving, wills that the oppressed be liberated."[82] For King, this also meant that blacks must be willing to sacrifice and join together in organized nonviolent actions to relentlessly resist racial discrimination and inequality.

Niebuhr's Critique of Gandhian Nonviolence

King was initially baffled by Niebuhr's critique of Gandhian nonviolence in *Moral Man*. Niebuhr argued that the social consequences of strategies of noncooperation and nonviolence, such as those implemented by Gandhi, were not totally different from those of violent resistance. He rightly saw that despite the claim of many pacifists, "nonviolence does coerce and destroy." This is not the intention of nonviolent resistance, but it is frequently a consequence.

Furthermore, Niebuhr maintained that Gandhi had confused *nonresistance* with *nonviolent resistance*.

In the early years of the South Afrikan struggle, Gandhi himself often used the terms *nonresistance* and *passive resistance* to characterize his work, and only later did he come to realize that such descriptions of their resistance work were actually misleading. An extended passage from *Moral Man* clarifies the point.

> [Gandhi] frequently speaks of his method as the use of "soul-force" or "truth-force." He regards it as spiritual in distinction to the physical character of violence. Very early in his development of the technique of non-violence in South Africa he declared: "Passive resistance is a misnomer. . . . The idea is more completely expressed by the term 'soul-force.' Active resistance is better expressed by the term 'body-force.'" A negative form of resistance does not achieve spirituality simply because it is negative. As long as it enters the field of social and physical relations and places physical restraints upon the desires and activities of others, it is a form of physical coercion. The confusion in Mr. Gandhi's mind is interesting, because it seems to arise from his unwillingness, or perhaps his inability, to recognise the qualifying influences of his political responsibilities upon the purity of his original ethical and religious ideals of non-resistance. Beginning with the idea that social injustice could be resisted by purely ethical, rational and emotional forces (truth-force and soul-force in the narrower sense of the term), he came finally to realise the necessity of some type of physical coercion upon the foes of his people's freedom, as every political leader must. "In my humble opinion," he declared, "the ordinary methods of agitation by way of petitions, deputations, and the like is no longer a remedy for moving to repentance a government so hopelessly indifferent to the welfare of its charge as the Government of India has proved to be. . . ." In spite of his use of various forms of negative physical resistance, civil-disobedience, boycotts and strikes, he seems to persist in giving them a connotation which really belongs to pure non-resistance. "Jesus Christ, Daniel and Socrates represent the purest form of passive resistance or soul-force," he declares in a passage in which he explains the meaning of what is most undeniably nonviolent resistance rather than nonresistance.[83]

83. Niebuhr, *Moral Man*, 242–43. Indeed, although the great abolitionist Frederick Douglass never advocated violence outright, he did come to the conclusion that in the enslaved Afrikans' struggle for

Niebuhr was not alone in grappling with this confusion. Gandhi also reported a similar struggle within himself, as he came to see that "passive resistance" and "nonresistance" were not accurate descriptions of the Indian struggle against British colonialism. He confessed that while in South Afrika he did not fully understand the meaning and implications of "passive resistance," although that was how he initially characterized their struggle. As the struggle progressed, he

freedom the method of moral suasion, i.e., the appeal to the conscience of whites, was not adequate to the task because white men of that period had an inadequately developed moral sense. As Douglass moved away from William Lloyd Garrison's nonresistance approach to abolition, he began to think more critically about the means of abolition of his people from enslavement. In addition, an interview he had with the radical abolitionist John Brown in 1847 made a strong impression on him, and lent further support to his growing distrust of the Garrison strategy of moral suasion as the only approach to black liberation. Clearly impressed with Brown, Douglass wrote that although Brown is "a white gentleman, [he] is in sympathy a black man, and as deeply interested in our cause, as though his own soul had been pierced with the iron of slavery" (Philip S. Foner, ed., *The Life and Writings of Frederick Douglass* [New York: International Publishers, 1975 {1950}], 2:49). Brown impressed Douglass by both condemning the institution of slavery and maintaining that "the slaveholders 'had forfeited their right to live, that the slaves had the right to gain their liberty in any way they could.' 'Moral suasion' could never liberate the slaves nor political action abolish the system." In addition, "Brown's belief that slavery was actually a state of war profoundly impressed [Douglass]. 'My utterances,' Douglass wrote later, 'became more tinged by the color of this man's strong impressions.' A year after his visit Douglass was echoing Brown's language, writing editorially that slaveholders had 'no rights more than any other thief or pirate. They have forfeited even the right to live, and if the slave should put every one of them to the sword to-morrow, who dare pronounce the penalty disproportionate to the crime, or say that the criminals deserved less than death at the hands of their long-abused chattels?'" In June 1849, Douglass startled an anti-slavery audience in Boston when he said: "I should welcome the intelligence tomorrow, should it come, that the slaves had arisen in the South, and that the sable arms which had been engaged in beautifying and adorning the South, were engaged in spreading death and devastation" (quoted in ibid., 50). This did not mean, however, that Douglass had completely relinquished faith in moral suasion. It did mean, however, that he now recognized both the need and the right of the enslaved to violently revolt against those who enslaved them. It was clear to Douglass that such a stance was consistent with that of the so-called Founding Fathers. By the late 1850s Douglass was a leading exponent of "militant abolitionism." By 1860 he was reasonably convinced that there was no peaceful solution to slavery. "I have little hope of the freedom of the slave by peaceful means," he wrote on June 29, 1860. "A long course of peaceful slaveholding has placed the slaveholders beyond the reach of moral and humane considerations. They have neither ears nor hearts for the appeals of justice and humanity. While the slave will tamely submit his neck to the yoke, his back to the lash, and his ankle to the fetter and chain, the Bible will be quoted, and learning invoked to justify slavery. The only penetrable point of a tyrant is the *fear of death* (51). See also Douglass, "Capt. John Brown Not Insane," in *The Life and Writings of Frederick Douglass*, ed. Philip S. Foner (New York: International Publishers, 1975 [1950]), 2:460; and Frederick Douglass, *Life and Times of Frederick Douglass* (New York: Collier, 1962 [1892]), 273, 505, for additional discussion on his conversation with John Brown and what the latter had to say about the means of the enslaved Afrikans' freedom.

noticed more and more that the term "gave rise to confusion and it appeared shameful to permit this great struggle to be known only by an English name."[84] Gandhi found that he increasingly disliked the term because it did not accurately convey his understanding of the Indian struggle. In a meeting with some Europeans, he found that many in the British world considered passive resistance to be a method of the weak. Some even believed that it could be characterized by hatred and may eventuate in other forms of violence.[85] Gandhi was also aware that supporters of women's rights in England identified their method as passive resistance, but their application of the principle in a number of ways contradicted what the Indian movement was all about, thus further contributing to the confusion around the meaning of the term. Gandhi reflected on this in 1917:

> "Passive resistance" conveyed the idea of the Suffragette Movement in England. Burning of houses by these women was called "passive resistance" and so also their fasting in prison. All such acts might very well be "passive resistance" but they were not "*satyagraha*." It is said of "passive resistance" that it is the weapon of the weak, but the power which is the subject of this article can be used only by the strong. This power is not "passive" resistance; indeed it calls for intense activity. The movement in South Africa was not passive but active. The Indians of South Africa believed that Truth was their object, that Truth ever triumphs, and with this definiteness of purpose they persistently held on to Truth. They put up with all the suffering that this persistence implied. With the conviction that Truth is not to be renounced even unto death, they shed the fear of death.[86]

Gandhi could only conclude that there was need to search the Indian language for a term that more accurately described their struggle against British imperialism. A contest was held for which a prize was offered to the person who suggested the best term. Maganlal Gandhi suggested the term *Sadagraha* (truth-firmness). Gandhi changed it to *Satyagraha* (truth-force, love-force, or soul-force), believing that it expressed with even greater clarity the nature of

---

84. Shriman Narayan, ed., *The Selected Works of Mahatma Gandhi* (Ahmedabad: Navajivan, 1928), 3:150.

85. M. K. Gandhi, *An Autobiography, or The Story of My Experiment with Truth* (Ahmedabad: Navajivan, 1927), 266.

86. Raghavan Iyer, ed., *The Essential Writings of Mahatma Gandhi* (New York: Oxford University Press, 1993), 308–9.

their struggle.[87] This term, Gandhi held, had nothing whatever to do with violence of any kind. He concluded that "things of fundamental importance to the people are not secured by reason alone but have to be purchased with their suffering."[88] From the standpoint of Afrikan American experience and history in the United States, this was quite a prophetic statement.

Gandhi differed from the nineteenth-century abolitionist Frederick Douglass, who appealed to nonviolence, but as a strategy only. Although Douglass did not counsel his enslaved people and (ostensibly) "free" blacks to take up arms against white oppressors, neither did he counsel them to accept blows without retaliating in kind. In addition, it made no sense to Douglass to be nonviolent with a man whose moral sensibility was not developed to the point that nonviolence would cause him to cease being violent. For Gandhi, on the other hand, the success of a campaign against injustice was not in the least dependent upon the moral conscience of the opponent. "Our nonviolence would be a hollow thing and worth nothing," Gandhi wrote, "if it depended for its success on the goodwill of the authorities."[89] For Gandhi, the moral sensibility of the opponent did not figure into the equation in any way. What was important was the nonviolent resister's attitude and level of commitment, not the disposition and response of the opponent.

WHAT NIEBUHR WAS ARGUING AGAINST

In any event, Martin Luther King's response to Niebuhr's critique of Gandhi and nonviolence was that a number of Niebuhr's statements "revealed that he interpreted pacifism as a sort of passive nonresistance to evil expressing naive trust in the power of love. But this was a serious distortion," King said. "My study of Gandhi convinced me that true pacifism is not nonresistance to evil, but nonviolent resistance to evil."[90] However, what Niebuhr actually argued—quite rightly—was that Gandhi himself—during the early period of struggle in South Afrika—often confused the meaning of nonresistance to evil and nonviolent resistance to evil. Frequently, when Gandhi referred to passive resistance and nonresistance to evil during the South Afrika struggle, he was actually describing nonviolent resistance to social evils. For, unquestionably, activities such as boycotting and civil disobedience were in fact types of

87. Gandhi, *An Autobiography*, 266.

88. Krishna Kripalani, ed., *All Men Are Brothers: Life and Thoughts of Mahatma Gandhi as Told in His Own Words* (New York: World Without War Publications, 1972), 82.

89. Ibid., 80.

90. King, *Stride*, 98.

resistance to social injustice. But during this period Gandhi used the language of "passive resistance" to describe it.

Gandhi was much influenced by the work of the Russian literary artist and pacifist-activist Leo Tolstoy, especially his stance that the key to understanding the Sermon on the Mount is found in the phrase, "resist not evil." Tolstoy accepted this at face value, and therefore insisted on a literal interpretation: "'Why had I always sought for some ulterior motive?' 'Resist not evil' means never resist, never oppose violence; or, in other words, never do anything contrary to the law of love.'"[91] Of course, this was precisely the stance that Niebuhr argued against so forcefully and relentlessly in *Moral Man*. For Niebuhr, the ethic of "resist not evil" is based on a perfectionistic ethic and an overly optimistic view of human nature, and might well be appropriate to a purely religious ethic, but not to sociopolitical ethics, or in the realm of power politics where a proponent of such a religious ethic would be eaten alive. Nevertheless, during his student days in England, Gandhi was much taken by Tolstoy's stance, as well as his book, *The Kingdom of God Is Within You*.

"Resist not evil." When Gandhi got involved in his people's struggle for freedom in South Afrika, he frequently used the language of passive resistance or nonresistance to describe their struggle—a struggle that actually resorted to strikes, boycotts, demonstrations, civil disobedience, and such. So they were actually resisting, not nonresisting.

It seems to me that what Reinhold Niebuhr was really arguing against in his critique of Gandhi, and especially the liberal interpreters of Gandhi, was that activities such as strikes and boycotts—necessary as they are in the social struggle for justice—are contrary to the spirit of a pure ethic of "resist not evil." According to Niebuhr, the minute that Gandhi and his followers resorted to such tactics, even though they were much more reasonable than explicit campaigns of violence, they were in fact engaging in coercive, not nonresistant, noncoercive tactics. Although the express intention may not have been to coerce oppressors, such tactics as Gandhi engaged in were indeed coercive. Nonviolent resistance *is* a form of constraint.

In addition, Niebuhr argued that people on both sides of the struggle suffered as a result of Gandhi's tactics. For example, when a cotton mill was closed down due to a protracted boycott or strike, it was not only the owners and management that suffered. The workers and their families suffered immensely as well, for it meant that they would be without an income to purchase basic necessities of life. This also meant that innocent children

---

91. Quoted in Branch, *Parting the Waters*, 85.

suffered, inasmuch as there was no family income as a result of strikes or boycotts. The difference between violent and nonviolent resistance is that the one is motivated by hatred, while the other is motivated by love. Nonviolent resistance may lead to a violent response from opponents, but this is never its aim. Moreover, Niebuhr was convinced that there is no intrinsic difference between violence and nonviolence in a social struggle; that once we admit coercion as an ethical factor there is no absolute demarcation between violent coercion and nonviolent coercion.

> The differences are pragmatic rather than intrinsic. The social consequences of the two methods are different, but the differences are in degree rather than in kind. Both place restraint upon liberty and both may destroy life and property. Once the principle of coercion and resistance has been accepted as necessary to the social struggle and to social cohesion, and pure pacifism [e.g., nonresistance] has been abandoned, the differences between violence and non-violence lose their absolute significance, though they remain important.[92]

What Reinhold Niebuhr sought to do in his critique of Gandhi and pacifism was to show that the pacifists were not necessarily more moral than the nonpacifists and those who were open to the idea of violence in certain contexts, such as a "just war." Nor were pacifists any more capable of living without sin than the nonpacifist, a point that Niebuhr made numerous times, but nowhere more poignantly than his "Open Letter to Richard Roberts" in 1940. He there argued that the difficulty with too many pacifists was that they were self-righteous in that they believed they could live in history without sinning.[93] This is not possible, of course, due to the fact that inordinate and sinful egoism expresses itself on every level of human existence.[94] Niebuhr conceded that not all pacifisms are of the naïve and sentimental type that rests on a superficial optimism regarding the goodness of human nature. And yet he lamented that too much of pacifism was of this type, to which he said: "Most of the pacifism I know is deficient in the 'tragic sense of life' and corrupts its perfectionism by offering its refusal to participate in conflict as a political

92. Niebuhr, "Non-Resistance and Non-Violent Resistance," in *Reinhold Niebuhr on Politics*, ed. Harry R. Davis and Robert C. Good (New York: Scribner's, 1960), 141. Niebuhr develops this provocative idea much more fully in *Moral Man*, 172, 179–80, 240–44.

93. Niebuhr, "An Open Letter (to Richard Roberts)," in *Love and Justice*, 270.

94. Ibid., 268.

alternative to the contest of power that is the very character of the political order."[95] According to Niebuhr, since we are all in this world, we affect and are affected by all that happens in it. That pacifists do not intentionally seek to do violence does not mean that their pacifist tactics somehow allow their hands to remain morally unblemished. Niebuhr saw this as the most serious problem with religious and secular pacifists alike. They naïvely believed that their particular approach to the social question was necessarily more moral and free of sin simply because they chose against violent means. Martin Luther King was in complete agreement with Niebuhr on this point, and rejected pacifisms that did not take the tragic aspects of human existence seriously, while believing they could somehow remain sinless. Reflecting on Niebuhr's influence in this regard, King wrote:

> After reading Niebuhr, I tried to arrive at a realistic pacifism. In other words, I came to see the pacifist position not as sinless but as the lesser evil in the circumstances. I do not claim to be free from the moral dilemmas that the Christian non-pacifist confronts, but I am convinced that the church cannot be silent while mankind faces the threat of nuclear annihilation. I felt that the pacifist would have greater appeal if he did not claim to be free from the moral dilemmas that the Christian non-pacifist confronts.[96]

Niebuhr was convinced that egoism and the tragic elements in history make it impossible for any human being or group to engage the social question without sinning. Just because one is a pacifist does not mean he is less susceptible to sin, or that he is without sin. For Niebuhr, both religious and secular pacifists wrongheadedly believed themselves to be more moral than nonpacifists; that they could live in the world without sinning; that they could somehow engage in political contests and still boast of clean hands in the area of morality. Indeed, Niebuhr's sense of realism about this is expressed in his view that "it may be necessary at times to sacrifice a degree of moral purity for political effectiveness,"[97] a point that King always had in mind during negotiating sessions with those who were standing in the way of civil rights for blacks.

Taylor Branch provides a helpful clarification regarding Niebuhr's critique of Gandhi and pacifism.

95. Ibid.
96. Carson, ed., *The Autobiography*, 27.
97. Niebuhr, *Moral Man*, 244.

> In his book [*Moral Man and Immoral Society*], Niebuhr attacked pacifists and idealists for their assumption that Gandhi had invented an approach that allowed religious people to be politically effective while avoiding the corruptions of the world. For Niebuhr, Gandhi had abandoned Tolstoy the moment he began to resist the color laws in South Africa. . . . Niebuhr applauded what Gandhi was doing but not the sentimental interpretations that placed Gandhians above the ethical conflicts of ordinary mortals. For Niebuhr, such a belief was dangerously self-righteous as well as unfounded.[98]

Martin Luther King believed, as did Niebuhr, that there was a huge difference between passive nonresistance to evil and nonviolent resistance to evil. Niebuhr's whole point was that nonviolent resistance is just as active, and in some ways just as coercive, as violent resistance. There is a coercive element in both. The chief difference between the two is that at the heart of violent resistance is hatred and disrespect for persons and dependence on physical force. On the other hand, nonviolent resistance is grounded in agape, respect for persons, and soul-force. Therefore, the *intention*—regardless of the consequences—is not to injure or violate the opponent in any way whatever. In addition, it elevates truth-force (or soul-force) to a place of prominence. King was in agreement with James Lawson that "love is the central motif of nonviolence."[99] Nonviolent resistance, according to King, does not submit to evil power, but rather is "a courageous confrontation of evil by the power of love, in the faith that it is better to be the recipient of violence than the inflicter of it. . . ."[100]

We can see from this discussion that King's early introduction to Niebuhr in seminary led him to disagree with him at several points, although on balance he was much influenced by him. In addition, we have seen that it is not entirely accurate to say that King's Christian realism emerged only after he read and studied Niebuhr. Niebuhr was baffling to King, until he finally began his doctoral studies at Boston University where he was befriended and mentored by Dean Walter G. Muelder. A Christian, personalist, democratic socialist, and pacifist, Muelder had mastered Niebuhr's ethics and his critique of pacifism. Although King took no courses under him,[101] it was Muelder who helped him

98. Branch, *Parting the Waters*, 85–86.
99. Quoted in ibid., 291.
100. King, *Stride*, 98. The latter part of King's statement is a point that feminist and womanist theologians and ethicists take issue with, i.e., that it is better to be the recipient of violence than to be the one inflicting it.

understand Niebuhr's critique of pacifism, his doctrine of human nature, and his interpretation of agape.

King was impressed with Niebuhr's admission that the oppressed have a higher moral right to resist and challenge the authority and power of their oppressors than the latter have to maintain their rule and privileges by force.[102] In addition, although Niebuhr, wrongly or rightly, counseled blacks against the use of violence because they were outnumbered and did not have access to a significant arsenal of weapons,[103] we have seen that he was just as forthright in saying that they would be foolish and naïve to trust in the moral sensibility of the white man in their quest for equality and social justice. Although King already had a sense of this truth before he read *Moral Man*, since he had learned it from his father's and grandfather's efforts to win blacks' freedom and equality through organized and determined struggle,[104] Niebuhr drove the point home with startling clarity.

Unfortunately, Martin Luther King did not react to the implication in Niebuhr's statement that blacks might not be able to force whites to grant them equal rights, for this seemed to imply Niebuhr's belief that racial inequality would exist permanently in the United States. King's level of hopefulness was such that this could not be a real consideration, but nearly fifty years after his assassination it seems reasonable that such a stance should be reassessed. Niebuhr's statement was made in 1932. Even in the early years of the twenty-first century, there is no evidence that blacks have a realistic chance of violently forcing whites to grant them full, enduring equality in a racism-free society. But nor is there reason and evidence to suggest that this can happen through nonviolent means.

It would seem that Niebuhr had whites' number on the issue of white-black equality. Any hope that blacks might have in this regard will be predicated on whether they are willing and have the resolve to be at least as realistic as Niebuhr was and to have the courage and will to act accordingly. Are racism and inequality permanent fixtures in the United States? King did not think so. However, a racism-free society and equality have not been achieved since his assassination. If racism is in fact permanent, what should blacks be doing differently than during the civil rights era? This and related questions will be addressed in the last chapter.

---

101. See Ansbro, *Martin Luther King, Jr.*, 23.

102. Niebuhr, *Moral Man*, 234.

103. Ibid., 253–54.

104. See Martin Luther King Sr. with Clayton Riley, *Daddy King: An Autobiography* (New York: William Morrow, 1980), 100, 104ff., 111, 123–24, 125.

King agreed wholeheartedly with Niebuhr's reinforcement of what he already knew, namely that blacks should not depend uncritically on the goodwill of whites in order to obtain social justice. Blacks had to depend first and foremost not on whites and the structures they control and benefit from, but on themselves, an emphasis we saw in A. D. Williams and Daddy King. This was the chief lesson that King learned from his support of what turned out to be a weak, watered-down, essentially meaningless Civil Rights Act in 1957.[105] After that decision, he came to the conclusion that blacks must be self-determined; that they must depend, first and last, on themselves and God, rather than wait passively for whites to decide when, or whether, they will do the right thing in race relations. And yet for all of this, it seems that King continued to believe to the end that white people would admit black people to a state of equality; and that racial discrimination would be significantly reduced, if not eliminated.

NIEBUHR'S ASSESSMENT OF KING

The admiration that King had for Reinhold Niebuhr was not one-sided. In 1959, Niebuhr wrote to thank him for an inscribed copy of *Stride Toward Freedom* and to say that he had read the book "with great enthusiasm" even before receiving the inscribed copy.[106] He characterized King as "the most creative Protestant, white or black."[107] At another time, Niebuhr expressed appreciation for both King and his nonviolent approach: "Dr. King's conception of the nonviolent resistance to evil is a real contribution to our civil, moral and political life."[108] He also applauded what he considered King's ability "to cure the Negro church of pietistic irrelevance and to engage it in the struggle for justice."[109] Critical of the majority of the white Protestant churches for their failure to join the civil rights movement and to act aggressively against racism and discrimination, Niebuhr again commended the efforts of King and the leadership he provided the black church: "Since the record of the white Protestant Church, except for a few heroic spirits, is shameful, one must record with gratitude that Negro churchmen have been conspicuous among

---

105. Branch, *Parting the Waters*, 221–22.

106. *The Papers* (2005), 5:102.

107. Quoted in D. B. Robertson, ed., *Love and Justice: Selections from the Shorter Writings of Reinhold Niebuhr* (Gloucester, MA: Peter Smith, 1976), "Introduction," 20.

108. Quoted in Ronald H. Stone, *Professor Reinhold Niebuhr: A Mentor to the Twentieth Century* (Louisville: Westminster John Knox, 1992), 234.

109. Niebuhr, "The Negro Minority and Its Fate in a Self-Righteous Nation," in *A Reinhold Niebuhr Reader*, compiled and edited by Charles C. Brown (Philadelphia: Trinity Press International, 1992), 122.

the leaders in the revolt. The Negro church in the person of Dr. Martin Luther King has validated itself in the life of the Negroes and of the nation."[110] Niebuhr praised King's "I Have a Dream" speech, delivered at the Lincoln Memorial on August 28, 1963, concluding that although he did not believe it would have a positive influence on hardcore racists (and it did not, and does not!), he believed it would influence the nation.[111] Elsewhere he said that King was "one of the great religious leaders of our time."[112] In addition, in a televised dialogue with literary artist James Baldwin after the tragic bombing of the Sixteenth Street Baptist Church in Birmingham, Alabama in September 1963 (just weeks after the March on Washington) which left four black children dead, Niebuhr commented that "King is one of the great Americans of our day." He was also careful to distinguish King's doctrine of nonviolence from pacifism.[113]

However, for all of his praise for King, Niebuhr was not as convinced as King that nonviolence was the *only*—or even the best—way in *every* situation to achieve social justice and equality of opportunity for blacks.[114] Niebuhr might well have feared that those in the *nonviolence is a way of life* camp may tend to unduly glorify cooperation and mutuality, which in his judgment *could* lead some to the uncritical acceptance of traditional injustices and a preference for the more subtle types of coercion (e.g., moral suasion and letter writing) to the more overt organized types.[115] Niebuhr wanted realism in social ethics, and therefore was adamant that the most adequate social ethic always takes seriously the insights of both the religious moralist and the political realist.[116] Both Niebuhr and King understood that ethical principles, as well as the harshness of current events and the insights of the political realist, must be taken into account if one desires to be politically responsible.

Nonviolence was not a way of life for Reinhold Niebuhr, as it was for Martin Luther King. Niebuhr was more interested in nonviolence as one

110. Niebuhr, "The Mounting Racial Crisis," in *A Reinhold Niebuhr Reader*, 109.

111. According to Charles C. Brown, Niebuhr wrote this to William Scarlett. See Brown, *Niebuhr and His Age: Reinhold Niebuhr's Prophetic Role in the Twentieth Century* (Philadelphia: Trinity Press International, 1992), 220.

112. Quoted in Stone, Professor Reinhold Niebuhr, 234. From "A Foreword by Dr. Reinhold Niebuhr," in *Dr. Martin Luther King, Jr., Dr. John C. Bennett, Dr. Henry Steele Commager, Rabbi Abraham Heschel Speak on the War in Vietnam* (New York: Clergy and Laymen Concerned About Vietnam, 1967), 3.

113. Brown, *Niebuhr and His Age*, 220.

114. Bennett, "Reinhold Niebuhr's Social Ethics," in *Reinhold Niebuhr: His Religious, Social and Political Thought*, 141.

115. Niebuhr, *Moral Man*, 233.

116. Ibid.

among many strategies for social change and the achievement of higher degrees of justice. To this extent, he was a pragmatic pacifist, but this is a far cry from the type of nonviolence advocated by King.

King's sense of realism was as keen as Niebuhr's in some ways, most especially regarding the persistence of racism in the United States. King unquestionably agreed with Niebuhr's sensitivity to blacks' desire to be free of all traces of racial discrimination. "The impatience of the Negro will not subside until the last vestiges of legal and customary inequality have been removed," Niebuhr wrote while reflecting on a stubborn, intractable race problem and blacks' determination to overcome it. "Revolutions," he said, "do not stop half way."[117]

In this chapter we have seen that on the home front, through the ministerial witness of his maternal grandfather and father, through teachings at Morehouse College, and through firsthand experiences of racism, Martin Luther King came face to face with ideas of Christian realism (with its emphasis on social sin, the limitations of reason and human imagination, and the facts of history and current events), although he did not then know that term. This homespun Christian realism was reinforced and given a strong theological foundation through King's study of Reinhold Niebuhr. It reinforced his sense of the need and obligation to resist injustice. Unlike Niebuhr, King concluded that such resistance should be done nonviolently.

Upon completing the formal requirements for his doctoral degree, King returned to the South with the intention of applying all he had learned in order to help his people. While he was still undergoing formal academic training, much was taking place in various places in the South, including the city of Montgomery, Alabama, to prepare the way for what was to come. In the case of Montgomery it was, in part, a certain eccentric but powerful and prophetic preacher and some fed-up, courageous, audacious black women who were paving the way. I now turn to an examination of their contributions and how they helped to shape King's ideas and practice.

117. Niebuhr, "The Mounting Racial Crisis," in *A Reinhold Niebuhr Reader*, 109. From *Christianity and Crisis* 23 (July 8, 1963): 121–22.

PART 3

A Preacher and Some Women Pave the Way

The two chapters in Part 3 (six and seven) take up the matter of people in Montgomery, Alabama who helped pave the way for the civil rights ministry of Martin Luther King. There were many contributors along the way, but I focus on a select few. One was the Rev. Vernon N. Johns, an outstanding pastor-prophet-preacher in the mold of the Hebrew prophets, who demanded that the powers do justice to his people, even as he commanded the members of Dexter Avenue Baptist Church to fight for their humanity, dignity, and civil rights. Chapter six focuses on his contributions. In chapter seven, we turn to an examination of the role and contributions of black women who courageously and determinedly cultivated the ground for King's coming; who had already drawn up plans for a boycott of the buses long before Rosa Parks was arrested. These women stood and protested even when it seemed to some of them that they were protesting and standing alone. Who were they, and what drove them? What was their relationship with King? Indeed, long before the arrest of Rosa Parks, many black women defied racist bus drivers by remaining in their bus seat.

Many years ago when I was a boy, I was told about the Montgomery bus boycott. I was led to believe that there was nothing complicated about who started it and who led it to successful conclusion. Rosa Parks, a seamstress at a local department store and secretary of the local branch of the NAACP, got on a bus to return home after work on Thursday, December 1, 1955. As the bus began to fill up with patrons the white bus driver demanded that some black passengers in the "Negroes only" section give their seats to white patrons who were standing. Mrs. Parks moved, but only to the window seat vacated by her seatmate. This made the driver furious. He then threatened to have her arrested if she did not move. She refused, was arrested, taken to jail, and charged with disorderly conduct. Word of her arrest spread rapidly throughout black Montgomery. Mrs. Parks was bailed out of jail and the wheels were set in motion by black leaders (read "black men"!) for a one-day boycott.

I was told further that after Rosa Parks's arrest and black leaders' talk of a boycott, a young, perspicacious black southern Baptist minister, Martin Luther King Jr., was nominated and voted to be president of the Montgomery Improvement Association (MIA), which would provide leadership for the boycott. In those days, we did not know a great deal about the details of King's background beyond his family upbringing and where he had gone to school. Writers on King during that period left us with the impression that he discovered and adopted Gandhi's doctrine of nonviolent resistance, and by the time he earned his Ph.D. in systematic theology he had mastered Gandhian ideas and techniques and accepted his method as his own, needing only the right time, place, and event to implement it. We were further led to believe that from the start of the boycott and King's leadership it was primarily based on Gandhi's ideas and techniques. But just how accurate was all this?

In those days, it did not occur to me and many others that Rosa Parks might not have been the first black person to be arrested for essentially violating Alabama's segregation ordinance. Indeed, there were those who claimed that she was in fact the first to be arrested for violating the segregation code.[1] The official arrest report said that she was arrested for disorderly conduct, not for violating the city's segregation ordinance. In addition, it did not occur to me that most—if not all—social movements do not generally emerge spontaneously, but as a culmination of many years of dissatisfaction and a general *fed-up-ness* on the part of an oppressed community. On a given day a particular incident—unplanned and unexpected—may erupt into what may seem like a spontaneous movement, but on closer inspection one easily sees that the event in question was merely the straw that broke the camel's back; that many related instances of similar injustices had occurred over many years, and it took that one incident, on that particular day, to cause an irruption and a movement.

Rosa Parks was a soft-spoken, gentle, respectful woman of high moral standards. Surely it could not be true that she was guilty of disorderly conduct

---

1. See Stephen B. Oates, *Let the Trumpet Sound: The Life of Martin Luther King, Jr.* (New York: Harper & Row, 1982), 65.

on a bus, or anywhere else. Quite possibly it took only minutes for news of her arrest to spread throughout the black community. Many were furious over Parks's arrest and the reported reason for it. Blacks in Montgomery knew full well that Rosa Parks was not the first black person to be arrested for refusing to relinquish her seat to a white person. They also knew that some black women had literally fought police officers who forcibly removed them from a bus for doing little more than what Mrs. Parks did (although Mrs. Parks, unlike many of the women, gave no verbal response at all to the bus driver's command). There were angry outbursts over some of those incidents. Indeed, we know now that earlier that year in March, a young high school girl, while on her way home from school, was forcibly removed from a bus for refusing to give her seat to a white woman. Fifteen-year-old Claudette Colvin fought with the police officers who violently removed her from the bus. Black women of the Women's Political Council (WPA) met with the mayor and city council about the matter, but the city fathers offered no resolution. Not very well known at the time, the young Rev. Martin Luther King Jr. was also present at that meeting. For reasons to be discussed subsequently, black male leaders decided that Colvin's case would not stand up as the test case they were looking for to challenge the segregation ordinance in court.

It was not just Rosa Parks's fatigue, frustration, and adamant refusal to stand up that prompted the boycott. It was this, in addition to the black community's long memory of the countless others who suffered insults to their humanity and dignity on the buses and throughout the entire Montgomery community because of racial discrimination and segregation laws. Moreover, blacks were incensed over the fact that no matter how religious, how moral, or sweet and gentle of spirit a black person may be, her sense of personhood and dignity could be crushed in an instant by the behavior of racist white people who uncritically carry out the policies and practices of racist institutions. "If one such as Rosa Parks is not safe," black Montgomery seemed to have reasoned after her arrest, "then no black person is safe."

The two chapters in Part 3 discuss the contributions of some of the forerunners to Martin Luther King's involvement and leadership during the Montgomery bus boycott. These include a certain preacher, a Pullman porter, and some bodacious, self-determined, fed-up black women, including two female teenagers. The names of these forerunners include but are not limited to: Vernon N. Johns, Edwin D. Nixon (hereafter E. D.), Mary Fair Burks, Jo Ann Robinson, Rosa Parks, Claudette Colvin, and Mary Louise Smith. The latter two were teenagers, ages fifteen and seventeen respectively, evidence that black youths were victimized by racial discrimination and segregation laws as much as black adults. It is also evidence that many black youths—from Montgomery to Memphis—were not hesitant to resist racist treatment and violence against their personhood.

We have seen that as a boy, Martin Luther King promised to help his father eradicate racism. After completing formal doctoral studies, he was called to be senior minister of the Dexter Avenue Baptist Church in Montgomery. It was not *his* plan to lead a bus boycott. Without question, King wanted to help his people and to keep the promise made to his father, but he had no idea what form that would take. Upon assuming pastoral responsibilities at Dexter, his primary aim was to be the best pastor he could be and to establish and give leadership to what he hoped would be a relevant and vibrant ministry. King had no desire to call attention to himself at the onset of his ministry. In fact, he even hesitated to tell E. D. Nixon that he would agree to join with other pastors to discuss what needed to happen after Rosa Parks was arrested. King quite possibly felt in the moment that he needed more time to get to know the city and how the powers-that-be operated. Ralph Abernathy recalled what King told him not long after he was appointed pastor of Dexter.

> For one thing, Martin said that he needed to spend several years in Montgomery, getting to know the city and its leaders, both black and white. He believed that he would have to establish his credibility in the black community before he could hope to lead them into a nonviolent crusade for freedom. He also wanted to gain the respect and trust of those progressive white leaders whose help might prove invaluable in the struggle. All of this would take two or three years at the very least.[2]

When Nixon phoned Abernathy, King, and other black ministers to elicit their involvement in the planning of a possible bus boycott, King was reportedly the only one to initially hesitate to give his consent. Nixon recalled that King was the third person that he phoned, and that he essentially stalled: "Brother Nixon, let me think about it awhile, and call me back."[3] King presumably hesitated because he felt that he had not been in the city long enough and thus was not familiar enough with the most pressing social issues in Montgomery, or how the powers operated. Once King consulted with Abernathy, he gave Nixon his

2. Ralph David Abernathy, *And the Walls Came Tumbling Down: An Autobiography* (New York: Harper & Row, 1989), 130.

3. Quoted in Howell Raines, *My Soul Is Rested: Movement Days in the Deep South Remembered* (New York: G. P. Putnam's Sons, 1977), 45.

consent, but stated that because of a prior commitment he could not attend the first meeting. However, he agreed to the meeting being held at Dexter.

King ultimately joined with other black pastors to discuss the possibility of a boycott. However, looking back, he said that had he been asked sooner to get involved in what came to be the bus boycott he would have fled in the other direction. Stanley Levison, a close confidant, advisor, fundraiser, speechwriter, and King's "closest white friend," reported that after the successful conclusion of the boycott King remarked:

> "If anybody had asked me a year ago to head this movement," he said quietly, "I tell you very honestly, that I would have run a mile to get away from it. I had no intention of being involved in this way. As I became involved, and as the people began to derive inspiration from their involvement, I realized that the choice leaves your own hands. The people expect you to give them leadership. You see them growing as they move into action, and then you know you no longer have a choice. You can't decide whether to stay in it or get out of it. You must stay in it."[4]

However, none of this is to say that King had not already been deeply involved in the Montgomery community *before* talk of a boycott.

Not long after King began his ministry at Dexter, he began familiarizing himself with the local context, including specific instances of how blacks were treated generally, and more particularly on the buses. He also had occasion to have firsthand experience with the racism and insensitivity of the mayor and city leaders, such as the meeting he attended with representatives of the WPC after the Colvin bus incident. Therefore, it would be a mistake to conclude that because King hesitated to give Nixon a positive response, he did so because he was not interested or did not want to get involved. He was already involved in social issues that concerned Montgomery blacks. Furthermore, because King's was a more pensive nature; because he was truly a man of ideas, and because of his temperament, it should not be difficult to understand the idea that he really did need time to observe what was going on, and as far as possible to think things through. In addition, that he declined the invitation to be president of the Montgomery chapter of the NAACP should not be taken to mean that he exhibited "a marked lack of interest in political activity," as some have erroneously claimed.[5] After all, King was the new pastor of a church and rightly

---

4. Quoted in Stewart Burns, *To the Mountaintop: Martin Luther King, Jr.'s Sacred Mission to Save America 1955-1968* (New York/San Francisco: HarperSanFrancisco, 2004), 148.

was eager to get to know the members and to put the church's ministry on a solid foundation. This would require a tremendous amount of the new pastor's time and energy. Called by Dexter to be its pastor, he was obligated to put in the necessary time and energy to establish a sound ministry. This was critical in the early stage of his ministry.

In addition, and to King's credit, he joined the local NAACP shortly after arriving in Montgomery. In this regard, he followed the example of his maternal grandfather and father. Both men strongly urged the members of Ebenezer Baptist Church to join the NAACP and to vote. A. D. Williams was a charter member and the president of the local affiliate. In addition, King strongly urged every member of Dexter Avenue Baptist Church to become a registered voter and a member of the NAACP. King was also elected vice president of the interracial Alabama Council of Human Relations. But that was not all. King also organized the Social and Political Action Committee (SPAC) at Dexter to hold public forums on pressing social issues, and also to keep him and the congregation informed. These things all occurred *before* King received that first telephone call from E. D. Nixon. This can only mean that he was already involved politically in Montgomery, and that even at that point his involvement exceeded that of many of his ministerial colleagues who had been longtime residents. King clearly had a plan for getting involved politically in Montgomery and was working that plan according to his own timetable. He was unaware, however, that cosmic and divine forces had another timetable for him to follow.

Womanist theologian Cheryl Kirk-Duggan helpfully comments that "King arrives at a pivotal moment in history, when the network was already in place to launch a movement."[6] Although much groundbreaking work had already been done in the Montgomery black community to prepare the way for King, we will learn about the specific contributions of some of the trailblazers and torchbearers and their importance to the ensuing civil rights movement. Because the significance of black women's contributions was frequently ignored or at best downplayed until more recent scholarship on King and the

5. See Marisa Chappell, Jenny Hutchinson, and Brian Ward, "Respectability, Class and Gender in the Montgomery Bus Boycott and the Early Civil Rights Movement," in *Gender and the Civil Rights Movement*, ed. Peter J. Ling and Sharon Monteith (New Brunswick, NJ: Rutgers University Press, 2004), 91.

6. Cheryl Kirk-Duggan, "Drum Major for Justice or Dilettante of Dishonesty: Martin Luther King, Jr., Moral Capital, and Hypocrisy of Embodied Messianic Myths," in *The Domestication of Martin Luther King, Jr.: Clarence B. Jones, Right-Wing Conservatism, and the Manipulation of the King Legacy*, ed. Lewis V. Baldwin and Rufus Burrow Jr. (Eugene, OR: Cascade Books, 2013), 111.

civil rights movement, special attention will be given these. Brief consideration will be given the contributions of black youths of Montgomery, as well as black youth participation in subsequent civil rights campaigns.

On September 1, 1954, Martin Luther King assumed full-time ministerial duties at Dexter Avenue Baptist Church. He was awarded the Ph.D. in systematic theology in absentia on May 31, 1955. Nearly two months later, he flew to New Orleans at the invitation of Dillard University president Albert W. Dent to be interviewed for dean of the new university chapel. One month later, fourteen-year-old Emmett Till of Chicago was brutally murdered and disfigured by white racists near Money, Mississippi, while he was visiting his uncle. This was a murder that King agonized over, so much so that we find him referencing it directly or indirectly in many speeches and sermons throughout much of his civil rights ministry.

I have already mentioned young Claudette Colvin's bus experience that led to her arrest. In October of 1955, seventeen-year-old Mary Louise Smith was arrested for violating the segregation code on city buses. Then December 1 arrived. It was an unusually warm day for that time of year in Montgomery. Mrs. Rosa Parks boarded a city bus to go home at the end of her workday. It was to her just another Thursday afternoon. She was tired at the end of her workday, but no more than usual. However, Mrs. Parks recalled that her fatigue was exacerbated by a nagging sense of being sick and tired of racist and discriminatory attacks on her personhood and sense of dignity. That day she followed the custom of sitting in the "Negro section" of the bus. Although seated in that area in compliance with city and state ordinances, blacks were nevertheless required by custom to give their seat to any white passenger that wanted it. To add insult to injury, black patrons had to deposit their fare at the front of the bus, exit the bus, and reboard at the rear of the bus. And as if this was not insulting enough, it was not uncommon for bus drivers to drive off before they could reach the rear door, an experience that Rosa Parks herself had had.

On that Thursday afternoon, Rosa Parks had not planned to do anything different than she had done hundreds of times when she boarded a city bus in Montgomery. When the bus driver, James F. Blake, stopped to pick up several white passengers and ordered blacks sitting just behind the "whites only" section to give up their seats, most did so promptly. (When she first got on the bus she had not noticed that Blake was the same driver who had driven away about twelve years earlier as she was trying to reboard at the rear of the bus.[7]) But something that day would not allow Mrs. Parks to move, except to slide into the window seat vacated by another black passenger. She had no intention of being either a troublemaker or a trailblazer that day. On reflection, she said that she "did not get on the bus to get arrested," but to go home.[8] She was not looking for trouble or a fight. She was simply tired of the disrespect and abuse; tired of passively taking it, and on that particular day she had simply had enough. Indeed, in 1956 she told interviewer Sidney Rogers that "the time had come 'when I had been pushed as far as I could stand to be pushed. . . . I had decided that I would have to know once and for all what rights I had as a human being and a citizen.'"[9] As a representative of the NAACP she had indeed participated in some of the fruitless conversations between the WPC, the mayor, and bus officials, and saw clearly that city and bus officials were not at all serious about addressing blacks' numerous complaints about their inhumane treatment on the buses. Mrs. Parks was without question a bundle of nerves and emotions when she was arrested.

Although admittedly physically tired that late Thursday afternoon, Rosa Parks was even more tired of the humiliation that she and other black patrons—principally women who rode the bus to and from their domestic jobs—experienced as a result of the treatment by the bus drivers. Parks later reflected: "People always say that I didn't give up my seat because I was tired, but that isn't true. I was not tired physically, or no more tired than I usually was at the end of a working day. I was not old. . . . No, the only tired I was, was tired of giving in."[10] Many years later, in 1991, she said that she refused to obey the bus driver's command "because I was so involved with the attempt to bring about freedom from this kind of thing. . . . I felt just resigned to give what I could to protest against the way I was being treated, and felt that all of our meetings, trying to negotiate, bring about petitions before the authorities . . . really hadn't done any good at all."[11] Ironically, by remaining in her seat Rosa Parks—and all of the black women who had done similarly before her—was really "sittin-in" for the freedom of all black people. This was essentially Rosa Parks's version of the sit-in (to be made popular in 1960).

7. Lynne Olson, *Freedom's Daughters: The Unsung Heroines of the Civil Rights Movement from 1830 to 1970* (New York: Scribner, 2001), 107.

8. Rosa Parks with Gregory J. Reed, *Quiet Strength* (Grand Rapids: Zondervan, 1994), 23.

9. Quoted in Stewart Burns, "Montgomery Bus Boycott," in *Black Women in America: An Historical Encyclopedia*, ed. Darlene Clark Hine (Brooklyn: Carlson, 1993), 2:808. From interview with Sidney Rogers (1956).

10. Rosa Parks with Jim Haskins, *Rosa Parks: My Story* (New York: Dial, 1992), 116.

11. Quoted in Burns, "Montgomery Bus Boycott," in *Black Women in America*, 2:808. From *Black Women Oral History Project*, 10 volumes, ed. Ruth Edmunds Hill (Westport, CT: Meckler, 1991).

Reflecting on what she remembered about Parks when they were schoolgirls, Mary Fair Burks commented on her decision to remain seated: "I became convinced that she refused to give up her seat not only because she was tired, but because doing so would have violated her humanity and sense of dignity as well as her values regarding right and wrong, justice and injustice."[12] Burks remembered that while growing up together, Parks was very principled. Her personality was such that she would not ordinarily defy authority as she did that day, but once she set her mind on a particular course of action there was no turning back.

Since Parks refused to give up her seat, custom required that the bus driver summon a police officer. She was immediately handcuffed and placed under arrest for disorderly conduct. Unknown to her at the time, she was actually *making* history. Precisely at the moment of saying that she would not give up her seat, Rosa Parks knew that she had the strength of her ancestors with her.[13] Her decision was not hers alone, nor was she alone in remaining seated. The spirits of black ancestors crowded in the seat with her. She was not alone, although no other black or white patron joined her silent protest.

Rosa Parks did not awaken that Thursday morning with the intention of becoming the NAACP's Jim Crow test case in the southern judicial system. She paid her fare like everybody else on the bus, and in compliance with the law, seated herself in the "colored only" section. Everything she did was in strict compliance with local and state law. But when she was told to give up her seat to a white passenger she knew on that particular day that she had had enough. "A lifetime's education in injustice—from her grandfather's nightly vigils to the murder of Emmett Till—had strengthened her resolve to act when the time came. What arose in Parks that fateful evening was her belief in what Dr. Martin Luther King, Jr., often said: that 'some of us must bear the burden of trying to save the soul of America.'"[14] When the bus driver used an unjust system to try to get her to move that day, Rosa Parks felt that it was her "burden" to remain in her seat, no matter the consequences.

There were many forces at work both before and during that fateful day in Montgomery. Unquestionably, the events leading up to and following the arrest of Mrs. Parks were events whose time had come. It was not solely the arrest of Rosa Parks that caused the chain of events that followed. Much had

12. Mary Fair Burks, "Trailblazers: Women in the Montgomery Bus Boycott," in *Women in the Civil Rights Movement: Trailblazers & Torchbearers 1941-1965*, ed. Vicki L. Crawford et al. (Bloomington: Indiana University Press, 1993), 72.

13. See Douglas Brinkley, *Rosa Parks* (New York: Lipper/Viking Books, 2000), 107.

14. Ibid., 109.

already happened in Montgomery prior to that day. Much was in process of occurring, not least a growing sense of utter frustration experienced by the Montgomery black community over the segregation laws, and a desperate sense of wanting to do something about it.

Indeed, many black women in Montgomery were already united around the bus segregation issue prior to Mrs. Parks's arrest. The WPC had already formulated plans to initiate a bus boycott, even if the black male leadership of Montgomery refused to do so after Mrs. Parks was arrested. In an interview in 1980, Mrs. Parks recalled having heard that some students at the all-black Alabama State College in Montgomery had already been talking about initiating their own boycott of the city buses.[15] Notwithstanding this, powerful forces—cosmic, divine, and human—had been at work for a long time in preparation for December 1, 1955. Martin Luther King acknowledged the truth of this idea at one of the early mass prayer meetings after the boycott began. At First Baptist Church where Ralph Abernathy was senior pastor, King told those gathered that long before he arrived much had already happened in Montgomery to prepare the way for what was now occurring. He therefore acknowledged that it was not he who started the movement, and he could not stop it. Rather, King said, the time was simply ripe for such a movement. Even had he not arrived on the scene, he said, the Montgomery movement would have occurred.[16] King believed that it was not just a matter of human forces at work, but cosmic and divine forces as well.

Interestingly, even at this early stage in his ministry King was apprehensive about being seen as the center of attention in the movement, or as "the movement." He constantly downplayed the media's tendency to characterize him in this way. He would later insist that he was a "symbol" of the civil rights movement, not the movement itself. King argued that the Montgomery movement had to occur, since God is not deaf to the cries and pain of oppressed people, an idea that is deeply rooted in the prophetic tradition of the Jewish and Christian faiths, as well as the black religious tradition. In addition, there had been other people in the Montgomery black community—female as well as male—whose voices of protest preceded King's arrival, not least the Rev. Vernon Johns, E. D. Nixon, the dedicated and courageous women of the WPC, and a few fearless, committed whites, for example, Juliette Morgan, and Virginia and Clifford Durr.

15. Interview with Rosa Parks by Steven M. Millner, January 20, 1980, in *The Walking City: The Montgomery Bus Boycott, 1955-1956*, ed. David J. Garrow (Brooklyn, NY: Carlson, 1989), 563.

16. Clayborne Carson et al., eds., *The Papers of Martin Luther King, Jr.* (Berkeley: University of California Press, 1997), 3:114.

It is important that we always remember that Rosa Parks was not the first black person—woman or man—to be arrested for defying the command to vacate her bus seat for a white patron. Countless blacks had refused to do this and were arrested, not least the two young people previously named. While the time is always right to do the right thing, the arrest of Rosa Parks and the swift reaction of Montgomery's black community was a reminder to all human beings that a force much greater than theirs was guiding the course of events in the world.

History has frequently revealed how particular injustices may exist for long periods of time, and only after a magnificent confluence of events and forces come together is a movement mounted to expose and eradicate the wrongs. This is what happened in Montgomery, Alabama. It may be strange that the movement occurred only after Martin Luther King Jr. was called by God to be a minister in that city. King's explanation was that he had been tracked down by the *Zeitgeist* (the Spirit of the times). He was convinced that it was all a part of God's program and plan.

Arguably, few played a more significant role in breaking ground for Martin Luther King and what came to be the civil rights movement than the venerable, brilliant, albeit eccentric, Vernon Napoleon Johns. Johns came declaring as fearlessly and boldly as the Hebrew prophets "thus says the Lord," about the need to do justice, to love kindness, and to walk humbly with God. Perhaps Charles Emerson Boddie has said it best: "As John the Baptist was 'the voice of one crying in the wilderness, make straight the way of the Lord,' Vernon Johns fallowed the ground which provided the seedbed for the germination of the great movement led by another, whose name was Martin Luther King, Jr. . . . The martyred leader's ministry was found acceptable largely because Vernon Johns had already passed that way."[17] In a way, Johns prepared Dexter Avenue Baptist Church as well as the city of Montgomery for King's arrival. God is *never* without a witness, in any era of history. Nor is God ever absent, but is always present in and concerned about what happens to human beings in the world. For, all people, without exception, belong to God, and God is concerned about the well-being of every person.

Every *witness* has a role to play in the movement toward the realization of God's purposes in the world. Vernon Johns does not get the recognition and credit given King. The commitment and obedience to God exhibited by Johns and many other lesser-known persons in Montgomery, however, paved the way for the massive bus boycott, and what became the civil rights movement.

17. Charles Emerson Boddie, *God's "Bad Boys"* (Valley Forge, PA: Judson, 1972), 70.

What was the role of Vernon Johns? What were the contributions of some of the black women of Montgomery—they who suffered most frequently the indignities of the city's bus drivers? Even though they *chose* to defer to black male leadership once the boycott began, black women of all social classes and ages in Montgomery were the real motivating and driving force that both started and sustained the boycott. I begin by considering the role of Vernon Johns, organic intellectual in his own right, that is, one who intentionally, powerfully, and persuasively linked mind and ideas with social struggle and the sense of obligation to make better persons and a better society. Vernon Johns was also the consummate preacher and prophetic social gospel pastor.

6

Vernon Napoleon Johns: "God's Bad Boy"

Martin Luther King's ministry in Montgomery did not begin in a vacuum. One's life evolves and builds on what has gone before. Consequently, King inherited a sound protest tradition from his predecessor at Dexter Avenue Baptist Church, the Rev. Vernon Napoleon Johns (1882–1965). His tenure at Dexter lasted only four years (1948–53). King entered seminary in 1948, and completed the formal requirements for the Ph.D. in 1953.

Let there be no doubt that Vernon Johns was a true prophet in the tradition of Amos, Isaiah, Jeremiah, Micah, and Hosea. It was the prophet in Vernon Johns that kept him in hot water with the members of Dexter, and the powers-that-be in white Montgomery. Where the issue of racial justice was concerned, he simply could not, and did not, hold his peace or his tongue.

There was also the matter of Johns's eccentricities. For example, he grew up on a farm in Virginia and loved farming all his life. Although a brilliant and masterful preacher, he also remained a farmer at heart. There was nothing wrong with this in itself, except that Johns had the habit of selling his produce and fish out in front of Dexter right after church services. This practice both distressed and embarrassed most of his refined, middle- to upper middle-class parishioners, even though his primary purpose was noble enough, namely to arouse in his people the spirit of protest against racial discrimination, as well as to instill in them a desire for economic freedom. Johns deplored the fact that his people bowed and kowtowed to white people, and that they were primarily consumers, rather than producers and entrepreneurs. Moreover, he wanted his people to understand—especially those who were embarrassed by his selling produce and fish in front of the church—that there is dignity in any honest work.[1]

Like any good pastor, Johns had a vision for the Dexter ministry that he hoped the congregation would eventually see as a shared venture. Economic self-sufficiency was a large part of that vision and the foundation for the ministry he hoped to establish; a ministry that had four goals:

> to persuade members that God often sent messages to the world through the humble and disavowed; to convince congregants of the natural relationship between "true" religion and social progress; to help congregants realize that self-sufficient economic development was indispensable to Christian living and in the struggle for racial equality; and, most important, that the dogma and doctrine of religion were futile, even immoral, without action. To achieve these goals, Johns harnessed the power of the pulpit, sharing his beliefs and passions with Dexter Avenue members in his Sunday morning sermons.[2]

Johns did not merely preach about black self-determination and the all-important need for economic self-sufficiency, he took his own advice and went into action. He dug a garden behind the parsonage, where he grew vegetables and sold them.

Although the Dexter congregation had no sense of appreciation for his produce-selling tactics after worship service, Vernon Johns was one of the most brilliant scholar-pastors of any race of his day. Born near Farmville, Prince Edward County, Virginia, he was trained at Virginia Seminary (1912–14) and at Oberlin School of Theology (1915–19). Ordained in 1918, Johns studied social gospel theology at Oberlin and became a provocative and profound social gospel preacher. He studied social gospel theology primarily under Dean Edward Increase Bosworth at Oberlin. Steeped in social gospel theology, Bosworth taught a course, "The Social Significance of the Teachings of Jesus," which was required during Johns's time at Oberlin.[3] It is significant to note that Walter Rauschenbusch, to whom Oberlin had given an honorary doctorate,[4] was invited by Oberlin College president and social gospel advocate, Henry Churchill King, to be a visiting professor in the fall of 1917.[5] It was an impossible assignment, really, since he lectured four times on Mondays and Tuesdays, and then boarded an overnight train back to Rochester to arrive in

1. Houston Bryan Roberson, *Fighting the Good Fight: The Story of the Dexter Avenue King Memorial Baptist Church, 1865-1977* (New York/London: Routledge, 2005), 89.

2. Ibid., 95.

3. Ibid., 90.

4. Christopher H. Evans, *The Kingdom Is Always but Coming: A Life of Walter Rauschenbusch* (Grand Rapids: Eerdmans, 2004), 283.

5. Ibid., 291.

time to teach two classes on Wednesday morning.[6] He did this for two straight months. The experience wreaked havoc on his health, but he needed the money. In any event, Vernon Johns was enrolled as a student during the period that Rauschenbusch taught at Oberlin, and quite possibly enrolled in a course with him.[7] Even if he did not enroll in the class with Rauschenbusch, he very likely heard him speak or lecture. In any case, like the one who would succeed him at Dexter, Vernon Johns was a race-sensitive social gospel advocate. He did not ignore racism and its brutal effects on blacks. This was quite different from the social gospel that was advocated by most whites, including Rauschenbusch. In addition, Johns was the first black person to publish a sermon ("Transfigured Moments") in the outstanding series, *Best Sermons*.[8]

Vernon Johns claimed to live by his mother's dictum: "If you see a good fight, get into it."[9] Unquestionably, Johns was without peer when it came to preaching prophetic sermons on God's imperative and expectation that justice and righteousness be done in the world. Like his immediate successor at Dexter, and in true social gospel fashion, Johns rejected any and all attempts to separate religion and ethics. He therefore preached prophetic sermons to his congregation that challenged them to apply the Christian message to social problems that adversely affected them. Additionally, Johns never hesitated to tell whites of Montgomery, including the chief of police and a Grand Jury, what he believed to be God's truth. In fact, there was even an incident in which Johns refused to obey the local and state segregation ordinance regarding public transportation. One day, he boarded a bus, paid his fare, and flat out refused to abide by the custom of leaving the bus and reboarding from the rear. Instead, he simply paid his fare, took a seat, and refused to move. The driver angrily declared that the bus would not move until Johns complied with his command. Johns finally said that if he had to leave the bus and reboard from the rear he would not ride the bus. Finally yielding, he even managed to get

6. Paul M. Minus, *Walter Rauschenbusch: American Reformer* (New York: Macmillan, 1988), 185.

7. This author contacted Oberlin's registrar (Liz Clerkin) several times during the 2012–13 school year to ascertain the name of the course taught by Rauschenbusch, and to verify whether Johns was officially enrolled in it. At my offer to pay to have this searched and verified, the registrar promised to implement the process. As of May 28, 2013, I have not received confirmation. Since it is known that Johns was officially a student at Oberlin during the fall of 1917 when Rauschenbusch taught there, and because his teacher-mentor, Edward Increase Bosworth, was himself a strong proponent of the social gospel, it is difficult to believe that he did not advise Johns to take the course with the premier social gospel advocate in the theological academy at that time.

8. See Vernon Johns, "Transfigured Moments," in *Best Sermons 1926*, ed. Joseph Fort Newton (New York: Harcourt, Brace and Company, 1926), 335–50.

9. Quoted in Roberson, *Fighting the Good Fight*, 88.

his money back, itself an amazing feat at that time. In addition, always the prophet, as he was leaving the bus Johns beckoned to blacks and well-meaning whites who also disagreed with the segregation ordinance and dehumanizing customs associated with it, to get out of their seats and follow him as a matter of conscience and protest. He was not at all surprised that not one person—white or black—left the bus with him.[10] And of course, much to the disappointment and embarrassment of many of the members at Dexter, Johns railed against racism and segregation from the pulpit during his entire tenure as senior pastor. He left the "feel good" sermons to other ministers in the city. His calling was to preach to the people a kind of "thus says the Lord" about the need to do justice. To the extent that Johns wanted his people to feel good about themselves as human beings and to enhance their sense of dignity, we can say that his prophetic sermons were "feel good" sermons of a much different type than those generally preached by ministers, regardless of race. Johns was determined to not let the good people of Dexter be at ease in what he saw as a very troubled Zion; would not allow them to deceive themselves into thinking that their level of educational attainment and social status somehow meant that they were excused from resisting social evil that affected the entire race.

Part of the significance of Vernon Johns's bus encounter is that while he may not have been the first black patron to refuse to obey the command of a city bus driver in Montgomery, it is a reminder that the refusal of Rosa Parks, Claudette Colvin, and Mary Louise Smith to give up their seats to white patrons in 1955, were not the first acts of black defiance on the city buses, nor as we will see, was Johns's. Despite the fact that frequently the incidents went unreported, blacks in Montgomery, generally women (since many of them rode the buses to and from their domestic jobs), often defied the practice of the bus company. At times these women were insulted and hit by bus drivers and/or police officers before being arrested and jailed; at times the women got the better of those trying to forcibly remove them from the bus; at times they essentially boycotted the buses, refusing to ever ride again after their ordeal. Such was the experience of Viola White, for example, in 1944, eleven years before Rosa Parks was arrested,[11] and several years before the Johns bus incident. Individual blacks, especially women, had been boycotting Montgomery city buses for a long time. So common were bus incidents involving black women that the press did not even consider them newsworthy. Indeed, frequently such

---

10. Taylor Branch, *Parting the Waters: America in the King Years 1954-63* (New York: Simon & Schuster, 1988), 14.

11. Darlene Clark Hine and Kathleen Thompson, *A Shining Thread of Hope: The History of Black Women in America* (New York: Broadway Books, 1998), 274.

incidents even seemed to go unnoticed by Montgomery's black male leadership. It was nearly an everyday occurrence, the social reality of the time, and thus seldom noticed since it was deemed to be normal.

Vernon Johns's act of defiance during the bus incident was unquestionably intentional. He was making a political, and even more importantly, a theological statement, and in a way that others, even ministers, had not the courage to do. His action served as a reminder that as human beings and citizens of the United States, and as persons imbued with God's image, black people had every right to be treated as equals to whites, but more importantly, to be treated as full-fledged human beings.

Johns made his witness that day on the bus. Lewis Baldwin has aptly described Vernon Johns as "imposing, scholarly, and controversial."[12] He was in fact an amazing admixture of these traits, although I would add that Johns was also "ethically prophetic," that is, he prophesied in the tradition of the Hebrew prophets of the eighth century bce, and thus did not soften his prophetic critique, whether from the pulpit at Dexter, or in the presence of the powers. He was constantly reminding the people and the powers about God's requirement that justice be done in righteous ways. In addition, he was intrepid and courageous as well as faithful to God's *call*. He *dared* to speak in God's name, and insisted that God is a God of justice, righteousness, compassion, and wrath. Johns paid the price for it, but he never wavered from speaking God's truth to church members, the authorities in Montgomery, and wherever he went.

Just as Vernon Johns did not let whites off the moral hook, he was not soft with his congregation and other members of the black community regarding racial segregation. Unquestionably, he was the quintessential preacher-prophet-scholar. He preached the prophetic word of God like no other, educating the Dexter parishioners as to divine expectations in segregated Montgomery. He was relentless in this regard, and as long as the people continued to occupy the pews on Sunday morning there was no place to hide, and no way to avoid hearing what "thus says the Lord." We can be sure that while some members revolted and ceased coming to church during the remainder of Johns's tenure as pastor, just as many, if not more, revolted but continued to come because they knew deep within that their pastor was right, was only being faithful to God, and was trying to get them to be faithful as well. So by the time Martin Luther King arrived as Dexter's pastor, the members were already more acquainted with prophetic and social gospel preaching than many wanted to be.[13]

12. Lewis V. Baldwin, *There Is a Balm in Gilead: The Cultural Roots of Martin Luther King, Jr.* (Minneapolis: Fortress Press, 1991), 183.

13. Roberson, *Fighting the Good Fight*, 106.

Vernon Johns had an incisive and analytical mind. Moreover, as pastor of Dexter he would allow no one to dictate what he should or should not teach, preach, or prophesy in or out of the pulpit. Instead, he insisted on the freedom to speak God's truth, as he understood it. We will see that this was a characteristic trait of Martin Luther King as well, although difference in temperament, personality, character, and socio-economic upbringing prompted him to preach God's word less abrasively than Johns presumably did. The personalities of Johns and King were different, but the message they preached and taught was the same, namely, that blacks are fully human and morally autonomous beings created in God's image, loved and cared for by God, and thus deserving of total freedom and respect as human beings. They also taught that blacks had to take the initiative and demand their rights, rather than passively wait for potential white liberators. They had to look to themselves if liberation was to come. Johns and (later) King also insisted that blacks must hold themselves accountable for their interpersonal and intracommunal actions as well. Johns had no patience with blacks who thought they were better than other blacks because of their education and/or social class. Nor did he have patience or take kindly to members whose church attendance was sporadic at best, and he cared little for their status or title. On one occasion, Harper Council Trenholm, president of Alabama State College, showed up to church after the service began. On that occasion, "Johns stopped the Sunday morning service, declaring, 'I want to pause here to give Dr. Trenholm a chance to get seated on his semi-annual visit to church.'"[14] Not surprisingly, Trenholm was among those who chose not to return to Dexter until Johns was no longer the pastor. He in fact only returned when King was installed as pastor.

When Vernon Johns saw evidence of injustice, in or outside the Dexter congregation, he did not hesitate to name it, including the culprit. For example, he did not hesitate to publicly chastise R. T. Adair, a prominent doctor and longtime member at Dexter, in the presence of the entire congregation after he shot and killed his wife on suspicion of adultery. Adair had received little more than a slap on the wrist by police and the white judicial system for the murder, and did not spend a single night in jail for his crime against Mrs. Adair and black humanity. Johns took this to mean that the black community had to take Adair to court and hold him accountable for his actions. What Johns did when Adair returned to church shocked and rattled most of the members at Dexter. Taylor Branch provides an account of what happened.

14. Ibid., 103.

But when Adair next took his customary seat at Dexter, Johns sprang quickly to the pulpit. "There is a murderer in the house," he announced to a stunned congregation. "God said, 'Thou shalt not kill.' Dr. Adair, you have committed a sin, and may God have mercy on your soul." Johns stared down at Adair in solemn judgment, with one eye in a menacing twitch caused by a childhood kick from a mule. Then he sat down.[15]

Nor did Vernon Johns ever hesitate to criticize congregants for their conspicuous consumption and a seeming unending greed for status at any cost. Coretta Scott King reports that according to her husband (who knew Johns by reputation, and also met him), Johns's "main purpose was to rock the complacency of the refined members of the Dexter Avenue Baptist Church—in whatever way he could."[16] By all accounts Johns succeeded in this.

Vernon Johns was just as fearless and demanding regarding whites. Police brutality against blacks was rampant in Montgomery. Johns was particularly angered when police nearly beat a black man to death with a tire iron when he was stopped for speeding. But what angered him most was that white and black onlookers said and did nothing to stop or at least try to minimize the severity of the beating. He did not hesitate to bring this to the attention of the Dexter faithful in his sermons. In another case, a black man was sentenced to death for allegedly robbing a white woman of $1.95. Luckily for him, the governor later commuted the sentence. This demeaning and cheapening of black life by whites prompted Johns to preach provocative sermons with titles such as: "It's Safe to Murder Negroes in Montgomery" (after a black man was lynched and a number of other blacks were killed by the police); "When the Rapist Is White"; and "Segregation after Death." These titles appeared in large bold print on the church bulletin board outside the church for all residents of Montgomery to see. The church was located near the Alabama State Capitol and Supreme Court. Johns's real target audience for those sermon title advertisements was white residents, including the police and other powers-that-be. The publicizing of such sermon titles got Johns summoned to the office of the chief of police. Indeed, he was summoned before the all-white Grand Jury for advertising "It Is Safe to Kill Negroes in Montgomery." He was charged with "inciting a riot and subpoenaed to appear . . . to show cause why he should not be indicted."[17]

15. Branch, *Parting the Waters*, 15.

16. Coretta Scott King, *My Life with Martin Luther King, Jr.* (New York: Holt, Rinehart & Winston, 1969), 95.

17. V. P. Franklin, *Martin Luther King, Jr.* (New York: Park Lane, 1998), 28.

Johns responded that until a suspect was arrested, the sermon title "was merely a statement of fact."[18] He was released by the Grand Jury. However, before preaching the sermon, Johns boldly sent letters to the city commissioners inviting them to send twelve of their best police officers to join the worship service when he preached that sermon. The night before the sermon was to be preached, "a cross was burned at the church, and the story got into the papers early Sunday morning: 'Cross Burned at Dexter Avenue Baptist Church.'"[19] To Johns's surprise, and much to the chagrin of the police, the service was very well attended, although the policemen who arrived remained in their parked cars across the street from the church. Because Johns had the sanctuary windows lowered so the overflow crowd could hear, the policemen undoubtedly heard every word.[20] And they most assuredly were not pleased with what they heard. For in the sermon, Johns did not hold back. He rocked the congregation that day:

> No man is fit to be alive until he has something for which he would die. . . .
>
> Two days from now my son's going to Korea, to fight, so many thousands miles away and yet he's fighting for those people for those things which he has been denied here. . . . I just as soon for him to die here as to die over there, and by dying here he will be dying for his own cause.
>
> God never spoke about justifiable homicide. He said "Thou shalt not kill." He didn't say thou shalt not kill, unless you've got an excuse. He didn't say thou shalt not kill, unless you are a police officer. And he most assuredly did not say thou shalt not kill, unless you're white.
>
> I'll tell you why it's safe to murder Negroes. Because Negroes stand by and let it happen. Do you know what occurred to me as I watched that cross burning in front of the church? When the Klan burns a cross it's a message. The next step is lynching.
>
> As I watched that cross it occurred to me that what we call the crucifixion is just that—a lynching. Isn't it ironic? Everything we worship was made possible by a lynching. Because at that ultimate moment of death Jesus spoke the words that transformed a lynching

18. Ibid.

19. Lamont H. Yeakey, "The Montgomery, Alabama Bus Boycott, 1955-56," Ph.D. diss., Columbia University, 1979, 103.

20. Ibid., 104.

into the crucifixion. That made Jesus the redeemer, not the condemner. Jesus said Father forgive them for they know not what they do. But you know what you do. And the white police officers who are free day after day to murder Negroes know what they do. And when you stand by and watch your brothers and sisters being lynched it's as if you stood by while Christ was being crucified.[21]

After this experience, Johns did not hesitate to criticize police brutality and police shootings of blacks whenever the occasion called for it. It has been said of the Hebrew prophets that they were among the most peculiar and disturbing personalities to ever appear on the stage of history. Vernon Johns was no different. He was in the best sense both pastor and prophet, and possessed the uncanny ability to know when to comfort his people, and when to challenge them with his sense of what the God of the Hebrew prophets expects of them. During one of the most dangerous periods of U.S. history in arguably the most dangerous place in the country, Johns's courage was simply amazing.

And yet, to an extent and degree that most pastors—of any race—were not, Vernon Johns was the chief exemplar of the prophet in the tradition of the Hebrew prophets. He was truly one of "God's bad boys," in the sense that he not only could tell the gospel story for his day and location in a way that really got the attention of his hearers and left them speechless and feeling convicted, but he was relentless in applying it to both church and world while insisting that these be brought into line with what the Lord thus says. "Vernon Johns was considered one of those 'crazy Negroes, who the white folks didn't mess with.' He was one of the few persons 'who walked up and down the street and did whatever he wanted to do.'"[22] Like Martin Luther King who succeeded him, Johns lived by the conviction that those who prophesy in the manner of the Hebrew prophets inevitably bear heavy crosses, the very reason that most ministers—of any race—avoid preaching prophetic sermons and doing prophetic ministry. None was more committed to such radical social gospel ministry than Vernon Johns. Martin Luther King himself was much influenced by his witness and his prophetic preaching.

Vernon Johns's commitment to social gospel ministry was merely a continuation of a long tradition of black preachers' commitment to applying Christian principles to social problems that adversely affected their people.

21. Quoted in Charles E. Cobb Jr., *On the Road to Freedom: A Guided Tour of the Civil Rights Trail* (Chapel Hill: Algonquin Books, 2008), 213. From http://www.vernonjohns.org.
22. Quoted in Yeakey, "The Montgomery, Alabama Bus Boycott," 104. From interview with James Pierce in the *Statewide Oral History Project, Alabama* 3, no. 047: 5.

We see strong evidence of this in many places in the classic text by Mays and Nicholson, *The Negro Church* (1933). One example will have to suffice. The authors share a sermon by a black minister who preached on the social implications of the kingdom of God. The minister argued that as much as people talk and pray about the kingdom of God and their desire to see it actualized in the world, the reality is that they do not want to see this happen, for if they did they would do what they could to create openings for its occurrence. The minister said in part:

> If I understand what is meant by the Kingdom, it means the existence of that state of society in which human values are the supreme values. It means the creation of a world in which every individual born into it would be given an opportunity to grow physically, to develop mentally and progress spiritually without the imposition of artificial obstructions from without. Everything in the environment would be conducive to developing to the nth degree the individual's innate powers. At the center of our social, religious, political and economic life would be not a selfish profit motive, not a prostituted conception of nationalism, not a distorted notion of race superiority; but at the center of our lives would be the sacredness of human personality; and whatever we did, the chief aim would be to protect life and improve it. If this is the meaning of the Kingdom, then frankly, we must admit that we do not want it.[23]

The minister was certain that if people were serious about the kingdom of God on earth, the United States and other nations would not continue to commit vast portions of their budgets to fighting wars; would not rush to dominate natural and economic resources all over the world, but would share equitably the bounties of God's world. Indeed, the minister argued, the kingdom of God on earth would mean that no race of people would seek to dehumanize and dominate any other race. That blacks continue to be dominated and oppressed by whites was clear indication to the minister that the United States had no interest in eradicating racial discrimination.

The first step to actualizing the kingdom is for individuals to assume responsibility for making it happen. Individuals cannot do it alone, but must work cooperatively with each other and God. Indeed, often there is need for the

---

23. Benjamin E. Mays and Joseph W. Nicholson, *The Negro Church* (Salem, NH: Ayer, 1988) [originally published New York: Institute of Social and Religious Research, 1933], 64.

prophetic voice of one crying in the wilderness to incite people's passion about the work of the kingdom, what it means, and what it requires.

I have learned from my own experience and study that neither nonreligious institutions, nor churches and other religious organizations, regardless of race-ethnicity and/or class, want prophets for pastors. Rather, they prefer and generally get the type of pastors who are more committed to comforting parishioners and making them feel good, often in their wrongdoing, since they do not challenge such behavior through prophetic preaching. M. C. Sutherland has rightly said that "unlike the pastor, the prophet does not merge with his community."[24] When Sutherland was asked whether Vernon Johns thought of himself as a prophet, he responded: "He didn't say it, but he acted it."[25] In a 1920 letter to one of his Oberlin mentors, George Fiske, however, Johns described himself as "a prophet and dreamer, leaving the more practical affairs to those who have more time and love for details."[26] Sutherland recalled that Johns was neither a braggart nor arrogant in his role as prophet, and in any case he did not, like many pastors, put himself at the center of ministry, such that everything done by a church centers on him as if he were the Savior of the world.

Coretta King relates yet another story about Johns, told to her by her husband, a story that must have been as hilarious as it was disconcerting to those in attendance at a certain wedding. According to Mrs. King:

> One time Dr. Johns was performing a very staid and elegant wedding ceremony for one of the most outstanding Negro families in Montgomery. The church wedding had been proceeding, but just before the marriage was final, the minister stopped. He peered up and said, "I would like to announce that right after the wedding there will be a watermelon cutting in the church basement. It will be twenty-five cents a slice, and for all you economical-minded people who order half a melon, the price will be a dollar fifty." Then, without stopping for a minute, Dr. Johns continued, "I now pronounce you man and wife."[27]

24. Patrick L. Cooney and Henry W. Powell, "Montgomery, Later Years, 1950-1952," in *The Life and Times of the Prophet Vernon Johns: Father of the Civil Rights Movement*, unpublished book, 3.

25. Ibid.

26. Quoted in Roberson, *Fighting the Good Fight*, 95. From Vernon Johns to George Fiske (letter), August 5, 1920, Oberlin College Archives, Oberlin, Ohio.

27. Coretta Scott King, *My Life with Martin Luther King, Jr.*, 95.

For a long time after that incident, the bride complained about how Johns had ruined her life by announcing during her wedding that there would be a watermelon sale immediately thereafter.[28] Who can doubt that Vernon Johns himself would make a fascinating study!

Despite Johns's diehard seriousness about things that pertain to ministry, he also had a great sense of humor, not least illustrated in the story just retold. Indeed, Martin Luther King himself had occasion to be on the receiving end of Johns's humor. One such instance was when Johns wrote to King, then president of the Southern Christian Leadership Conference and Associate Pastor of Ebenezer Baptist Church in Atlanta, and requested support for his farm cooperative, Farm and City Enterprises, a venture in which the Montgomery Improvement Association had invested $11,000. Johns also asked that King and Wyatt Walker assist in arranging speaking engagements for him. His humor is quite apparent in the opening paragraph of his letter.

> If you could see what I have done with a dozen or more swank audiences over the US that tried to get you and couldn't—you would start referring them to me when you couldn't accept. Maybe not. It takes a mighty big man to enjoy hearing an audience say how glad it is the invited speaker couldn't get there! You will take this of course with a pound of salt![29]

Most of the members at Dexter resented Vernon Johns's almost constant ranting and raving about what the Lord thus says. Johns was "committed to telling people what he believed they needed to hear, confident that 'whether they hear or refuse to hear, they will know that there hath been a prophet among them.'"[30] Johns understood what most ministers did not, namely that as a Christian minister his responsibility was to speak the gospel truth. It was the responsibility of the hearers to respond accordingly. There was, however, a cadre of members at Dexter, including members of the WPC who readily received Johns's strong messages, even though they did not always agree with his methods.[31] Thus, not all were pleased or happy to see Johns leave. At least one writer contends that "[m]any, perhaps a slight majority in the church, saw his leaving as regrettable. Some people even cried when he resigned."[32]

28. Branch, *Parting the Waters*, 1001n902.

29. Clayborne Carson et al., eds., *The Papers of Martin Luther King, Jr.* (Berkeley: University of California Press, 2005), 5:455.

30. Roberson, *Fighting the Good Fight*, 86.

31. Ibid., 84–85.

Vernon Johns was also an embarrassment to many members at Dexter because of his inattentiveness to dress. For example, it was not unusual for him to show up in mix-matched socks and untied shoes. Nor was it unusual to see him out on the street dressed like a common day laborer, "taking orders for watermelons."[33] Moreover, the fact that he was short tempered, no nonsense, and adamant about addressing every injustice that came to his attention also caused problems for him with many members. Notwithstanding such behavior and the criticisms elicited by it, he still laid a significant social protest foundation for the one who would be his immediate successor at Dexter, even if many of the members did not appreciate what he did. Nevertheless, in this regard Johns was the forerunner to King and what came to be known as *the movement*.

I do not consider it a serious criticism that Vernon Johns was not able to elicit from the vast majority of the Dexter congregation the response he wanted. It has to be remembered at all times that Johns was a persistent and courageous bearer of the prophetic word of God. Anybody that knows anything at all about the church knows that most members have no sense of appreciation for such a powerful, convicting word as that uttered by the Hebrew prophets and those who take their message seriously. History teaches us that only a faithful few will hear and receive the prophetic word, and alter their practice accordingly. There were a few of these types in the Dexter congregation when Johns was pastor. The contributions of two of these, Professors Mary Fair Burks and Jo Ann Robinson of the Women's Political Council, will be discussed in the next chapter. Johns broke ground for what was to follow. Rufus Lewis was surely right when he said that "Johns prepared 'Negroes for confrontation. . . . His role can be defined as one who prepared the blacks in Montgomery for the things that they did further on.'"[34]

The truth is that one such as Vernon Johns could not long remain pastor of any church, let alone a middle- to upper middle-class one like Dexter Avenue Baptist Church. Taylor Branch put it this way: "His behavior pitched the entire church into four years of awe, laughter, inspiration, fear, and annoyance. For [R. D.] Nesbitt, the responsible deacon, Johns became the most exquisite agony he had ever known in the church."[35] On four different occasions Johns submitted his resignation and threatened to leave if matters were not settled his way. Each time the board conceded, and Johns remained. When he submitted his resignation a fifth time the board simply accepted it. Johns in fact tried to

32. Yeakey, "The Montgomery, Alabama Bus Boycott," 110.
33. Quoted in ibid., 106. From Yeakey's interview with Robert Nesbitt Sr., November 26, 1976.
34. Yeakey, "The Montgomery, Alabama Bus Boycott," 111n1.
35. Branch, *Parting the Waters*, 7.

withdraw his letter of resignation,[36] but the board had had enough, and he was out.[37]

Others also paved the way for the social-activist ministry of Martin Luther King, but it is fair to say that Vernon Johns was in a class by himself. Indeed, dean of all preachers (regardless of race-ethnicity) Gardner C. Taylor was instructive when he remarked about Johns: "I think he was the principal forerunner of the whole civil rights movement."[38] Taylor went on to say that a reason for this was that during this period it could be said of no other black person that his "whole career was focused in such a white heat fashion upon this one matter of the plight of blacks."[39]

LIFE AND MINISTRY AFTER DEXTER

Although Vernon Johns lost the Dexter pastorate after barely four years, that did not end his prophetic proclamations and practice, or his commitment to a gospel that he believed required ministers to lead the fight against injustice, and to focus on both the spiritual and material well-being of the whole person. It is not clear whether white proponents of the social gospel knew of Vernon Johns, although it is difficult to believe that some did not. It is quite apparent, however, that more than his white counterparts in ministry, Johns's own ministry and behavior actually reflected the basic liberal-progressive principles of the Christian faith. Furthermore, and also unlike white ministers, Johns was relentless in seeking the eradication of racism, a practice that would be just as prevalent in the ministry of Martin Luther King. Make no mistake here. Vernon Johns's ministry was a social gospel ministry in the best sense of the word, and he did not mince words in his challenges to white clergymen.

In a meeting of white and black Baptist ministers in Baltimore, Maryland in 1960, Johns lost patience when a white pastor preached a nice little sermon "on the theme of Christian salvation, of being 'washed in the blood of the Lamb.'"[40] Selected by his black peers to speak next, the white preacher hardly uttered his last words before Johns, who also had an inclination toward the theatrical, leaped to his feet and said: "The thing that disappoints me about the Southern white church is that it spends all of its time dealing with Jesus after

---

36. Franklin, *Martin Luther King, Jr.*, 28.
37. Yeakey, "The Montgomery, Alabama Bus Boycott," 109.
38. Quoted in Cooney and Powell, "Montgomery, Later Years, 1950-52," 11.
39. Ibid.
40. Quoted in Branch, *Parting the Waters*, 339.

the cross, instead of dealing with Jesus before the cross."[41] Clearly embarrassing both white and black preachers at the gathering, Johns continued:

> "You didn't do a thing but preach about the death of Jesus. If that were the heart of Christianity, all God had to do was to drop him down on Friday, and let them kill him, and then yank him up again on Easter Sunday. That's all you hear. You don't hear so much about his three years of teaching that man's religion is revealed in the love of his fellow man. He who says he loves God and hates his fellowman is a liar, and the truth is not in him. That is what offended the leaders of Jesus's own established church as well as the colonial authorities from Rome. That's why they put him up there"[42] [on the cross].

Johns was clearly rejecting the Anselmian "satisfaction" theory of salvation in his remarks. According to this theory, God gave up Jesus to die so that human beings would not have to suffer eternal punishment for sin. Implied in this is the strange notion that God actually willed the death of God's son, an idea that did not sit well with Johns.

The focus of Vernon Johns, on the other hand, was on what Jesus did on this side of the grave and what remained to be done in the world. He was interested in what Jesus taught, how he lived, and what this must mean for those who followed him. Johns was convinced that Jesus was killed by the powers-that-be precisely because of the way he lived and what he expected of his followers. It was a political lynching. Jesus *lived* the Sermon on the Mount. Thus, Johns wanted to focus on what Jesus did *before* the cross, not after he was crucified. Therefore, to a stunned group of white and black ministers he went on to say: "There is a world of disparity between the idealism of Jesus and the practices of men. But Jesus is not crazy. We are crazy. The church has not formally denounced the Sermon on the Mount. It has merely let it slide. I want to deal with Jesus before the cross. I don't give a damn what happened to him after the cross."[43] Not surprisingly, Johns was forced to resign his position at the Maryland Baptist Center, which was jointly sponsored by white Southern Baptists and the all-black National Baptist Convention. The Center sought to provide adult education for black preachers, but apparently the methods and contents of that education had to be approved in advance by whites.

41. Quoted in ibid.
42. Quoted in ibid., 340.
43. Quoted in ibid.

Like the Hebrew prophets, Vernon Johns deplored any "religion without reverence or justice, and government entirely void of discipline or even the capacity for watchfulness, which is apt to be the crudest and surest form which godless government assumes."[44] The respect and appreciation that Johns had for the Hebrew prophets kept him in hot water with organized religious authorities, his own congregants at Dexter, and the local secular authorities in Montgomery.

The Hebrew prophets were for Vernon Johns among the most significant, readily active persons in what he affectionately called "the Book" (the Bible). The prophets were "God's 'standing servants,'"[45] he declared. This meant that when God's word came there was no need to waste precious time making preparation to deliver God's message, which so frequently happens among those who claim to be the faithful. Because they were God's "standing servants," the prophets had a clear sense of the urgency of God's word and the need to be expeditious in conveying it to the people and/or rulers. They understood, as did Johns, that God was concerned about basic issues of human living, relating, and behaving in the world, not the formulation and exactness of creeds, ethical theories, and theologies. Nor were the Hebrew prophets concerned to placate the people and the nation through their words, which means they were frequently seen to be abrasive and inconsiderate since they did not sugarcoat their speech.

Vernon Johns was convinced that the prophet, whether Moses, Daniel, Deborah, Jeremiah, Amos, Micah, or Isaiah, was the "glad ally of the weak against the strong." Although the vast majority of ancient and present-day religious people find this exceedingly difficult to do, Johns held that "almost invariably the Old Testament prophets are found defending the poor against the rich or the weak against the strong."[46] In this, Johns was a forerunner to what we know today as black liberation theology. Indeed, he argued that the entire Bible is nothing short of the *friend of the poor and the oppressed*.

Vernon Johns, not unlike the white social gospel leader Walter Rauschenbusch, categorically rejected the claim that the Bible conveys the view that religion and politics do not mix or should somehow be kept apart, as if the two realms they represent have a different source and different sets of morals by which to abide.[47] Instead, Johns supported the biblical view that conveys the idea that there is but one world, and the God of the Hebrew prophets

44. Vernon Johns, "Prophetic Interference in Old Testament Politics," in *Human Possibilities: A Vernon Johns Reader*, ed. Samuel Lucius Gandy (Washington, DC: Hoffman, 1977), 37.

45. Ibid., 26.

46. Ibid., 33.

is its Author and chief caregiver. Therefore, the entire world is required to abide by God's expectation that justice and righteousness be done. There is no restrictionism such that divine mandates are relevant only to specific spheres of the world. The "thus says the Lord" of the Hebrew prophets is relevant to every realm of human existence or to none at all.

Ethical prophecy[48] contends that even the decisions and actions of political rulers are accountable to the God of the universe, particularly when they govern in ways that are contrary to what God requires. Similarly, Vernon Johns maintained that one of the nine indisputable assumptions of the Bible is "That God, an Invisible Personal Intelligence, Has Unimpeachable Authority Everywhere."[49] Acknowledging the humanity of the prophets, Johns believed their fearlessness and composure "in the presence of tyrants who wielded all the destructive powers known to man is evidence of their faith in the Supremacy of the Invisible Power which they represented."[50]

It is important to remember that all that is known about Vernon Johns suggests that he himself possessed the traits of the ethical prophet. He spoke forthrightly what he took to be God's truth, and without trying to devise language that would make it more palatable either to religious or secular powers, or even to his congregants. One did not leave a church where Johns preached having to wonder about what he was really trying to say. There was no sugarcoating his speech. One might not agree with or even like what he said, but one understood in no uncertain terms what Vernon Johns preached. R. T. Adair, Harper Council Trenholm, and many others could attest to that. It is no wonder that the church membership was way down by the time King arrived as senior minister.[51] The Dexter faithful knew exactly what Vernon Napoleon Johns preached each Sunday.

Determined to fight to the death to eradicate injustice against his people, Johns had no patience with diplomacy, whether he was addressing white racists, or his own people, whom he loved dearly. He knew how precious time was,

47. See Walter Rauschenbusch, *Christianity and the Social Crisis* (New York: Macmillan, 1907), 42–43. According to Rauschenbusch: "Whoever uncouples the religious and the social life has not understood Jesus" (48).

48. For the most thorough discussion of this type of prophecy, see Mary Alice Mulligan and Rufus Burrow Jr., *Daring to Speak in God's Name: Ethical Prophecy and Ministry* (Cleveland: Pilgrim, 2002), and Burrow, *God and Human Responsibility: David Walker and Ethical Prophecy* (Macon, GA: Mercer University Press, 2003).

49. Johns, "Prophetic Interference in Old Testament Politics," 27.

50. Ibid., 36.

51. See Yeakey, "The Montgomery, Alabama Bus Boycott," 39n1.

and thus was focused on one thing only—conveying the truth. Boddie has written about this.

> His abrasiveness is revealed in the following vignette. Over the remains of an unfortunate Charlestonian who died in a brawl, came forth these exact, incredible, and only words: "Anyone who stops by a grog shop with his paycheck instead of going straight home to his wife and family with it ought to be struck over the head with a ball bat and killed. The benediction will take place at the cemetery."
>
> One can see why the Reverend J. Raymond Henderson suggested that Vernon Johns be endowed to do nothing but traverse the country irritating the Negro.[52]

Lamont Yeakey tells of another instance in which Johns was preaching a funeral, "and 'the family was hollering and carrying on.' Johns told the undertaker, 'Open up this casket, let me see this man. I ain't never seen this man, this Niggra in church before. I just want to see what these folks hollering about.'"[53] Obviously such practices did not endear him to many members, and most certainly bereaved family members.

The ethical prophet is obligated to convey God's word of truth to the people and the nation. Such a person knows that God's word is more important than anything else, including uppity well-to-do people who would rather not hear it. Vernon Johns, like other ethical prophets, was criticized for being "curt and abrasive" and for being too "direct and to the point"[54] during his ministry at Dexter. Those who criticize the ethical prophet in this way fail to understand the true nature of this prophet. Vernon Johns did not preach the tough words of prophecy to his people out of hatred. On the contrary, he preached as he did out of deep love for them and in strict obedience to the One who called him. He preached the truth in love, and out of devotion to his God.

Above all else, Vernon Johns demanded that justice be done, and that racism in all its forms be eradicated. He saw love as the ultimate Christian imperative, but he was just as adamant that justice must be done first and foremost, for love required that justice be done.[55] He knew that people, including Christians, frequently spoke of their love for others, but what they said, no matter how eloquently or passionately, tended not to be consistent with

---

52. Charles Emerson Boddie, God's "Bad Boys" (Valley Forge, PA: Judson, 1972), 72.
53. Quoted in Yeakey, "The Montgomery, Alabama Bus Boycott," 107.
54. See Yeakey, "The Montgomery, Alabama Bus Boycott," 107, 108, 110.
55. Boddie, God's "Bad Boys," 71.

their behavior. In this sense too, Johns anticipated black liberation theologians, for instance, James H. Cone, who later argued that what oppressors *do* is the best indicator of what they really believe. In other words, mere verbal language and ideas are cheap if not made to live through action or behavior. White pastors and Christians often preached and talked about love for the neighbor in Vernon Johns's day, but saw no incongruity between such speech and their racist behavior toward their black neighbor. They might well have loved humanity in general or in some abstract sense, but their actual treatment of black people was a far cry from what Christian love means and requires.

I believe that in large measure it is precisely because of Vernon Johns's unwillingness to compromise God's truth and to tone down his language that he has been relatively ignored in textbooks on preaching and in seminary courses on preaching, even though he was without peer as preacher. Most white homiletics professors know virtually nothing about Vernon Johns, which explains, largely, why most seminary-trained white preachers know nothing about him. Johns had the uncanny gift of "killing his audience," even as "he was thrilling it." He put his entire being, that is, "brain power, lung power, and body power" into the sermon. Boddie amplifies this point.

> As preacher, no living person seemed to be able to "flesh out" the homiletical bones with such skill and originality and to throw kisses at the Pleiades with such astounding aplomb and deftness. His sermonic cadences seemed almost as though they were set to music, and the bodily surges associated with his delivery would induce audience sympathetic vibration worthy of a Howard Thurman.[56]

Moreover, Boddie writes: "He inspired students, unstuffed shirts, tweaked aristocratic noses, and punctured captiousness, infuriating, spellbinding, overpowering, and making use of every weapon in his God-supplied arsenal. The man was the epitome of sheer brilliance, grandiloquence, and perspicacity."[57] In many ways, Vernon Johns was a tough act for anyone to follow, including Martin Luther King.

THE MARTIN LUTHER KING–VERNON JOHNS CONNECTION

Martin Luther King succeeded Vernon Johns as pastor of Dexter Avenue Baptist Church. Ironically, on the day that he was to preach his trial sermon,

56. Ibid., 69.
57. Ibid.

King gave Johns a ride from Atlanta to Montgomery.[58] Upon arrival, Johns prevailed upon King to join him at Ralph Abernathy's home for dinner. During this time, Johns reportedly gave King a sage piece of advice about Dexter. King was advised that should he receive the call, "he must act quickly in establishing his program, giving the deacons as little opportunity as possible to challenge him."[59] Indicators are that afterward King considered Johns to be more than a mere casual acquaintance, and at one point even asked him for copies of his sermons. Johns promised to send them but never did. In part, his failure to do so might have been related to the fact that he claimed to have lost a vast quantity of his papers in a house fire. It might also be related to the fact that Johns seldom wrote out his sermons. In any case, if Johns did write out most of his sermons it was to King's deep disappointment that they did not find their way to him.[60]

Martin Luther King had heard stories about Johns's prophetic and sometimes eccentric behavior at Dexter and throughout the Montgomery community. There is no question that he had much respect for the witness and ministry of his predecessor. This is the sense one gets from what King wrote in *Stride Toward Freedom*:

> Vernon Johns . . . was a brilliant preacher with a creative mind and an incredibly retentive memory. It was not unusual for him to quote from the classics of literature and philosophy for hours without ever referring to a manuscript. A fearless man, he never allowed an injustice to come to his attention without speaking out against it. When he was still pastor, hardly a Sunday passed that he did not lash out against complacency. He often chided the congregation for sitting up so proudly with their many academic degrees, and yet lacking the very thing that degrees should confer, that is, self-respect. One of his basic theses was that any individual who submitted willingly to injustice did not really deserve more justice.[61]

King was also aware of the eloquence and the power of Johns's preaching, and was much impressed by it. Indeed, as preacher, King was variously influenced by the sermons of both white liberals, for example, Harry Emerson Fosdick, Robert J. McCracken, Frederick M. Meek, and George Buttrick,[62] and many

---

58. Branch, *Parting the Waters*, 104–5.

59. Roberson, *Fighting the Good Fight*, 118–19.

60. Branch, *Parting the Waters*, 902.

61. Martin Luther King Jr., *Stride Toward Freedom* (New York: Harper & Row, 1958), 38.

62. *The Papers* (2007), 6:3.

black preachers of various denominations. But by far, when it came to actual preaching and pulpit demeanor it was black preachers who influenced King most, and who he most emulated. These included such giants as Vernon Johns, Sandy Ray, Howard Thurman, Benjamin E. Mays, and Daddy King. This point is supported both by family members and close friends of King's.[63] Although Vernon Johns was the prophet's prophet, we saw earlier that he also exhibited a strong sense of humor in his preaching, another trait that King admired and took as his own.[64]

Like Vernon Johns, Martin Luther King was also made of the stuff of the eighth-century prophets, although he was an entirely different personality. Here I part company with those who contend that Johns, not King, was a prophet, and that King was more of a tactician who sought to apply "the strategy of the prophet Vernon Johns."[65] It is one thing to present the quite reasonable argument that Johns and King were different personalities with different gifts, and who accomplished different things in their respective tenures as pastor at Dexter. But it is quite another matter to argue, wrongly in my view, that because King's speech and temperament were not as abrasive and explosive as Johns's, only the latter was a prophet.[66] It is more reasonable to argue that the two men had different gifts and did different things; that neither was in this sense "better" or "worse" than the other, but that their efforts essentially complemented each other's.[67] Somebody had to break ground or blaze the trail in order to prepare the way for what was to come. That was Vernon Johns's role. On the other hand, somebody also had to cultivate the ground in order to prepare it to bring forth fruit. That was King's role. According to James Pierce, "Johns came here and pulverized this particular soil [at Dexter Avenue Baptist Church]. He not only pulverized it, but planted it, and out from that came men of courage, women of courage. Martin Luther King only had to find a rallying place for other people. . . ."[68]

Vernon Johns might well have been eccentric, but it would be grossly erroneous to use such a characterization to undermine or dismiss the profoundly important work he did for the black church in general, for Dexter Avenue Baptist Church in particular, for the city of Montgomery, Alabama, and for the

63. Baldwin, *There Is a Balm in Gilead*, 299.

64. Ibid., 299–300.

65. Cooney and Powell, "Vernon Johns' Final Years," in *The Life and Times of the Prophet Vernon Johns*, ch. 27, 11.

66. Ibid.

67. Ibid.

68. Ibid.

emerging civil rights movement. Indeed, even some of the members of Dexter grew to appreciate Johns and his contribution, albeit *after* he was no longer their pastor! For example, in a series of articles written for the hundredth anniversary of Dexter with an emphasis on its pastors, Thelma Austin Rice wrote:

> In his perennial militancy in speech, action and from his pen for racial equality for all men, Rev. Johns rocked the Montgomery community with far reaching consequences elsewhere in this great land of ours. . . . Through his teachings and his precepts, he aroused not only the Dexter family but hundreds of citizens of Montgomery to the changes that had taken place and to those which were still taking place in the relationships of mankind and emphasized the concept of human fellowship that would know no narrow racial, religious, or national boundaries. He kindled a strong flame of thoughts of the importance that every individual should have in the affairs of the world. [69]

Unlike Vernon Johns, Martin Luther King was more polished and inclined to political compromise within and outside the church. King's temperament and philosophy were such that he was more inclined toward group decision making, and thus toward compromise. Johns was more prone to make decisions alone.

For good or ill, Ralph Abernathy pulled King aside when he arrived as Dexter's pastor and advised that if he expected to survive there, he would be wise to work harder at being a pastor than a prophet.[70] In other words, it would be better that he not make waves and ruffle the feathers of the good people of Dexter, but rather care for them as a shepherd would his flock. Abernathy also advised King to involve himself in the guts of the ministry at Dexter, that is, to be involved in all of the various ministries there. In any case, Abernathy's point was—quite correctly—that prophets of the likes of Vernon Napoleon Johns generally end up having no church, no congregation to which to prophesy. On this point, Abernathy may have been politically and strategically correct, but he was not being consistent with the prophetic tradition of the Jewish and Christian faiths, and the black religious tradition. More important, Abernathy was not morally and religiously correct. For when God speaks, who can but prophesy (Amos 3:8)? Furthermore, Vernon Johns did not need a local congregation in order to speak what "thus says the Lord,"

---

69. Quoted in Cooney and Powell, ch. 27, 1.
70. Branch, *Parting the Waters*, 109.

for wherever he went he prophesied what he believed to be God's truth. His immediate successor at Dexter was not different in this regard.

We have seen that Vernon Johns played a key role in paving the way for Martin Luther King and the movement that made, and was made by, him. But Johns was not the only trailblazer. Because of more recent scholarship on the civil rights movement we know more clearly the significant and dangerous trailblazing work done by black women in Montgomery and other places in the Deep South, as well as the North. What did black women contribute toward paving the way for Martin Luther King, and how did their contributions inform his *practiced* ideas?

7

Black Women Trailblazers

Rosa Parks was devoted to civil rights for her people. In preparation for the work she would do with the Montgomery branch of the NAACP she participated in a leadership training workshop led by the venerable Ella Baker (of the National NAACP Office in New York City) held in Atlanta, Georgia in March 1945. Parks later confided that Baker made a huge impact on her, especially in the matter of trying to obtain justice for black people throughout the South. The theme of that leadership workshop was "Give People Light and They Will Follow the Way."[1] This was reflective of Baker's own leadership philosophy, preferring communal-grassroots leadership over the individual charismatic leader model that was the preference of most people, including—and especially—black Baptist ministers and Martin Luther King. Baker would later serve as director of the Southern Christian Leadership Conference after its establishment in 1957, and would clash regularly with King and SCLC board members—all black pastors—over leadership style. Later, in 1955, at the encouragement and with the assistance of a white woman activist for racial justice and the vote for women and blacks, longtime Montgomery resident Virginia Durr, Parks also attended a two-week workshop for civil rights and labor activists at the Highlander Folk School in Monteagle, Tennessee. Parks was committed to doing whatever she could, not for herself, but for those who would come after her, namely black youths. Indeed, by this time she cared little for white people as a race, so fed up was she with racial discrimination and all that came with it. Before going to Highlander, she believed that solving the race problem was hopeless. After her two-week stay, she had internalized "the message hammered home by Highlander: Real social change could come only from grassroots pressure, not from 'some government edict or some Messiah.'"[2]

1. Barbara Ransby, *Ella Baker and the Black Freedom Movement: A Radical Democratic Vision* (Chapel Hill and London: University of North Carolina Press, 2003), 142.

After news of Rosa Parks's arrest spread throughout the Montgomery black community on December 1, 1955, black women decided that enough is enough. These women already had in place an organization that could mobilize reaction against this most recent assault on black personhood in general, and black womanhood in particular. The Women's Political Council was founded by Mary Fair Burks in 1946,[3] and thus had been functioning for about two years before Vernon Johns was appointed pastor of Dexter Avenue Baptist Church.[4] Burks, professor and chair of the English department at the all-black Alabama State College, was the WPC's founding president. Following a car accident in 1946, Burks was falsely accused of causing the accident, clubbed by a policeman, and then unjustly arrested. In part, this incident was a contributing factor to her founding the WPC, which was also a response to the refusal of the League of Women Voters in Montgomery to admit black women. The initial purpose of the organization was to address the race problem in Montgomery, more specifically, "to foster women's involvement in civic affairs, to promote voter registration through citizenship education, and to aid women who were victims of rape or assault."[5]

For a long time, Burks had a burning desire to do something about racial segregation, but she did not know what to do or how to get started. She said that she got inspiration to move forward from a Vernon Johns sermon. She recalled that Sunday sermon, which inspired her—the day of the car accident:

> I had no idea until Vernon Johns, pastor of Dexter Avenue Baptist Church, mounted one of his scathing attacks on the complacency of

2. Lynn Olson, *Freedom's Daughters: The Unsung Heroines of the Civil Rights Movement from 1830 to 1970* (New York: Scribner, 2001), 106.

3. Mary Fair Burks, "Trailblazers: Women in the Montgomery Bus Boycott," in *Women in the Civil Rights Movement: Trailblazers and Torchbearers 1941-1965*, ed. Vicki L. Crawford, Jacqueline Anne Rouse, and Barbara Woods (Bloomington: Indiana University Press, 1993), 79. Although Burks says the founding meeting was in 1946, Stewart Burns contends that the WPC was founded in 1949. This might well be little more than a typo. See his "Women's Political Council, Montgomery, Alabama," in *Black Women in America: An Historical Encyclopedia*, ed. Darlene Clark Hine (Brooklyn, NY: Carlson, 1993), 2:1279. Jo Ann Robinson seems to concur with Burks, noting in her memoir that when she first met Burks in 1949 the WPC had already been in existence for some time. See Robinson, *The Montgomery Bus Boycott and the Women Who Started It*, ed. David J. Garrow (Knoxville: University of Tennessee Press, 1987), 10.

4. Burks, "Trailblazers: Women in the Montgomery Bus Boycott," in *Women in the Civil Rights Movement*, 74–75.

5. Stewart Burns, "Women's Political Council, Montgomery, Alabama," in *Black Women in America: An Historical Encyclopedia*, ed. Darlene Clark Hine (Brooklyn, NY: Carlson, 1993), 2:1280.

his affluent membership. I looked around and all I could see were either masks of indifference or scorn. Johns's attacks, his patched pants, and his Thoreauvian philosophy of plain living and high thinking did not endear him to his congregation. I was a feminist before I really knew what the word meant and so I dismissed the hard-faced men, but I felt that I could appeal to some of the women. . . . I believed I could get enough . . . women together to address some of the glaring racial problems. Thus the idea of the Women's Political Council was born on that Sunday morning following my arrest.[6]

Burks was a member of Dexter Avenue Baptist Church during the tenure of both Johns and King. Her founding of and leadership in the WPC was one clear indication that some Dexter members actually listened to Vernon Johns and took seriously his messages about the need for Christians to apply their faith to the everyday affairs of life, and especially to social justice issues.

Jo Ann Robinson, also a member of Dexter and an English professor at Alabama State College, succeeded Burks as president of the WPC in 1949. It was under her leadership that the idea of a one-day boycott of the buses was conceived. This should not be taken to mean that the idea was solely Robinson's, as Taylor Branch seems to imply.[7] Rather, my reading of Robinson's memoir suggests that the idea, as well as the distribution of leaflets announcing the boycott, had been discussed by the women of the WPC. I therefore interpret this to mean that Robinson was acting not as a lone wolf, but on behalf of her colleagues in the WPC.[8]

It is said that when Robinson became president of the WPC, "she made bus desegregation its primary goal."[9] Burks said that under Robinson's leadership they focused their energy on bus abuses; met with the City Commission a number of times about bus and related abuses against blacks; "and precipitated the bus boycott."[10] It is significant that some of the women in the WPC,

6. Burks, "Trailblazers: Women in the Montgomery Bus Boycott," 78.

7. Taylor Branch, *Parting the Waters: America in the King Years, 1954-63* (New York: Simon & Schuster, 1988), 132.

8. Jo Ann Robinson, *The Montgomery Bus Boycott and the Women Who Started It: The Memoir of Jo Ann Gibson Robinson*, ed. David J. Garrow (Knoxville: University of Tennessee Press, 1996), 45. When Mary Fair Burks read this page she interpreted it to mean that Robinson credits herself as the sole instigator of the one-day boycott. See Burks, "Trailblazers: Women in the Montgomery Bus Boycott," 75.

9. Darlene Clark Hine and Kathleen Thompson, *A Shining Thread of Hope: The History of Black Women in America* (New York: Broadway Books, 1998), 274.

10. Burks, "Trailblazers . . . ," 75.

including Robinson and Burks, were also members of the Women's Political Group at Dexter Avenue Baptist Church, a committee that King established. One cannot help but wonder to what extent King was influenced by these women, though he most assuredly must have been. They were highly educated, intelligent, and outspoken, which suggests that they demanded to be heard by their pastor and other male leaders at Dexter. King was surely impressed with the leadership and political savvy of Jo Ann Robinson. By all accounts, by December 1955 the WPC was without question "the largest, best-organized, and most assertive black civic organization" in Montgomery.[11] The boycott idea originated not with Martin Luther King, nor with any of the other black male leaders in Montgomery, but with the women of the WPC.

Black women in Montgomery had surely had enough of dehumanizing treatment on the city buses. Arrested on Thursday, December 1, 1955, Rosa Parks was to be arraigned the following Monday. The day of Parks's arrest, Jo Ann Robinson scribbled on a piece of paper the words: "The Women's Political Council will not wait for Mrs. Parks' consent to call for a boycott of city buses. On Friday, Dec. 2, 1955 the women of Montgomery will call for a boycott to take place on Monday, Dec. 5."[12]

As with a number of the women in the WPC, Robinson was both keen-minded and politically shrewd. She knew how to play the game. Lawrence D. Reddick pointed to this fact in *Crusader Without Violence: A Biography of Martin Luther King, Jr.*, thereby helping us get a sense of her acumen and her political astuteness.[13]

> She is a quick thinker and extremely creative in formulating ways of getting things done. At many a conference, when the "enemy" made a calculated maneuver, it was Jo Ann who first spotted the move and countered it. Once the Mayor of Montgomery was appointing eight white persons and three Negroes to a committee on the basis of the number of organizations represented in the meeting. Jo Ann immediately saw what this meant and politely interrupted the mayor to point out that actually there were as many Negro organizations

11. Stewart Burns, *To the Mountaintop: Martin Luther King, Jr.'s Sacred Mission to Save America 1953-1968* (New York: HarperSanFrancisco, 2004), 20.

12. Quoted in Olson, *Freedom's Daughters*, 111.

13. Unfortunately, throughout his discussion of Robinson's contributions to the Montgomery campaign, Reddick refers to her only by first name, something he does not do consistently when referring to male contributors.

as white organizations represented in the meeting. The committee became eight to eight.[14]

Most of the women in the WPC had actually wanted to boycott the buses after fifteen-year-old Claudette Colvin was abused and arrested by police on March 2nd of that year for refusing to give up her bus seat. A very smart high school student who wanted to become a lawyer in order to help her people better negotiate a racist criminal justice and judicial system, Colvin was on her way home from school. When she refused the bus driver's command to give her seat to a white patron, the police were summoned and she was eventually "kicked" and forcibly removed from the bus. Colvin testified that "they just drug me out."[15]

Two important things happened after Colvin's arrest. First, the women in the WPC almost immediately began discussions about the possibility of organizing a boycott of the buses. Although there was no planned, organized boycott at that time, it is significant that the women were talking about it as early as March 1955, nine months before Rosa Parks was arrested. The second thing that happened was that Colvin's subsequent conviction angered the black community in Montgomery. Perhaps because Colvin was a child of the black community, her arrest unified black residents, as never before. "In a spontaneous protest, large numbers refused to use the buses for several days."[16] This was a significant, although mostly unnoticed event, especially in the white community. It was an early indicator, however, that Montgomery's black residents were not only getting fed up with their treatment on the buses and throughout the city. Significantly, it was also an indication that they could come together in protest. The stew was brewing.

Unlike many of her classmates at the all-black Booker T. Washington High School in Montgomery, Claudette Colvin was much influenced by her teacher, Mrs. Geraldine Nesbitt, a member of the Dexter Avenue Baptist Church. Nesbitt instilled in her students the importance of thinking for themselves, and sought also to awaken their sense of race pride and self-worth.[17] This explains, at least to some extent, why Colvin could tell the arresting police officer that she refused to give her seat to a white passenger because she "was just as good as any white person" and therefore she "wasn't going to get

14. L. D. Reddick, *Crusader Without Violence* (New York: Harper & Brothers, 1957), 118.

15. See Colvin's court testimony in *Daybreak of Freedom: The Montgomery Bus Boycott*, ed. Stewart Burns (Chapel Hill: University of North Carolina Press, 1997), 75.

16. Burns, "Women's Political Council, Montgomery, Alabama," in *Black Women in America*, 2:1280.

17. Burns, *To the Mountaintop*, 4.

up."[18] This defiance on the part of a black youth was also a sign of what was happening to and within other black youths throughout the city. They were young people, students, but in some ways they were just as affected by acts of racial discrimination as their parents and other black adults. Colvin's action was an indication that black youths were fed up, too.

The women in the WPC, although furious over what happened to Colvin, were dissuaded from implementing a boycott at that time. Not all of the women agreed with this decision, however. E. D. Nixon claimed that Colvin was pregnant, and thus he argued that from a moral standpoint she was not a good Jim Crow test case for the courts. Some of the women of the WPC, especially Robinson and Burks, were seething with anger about this reaction on the part of the black male leadership. Robinson and Burks insisted that it was not Claudette Colvin's morality that was at issue, but that of the bus company, city officials, and the white community of Montgomery. Looking back years later, Robinson said that the men "were afraid." "Women [read 'black women'] are more daring when it comes to what we face," she said.[19] Not surprisingly, some members of the WPC agreed with Nixon, who might well have stretched the truth regarding Colvin's pregnancy. A few years after the bus incident, Colvin said that Nixon's claim that she was pregnant at the time of her arrest was false, and at best a cover for his social-class bias. She said she became pregnant only later that year, long after the bus incident.[20] Colvin argued, in any case, that Nixon did not want to use her as a test case primarily because she lived in one of the most economically depressed areas of Montgomery. Her parents were dirt poor. Colvin put it this way: "We weren't in the inner circle. The middle-class blacks didn't want us as a role model."[21]

We can be sure, however, that most members of the WPC were absolutely convinced that the issue was the city's segregation ordinance, not whether Claudette Colvin was pregnant, or whether some other young woman's father was a drunk.[22] The latter reference is to Mary Louise Smith, the seventeen-year-old who was similarly arrested in October 1955, just weeks before Parks was arrested. Smith recounted the incident on the bus: "[The driver] asked me

18. Quoted in ibid., 5.

19. Quoted in Burns, "Montgomery Bus Boycott," in *Black Women in America*, 2:807. From Jo Ann Robinson, interview by David Garrow (April 5, 1984).

20. Colvin had gotten pregnant by a married man two or three months after the bus incident, according to Burns, *To the Mountaintop*, 9. Burns also reports that her parents were hesitant about having their daughter's reputation be scandalized in a public display in the racist courts of Montgomery.

21. Quoted in Olson, *Freedom's Daughters*, 95.

22. This was the rationale for not using Mary Louise Smith as a judicial test case. Smith had been arrested in October 1955 for refusing to give her seat to a white patron.

to move three times. And I refused. I told him, 'I am not going to move out of my seat. I am not going to move anywhere. I got the privilege to sit here like anybody else does.'"[23] According to Jo Ann Robinson, Smith's arrest and ensuing case went almost unnoticed, because the case was not publicized until after her arrest and conviction. She paid her fine and continued to ride the bus.[24] However, Smith would become one of five black women plaintiffs who filed a federal lawsuit (*Browder v. Gayle*) against Montgomery's and the state of Alabama's bus-segregation statute.

The truth is, the women of the WPC had grown weary of the black male leadership's imposed criterion of finding the perfect judicial test case against Alabama's segregation ordinance. The women no doubt felt that those who were more often the subjects of dehumanizing treatment should be the ones to decide when, where, and how to protest and resist. What we need to remember, then, is that even before Rosa Parks was arrested, black women of Montgomery were ready to revolt. This is consistent with King's reflection that the Montgomery movement would have ignited even if he had not gone there or had not gotten involved. The movement might well have taken a different course, he reasoned, but there would have been a resistance movement in Montgomery. Out of his faith, King knew almost instinctively that cosmic and divine forces were at work in Montgomery and that the time was simply ripe for change. Whatever the case, the women of the WPC kept their plans for a boycott close at hand, needing only to activate and implement them when Rosa Parks was arrested.

There is no question that certain actions of the WPC actually anticipated the now-famous Montgomery bus boycott by at least a year and a half. For example, in what may be the first significant step to make real her promise to fight for desegregation of the buses, Jo Ann Robinson composed a letter on behalf of the WPC on May 21, 1954, and sent it to the mayor. The letter reminded Mayor William A. ("Tacky") Gayle that three-fourths of those who ride the city buses were black, and that without their patronage the bus company could not remain solvent. It was therefore good business sense, if nothing else, she argued, to work toward more humane and respectful treatment of black passengers within the parameters of the law. It is instructive to point out that there was at this time no challenge made against the state's

23. Quoted in Russell Freedman, *Freedom Walkers: The Story of the Montgomery Bus Boycott* (New York: Holiday House, 2006), 21.

24. See "Excerpts from Jo Ann Robinson's Account of the Boycott," in *Let Nobody Turn Us Around: Voices of Resistance, Reform, and Renewal*, ed. Manning Marable and Leith Mullings (Lanham, MD: Rowan & Littlefield, 2000), 378.

segregation ordinance. At this juncture, the WPC sought fair treatment of black patrons under the existing segregation laws.[25] This would also be the initial tactic of King and other leaders once the boycott did get under way more than a year later. Like Robinson and the WPC, King and the MIA did not initially challenge the state's segregation codes, but only *requested* that the city and the bus company obey existing law. However, all quickly found that even this was too much to expect. So at the start, the WPC, and later the boycott leaders, initially wanted only that black passengers be treated with the same degree of respect as their white counterparts, and that the bus drivers honor the law. Separate but equal treatment—the law—is what they asked for, for this was the law of the land since the landmark case of *Plessy v. Ferguson* in 1896, which wrote the "separate but equal" clause into the Constitution of the United States. In *Brown v. Board of Education of Topeka, Kansas*, the Supreme Court overturned *Plessy* on May 17, 1954 (four days before Robinson's letter was written to Mayor Gayle), making "separate but equal" in public accommodations unconstitutional.

In her letter to Mayor Gayle, Robinson included the three things that the representatives of the WPC had previously put before the mayor and the city council in March 1954: 1) That city buses stop at every corner in residential sections of black communities, as they did in white neighborhoods; 2) That the custom of blacks paying at the front of the bus, and then being required to leave the bus, walk to the rear, and board from there, be discontinued, since it was not in compliance with the law; and 3) That the bus company enforce the policy that blacks seat from the rear toward the front of the bus, and for whites to seat from the front to the rear until all seats are occupied in the "whites only" section.[26] The significance of the latter is that blacks seated in the "colored-only" section would no longer be required to give their seats to white patrons when all seats in the whites-only section were occupied. However, this would mean that some white passengers would invariably have to stand while blacks were seated in the blacks-only section, a scenario that city and bus officials could not allow.

Not entirely unexpected, Robinson's letter to the mayor said that while members of the WPC were pleased to report that buses were making more stops in black communities, there had been no compliance with their other two requests. Because blacks, especially women, who rode the buses in larger

25. See "A Letter from the Women's Political Council to the Mayor of Montgomery, Alabama," in *The Eyes on the Prize Civil Rights Reader*, ed. Clayborne Carson, David J. Garrow, Darlene Clark Hine, et al. (New York: Penguin, 1991), 44–45.

26. See ibid., 44.

numbers, were so frequently humiliated and disrespected by drivers, Robinson said, many were already making arrangements to ride in cars with friends rather than continue riding the buses. She also reported that there were discussions among more than a dozen black organizations about staging a citywide boycott of the buses. Robinson argued that blacks were only asking to be treated with respect and decency like any other paying passengers. If bus officials and drivers comply with this, she said, there would be no reason to boycott. Significantly, Robinson said that it would be the actions of the mayor and the city council that would determine whether a boycott would take place. The decision to boycott was not that of the black community. However, Robinson also made it clear that the WPC was not opposed to supporting a boycott. This was in March 1954, nearly a year and a half *before* the arrest of Rosa Parks, and approximately two months before the Supreme Court reversed the "separate but equal" ruling in *Plessy*.

There was nothing radical about either the presentation made to Mayor Gayle and the city council, or the earlier letter written by Jo Ann Robinson. However, both actions were indicative not only of Robinson's determination and activism, but that of a major black women's organization. Most of the members of the WPC were also members of local black churches, including the church where King was pastor. And remember, Mary Fair Burks, founder of the WPC, received her inspiration to do something about racial segregation from a sermon preached by Vernon Johns.

As we go forward we need to keep all of this in context. Robinson's letter to Mayor Gayle did not challenge the state's segregation ordinance. However, back of her mind was the realization that this was where the real battle lay.[27] Blacks had to challenge the constitutionality of the segregation laws, a goal that Robinson shared with Attorney Fred Gray from the beginning, even though her earlier letter to Mayor Gayle made no mention of this. Looking back more than forty years later, Robinson reflected that "the women of the WPC had started the boycott, and we did it for the specific purpose of finally integrating those buses."[28] Moreover, Robinson said: "We had planned the protest long before Mrs. Parks was arrested. There had been so many things that happened, that the black women had been embarrassed over, and they were ready to explode."[29]

27. See Fred Gray, *Bus Ride to Justice* (Montgomery, AL: Black Belt, 1995), 68–73.

28. Quoted in Olson, *Freedom's Daughters*, 123.

29. Quoted in David Garrow, *Bearing the Cross: Martin Luther King, Jr. and the Southern Christian Leadership Conference* (New York: William Morrow, 1986), 6.

Indeed, Robinson had herself been threatened and humiliated by a bus driver who ordered her to vacate her fifth-row seat at a time when there were "only three people riding the entire bus." The driver also threatened to strike her when he believed she did not comply quickly enough to his command.[30] Robinson, born on a small cotton farm near Culloden, Georgia in 1912, had only lived in Montgomery a few weeks. She was preparing to go to Cleveland, Ohio to visit relatives for the Christmas holidays in 1949. She told David Garrow about her experience.

Not familiar with the city bus policy that did not permit blacks to sit in the first ten rows, even if she was the only passenger on the bus, Robinson was ordered to vacate her seat. Tearful and emotional, she told David Garrow in an interview: "He was standing over me, saying 'Get up from there! Get up from there,' with his hand drawn back."[31] Robinson was devastated. Confused and momentarily disoriented, the only thing she could think to do was leave the bus. Looking back on the experience, she said: "I felt like a dog. And I got mad, after this was over, and I realized that I was a human being, and just as intelligent and far more trained than that bus driver was. But I think he wanted to hurt me, and he did . . . I cried all the way to Cleveland."[32] But Robinson promised herself that she would not soon forget the incident, and would do whatever she could to urge the Women's Political Council to address the dehumanizing practices of the bus company. She did not forget, nor was she satisfied with just being embarrassed and incensed over how she was treated. Jo Ann Robinson knew instinctively that it was not enough to exhibit an emotional outburst. She had to find a way to protest the injustice with the express aim of eradicating it. She would not forget the incident, and her desire to do something about it.

Although E. D. Nixon and other black male leaders rightly believed that Robinson and the women of the WPC could not pull off a successful, sustained boycott without the support of black ministers (read "black men") in the city, David Garrow contends that not a few people in Montgomery's black community knew that it was black women, more than the black male leadership, who "had been the driving force behind all of the black community efforts of the last few years,"[33] and even after the arrests of Claudette Colvin, Mary Louise Smith, and Rosa Parks in 1955.

Indeed, more than a few black women shared the sentiment of Gladys Moore when she talked about the role of women in the bus boycott and

30. Robinson, *The Montgomery Bus Boycott and the Women Who Started It*, 49, 24–25.
31. Garrow, Foreword, in ibid., xiii.
32. Ibid.
33. Garrow, *Bearing the Cross*, 17.

who actually started it. "Wasn't no man started it," she said. "We all started it over night."[34] Other black women domestics shared this view, insisting that the black male leadership, including King, did not start the boycott, and therefore they could not stop it. In this regard, a black woman told Afrikan American reporter Ted Poston: "They didn't really start it, you know. And they can't end it either. The people, the plain, ordinary Negro people here started this thing and only they can stop it."[35] Erna Dungee Allen, MIA financial secretary, corroborated this: "We [women] really were the ones who carried out the actions."[36] It was the women who "passed the ideas to men to a great extent," she said.[37] In addition, Gladys Moore had herself experienced abusive treatment from white bus drivers. She was what is known today as a womanist,[38] inasmuch as she was bold, self-determined, responsible, thought for herself, talked back to the powers (including abusive white bus drivers), "ignored or defied commands, reported drivers to the manager, or occasionally engaged in physical self-defense. More and more often they refused to give up their seats to white people."[39] Periodically, like young Claudette Colvin, black women not only refused to give their seats to whites, but even resisted the police when summoned by bus drivers. When a bus driver commenced beating on Mrs. Epsie Worthy in 1953 because she refused to pay another fare after having transferred from another bus, she fought back with everything she had to give, "and she gave as much as she took."[40] So by the time Rosa Parks was arrested, black women's cup of endurance had fissured to the point of impossible

---

34. Quoted in Burns, *To the Mountaintop*, 105.

35. Ted Poston, "The Negroes of Montgomery," in *Reporting Civil Rights Part One: American Journalism 1941-1963* (New York: Library of America, 2003), 270.

36. Quoted in Burns, "Montgomery Bus Boycott," in *Black Women in America*, 2:808.

37. Quoted in ibid.

38. In her book, *In Search of Our Mothers' Gardens: Womanist Prose* (New York: Harcourt Brace Jovanovich, 1983), xi, Alice Walker defines womanist as "a black feminist or feminist of color." A womanist is self-determined, sassy, responsible, in charge, and talks back. She is characterized by "outrageous, audacious, courageous or *willful* behavior" (ibid.). The term *womanist* is frequently used "to reflect an understanding of race, gender, and class that is grounded in a 'commitment to the survival and wholeness of entire people—men and women—as well as to a valorization of women's works in all their varieties and multitudes" (Vanessa Sheared, "Giving Voice: An Inclusive Model of Instruction—A Womanist Perspective," in *The Womanist Reader*, ed. Layli Phillips [New York: Routledge, 2006], 272). A womanist is concerned to address and eradicate not merely the oppressions affecting women, but those affecting all people.

39. Burns, *To the Mountaintop*, 105.

40. Robinson, *The Montgomery Bus Boycott and the Women Who Started It*, 22.

repair. They needed a new cup, and such a cup could be accessed only if they mounted a determined resistance to the injustice they suffered on the buses.

Nevertheless, as strong as the WPC was as a civic organization and as committed as its members were, it was clear to all concerned, including the women, most who were church members themselves, that they would need the support of black pastors. For as pastors of churches, they had access to the best means of keeping the black community informed. They could do this effectively from the pulpit. And yet we should understand that many of the pastors themselves would be reluctant participants in the boycott. Even more so, many of the black ministers were initially hesitant to be speakers at the first mass rally to be held at the Holt Street Baptist Church after Rosa Parks was arraigned on December 5. Some of the pastors did not even want their names mentioned, for fear of retaliation from the white community.[41]

The real initiative and leadership in the early stages of the Montgomery bus boycott, therefore, did not come from the vast majority of black ministers. Nor did it come from other black males in the city, although the trailblazing efforts of Vernon Johns were a significant exception. Besides this, no black male—pastor or otherwise—agreed to be one of the plaintiffs in the suit that was filed in federal court on February 2, 1956, challenging Alabama's segregation ordinance in public transportation. Only black women consented to be plaintiffs.[42]

As noted previously, the initiative and leadership came from the people, especially black women. At least a partial explanation for this scenario is often linked to the belief that since the time of American slavery the black male was thought to be a threat to white society, and thus the pattern developed of many being less outspoken in the public arena than black women. The thinking seemed to be that black women were less of a threat, and therefore had more freedom to speak out, a point made by Johnnie Carr who had grown up in Montgomery, and was a close friend of Rosa Parks. Reflecting on the Montgomery struggle in 2006, a ninety-five-year-old Carr said that had black women not done what they did, King and other male leaders would not have accomplished all that they did. She went on to say: "Women weren't given the opportunity to be out in front. . . . Black men could not speak out. They had to worry about being killed. We were able to speak out more."[43] Juanita Abernathy, wife of Ralph Abernathy, echoed this view, saying that

41. Olson, *Freedom's Daughters*, 115.

42. Ibid., 123.

43. Quoted in *On the Road to Freedom: A Guided Tour of the Civil Rights Trail*, ed. Charles E. Cobb Jr. (Chapel Hill: Algonquin Books, 2008), 216.

black women "always had a certain amount of freedom that wasn't given to black males."[44] Of course, notwithstanding this, there were always black men, for example, Vernon Johns, who spoke out regardless of their awareness of the potential danger to themselves and their families. But prior to the bus boycott these were exceptions. For example, in the early days of the boycott it was generally the case that black ministers had to be *pulled* along by their church members. By Jo Ann Robinson's account, black church members were committed to supporting the boycott with or without their pastors. She claimed further that it was precisely because of this that the ministers then "decided that it was time for them, the leaders, to catch up with the masses."[45] Indeed, when it seemed that the boycott had stalled, and several of the ministers asked if it would not be best to call it off, King reminded them all as to who was really in charge. "[I]f we went tonight and asked the people to get back on the bus, we would be ostracized," he said. "They wouldn't get back. . . . I believe to the bottom of my heart that the majority of Negroes would ostracize us. They are willing to walk."[46] This was the stance of domestic worker Gussie Nesbitt, who had her fill of insults from bus drivers and said that she participated in the boycott. She walked, because she wanted to do her part to make things better. "I didn't want somebody else to make it better for me," she said. . . . "I walked. . . . I was tired, but I didn't have no desire to get on the bus."[47] Nesbitt spoke for the majority of the boycotters, which means that King read the situation perfectly. The people were not ready to return to the buses.

On a number of occasions when black ministers were asked to volunteer as plaintiffs in the federal court case against the bus company, or to volunteer to go to jail, they made excuses as to why they could not do so. At one point, King himself called for just one pastor to volunteer to join the women as plaintiffs, saying "I think it is very important in throwing sentiment our way if we have a minister as a plaintiff. Who will volunteer?"[48] No one did so. On another occasion the Montgomery County Grand Jury indicted eighty-nine bus boycott leaders for violating an old law prohibiting conspiracy to interfere with a legitimate business. Of these, five were women: Rosa Parks, Jo Ann Robinson, Euretta Adair, Jimmie Lowe, and Irene West.[49] When the Rev. Solomon Seay, pastor of the Mount Zion AME Zion Church, shouted "Let's all

---

44. Quoted in ibid.

45. Quoted in Olson, *Freedom's Daughters*, 114.

46. Quoted in ibid., 122.

47. Henry Hampton and Steve Fayer (with Sarah Flynn), *Voices of Freedom: An Oral History of the Civil Rights Movement from the 1950s Through the 1980s* (New York: Bantam, 1990), 26.

48. Quoted in Burns, *To the Mountaintop*, 44.

go to jail," there was an eerie silence in the room, and when the vote was called, no pastor agreed to go to jail with him, although nonclergy persons present voted to do so.[50] This was a perfect instance of the pew leading the pulpit.

Solomon Seay was known for his deep commitment and devotion to social gospel ministry. He was also fearless before religious and secular powers. Not known as one to initiate or invite protest and/or controversy, he was always ready to respond.[51] Seay was convinced that blacks' racial predicament would be resolved only through black self-determination; when they make up their minds that they have had all they intend to take. He was also no stranger to the practice of standing alone for what he believed to be right.[52] Even before King's arrival in Montgomery, Seay was known as one of the most fearless among black leaders.

Notwithstanding King's initial apprehension when E. D. Nixon first phoned him, it is important to point out that when the boycott came to a successful conclusion, King did not claim for himself that which he did not deserve. He received numerous accolades and much praise for his role as leader, but he always knew who started and organized the boycott, and he remembered his own early reluctance to get involved. King would have agreed with Mary Fair Burks's assessment that the "trailblazers" of the Montgomery movement were Rosa Parks, Jo Ann Robinson, and other women in the WPC. My sense, however, is that Burks also saw Vernon Johns as a lonely trailblazer whose witness anticipated that of the women of the WPC. Trailblazers are pioneers. So was Vernon Johns. So were the women of the WPC. It has been argued that King was one who came after the trailblazers, that is, he was a "torchbearer."[53] However, the record is absolutely clear that once King got involved he was in it for the duration, and none could match his eloquence and his ability to hold the black community of Montgomery together (although this too was ultimately a shared effort).

Jo Ann Robinson observed that prior to the arrest of Rosa Parks, one thing was clear. Most members of the WPC had all but lost patience with the tendency of the black male leadership to seek "compromise with officials for better treatment" on the buses, while mostly black women were "still

49. Clayborne Carson et al., eds., *The Papers of Martin Luther King, Jr.* (Berkeley: University of California Press, 1997), 3:235, 240.

50. Burns, *To the Mountaintop*, 72.

51. Lamont Yeakey, "The Montgomery, Alabama Bus Boycott, 1955-56," Ph.D. diss., Columbia University, 1979, 85.

52. Ibid., 89.

53. Olson, *Freedom's Daughters*, 131.

enduring embarrassing experiences each day."[54] The continued degradation and inhumane treatment of black women was getting to be too much to bear. The arrest of Rosa Parks was simply the last straw. Robinson and the members of the WPC decided that they would wait no longer, but would initiate a one-day boycott.[55]

With the assistance of John Cannon, chairman of the business department at Alabama State College and two of her students, Robinson organized the printing and distribution of thousands of leaflets announcing the boycott and urging blacks not to ride the buses on the designated day. Summoned to the College president's office after the leaflets were distributed, Robinson knew she was on the verge of losing her job for her part in the project. For it was, after all, a state-supported institution. Although the president, Dr. Harper Council Trenholm, was black and a deacon at Dexter, they both knew it was not politically feasible to involve the College in any way. Trenholm reacted angrily and threatened to fire her until Robinson assured him that the school had not been implicated.[56] She said that her fear of reprisal from the president was soon relieved, since Trenholm, she said, became a strong and steady behind-the-scenes supporter.[57] The problem, however, was that she could not predict how long his support would last, especially if the governor and the Board of Education brought pressure to bear on him because of faculty members' involvement in civil rights activities. Unfortunately, such pressure was in fact brought to bear, and Trenholm, much the institutional man and much more politically conservative than Robinson, caved. Trenholm had succeeded his father as president of Alabama State in 1925. He remained as president until December 1962.[58]

THE PRICE OF FREEDOM

It would be an egregious error to conclude that there were no repercussions for Robinson, Mary Fair Burks, and others in the WPC who taught at Alabama State College. Not long after the Supreme Court ruled against the state of Alabama's segregation ordinance in *Browder v. Gayle* on November 13, 1956, members of the Alabama state legislature began showing up in WPC women's classes at the College and taking notes. This included not only Robinson and

54. Robinson, *The Montgomery Bus Boycott and the Women Who Started It*, 40.

55. Ibid., 45.

56. See Steven Millner's interview with Robinson (August 10, 1980) in *The Walking City: The Montgomery Bus Boycott, 1955-1956*, ed. David Garrow (Brooklyn, NY: Carlson, 1989), 570.

57. Robinson, *The Montgomery Bus Boycott and the Women Who Started It*, 50–52.

58. Yeakey, "The Montgomery, Alabama Bus Boycott, 1955-56," 74.

Burks, but other women faculty members who were members of the WPC. The obvious intention was to intimidate the women. "Then, in February 1960, an investigation of a student sit-in at the state capitol—in which Robinson and Burks had not been involved—cost the two women their jobs."[59] Martin Luther King was certain that they and others involved would not be fired outright by the president, but would be eased out, meaning that some, at least, would be allowed to resign at the end of the school year.[60]

Lawrence D. Reddick, first King biographer, was also on the faculty and was very much involved in the protests. Reddick had actually tendered his resignation effective the end of August, but state officials and the governor were determined to make an example of him, and Governor Patterson ordered Trenholm to fire him "before sundown."[61] After several other professors were fired, Burks and Robinson left Montgomery in 1960. They took teaching positions in Maryland and California, respectively.[62]

President Trenholm announced that he would "purge" the institution of all "disloyal" faculty members who in any way participated in the student protests and who would not remain loyal to the state's segregation ordinance. King wrote Governor Patterson to express his dismay over the promise that he "extracted from president Trenholm . . . that the students . . . would not participate in any more anti-segregation demonstrations and that the faculty . . . would remain loyal to Alabama segregation laws."[63] King sent copies of the letter to A. Philip Randolph and Roy Wilkins, explaining that he had "felt compelled to get some word to the Governor which would indirectly condemn Mr. Trenholm for taking such a cowardly position."[64] At King's urging, both Randolph and Wilkins sent similar letters to Patterson. King's condemnation of Trenholm was reminiscent of Vernon Johns's public castigation of both R. T. Adair and Trenholm.

As a result of Trenholm's action, Burks wrote to King requesting assistance in finding employment in the fall of 1960. King wrote back from Atlanta expressing his intention to do all in his power to assist the unemployed professors (eleven in all) in finding teaching positions elsewhere. He also expressed his deep disappointment in Trenholm for failing to take the high road by standing up to the governor and state school board. King said of his

59. Olson, *Freedom's Daughters*, 131.
60. *The Papers* (2005), 5:407.
61. Ibid., 5:472n1.
62. Burns, "Women's Political Council, Montgomery, Alabama," in *Black Women in America*, 2:1280.
63. *The Papers*, 5:496.
64. Ibid., 5:495n2.

former deacon: "I had hoped that Dr. Trenholm would emerge from this total situation as a national hero. If he would only stand up to the Governor and the Board of Education and say that he cannot in all good conscience fire the eleven faculty members who have committed no crime or act of sedition, he would gain support over the nation that he never dreamed of. And indeed jobs would be offered to him overnight if he were fired."[65]

King was not only critical of Trenholm's decision to terminate faculty members who supported civil rights protests. Along with the executive board of SCLC, he wrote a letter of protest to Governor John Malcolm Patterson on April 14, 1960. The letter expressed their "deep concern" about published reports of purging Alabama State College of faculty members who had supported the student sit-ins and other forms of protest. The letter called for Patterson "to insure the protection of teachers against such fantastic charges and a fair trial for them in the event the charges should be raised."[66] In addition, the letter pledged SCLC's support of any professor whose academic freedom and right to citizenship was violated. Other than ordering that Reddick be fired there is no evidence that the governor acted on King's requests.

King also wrote letters to the leaders of the ACLU (Patrick Murphy Malin), NAACP (Roy Wilkins), and American Federation of Teachers (Carl J. Megel) to alert them to what was happening at Alabama State College. He urged them to voice loud public protests of the governor's efforts to purge the faculty.[67] Each leader complied with King's request, thus helping to bring national attention to the matter.[68]

Years later, Robinson, "the Joan of Arc of the Montgomery Bus Boycott,"[69] said: "Everybody who had been involved in either protest paid for it."[70] The reference to the contributions of black women to the Montgomery struggle is significant and should not be taken lightly or forgotten. Many years passed before scholars, led by black women, began highlighting these contributions and focusing on the roles played by women. Indeed, not only was it black women who proposed the boycott, began discussing and planning for one when young Claudette Colvin was arrested, and printed and distributed about

65. Ibid., 5:407. Governor Patterson also threatened to recommend the termination of president Trenholm for failing to fire all faculty members who were sympathetic toward the student sit-ins (*The Papers*, 5:472).

66. Ibid., 5:425–26.

67. Ibid., 5:471–72.

68. Ibid., 5:471n2.

69. Burks, "Trailblazers . . . ," 76.

70. Quoted in Olson, *Freedom's Daughters*, 131.

fifty thousand leaflets announcing the one-day boycott.[71] They also, more than black men, filled the churches during the numerous mass meetings,[72] later termed prayer meetings by King, because of the need to convey spiritual support to the protesters, and because there were rumors that public officials were considering issuing a ban against mass meetings. The thinking was that it was unlikely that a ban would be placed on prayer meetings.[73] Indeed, it was black women of Montgomery who handled most of the important daily mechanics of the boycott. Stewart Burns has put it in a helpful way:

> Although Martin Luther King, Jr., and other male leaders, particularly ministers, took over the visible leadership of the boycott after it began, several WPC activists—including Robinson, Burks, Irene West, and Euretta Adair—played crucial roles in organizing and sustaining it. They served on all major committees, shared in planning and strategy, helped to manage the car pool system, and handled many of the boycott's day-to-day details. Robinson negotiated skillfully with white officials concerning the bus demands and edited the monthly newsletter.[74]

Without question, it was a long time before black women's contributions to the Montgomery struggle were adequately and appropriately recognized by black male scholars. The pattern of black male failure to acknowledge and celebrate the leadership and other contributions that black women made to the civil rights movement continued beyond the Montgomery struggle. Although "sexism" was not a term that was in vogue during that period, there is no question that black male chauvinism and sexual discrimination were prominent in early civil rights organizations, including the Montgomery Improvement Association and the Southern Christian Leadership Conference.

SEXISM AND THE MONTGOMERY STRUGGLE

In principle, there is no place in Martin Luther King's theological social ethics, and especially in his personalism and beloved community ethic, for male chauvinism and sexism. And yet, this social evil was prominent in the daily

71. See Steven M. Millner's interview with Jo Ann Robinson, August 10, 1977, in *The Walking City*, ed. Garrow, 569.

72. Branch, *Parting the Waters*, 149.

73. See Rustin's letter to Arthur Brown, February 23, 1956, in *I Must Resist: Bayard Rustin's Life in Letters*, ed. Michael G. Long (San Francisco: City Lights, 2012), 166.

74. Burns, "Women's Political Council, Montgomery, Alabama," in *Black Women in America*, 2:1280.

operations of the MIA and later, SCLC. Patriarchy was, and continues to be, endemic to this society and its institutions.

Stewart Burns reports what could be a glaring instance of sexism when the boycott ended. Early the next morning after the boycott was officially ended on December 20, 1956, E. D. Nixon, Ralph Abernathy, and Glenn Smiley arrived at King's home to board the first desegregated bus, which not one of them had ever ridden in Montgomery. Burns contends that Rosa Parks was present as well.[75] However, this claim is not consistent with what Parks herself remembered. In *My Story* (1992), Parks wrote: "Dr. King, the Reverend Abernathy, Mr. Nixon, and Glen [*sic*] Smiley, one of the few white people in Montgomery who had supported the boycott, made a great show of riding the first integrated bus in Montgomery. Some of the books say I was with them, but I was not. I had planned to stay home and not ride the bus, because my mother wasn't feeling well."[76] When the bus arrived, King and Abernathy sat in the previously whites-only section as reporters took pictures. Rosa Parks, however, deemed by Mary Fair Burks as the "patron saint"[77] of the boycott and the one whose arrest precipitated it, was noticeably absent on that desegregated bus. It is unclear whether Mrs. Parks was actually invited to meet at King's house to board that bus. She did not say whether she was in fact invited, only that she had "planned to stay home" because of her mother's illness. My own sense is that had she been invited she would have said so when looking back on the incident after thirty-six years, even had she decided against joining the men because of her mother's illness. Although it might well be that Parks was merely adhering to the tradition of black women by deferring to black males in public leadership matters, thus choosing to remain in the background, the incident has the smell of sexism about it. Nevertheless, we do know that when reporters from *Look* magazine asked later that morning if they could photograph Parks boarding buses downtown she readily consented.[78] The reluctance and ultimate refusal of the MIA to hire Mrs. Parks in a paid position at a time when she desperately needed a job[79] might also be evidence of sexism, or at the very least an indication of insensitivity among the black male leadership.[80]

75. Burns, *To the Mountaintop*, 145.

76. Rosa Parks with Jim Haskins, *My Story* (New York: Dial, 1992), 157.

77. Burks, "Trailblazers . . . ," 76.

78. Parks, *My Story*, 157.

79. Olson, *Freedom's Daughters*, 129.

80. It is worthwhile to note that when it came to the attention of King that Parks was in dire financial straits, he encouraged the MIA to assist her. By this time he was serving as co-pastor of Ebenezer Baptist

Rosa Parks would again be slighted when the SCLC invited her to participate in the March on Washington for Jobs and Freedom on August 28, 1963. On that occasion, Parks was disappointed when, upon her arrival she discovered that none of the other movement women who were present, for example, Ella Baker, Septima Clark, Daisy Bates, and Diane Nash Bevel, were allowed to march with the men, "nor were any women invited to speak on the program." Anna Hedgeman, who worked with the committee that planned the march, recalled that one week before the march the final program was presented for discussion. No woman was listed as a speaker. Hedgeman wrote A. Philip Randolph and the other members of the so-called "Big Six" (Martin Luther King, John Lewis, James Farmer, Roy Wilkins, and Whitney Young) to express her shared concern with other black women about this gross omission. By the time of the final meeting of the planning committee she had not received a single response from her male colleagues, noting that it was "significant that not even the rebellious youth leader [John Lewis] thought of the role which women had played in the present phase of the continuing Negro revolution."[81] At the end of that last meeting, Hedgeman asked if she could read a statement. She chided the "Big Six" for failing to give women "the quality of participation which they have earned . . . ," and suggested that they permit at least one "Negro woman to make a brief statement. . . ."[82] She suggested Myrlie Evers (wife of slain civil rights worker Medgar Evers), or one of the younger, more militant civil rights leaders, for example, Diane Nash Bevel. On March day the wives of civil rights leaders and other black women were asked to sit on the platform and Daisy Bates was asked to present brief remarks. Hedgeman recalled that Rosa Parks was introduced to the crowd, "but almost casually. We grinned; some of us, as we recognized anew that Negro women are second-class citizens in the same way that white women are in our culture."[83] Considering what black women had done from Montgomery up to the March, it was a bitter pill for them to swallow. "'All I remember Rosa saying,' Bates recalled, 'is that *our time will someday come.*'"[84]

Only looking back after more than forty years was Clarence Jones (King's lawyer, fundraiser, confidant, and sometime speechwriter) able to

Church and president of the SCLC in Atlanta. As early as August 1957 the press had criticized the MIA's failure to assist Parks (see *The Papers*, 5:389n1, 2).

81. Anna Arnold Hedgeman, *The Trumpet Sounds: A Memoir of Negro Leadership* (New York: Holt, Rinehart & Winston, 1964), 178.

82. Ibid., 179.

83. Ibid., 180.

84. Quoted in Douglas Brinkley, *Rosa Parks* (New York: Viking, 2000), 185 (my emphasis).

say—somewhat casually it seems—"that the choice [to exclude women as major speakers] was very much a slight to the concept of 'equality for everyone,' which was the true theme of our demonstration."[85] Writing further in his book, *Behind the Dream: The Making of the Speech That Transformed a Nation* (2011), Jones implies that during the planning and discussion phases of the March on Washington he was disturbed by the male slighting of women's participation. "When I first heard about the issue," he writes, "I had an immediate reaction *that I kept to myself.*"[86] He alludes to the idea that his own gender sensitivity somehow exceeded that of his male colleagues on the planning committee, and that his only mistake was in remaining silent.

As it turned out, a number of the more prominent women civil rights leaders were introduced to the vast crowd that day, for example, Dorothy Height, Fannie Lou Hamer, Dorothy Cotton, and Gloria Richardson, but they were not allowed to speak. On reflection, Jones claims that he wishes some of them had been speakers that day. However, one does not get the sense that Jones believes—even today—that any of the women were *entitled* to speak. He certainly thought that John Lewis, the youngest of those slated to speak, was "*entitled.*"[87] In fairness, we should remember that Jones himself was not a part of the March planning committee, which is why he could say that when he first *heard* about the exclusion of women speakers he was immediately concerned, but said nothing. What may be more important is how this presumed supporter of the inclusion of women reacts when he gets the opportunity to be one of six or seven advisors to King as he thought through what came to be the "I Have a Dream" speech.

It is also of interest to note that Martin Luther King's cast of consultants for the writing of his speech for the March was all male, including Jones, who did not raise a fuss over the failure to include women, thereby missing a second opportunity to speak up. The other members were Cleveland Robinson, Ralph Abernathy, Walter Fauntroy, Bernard Lee, Lawrence Reddick, and Bayard Rustin. King had already received written notes with suggestions from Andrew Young and Wyatt Walker.[88] It is not known whether he received any written or verbal ideas from women. Not a single woman was present at that meeting on the eve of the March as ideas were solicited by King for his speech. Nor is there evidence that any of the men, including King, raised the issue of and the

85. Clarence B. Jones and Stuart Connelly, *Behind the Dream: The Making of the Speech That Transformed a Nation* (New York: Palgrave/Macmillan, 2011), 101.

86. Ibid. (my emphasis).

87. Ibid., 102.

88. Ibid., 55, 59.

absence and exclusion of women. Moreover, Clarence Jones does not seem to have been disturbed by this omission. If he was, one gets no sense of it from reading *Behind the Dream*.

Be that as it may, Coretta Scott King was aware that her husband had issues concerning women, especially in the public sphere. But she also felt that he had a sense of the need for women to be organized. At least this is what she told literary artist Alice Walker in 1971. Walker reflects: "She says that she and Martin used to talk a lot about trying to organize women and she regrets that he never had time to get around to addressing women as women."[89]

It is significant to note that one of Coretta Scott King's challenges to King scholars and former movement activists at a symposium on King as leader, and his legacy in 1986, was that they needed to take up the question of how King saw women and their role in the struggle. Clearly implying that her husband had limitations in this regard, and that planners of the conference failed to invite a critical mass of women to read papers on King, Mrs. King chided the group, saying that "we have yet to deal with how Martin Luther King, Jr., saw women and how he dealt with women and women's roles. The next time we have a conference on him I want to see more women scholars."[90] The only two women contributors were Mrs. King and Mary Frances Berry. The fourteen men included James Cone, Cornel West, Clayborne Carson, David Garrow, John Hope Franklin, and Vincent Harding, among others.[91] Mrs. King was clearly a woman with her own voice, and who had the courage to speak her own prophetic critique.

Very much a man of his day, Martin Luther King was sexist and did not always seem sympathetic to women having leadership roles in the public arena, including his own organization. True, Ella Baker was selected as executive director of SCLC, but only begrudgingly. It was actually Bayard Rustin and Stanley Levison, advisors and confidants to King, who prevailed upon him to hire Baker. Baker scholar Barbara Ransby explains.

> The three men met at New York's La Guardia Airport while King was on a travel layover. King was initially reluctant to hire Baker,

89. Alice Walker, "Coretta King: Revisited," in *In Search of Our Mothers' Gardens* (New York: Harcourt Brace Jovanovich, 1983), 155.

90. Coretta Scott King, "Thoughts and Reflections," in *We Shall Overcome: Martin Luther King, Jr. and the Black Freedom Struggle*, ed. Peter J. Albert and Ronald Hoffman (New York: Da Capo, 1993), 255.

91. The other male contributors were Shun P. Govender, Louis R. Harlan, George M. Houser, Nathan I. Huggins, Richard H. King, Aldon D. Morris, Robert Parris Moses, and Howard Zinn. See *We Shall Overcome*, ed. Albert and Hoffman, 281, 282.

because he had a different profile of the type of person who should share the leadership role with him at the helm of the coalition. King indicated that he did not personally believe that the director had to be a minister, but he recognized that many of his clerical colleagues strongly held that conviction. Of course, choosing a minister also meant that the director must be a man.[92]

In any case, Rustin and Levison were insistent, and won the day. Baker was hired, but only on a temporary basis. In addition, she was given little support by King and the all-male board. Moreover, she was not provided the necessary funds and other resources—not even an office or office space—to get the new organization up and running.[93] She was essentially left to her own wits and know-how, both of which she had a great deal of as a result of her many years of organizing experience and work with the New York City branch of the NAACP. Notwithstanding this, Baker believed that King never gave her serious consideration for permanent director. "At one meeting, a minister from Nashville proposed that Baker be considered as a candidate for the job, but his suggestion fell on deaf ears. 'The officialdom didn't take it seriously,' Baker recalled."[94] Ransby rightly surmises that the problem was not unique to Baker, but was "a manifestation of the much larger problem of sexism within the church, the organization, and the culture."[95] The SCLC board was composed of black pastors—and black churches, like the rest of society, were known for their patriarchy. It is also important to note that Coretta Scott King also believed that Ella Baker was mistreated because she was a woman.[96]

It cannot be denied that Martin Luther King was sexist and that his sexism was a contradiction of his personalism and Christian principles. And yet, there is a complexity about his sexism that needs to be acknowledged and considered. This is not the place to examine the matter in detail, but it will be instructive to call attention to at least two instances in which King's words suggest that he was not as rigid—indeed that he was conflicted—in his views about women, both in the home and in the public sphere. And, of course, it goes without saying that Coretta Scott King believed that her husband was much more liberated in his views about the woman's role in the home than most men.[97]

92. Ransby, *Ella Baker*, 180.
93. Ibid., 181.
94. Ibid., 184.
95. Ibid., 184.
96. Coretta Scott King, *My Life with Martin Luther King, Jr.*, revised edition (New York: Henry Holt, 1993), 142.

On May 8, 1955, King preached a Mother's Day sermon at Dexter, "The Crisis in the Modern Family." He expressed the more liberal view that divorce may sometimes be necessary, and thus should not be dogmatically ruled out. In addition, he was certain that doing away with the custom of male headship could only add to the health of the family. "Men must accept the fact that the day has passed when the man can stand over the wife with an iron rod asserting his authority as 'boss,'" he told the congregation.[98] King went on to explain that this means "the day has passed when women will be trampled over and treated as some slave subject to the dictates of a despotic husband. . . . Women must be respected as human beings and not be treated as mere means. Strictly speaking, there is no boss in the home; it is no lord–servant relationship."[99] King was certain that the family is a cooperative enterprise, and that each member theoretically has something positive to offer. Even children should be appreciated and respected as persons who can also contribute constructively to the family.

Although King believed that Christianity did much to lift the status of women to "dignity honor and respect," I would say that he is very much the traditionalist when he goes on to say that this is one of the most significant contributions of Christianity. He gives Christianity more credit than it is due. For time and again, history and experience have shown that, not Christianity and the church as such, but some minority segment of them has been responsible for the type of progress to which King refers. Only after the fact, usually many years later when the tension is gone, does Christianity or the church declare that *it* was responsible for the good that arose from the struggle.[100]

At any rate, six years after the aforementioned Mother's Day sermon, King talked about some of the secrets of a happy marriage. His discussion about the differences between man's nature and woman's nature is clear indication of his conflicted sense about the role(s) of men and women. In fact, King's discussion is based on traditional conservative views. He argues that tension arises in the marital relationship most often because one or the other or both partners "never learned that a man and a woman differ decidedly in taste, opinion and

---

97. See Coretta Scott King, *My Life with Martin Luther King, Jr.* (1969), 60, 91.

98. *The Papers* (2007), 6:212.

99. Ibid.

100. See Walter Rauschenbusch, *Christianity and the Social Crisis* (New York: Macmillan, 1907), 150. See also Frederick Douglass, "Emancipation of Women," Speech at the Twentieth Annual Meeting of the New England Woman Suffrage Association, Tremont Temple, Boston, May 28, 1888, in *Frederick Douglass on Women's Rights*, ed. Philip S. Foner (New York: Da Capo, 1992), 119.

temperament."[101] Unfortunately, he goes on to clarify his meaning in glaringly traditional terms.

> A man's wold [sic] is largely one of action. He is never happy unless he can measure his success or failure in terms of conquest in the exterior world. On the other hand, despite all her success in the exterior word [sic], a woman is never happy outside an emotional world. She is most at home in the world of love and maternity. Woman is subjective, realistic, concrete. Man is objective abstract and general. Every woman has her world of love, devotion and sympathy, and wise is the man who understands and appreciates it. Man has his world of action and creativity and wise is the wife who understands it.[102]

WOW! This sounds quite different from King's strong counsel against headship six years previous.

In February 1958, and again in November 1967, we find King praising women (read "white women") for their struggle to gain the vote. Discussing the need and importance of determined protest and struggle against any practice that undermines one's humanity, dignity, and citizenship, King said that after many long, tough years of struggle, "the glorious fight for women's suffrage succeeded. . . ."[103] Unfortunately, this victory did not include blacks, who still did not have the vote. King pointed out that the lesson for blacks was that they had to keep their eyes on the goal and that their struggle must be unrelenting until the goal is achieved.[104]

Returning to this theme during a Birmingham, Alabama press conference on November 4, 1967, five months before he was assassinated, King said that as they anticipated the Poor People's Campaign they had to be as determined and persistent as those disenfranchised women who fought so valiantly for the vote. He said to the audience gathered: "Do you know there was a time in this nation when women could not vote? Do you think they just sat down and sent petitions up and letters, and say we ought to vote? What did they do; they went to Washington. They went through the halls of Congress . . . and they plagued Congress and this nation so much until they got the right to vote."[105]

---

101. *The Papers*, 6:432.

102. Ibid.

103. Ibid., 4:368.

104. Ibid.

105. King, Press Conference, Birmingham, November 4, 1967, King Library and Archives, 5.

Like those women, King said that there would be neither peace nor tranquility in the nation until it comes to terms with the demands of blacks and the poor of all races.

Martin Luther King criticized the outmoded practice of headship, explained in quite conservative terms the difference between man's nature and woman's nature, and praised white women for their gallant struggle for the franchise. Although he was at best conflicted about his views on women, especially in the public arena, we were also told by his wife that she and her husband actually discussed and saw the need for women to organize politically. Sadly, King did not get around to pursuing this in concrete ways.

Victory at Last

The majority opinion of the federal judges in the case of *Browder v. Gayle* was that the rejection of "separate but equal" in *Brown* went well beyond public schools to other areas of society, including public transportation. Aurelia Browder was one of four plaintiffs in the case. The other three were Claudette Colvin, Susie McDonald, and Mary Louise Smith. A fifth plaintiff, Jeanetta Reese, told the press the day after the lawsuit was filed that she was tricked into signing the complaint by defense attorney, Fred Gray, and that she wanted "nothing to do with that mess."[106] Reese was likely afraid of white reprisal. Nevertheless, the panel of federal judges decided to suspend enforcement of their ruling pending the forthcoming Supreme Court ruling on the city's appeal. That ruling came five months later on November 13, 1956, while King and other leaders were on trial for operating a private enterprise (car pool) without a license. The Court ruled that Alabama's state and local segregation ordinances were in violation of the U.S. Constitution.[107] Although this was only the beginning, it was a significant victory that helped launch King's civil and human rights ministry.

We need to remember at all times that as a human being Martin Luther King was not perfect, and from time to time he attested to this fact from the pulpit at Ebenezer Baptist Church and other places. He made mistakes along the way in both his private and public life, and one could tell from various sermons, especially during the last two years of his life, that he was engaged in an internal warfare with some of his moral shortcomings. We get a sense of this struggle in his March 3, 1968 sermon, "Unfulfilled Dreams," preached at Ebenezer Baptist Church. Here we find him saying to the congregation: "You don't need to go

106. Quoted in Burns, *To the Mountaintop*, 70.

107. Robert Bleiweiss, *Marching to Freedom* (New York: New American Library, 1968), 74.

out this morning saying that Martin Luther King is a saint. Oh, no. I want you to know this morning that I'm a sinner like all of God's children. But I want to be a good man. And I want to hear a voice saying to me one day, 'I take you in and I bless you, because you try. It is well that it is within your heart.'"[108] This notwithstanding, King exhibited a powerful sense of being *called* by God to do the work he did. It was his strong sense of commitment to the call to ministry that caused him to be driven to God and to what he understood to be God's will for his life and for the world. King's sense of call and commitment gave him the courage to stay the course, no matter how difficult things were for him personally, and as he tried to provide leadership in the struggle to actualize the beloved community.

Although Martin Luther King was most assuredly many things, by his own admission, he was first, foremost, and last *a Christian minister*, a point that he proudly acknowledged.[109] In the sermon, "Why Jesus Called a Man a Fool," preached in 1967, King said that ministry was his greatest vocational call, and that all he did as civil and human rights leader was done because he considered it a part of his ministry. At the end of the day, he did not expect to be remembered as a politician, academician, or even civil rights leader. Rather, his greatest expectation was that he be remembered as a minister of the gospel of Jesus Christ.[110] After all, he was proud to say, his father, maternal grandfather and great grandfather, his only brother, and his father's brother were all preachers.[111] King undoubtedly believed ministry to be the greatest vocation in the world.

There is no question that despite his sharp challenges, criticisms, and periodic disappointments, Martin Luther King loved the church, and most especially the black church. Lewis Baldwin's powerful and definitive book on King's ecclesiology, *The Voice of Conscience: The Church in the Mind of Martin Luther King, Jr.* (2010), is the strongest testament to this fact. The church was not, for King, an end in itself. It was, among other things, a significant means to establishing the beloved community. He also believed that the church should model within its membership what such a community should look like. As a Christian minister, King saw it as his responsibility to do all in his power to steer the church and its human and other resources in the direction of the community of love.

108. King, "Unfilled Dreams," in *A Knock at Midnight*, ed. Clayborne Carson and Peter Holloran (New York: Warner Books, 1998), 198–99.

109. King, "The Un-Christian Christian," *Ebony*, August 1965, 77.

110. King, "Why Jesus Called a Man a Fool," in *A Knock at Midnight*, 146.

111. Ibid., 159.

Although King accepted his role as Christian minister and social activist, he also dreamed of the time when there would be fewer demands on him in the civil and human rights movement. His hope was that he would one day be able to teach in a university or seminary.[112] Indeed, upon completion of his formal studies for the Ph.D., King had offers to teach in institutions such as Morehouse College, and was even offered the position of dean of the chapel at Dillard University. Samuel Proctor considered offering him the position of dean of the school of religion at Virginia Union University. At the end of the Montgomery struggle he was offered a faculty position at Garrett Evangelical Theological Seminary, but duty of another type was calling. So King continued to follow the call to ministry.

By the time that Martin Luther King arrived on the scene in Montgomery, and prior to being cast into the leadership of the bus boycott, the ground had already been pulverized. The participants in this groundbreaking included a fired-up, prophetic, brilliant, sometimes unconventional and eccentric country preacher in the personage of Vernon Napoleon Johns. They also included some professional and nonprofessional black women, including many domestics. Claudette Colvin and Mary Louise Smith, both teenagers, also played a significant part in helping to pave the way for King. All of these were what Mary Fair Burks called trailblazers. They led the way, breaking ground in the wilderness for what was to be the main event.

Martin Luther King was one of a number of torchbearers whose task it was to organize and lead the people to the promised land of freedom and justice. But before he could do that, he had first to be reintroduced to Gandhian ideas and to be trained in Gandhian techniques of nonviolence. He would then meld these into what had already been central to his ministry up to that point, namely, agape love. This is a good segue to an examination of the meaning of Gandhian nonviolence and Christian love for King, and how he integrated these to form his own unique brand of nonviolence.

112. *Playboy* Interview: Martin Luther King, Jr., in *A Testament of Hope: The Essential Writings of Martin Luther King, Jr.*, ed. James M. Washington (New York: Harper & Row, 1986), 375.

PART 4

Christian Love and Gandhian Nonviolence

Part 4 takes an in-depth look at the roots of King's understanding of Christian love, from the teachings and example of his mother and maternal grandmother, to his formal study of love in the academy. King frequently discussed the difference between the three Greek forms of love—*eros, philia,* and *agape.* He sometimes spoke of other types or levels of love, for example, *motherly love, humanitarian love,* and *utilitarian love,* but he was certain that agape is the highest form of love, and thus is the source of all other types. King saw agape as being applicable not only to individuals, but to groups and nations as well. Consequently, as we saw in chapter five, he rejected what he saw as ethical dualism in the thought of Reinhold Niebuhr, who claimed that love is applicable to individuals, but not to groups (especially to nations), where justice is the most we can hope for.

In addition to identifying and examining the formal elements of King's doctrine of nonviolence, and considering his approach to training for nonviolent demonstrations, the chapters in Part 4 try to sort out what King actually knew about Gandhi and his techniques when the Montgomery bus boycott began. Was he a Gandhian when he arrived in Montgomery? At what point, and for what reason, did King begin to explicitly implement Gandhian ideas and techniques during the boycott? How did King's doctrine of nonviolence begin to take shape once he incorporated agape, as well as black cultural and religious ideas and practices, with Gandhian ideas?

Although Martin Luther King was committed to nonviolence absolutely, there was never a time when he favored anarchy. Because of his early experiences of racism, the influence of his father and maternal grandfather, his teacher-mentors at Morehouse College, and the insights gleaned from the study of Reinhold Niebuhr, King held a realistic view of human nature and human destiny. This led him to the view that as long as human beings are human beings—with their inclinations to selfish interest, pride, and unwillingness to share power and privilege without being made to do so—there will be need for what he called "the intelligent use of police power."[1] He came to believe that there would never be a time when there would be no need for checks of some kind on human behavior—individual and corporate.[2] For King, it was a real travesty when local police forces, who were ostensibly devoted to law and order and the rule of law, were seen either participating in violence against nonviolent demonstrators and Freedom Riders, or simply observing such violence without attempting to stop it. But it was clear in King's own mind that human nature is such that the intelligent use of police force could prevent anarchy.

We will see that a mature Martin Luther King would have nothing to do with violence, not even the self-defensive type. On more than one occasion he stated unequivocally: "I am committed to non-violence absolutely, not merely as a technique or a passing strategy but as a way of life. For this reason . . . I don't think that I would use violence in self-defense."[3] However, as we will see below, this was not always the case with him.

KING'S ETHIC OF SELF-DEFENSE

Part of King's southern cultural heritage made him amenable to possessing weapons for self-defense, and when he returned to the South for his first pastorate he was still open to the ethics of self-defense. Let's be clear. King was not a Gandhian when he arrived in Montgomery. In his move toward absolute nonviolence, King gave up self-defensive violence. However, it would be inaccurate to suggest that the mature King closed himself off entirely to self-defense. The important point is that he was insistent that it must be self-defense of the nonviolent type. When a nonviolent demonstrator curls up in a fetal position and covers her head and face with her arms and hands when she

---

1. Martin Luther King Jr., *Redbook Magazine* Interview, November 5, 1964, King Library and Archives, #7, 8.

2. Ibid.

3. Ibid., #3, 4.

is about to be clubbed, for example, she is defending herself nonviolently and without retaliating against the perpetrator.

Martin Luther King was fundamentally committed to the Kantian, Afrikan American principle of the inherent worth of persons as such. Accordingly, persons have inherent worth by virtue of being persons. Thus, one need not be a theist—indeed one may be an atheist—in order to believe in the inviolable dignity of human beings. However, the Christian version of this idea goes considerably further, in that it sees God as the ground or source of inviolable worth. Human beings possess inalienable worth because they are created, sustained, and loved by God. In any case, the person is required to acknowledge and respect her own innate dignity even as she respects that of others. She is also required to recognize every person as an end in herself and not a mere means only. One who understands the meaning of this also understands that she must be willing to defend self and other selves at all cost, although—King would insist—nonviolently.

In the early weeks of the Montgomery bus boycott, there was no obvious Gandhian influence on King, nor did he include Gandhian ideas in sermons and speeches in the first mass prayer meetings. Bayard Rustin discovered this as well when he first met King in late February 1956. He found that King essentially adhered to an ethic of self-defense. At this time, King believed that one was never to incite or initiate violence, but one had a right to defend oneself and one's family. Consequently, not only King, but many of the participants in the bus boycott owned guns. On February 1, 1956, King in fact applied for and was denied a gun permit for himself and those who patrolled around his house.[4] Moreover, we will see in chapter eight that the ownership of guns and knives among southern blacks and whites was not uncommon during this period. It was a southern custom dating from the period of American slavery, but adopted by blacks in the Reconstruction years (1867–77). Guns and knives in the possession of poor whites and blacks in the South were as common as the clothing on their backs. An obvious danger of such high incidence of bearing arms was that it made it much easier for blacks to be violent toward each other, especially when they were prevented from legitimately retaliating against the violence of white racists. During his time in Montgomery and in later years, Martin Luther King would have occasion to criticize blacks and to lament the practice of black-against-black violence and homicide. Writing in his last published book before he was assassinated, King said that "a check of hospitals

4. Clayborne Carson et al., eds., *The Papers of Martin Luther King, Jr.* (Berkeley: University of California Press, 1997), 3:120n2.

in any Negro community on any Saturday night will make you painfully aware of the violence within the Negro community."[5] Understandably, he strongly advocated for the discontinuation of this practice.

THE GANDHIAN INFLUENCE

In his study of Gandhi, King discovered what he considered the most reasonable method for an oppressed people to address and eradicate the social problems that were crushing their humanity and sense of dignity. Although the legacy of the influence of nonviolence can be traced to King's parents and maternal grandparents, we saw that he had his first theoretical encounter with this way of addressing social evils when he read and was much influenced by Thoreau's "Essay on Civil Disobedience." Although during this time King was not intentionally searching for such a method to address injustice, his reading of Thoreau's essay left an indelible imprint on his mind. He surely remembered this essay when he first read Gandhi. We do not know for certain when he first read Gandhi. David R. Collins claims that this first happened when King was in high school, and that he eagerly shared at the family dinner table what he had read about Gandhi.[6] At this writing, however, I have not been able to locate evidence to substantiate this claim. But in addition, it is not clear whether King actually read and studied Gandhi systematically while he was in seminary and/or graduate school, or whether this only happened later. What is clear is that Gandhi's social philosophy and doctrine of nonviolence as a way of life suggested to King the relevance of nonviolence to addressing the social problems facing black people in the Deep South. And yet, we will see that there was a period during the early weeks of the Montgomery bus boycott when King had either forgotten about Gandhi entirely, or he simply had no idea how to implement Gandhian techniques. After all, he had heard Mordecai Johnson lecture on Gandhi in his senior year in seminary and claimed to have enthusiastically gone out to purchase half a dozen books by and about him. He had not actually been *trained* in the techniques of Gandhian nonviolence, and would not receive such training until about two months after the startup of the Montgomery bus boycott. Prior to this training the focus had been on what King as pastor knew best, namely the love ethic of the Sermon on the Mount. From the beginning, the spirit of Christian love was the regulating ideal in the

5. King, *Where Do We Go from Here: Chaos or Community?* (Boston: Beacon, 1967), 64. See also 125.
6. David R. Collins, *Not Only Dreamers: Martin Luther King, Sr. and Martin Luther King, Jr.* (Elgin, IL: Brethren, 1986), 95, 96, 107.

Montgomery bus boycott, but initially there was virtually no evidence of the appropriation of explicit Gandhian ideas and techniques.

King's intellectual journey toward nonviolence began in earnest at Crozer Theological Seminary and continued throughout his doctoral studies at Boston University. King said, in "Pilgrimage to Nonviolence," that when he completed his formal training for the Ph.D. in 1954, he left Boston with the conviction that "nonviolent resistance was one of the most potent weapons available to oppressed people in their quest for social justice."[7] But this is actually a misleading statement, considering what happened when the bus boycott began a little over a year later. For had King been as convinced of the potency of nonviolence in the struggle for justice as he said, one must wonder why he did not implement Gandhian nonviolence in the first weeks of the bus boycott. While it is certainly the case that he had no direct practical experience with implementing Gandhian techniques of nonviolence by the time he arrived in Montgomery, it is baffling that he admittedly did not even use the language of nonviolence, for example, *nonviolent resistance to evil*, *passive resistance*, and so on, that was so prominent in Gandhi's voluminous writings. This would not happen until Bayard Rustin and Glenn Smiley arrived in Montgomery. Rustin arrived about eight weeks into the bus boycott, and Smiley followed approximately two weeks later. Literary artist and Fellowship of Reconciliation (FOR) board member Lillian Smith has said that she believed that with his experience in Gandhian techniques, Rustin, then the executive secretary of the War Resisters League in New York City, could probably be of help to King. Smiley was sent by the FOR on a fact-finding mission to Montgomery to see how or whether that organization could assist King and the leaders of the boycott.

Prior to the arrival of Rustin and Smiley, King's approach was essentially a nonviolent one, but it was based, not explicitly on Gandhian principles and techniques, but on the love ethic of the Sermon on the Mount. This should not be taken to mean that King had completely forgotten about Gandhi. Indeed, even had this been the case, a fraternity brother, Walter C. Carrington, praised the work of Gandhi in a letter written to King less than one month into the boycott: "In the hands of Gandhi civil disobedience proved to be a potent political weapon. It may also prove to be such in the hands of the Southern Negro."[8] Carrington also wrote of the great potential of "large scale, well disciplined, non-violent civil disobedience to segregation laws. . . ."[9] At this

---

7. Martin Luther King Jr., *Stride Toward Freedom* (New York: Harper & Row, 1958), 101.

8. *The Papers*, 3:89.

time, barely twenty days into the boycott, King did not know what to do with this information since he had not actually been trained in Gandhian techniques. What is important for our purpose, however, is that even had King forgotten about Gandhi after his academic studies, Carrington's letter reminded him.

It is no small matter that Carrington's letter expressed the possibilities of Gandhi's method for the bus boycott. In the meantime, King required that the boycotters not strike back physically if attacked by racist whites. By all means, however, they were to resist, but the resistance was to be a nonviolent refusal to ride the buses. We will see, however, that this was not the pattern that was initially followed even by King when it came to the matter of self-defense.

Carrington's letter surely awakened or stimulated King's memory and appreciation for what he had learned about Gandhi through the lectures by Mordecai Johnson and what he might have learned about him through independent reading, as well as during his student days at Boston University. This may help to explain why King resonated so quickly and easily to Gandhian ideas and techniques later taught him by Rustin and Smiley. These men were just what King needed, and appeared at just the right time. Forces bigger than him and other human beings were at work, providing what he needed. Lillian Smith's recommendation that Rustin go to Montgomery to offer King some advice about Gandhian techniques was on point. Indeed, Rustin himself marveled at how quickly King caught on and began using Gandhian language about nonviolence, as well as implementing Gandhian ideas and techniques.

KNOWLEDGE OF GANDHI BEFORE MONTGOMERY

What King knew of Gandhi during the early weeks of the bus boycott was based primarily on the lecture he heard Mordecai Johnson deliver during his senior year in seminary, what he gathered from conversations with Dean Walter Muelder at Boston University regarding Reinhold Niebuhr's critique of Gandhi's nonviolence, and discussions with his black peers in the Dialectical Society during his doctoral studies. In the two versions of his brief intellectual autobiography, "Pilgrimage to Nonviolence," King implies that he actually read and studied Gandhi systematically while he was in seminary. In the *Stride Toward Freedom* version of "Pilgrimage," he implies that very shortly after hearing Mordecai Johnson's lectures on Gandhi he began reading the books he purchased by and about Gandhi. "As I read I became deeply fascinated by his campaigns of nonviolent resistance," he wrote. "As I delved deeper into the philosophy of Gandhi my skepticism concerning the power of love

9. Ibid.

gradually diminished, and I came to see for the first time its potency in the area of social reform. Prior to reading Gandhi, I had about concluded that the ethics of Jesus were only effective in individual relationship. . . . But after reading Gandhi, I saw how utterly mistaken I was."[10] From this, the reader is left with the impression that King arrived at this conclusion not long after the Johnson lecture and his follow-up readings. King, it should be remembered, was writing these reflections ten years after the fact, and therefore the way he wrote about this leaves the reader wondering whether his in-depth reading and reflections on Gandhi occurred while he was still a student, or afterward, perhaps during the Montgomery bus boycott. Although there is no evidence that King intentionally sought to mislead readers, what he wrote in "Pilgrimage" was in fact misleading, inasmuch as he implied that his systematic reading and pondering of Gandhi's ideas occurred while he was still in school.

In the *Strength to Love* version of "Pilgrimage," King again implies that he was introduced to the life and teachings of Gandhi in seminary. "As I read his works," he said, "I became deeply fascinated by his campaigns of nonviolent resistance. The whole Gandhian concept of *satyagraha* . . . was profoundly significant to me." He goes on to say:

> As I delved deeper into the philosophy of Gandhi, my skepticism concerning the power of love gradually diminished, and I came to see for the first time that the Christian doctrine of love, operating through the Gandhian method of nonviolence, is one of the most potent weapons available to an oppressed people in their struggle for freedom. *At that time, however, I acquired only an intellectual understanding and appreciation of the position*, and I had no firm determination to organize it in a socially effective situation.[11]

Since King was giving an account of thinkers and intellectual ideas that most influenced him while he was in seminary and graduate school, the clear implication that one gets from the two "Pilgrimage" accounts is that he actually read and studied a significant amount of Gandhi's writings while he was in school. Indeed, in response to a letter written by George Hendrick inquiring about the influence of Gandhi on his thinking, King wrote on February 5, 1957 that there was "a definite influence." In addition, he "claimed to have read most of Gandhi's major works and Thoreau's 'Essay on Civil Disobedience' prior to

10. King, "Pilgrimage to Nonviolence," in *Stride*, 96, 97.

11. King, "Pilgrimage to Nonviolence," in *Strength to Love* (New York: Harper & Row, 1963), 138 (my emphasis).

coming to Montgomery."[12] But as we have seen, other than having actually read Thoreau's essay while in college, his claim about the amount of material he read on Gandhi is misleading. No evidence has yet surfaced to verify how much of Gandhi's work was actually read by King during his student days, let alone his claim to have read most of his writings during that period.

Considering that Martin Luther King was a full-time student, who often carried a heavy load of courses in seminary, while sometimes simultaneously taking philosophy courses at the University of Pennsylvania, it would not be unreasonable to say that he likely skimmed one or more of those books he purchased after the Johnson lecture, but did not put much sustained energy into reading them from cover to cover and actually studying them. The argument I am presenting is different from the claim made by Kenneth L. Smith and Ira Zepp Jr., namely, that King purchased those books on Gandhi and "read them intensively."[13] There is no way that these authors could have known this with certainty unless King told one or both, but no evidence has been found that he told either man, and even had he done so we would still have reason to wonder whether corroborating evidence exists, especially since all three men are no longer living.

In a written assignment titled "Six Talks in Outline," for George W. Davis's course on Christian Theology for Today in the fall of 1949, King named Gandhi as one of four men "who greatly reveal the working of the Spirit of God." However, he wrote nothing of substance about Gandhi or the other three personalities included in the outline—David Livingstone, Albert Schweitzer, and Jesus of Nazareth.[14] He listed their names and nothing else. In his senior year and final semester at Crozer, King appears to have written a paper for Kenneth Smith's course on Christianity and Society in which he reflected on pacifism, and stated his argument for rejecting absolute pacifism. In the paper's only comment about Gandhi he wrote: "That Gandhi was successful against the British is no reason that the Russians would react the same way."[15] It is a mystery as to whether King actually wrote a paper on Gandhi in Davis's course on the

---

12. *The Papers* (2000), 4:183n1. Hendrick had written to King on January 25, 1957. See George Hendrick (University of Colorado), "Letter to Martin Luther King, Jr.," Boulder, CO, 1 p. MLKP-MBU: Box 14A, 570125-008. King's response was sent from Dexter Avenue Baptist Church, Montgomery, Alabama: "Letter to George Hendrick," February 5, 1957, TLC, 1 p. MLKP-MBU: Box 14A, 570205-003.

13. Kenneth L. Smith and Ira Zepp Jr., *Search for the Beloved Community: The Thinking of Martin Luther King Jr.* (Valley Forge, PA: Judson, 1974), 47.

14. *The Papers* (1992), 1:249.

15. Ibid., 1:435.

Psychology of Religion in his senior year as Smith claims. If he did write such a paper, it has not yet surfaced.[16] Indeed, the course to which Smith referred was most likely Religious Development of Personality, since this, not Psychology of Religion, is the course listed in King's academic transcript.[17] There is presently no evidence that King actually wrote one or more full-length papers on Gandhi while he was in seminary.

Rev. J. Pius Barbour, a Morehouse man, Crozer's first black graduate, and close family friend and mentor to King while he was in seminary, claims that he heard King "argue nearly all night [at the Barbour house] about Gandhi and his methods against [Barbour's] thesis of coercion."[18] However, I have searched unsuccessfully to find corroborating evidence to support this claim. It is quite possible, however, that such a conversation occurred, especially if it happened soon after King heard the lecture on Gandhi given by Mordecai Johnson. King was known to frequent the Barbour house for his favorite southern home-cooked meals. Moreover, although he later turned to Dean Walter Muelder to help clarify Reinhold Niebuhr's critique of Gandhi's doctrine of nonviolence, I find it most interesting that one who claims in "Pilgrimage" to have been so impacted by Gandhi's views actually passed up the opportunity to enroll in the Seminar in Gandhi when he was a doctoral student.[19] The Boston University catalog of courses for 1951–53 indicates that this seminar was in fact offered during that period—the period when King was completing course work for his doctorate.

THE SERMON ON THE MOUNT

It cannot be denied that at least some of King's practices from the start of the bus boycott were consistent with Gandhi's teachings, even though he was not consciously thinking about Gandhi and his ideas. Only *after* the boycott had been in progress would King be explicitly taught and trained in Gandhian nonviolence. This teaching and training was done primarily by Bayard Rustin and Glenn Smiley. According to Stewart Burns, it was Smiley who also passed on to King a number of books to read about nonviolence, including Richard Gregg's popular book, *The Power of Nonviolence* (1935).[20] Interestingly, it did

16. Smith and Zepp, *Search for the Beloved Community*, 47. Smith claims to have read the paper, but recalled nothing about what King actually said beyond reference to a number of books and articles about Gandhi in the seminary library. See 47–48.

17. *The Papers*, 1:48.

18. Ibid. (1997), 3:171.

19. Ibid. (1994), 2:8n30.

not take King long to understand the significance of the difference between nonviolence as a strategy or tactic, and nonviolence as a principle or way of life. This might well have been due to the earlier knowledge he obtained about Gandhi while in school, as well as his practice of nonviolence in the early days of the bus boycott, practice that was based on the love ethic in the Sermon on the Mount.

King himself acknowledged that in the first weeks of the boycott he did not use the language of nonviolence, such as "nonviolent resistance," "noncooperation," and "passive resistance," which would have called to mind the name of Mahatma Gandhi. Rather, he said, "the phrase most often heard was 'Christian love.' It was the Sermon on the Mount, rather than a doctrine of passive resistance, that initially inspired the Negroes of Montgomery to dignified social action. It was Jesus of Nazareth that stirred the Negroes to protest with the creative weapon of love."[21]

This raises an interesting and important point. In at least two places, Wyatt Tee Walker contends that while King was influenced by a number of important theological and philosophical sources, none influenced him more than the Gospels and the principles of the Sermon on the Mount.[22] "The basis of Martin Luther King's ministry and mission," Walker declares, "was the ethics and morality of the Crucified Carpenter from Galilee."[23] While I have been hesitant to say that King was most influenced by any one single source, what Walker suggests is really quite novel and significant in King studies, and his point is very well taken. After all, King not only grew up in the church, but once it became clear to him that he was being called to ministry he (like southern Baptists generally) worked to become proficient in the use of the Bible such that by the time he began formal theological studies he knew that Book very well indeed, and his sense of ethics was much

20. Stewart Burns, *To the Mountaintop: Martin Luther King, Jr.'s. Sacred Mission to Save America 1955-1968* (New York: HarperSanFrancisco, 2004), 89. Although Smiley gave King a copy of Gregg's book, it is known that this was a text that King was familiar with during his student days at Crozer. The late Kenneth L. Smith, one of King's professors at Crozer, claims to have remembered reading a paper that King wrote on Gandhi in which he included Gregg's book in the bibliography. However, this paper has not yet surfaced in the King Papers Project. See Smith and Zepp, *Search for the Beloved Community*, 48.

21. King, *Stride*, 84.

22. See Wyatt Tee Walker, Introduction to "Rediscovering Lost Values," in *A Knock at Midnight*, ed. Clayborne Carson and Peter Holloran (New York: Warner Books, 1998), 3; and Walker, Foreword to *The Voice of Conscience: The Church in the Mind of Martin Luther King, Jr.* by Lewis V. Baldwin (New York: Oxford University Press, 2010), x.

23. Walker, Introduction to "Rediscovering Lost Values," 3.

informed by its teachings, as well as the guidance and example of his parents and maternal grandmother. The course that he took in Bible under George Kelsey at Morehouse was the beginning of his formal criticism of the Bible and how best to use it. Consequently, by the time he arrived at Crozer Theological Seminary he already had a deep appreciation for the Hebrew prophets and the ethical teachings of Jesus, and only honed that appreciation and understanding through the philological-historical-critical approach to the study of the Bible. Therefore, it is without question that King was not only influenced by the likes of Walter Rauschenbusch and the social gospel, Reinhold Niebuhr and Christian realism, and personalism (with its emphasis on God as personal, and the dignity of persons), but the Bible as well. What is even more interesting is that King gleaned a sense of each of these influences through his private and more formal study of the Bible. The Bible, especially the Sermon on the Mount, teaches the importance of the social gospel; it teaches about the centrality of sin (a trait of Christian realism); and it teaches about a God who is personal and has imbued human beings with the image of God, thus making them inherently sacred. The influence of the Bible is really quite a fascinating point, and warrants much more attention in King studies, a point that Lewis Baldwin made when he read the manuscript version of this book.

For now, suffice it to say that by the beginning of the bus boycott King's memory of Gandhian ideas was not as fresh as it was in seminary and during doctoral studies. Moreover, he was even less familiar with the concrete use of Gandhian techniques since he had had no training. But as a Christian minister, he knew a good deal about the requirements of the Christian love ethic in the Sermon on the Mount, as well as the doctrine of love in the Book of John. King, as well as most of those who regularly attended the mass prayer meetings, knew much about what the ethical teachings of Jesus required of them, and that responding nonviolently and in love to acts of violence was consistent with the ethics of the man from Nazareth. In addition, King's father and grandfather had stressed the Christian love ethic in their demonstrations for voting rights. It therefore made sense that in the early weeks of the Montgomery bus boycott, King appealed to what he knew best and thus was most comfortable with, namely the love ethic of the Sermon on the Mount.

It is of interest to note that the Sermon on the Mount also inspired Gandhi—more than any other aspect of Christianity. It was the Sermon on the Mount, he said, that "endeared Jesus to me."[24] Accordingly, Gandhi described Jesus as "the prince of passive resisters," although by this time he preferred

24. Robert Ellsberg, ed., *Gandhi on Christianity* (Maryknoll, NY: Orbis, 1991), 22.

to say that he was the prince of Satyagraha.[25] Gandhi further admitted that if the Christian message were only that conveyed by the Sermon on the Mount he would declare himself a Christian.[26] Clearly, for Gandhi, then, the message of the Sermon on the Mount, with its emphasis on love, was the essence of Christianity.

Stewart Burns seems to undermine the importance of the Sermon on the Mount for King, when he claims that the black social gospel as opposed to the white social gospel "was driven more by the Old Testament than by the New."[27] Burns's claim is that King was more influenced by the Hebrew prophets and their challenge of the sins of the nation, than the love ethic of the Second Testament. And yet, as we have just seen, King himself said that early on in the Montgomery campaign they were more influenced by the ethic of the Sermon on the Mount. King was most assuredly influenced by the Hebrew prophets. However, it is just as true to say that the black social gospel was inspired by *both* Testaments of the Bible: by the Hebrew prophetic tradition with its emphasis on justice and challenging the sins of the nation, as well as the ethic of unconditional love exhibited by the life and teachings of Jesus as illustrated most profoundly in the Sermon on the Mount. To be sure, Martin Luther King and black religion in general took sin, especially in the form of racism, much more seriously than white Christianity and white social gospel leaders ever did, but this should not be taken to mean that the black social gospel undermined the ethic of love found in the ethical teachings of Jesus. It did not. In addition, the truth is that Walter Rauschenbusch's version of the social gospel was also much influenced by the Hebrew prophets. He believed, not unlike King, that the Hebrew prophets are "the beating heart of the Old Testament."[28] Furthermore, there is no better discussion on the importance of the Hebrew prophets for social Christianity than what we find in the work of Rauschenbusch.

RECONNECTING WITH GANDHI

Martin Luther King reestablished connection with Gandhi in a number of ways during the bus boycott. At times, he was reminded about Gandhi through

---

25. Gandhi, "Satyagraha v. Passive Resistance," in *The Selected Works of Mahatma Gandhi* [*Satyagraha in South Africa*], ed. Shriman Narayan (Ahmedabad: Navajivan, 1968 [1928]), 3:157.

26. Ellsberg, ed., *Gandhi on Christianity*, 19.

27. Burns, *To the Mountaintop*, 92.

28. See Walter Rauschenbusch, *Christianity and the Social Crisis* (New York: Macmillan, 1907), ch. 1, "The Historical Roots of Christianity: The Hebrew Prophets."

unexpected correspondence received, such as the letter from an Alpha brother, Walter C. Carrington, dated December 21, 1955, barely two weeks into the bus boycott. Carrington told King that in the hands of Gandhi nonviolence proved to be a potent political weapon, and that his hope was that the same could be the case for blacks in the South.[29] Three months later, Dean William Stuart Nelson of Howard University wrote to King informing him of his meeting with Gandhi and his own commitment to nonviolence as the best means for blacks in their struggle against racism. He praised King for experimenting with nonviolence. By the time King heard from Nelson he had been committed to Gandhian principles and techniques for only a few weeks.[30] King also reconnected with Gandhi through his awareness of the witness of a white native of Montgomery, Juliette Morgan. There is presently no evidence that King and Morgan were acquainted.

Seldom is attention given to the significance of Morgan's long letter, "Lesson from Gandhi." A city librarian who had grown up in a well-respected, prominent Montgomery family and was a Phi Beta Kappa graduate from the University of Alabama, Morgan was sympathetic with Montgomery blacks in their quest for humane treatment. Her personality and temperament were such that she did not think of herself as a social activist, but her sensitivities toward humanity in general, and the left-outs in particular, compelled her to register her protests against perceived injustices. In this regard, she was much influenced by writer-social activist Lillian Smith. Morgan was a strong writer and chose that medium as the best means to express her discontent regarding the mistreatment of blacks. Her views were made known publicly through a series of strong letters to the editor in various Alabama newspapers, including the Montgomery *Advertiser*. Although whites retaliated against her for the pre-boycott letters, the retaliation was fierce after she wrote "Lesson from Gandhi," and subsequent letters. Even the mayor contributed to the ugliness directed toward Morgan by demanding that she be terminated as a city librarian. Although she survived this, she was warned to cease the letter-writing campaign. She endured virtually everything that was thrown at her: taunts, insults, threats from strangers, and old family friends turning their backs

29. *The Papers*, 3:89.
30. Ibid., 3:183.

on her.[31] And yet, we will see that she could not hold her peace, or relax her pen.

Morgan had earlier written an article in 1952, "White Supremacy Is Evil." In "Lesson from Gandhi," written in December 1955, before King actually thought seriously about utilizing Gandhian tactics in Montgomery, Morgan compared the bus boycott to Gandhi's "Salt March" from Sabamarti to the sea. This march was part of a boycott of the British government's salt monopoly. All salt had to be purchased from the government, a clear exploitation of the Indian people. Morgan believed that Montgomery blacks had taken a lesson from Gandhi, as well as Thoreau, although she rightly observed that blacks had a "greater prejudice to overcome" than what Gandhi and Thoreau experienced. Morgan believed that history was being made in Montgomery as a result of blacks' protest. In this regard, she wrote: "It is hard to imagine a soul so dead, a heart so hard, a vision so blinded and provincial as not to be moved with admiration at the quiet dignity, discipline, and dedication with which the Negroes have conducted their boycott."[32] Morgan went on to express her frustration over seeing so many editorials that went on endlessly about the legality or illegality of the boycott. It brought to her mind a boycott that ultimately led to the American Revolution. "They make me think of that famous [boycott] that turned America from a tea to a coffee drinking nation. Come to think of it, one might say that this nation was founded upon a boycott. . . . Instead of acting like sullen adolescents whose attitude is 'Make me,' we ought to be working out plans to span the gap between segregation and integration, to extend public services—schools, libraries, parks—and transportation to Negro citizens."[33] Furthermore, Morgan expressed dismay that the (initial) minimal requests of King and other boycott leaders (that buses stop at more street corners in the black community; that the customary practice of blacks purchasing their ticket at the front of the bus and leaving the bus to board from the rear be halted; and that drivers obey the law by not requiring that blacks in the "Negro" section give their seats to whites) were rejected by Mayor Gayle and the city council. She declared that the law, rather than be followed at this point, "ought to be changed." She was resentful of the abuses

31. Lynne Olson, *Freedom's Daughters: The Unsung Heroines of the Civil Rights Movement from 1830 to 1970* (New York: Scribner, 2001), 121. I have been much helped and enlightened by Lynn Olson's well-informed discussion on the contributions and trials of Juliette Morgan. Much of the discussion in this section is informed by what Olson has written.

32. Juliette Morgan, "Lesson from Gandhi," in *Daybreak of Freedom: The Montgomery Bus Boycott*, ed. Stewart Burns (Chapel Hill/London: University of North Carolina Press, 1997), 102.

33. Quoted in Olson, *Freedom's Daughters*, 121.

that blacks suffered at the hands of bus drivers, and said that on at least three occasions she was so disgusted at such treatment of blacks that she got off the bus. Morgan said she only wished she had done so more often.[34]

After Juliette Morgan wrote the Gandhi article, she was harassed almost incessantly by unsympathetic whites. Schoolkids threw rocks through her windows, and in the middle of the night people would ring her doorbell and run. But still she was not deterred, for not long after the boycott officially ended, she "wrote a letter to the publisher of the Tuscaloosa News, praising a speech he had given criticizing the White Citizens Council. 'You help redeem Alabama's very bad behavior in the eyes of the nation and the world,' Morgan said. 'I had begun to wonder if there were any men in the state—any white men—with any sane evaluation of our situation, with any good will, and most especially any moral courage to express it.'"[35] Of course, the publisher asked if he could publish the letter in his newspaper. Disregarding the earlier warning that she cease writing such provocative letters regarding the boycott and related issues, she gave her consent. Morgan was blasted for praising the boycott in "Lesson from Gandhi," but this paled in severity and significance to what she experienced when her letter appeared in the Tuscaloosa News.

Although only in her early forties, it has been speculated that the constant harassment by foes and former white friends alike, contributed to Morgan's suicide by an overdose of sleeping pills in 1957. Stewart Burns tells us that Morgan was "*the bus boycott's only known death.*"[36] Virginia Durr, longtime Montgomery resident and interracial activist since the late 1940s, was outraged when she heard about Morgan's suicide, for which she "laid the blame . . . squarely at the feet of white Southern men. 'This,' she declared, 'is Southern chivalry in all its glory.'"[37] Durr, who had been raised as a white supremacist in a well-to-do Montgomery family, underwent a radical conversion in matters of race when she met and was schooled and befriended by two outstanding black women social activist leaders, Mary McLeod Bethune and Mary Church Terrell. Bethune had been invited to join the Franklin D. Roosevelt administration after serving as president of Bethune-Cookman College in Daytona Beach, Florida. Terrell was a longtime civil rights and women's rights activist. Durr was fighting for white women's right to vote when she met Bethune, who informed her that white women had no power; their men had

34. Morgan, "Lesson from Gandhi," in *Daybreak of Freedom*, 102–3.

35. Olson, *Freedom's Daughters*, 127.

36. Burns, *To the Mountaintop*, 32 (my emphasis).

37. Olson, *Freedom's Daughter's*, 128.

the power. Therefore, Bethune informed her, white women would not succeed unless they came to see that their interests were similar to those of blacks, and they should join forces. Not only did Durr become friends with Bethune and Terrell, the women actually took her under their wing and schooled her about practical politics and race. Durr credited the two women "with transforming her feelings about blacks and starting her on her own tumultuous journey toward civil rights activism."[38] In addition, Durr came to reject her mother's teaching—and that of many southern whites—that black women are never to be called ladies. When she was in the presence of Bethune and Terrell, she knew that this was false advice, and that her mother and other southern whites did not know what they were talking about. Durr's stance was that Bethune and Terrell were ladies, or no women were.

Although it is not known when Martin Luther King learned about Juliette Morgan, there is no question that he knew about her contributions. He believed her efforts were important enough that he wrote about her in his first book:

> About a week after the protest started, a white woman who understood and sympathized with the Negroes' efforts wrote a letter to the editor of the *Montgomery Advertiser* comparing the bus protest with the Gandhian movement in India. Miss Juliette Morgan, sensitive and frail, did not long survive the rejection and condemnation of the white community, but long before she died in the summer of 1957 the name of Mahatma Gandhi was well-known in Montgomery.[39]

Morgan's stance and contribution was but one significant reminder to King that not all white people in Montgomery were against the boycott and desegregation efforts; that racism was a social, and not a metaphysical and biological phenomenon. Human beings are not born as racists, but are socialized to be racists. One *learns* to be a racist, which also means that one can learn to be other than racist. This was nowhere more evident than in the outstanding and fearless witness, contribution, and sacrifice of Juliette Morgan. Indeed, this should serve as a reminder that everybody who wills to do so can contribute something meaningful to struggles against oppression and injustice of all kinds. One need not be a Jo Ann Robinson, Mary Fair Burks, Vernon Johns, or Martin Luther King. One need only bring to bear on injustice whatever strengths and gifts one has. Not everybody has the temperament to be

38. Ibid., 102.
39. King, *Stride*, 85.

the type of social activist that King was. Indeed, King himself was often heard to say that everybody has something meaningful to offer toward the struggle for civil rights. If letter writing is one's strength, as it was for Juliette Morgan, then one should use that as the means to protest injustice, and like everything else, Martin Luther King would say, one should do it so well that no man, woman, or child, born, dead or alive, can do it better.

LEARNING ABOUT NONVIOLENCE

Lewis Baldwin has written about King's tendency to avoid violence as a child.[40] King's mother taught him that "hatred and violence must be replaced by love."[41] We saw earlier, that as a growing boy, he had been constantly reminded by his parents that it was his duty as a Christian to love, and not to hate white people, regardless of the racist attitudes and behavior of many. When the white parents of his boyhood friend would not allow them to play together because of their difference in skin color, King wondered how it would be possible for him to love the people who could do something as unthinkable and dreadful (in the mind of a six-year-old) as to separate him from one of his best friends.[42] The advice that his mother gave him was an example of the early influence of the love component in what would become his doctrine of nonviolence.

Mahatma Gandhi was assassinated in January 1948, while King was a senior at Morehouse College. We have seen that Mordecai Johnson was much influenced by the work of Gandhi. When Johnson was appointed president of Howard University, he recruited to the faculty three black men who were very attentive to, and inspired by, Gandhi's work: Benjamin E. Mays, Howard Thurman, and William Stuart Nelson. Each independently traveled to India and met with Gandhi. Mays's visit occurred four years before he was elected president of Morehouse College in 1940. He had a ninety-minute visit with Gandhi.[43] Larry O. Rivers contends that when Mays was appointed president of Morehouse he continued to encourage Morehouse men to study Gandhi and his

---

40. See draft of Lewis V. Baldwin's book manuscript, *Who Is Their God?*, ch. 1, 63–64. This manuscript, of which I have a draft copy in my possession, was published under the title *The Voice of Conscience: The Church in the Mind of Martin Luther King, Jr.* (New York: Oxford University Press, 2010).

41. Baldwin, *The Voice of Conscience*, 26.

42. *The Papers*, 1:362.

43. During this meeting Mays queried Gandhi as to how best to teach the masses to love to the point of being able to be nonviolent. Gandhi replied that nonviolence cannot be preached or taught, but must be practiced. "People do not gain the training by preaching," said Gandhi. "Non-violence cannot be preached. It has to be practiced. . . . Non-violence, when it becomes active, travels with extraordinary velocity, and then it becomes a miracle. So the mass mind is affected first unconsciously, then

work.[44] In addition, there is good reason to believe that Mays spoke of Gandhi fairly regularly in his Tuesday chapel talks. This means that it is quite likely that one of King's earliest introductions to Gandhi was actually during his student days at Morehouse. King's near-perfect chapel attendance increased his chances of hearing whatever Mays might have said about Gandhi. Indeed, Troy Jackson writes: "When looking for models and examples to hold up before his students at Morehouse, Mays found none more powerful than Gandhi's independence movement in India."[45]

When King read Thoreau's essay "On Civil Disobedience" at Morehouse, he had no way of knowing that civil disobedience would be a key tactic in what would become his philosophy of nonviolent resistance to evil. Nor did he know that Gandhi read Thoreau's essay in a South Afrikan prison in 1908, but *after* he had already engaged in a number of civil disobedience campaigns in South Afrika. Indeed, reacting to the claim that he derived his idea of civil disobedience from Thoreau, Gandhi was quick to say that this was inaccurate. "The resistance to authority in South Africa," he wrote, "was well advanced before I got the essay of Thoreau on Civil Disobedience" [from the prison library].[46] Gandhi actually preferred the term *civil resistance* to *civil disobedience*, believing that it more accurately reflected the meaning of his people's struggle in South Afrika.[47]

Having read Thoreau's essay in college, King was formally introduced to pacifist ethics as a student at Crozer. While there, he heard well-known pacifist Abraham J. Muste lecture on pacifism, but he was not converted by it. At the time, King was an adherent of the *just war theory*, prevalent in much of liberal thought, and believed that there may be times when war could serve a negative good, such as eradicating the Nazi regime of Adolph Hitler and a brutal dictatorship. He therefore repudiated what he then understood to be the pacifist stance. Moreover, King believed that just because Gandhian principles worked in South Afrika and India did not necessarily mean they would work in other places in the world, including the Deep South in the United States.

consciously" (Homer A. Jack, ed., *The Gandhi Reader* [Bloomington: Indiana University Press, 1956], 311).

44. See Larry O. Rivers, "James Hudson: Tallahassee Theologian and Campus Activist," *The A.M.E. Review* (October–December 2007): 47.

45. Troy Jackson, *Becoming King: Martin Luther King, Jr. and the Making of a National Leader* (Lexington: University of Kentucky Press, 2008), 44.

46. Quoted in Louis Fischer, *The Life of Mahatma Gandhi* (New York: Harper & Brothers, 1950), 87.

47. Fischer, *The Life of Mahatma Gandhi*, 87–88.

In a letter to Ingeborg Teek-Frank in 1959, King said that he had read most of Gandhi's writings and was happy to say that he had most of them in his personal library.[48] Even a cursory look at the select list of books in King's personal library confirms the presence of well over a dozen books by and about Gandhi.[49] While it is safe to say that he had read extensively about Gandhi by 1959, the reading of these texts occurred during and after the bus boycott, not during his student days.

TRACKED DOWN BY THE SPIRIT OF THE TIMES

Like Gandhi in South Afrika and later in India, Martin Luther King came to see that the emergence and practice of nonviolence from Montgomery to Memphis was an *experiment* that his people had to muster the courage to carry out.[50] He saw that while Gandhi provided the method for addressing social problems, Jesus Christ "furnished the spirit and motivation" through love.[51] Not only should one adhere to nonviolence, one should do so in the spirit of genuine love. Indeed, King came to see that nonviolent resistance was nothing short of *Christian love in action.*[52] The purpose of nonviolence was not to defeat the white man, and then to lord it over him or to treat him as he had treated blacks. Increasingly, King could see that nonviolence (rather than violence) made it easier to seek reconciliation after nonviolent demonstrations. King's primary aim was not to win or to be successful, but to be faithful to the God who *called* him to ministry. This may be why he told Bayard Rustin regarding the bus boycott when they first met: "It is not for me to say or for you to analyze whether I can win, my obligation is to do the right thing as I am called upon to do it. The rest is in God's hands."[53] King's sense of divine call was one of the key reasons he was able to persevere throughout his civil rights ministry; why he persevered even in the face of imminent danger and even death. He was determined to be faithful to his call and to the One who called him, and was his ever-present coworker and companion in the struggle for justice and equality. The God of his ancestors, the Hebrew prophets, and Jesus Christ was the source

48. *The Papers* (2005), 5:347.

49. Ibid. (2007), 6:629–55.

50. Clayborne Carson, ed., *The Autobiography of Martin Luther King, Jr.* (New York: Warner Books, 1998), 68.

51. Ibid., 67.

52. *The Papers*, 6:324.

53. Quoted in Howell Raines, *My Soul Is Rested: Movement Days in the Deep South Remembered* (New York: G. P. Putnam's Sons, 1977), 57.

of King's faith and determination to stay on task throughout the movement, no matter the cost.

We need to remember that Martin Luther King did not plan the incidents that led to the use of nonviolent resistance as a strategy, and later as a creed. Nor did he volunteer to serve as chief spokesperson and president of the Montgomery Improvement Association. Rather, he believed that God was somehow involved in the events that led to his leadership. What happened to King, a newcomer to the city of Montgomery, was not unusual. There is good reason to believe, for example, that many longtime black pastors in Montgomery saw King as a kind of scapegoat or as a way for them to avoid being asked to provide leadership to the movement that was being born before their very eyes. They knew that the one selected as the spokesperson would undoubtedly have many demands on his time, which could mean that the ministry at his local church could suffer. In addition, such a person would have to bear most of the severe scrutiny and blame when things went wrong, as well as be singled out, harassed, and threatened with death by racist whites in the city.

But more positively, as a newcomer, King did not carry the baggage that many local black ministers did. Nor would he be in a compromised position since he did not have the reputation of those who had accepted gifts from white authorities. He had no history of selling out, or of being a lackey for the white city fathers. To a large extent, then, King may have been chosen for the leadership of the MIA primarily because he was the new kid on the block. Other black pastors might very well have had their own selfish reasons for selecting King, and some may have even meant ill by their choice. We can be certain, however, that Martin Luther King thought more positively about the matter, believing that it was all part of a higher plan of which the God of his faith was the source.

Looking back, King said that he had been tracked down by the *Zeitgeist* ("the spirit of the times"). In addition, and most importantly, he essentially gave a theological interpretation to his selection as president of the MIA. For him it was not a mere accident, nor the result of a prank instigated by black pastors. Even if that was the case, King interpreted what happened quite differently. He considered his nomination and election as leader of the MIA to have been a result of divine initiative, thought, energy, and presence. In his view, he was selected because of God's action in that historic moment. King reasoned that what became the Montgomery bus boycott and the beginnings of the civil rights movement and his role in it was an idea whose time had come, and God was present and acting in what unfolded from the very beginning.

He was convinced that the boycott could not be explained entirely either by his presence or that of other black leaders in Montgomery. Something else was also at work; something much bigger than any individual or group. "The Montgomery story," King said, "would have taken place if the leaders of the protest had never been born."[54] This was his way of saying that the movement was not about him or any other individual as such, and that there was no purely human explanation for the Montgomery campaign. The God of the Hebrew prophets and Jesus Christ was the chief cause of what happened in Montgomery, and was present and active throughout.

A few weeks into the boycott, King straightforwardly told those assembled at a prayer meeting that he had nothing to do with the startup of the Montgomery movement, or the events leading up to it. He just happened to have been called as pastor of Dexter Avenue Baptist Church in Montgomery, Alabama, and thus just happened to be there when December 1, 1955 rolled around. Time itself was ready for change, he said, and that time—without any efforts on his part—had come to Montgomery. Initially, King just wanted to be a good pastor and to develop an effective ministry. He had no other agenda. He came to see, however, that cosmic and divine forces required more of him, and that if he worked cooperatively and determinedly with those forces and with human beings, that *more* would become a reality.

The discussion in chapter eight examines Martin Luther King's movement toward nonviolence in Montgomery, explores some of its basic features in the thinking and practice of the mature King, and discusses at length the importance of love in his mature doctrine of nonviolence. Such a discussion would be incomplete if there was not also a consideration of how the demonstrators were trained in the techniques of nonviolence. This is the focus of chapter nine.

Like Gandhi, Martin Luther King's thinking evolved from the idea of nonviolence as a mere strategy for social change to a firm conviction of nonviolence as a philosophy or way of life. How did King's evolving ideas in this regard influence his practice? Conversely, how did his practice and experiments with Gandhian ideas and the Christian doctrine of agape influence his emerging ethic of nonviolence? A discourse on the formal elements in King's concept of nonviolent resistance to evil will shed light on these and related questions.

54. King, *Stride*, 69.

8

Gandhian Influence and the Formal
Elements of King's Nonviolence

This chapter begins with a discussion on the general influence that Mohandas K. Gandhi had on Martin Luther King. Attention is also given the role that Bayard Rustin played in educating King about Gandhian ideas and techniques of nonviolence. There is consideration of the significance of Gandhian vows relative to King's commitment to nonviolence, and the focus then shifts to an extensive examination of basic Gandhian ideas and formal elements in King's doctrine of nonviolence.

Gandhi was not only the world's chief activist and proponent of the method of nonviolence in social struggles, but was nonviolence personified. During his senior year at Crozer, Martin Luther King drove to Philadelphia to hear Howard University president, Mordecai Johnson, lecture on Gandhi. King was so moved by Johnson's passion and what he said in his lecture that he claims to have immediately gone out to purchase a half-dozen books by and about the late Indian leader.[1] In an interview on "Front Page Challenge" in 1959, he said: "I read Mahatma Gandhi in my student days and got a great deal from him."[2] Notwithstanding this claim, it is not clear as to how much King actually read by and about Gandhi while in seminary and/or during doctoral studies. After all, after the Johnson lecture he only says that he went out and purchased the books, not that he actually read them, or how much of them he read. However, from what I can tell, it has generally been held by many that King actually read them, or at least major portions of them. I have found no corroborating evidence of

---

1. Martin Luther King Jr., *Stride Toward Freedom* (New York: Harper & Row, 1958), 96.

2. Clayborne Carson et al., eds., *The Papers of Martin Luther King, Jr.* (Berkeley: University of California Press, 2005), 5:193. "Front Page Challenge" was a popular weekly show on Canadian television (CBC) in the 1950s and 60s, featuring a panel of pundits who tried to guess the identity of a "guest" connected with a famous front-page news story. During the guessing period, the guest was visible to the audience but hidden from the panelists.

either of these scenarios. Indeed, we will see that neither Bayard Rustin nor Glenn Smiley seemed to think that King knew much at all about Gandhi and his ideas when they first met him.

Martin Luther King might well have heard much about Gandhian nonviolence in chapel talks given by Benjamin E. Mays at Morehouse College. On a trip to India approximately six years before King matriculated at Morehouse, Mays had a ninety-minute meeting with Gandhi. He had much more than a casual interest in Gandhi's ideas on nonviolence. Mays hoped that Gandhi's method could one day be applied to the problem of racism in the United States. However, notwithstanding what he may have heard about Gandhian nonviolence in chapel talks by Mays, it appears that it was during his student days at Crozer Theological Seminary that King got his first formal introduction to the method that would later become for him more than a mere strategy for social change. This method would ultimately become for him a creed or *a way of life*, but this would happen only after seminary and doctoral studies.

It really is not known just how much King knew about Gandhi and the Indian struggle before hearing the lectures by Johnson, although it is more than a notion that he probably first heard of him through Mays's chapel talks. Earlier in his career, Mays was invited by Mordecai Johnson to be dean of the Howard University School of Religion. Johnson was as much under the influence of Gandhian ideas as anybody in the United States at that time. Along with faculty colleagues Howard Thurman and William Stuart Nelson, Mays kept close tabs on Gandhi's nonviolent struggle for Indian independence from British imperialism. This is an important point because it establishes the Gandhian influence on Mays long before he was called to be president at Morehouse in 1940. In addition, at least one writer has stated outright that at Morehouse, Mays periodically lectured on Gandhi in Tuesday chapel talks.[3]

Larry O. Rivers offers the helpful assertion that while at Howard University, Mays, Thurman, and Nelson "identified Gandhian civil disobedience as a possible tactical answer to a need for a moral, love-centered method to attack segregation."[4] While still dean of Howard's School of Religion, Mays himself had spent ninety minutes in conversation with Gandhi during his trip to India in 1936.[5] Thurman and Nelson also made trips to India in 1936 and 1946, respectively. A strong advocate of nonviolence, Nelson's

3. See Houston Bryan Roberson, *Fighting the Good Fight: The Story of the Dexter Avenue King Memorial Baptist Church, 1865-1977* (New York: Routledge, 2005), 115.

4. Larry O. Rivers, "James Hudson: Tallahassee Theologian and Campus Activist," *The AME Church Review* 123, no. 408 (October–December 2007): 47.

concern about Hindu and Muslim relations in India prompted him to go there to join with Gandhi in a march to promote better relations between the two groups.[6] By association, all of this only adds to the depth of Mays's commitment to nonviolence, since both he and Nelson were deeply devoted to it during their time together at Howard.

It should therefore not be surprising when Rivers informs us that, after becoming president of Morehouse, Mays "continued to encourage students to learn [sic] study Gandhi's work in India."[7] When Gandhi was assassinated during King's senior year at Morehouse in 1948, Mays surely addressed the tragedy in his Tuesday chapel talks, just as he most likely spoke of Gandhi on many previous occasions. King was in attendance at virtually all of those chapel services, and thus would have heard the references to Gandhi and the Indian struggle for independence from British colonialism. In any case, if Rivers's assessment is accurate—and I see no reason to question it—Martin Luther King heard more than passing references to Gandhi and his method while at Morehouse, even if his youthful mind was not then able to see the possible connection to blacks' struggle in the United States.

King said that before hearing Mordecai Johnson's electrifying lecture, he had "despaired of the power of love in solving social problems."[8] He recalled that the reason for this might have been related to the fact that he had read and been challenged by the work of Friedrich Nietzsche, who argued that Christianity and its ethic of love was representative of the religion of the weak. Nietzsche was pessimistic about the power of Christianity to effect positive change in the world. Having read Nietzsche in seminary, while also witnessing the treatment of his people by whites who claimed to be Christians, it is not difficult to understand why the young seminarian reached the point of despair regarding the power of love in solving social problems. After all, the chief ethical imperative of Christianity is agape, which means that the lives and behavior of Christians should conform to its requirement to love God as they love self and others. Surely, racism and racial discrimination, so characteristic of too many white Christians even today, is not consistent with what agape requires.

5. See Benjamin E. Mays, *Born to Rebel: An Autobiography* (New York: Charles Scribner's Sons, 1971), 156–57. Although Mays said the year was 1936, a number of sources record 1937 as the year of his visit. See *The Gandhi Reader*, ed. Homer A. Jack (Bloomington: Indiana University Press, 1956), 309, where Mahadev Desai lists 1937.

6. See Nelson's letter to King (March 21, 1956) in *The Papers* (1997), 3:182–83.

7. Rivers, "James Hudson . . . ," 47.

8. King, *Stride*, 95.

Nevertheless, there is no question that the lecture that Mordecai Johnson gave on Gandhi was providential for young King. It is important to remember that despite what King says in "Pilgrimage to Nonviolence" about going out and buying those books by and about Gandhi, he did not at that time completely buy into Gandhian nonviolence. It was not quite clear to him in seminary and Boston University just how effective Gandhi's method could be in the United States if applied to the race problem. This was a much different context than what Gandhi encountered in South Afrika and later in India. In fact, even in seminary King wondered about the applicability of nonviolence in struggles for freedom from oppression in places other than India. King reasoned that just because the British reacted to Gandhian nonviolence as they did was no guarantee that the Russians would, for example.[9] In any event, there is no question that King did not completely forget the lecture on Gandhi, for as a doctoral student at Boston University, he would again reflect on the relevance of nonviolence, this time in light of having read and pondered Reinhold Niebuhr's critique of Gandhi's nonviolence (as discussed at length in chapter five). Although I have not found evidence that King studied Gandhi and nonviolence systematically during seminary and/or doctoral studies, he most certainly had the opportunity to do so at Boston University. We know, for example, that a course titled "Seminar on Gandhi" was offered while King was a doctoral student, but for reasons unknown, he did not enroll.[10]

In numerous places in his sermons, speeches, and writings, King calls attention to Gandhi's influence on his civil rights ministry, once characterizing him as "the Saint of India."[11] However, when the bus boycott began, he only preached the love ethic of the Sermon on the Mount, while simultaneously adhering to an ethic of self-defense. During the first weeks of the boycott, he was not opposed to retaliatory self-defense to protect himself and/or his family, a stance that was very much a part of Deep South culture. King did not relinquish his position on self-defense until after conversations with Bayard Rustin on Gandhi's doctrine of nonviolence as a way of life.

EARLY IMPACT OF BAYARD RUSTIN

In a letter to Carroll Bowen of Oxford University Press on February 21, 1956, Bayard Rustin stated the need to postpone a publication because he had been summoned to Montgomery, Alabama "to consult with Negro leaders about

9. *The Papers* (1992), 1:435.

10. See ibid. (1994), 2:8n30.

11. Ibid. (2007), 6:508.

the possibility of setting up a workshop, the purpose of which is to bring the Gandhian philosophy and tactic to the masses of Negroes in the South."[12] Rustin considered such instruction and training in Gandhian nonviolence to be the only way to avoid widespread violence that might occur because of the boycott. When Rustin arrived in Montgomery, King was out of town, so he initially conferred with King's friend and ministerial colleague, Rev. Ralph Abernathy of First Baptist Church. Rustin would only have two weeks to make his initial contribution to the Montgomery struggle, for just two days after he sent his colleagues at the War Resisters League a report of his activities in Montgomery, they, along with A. Philip Randolph and new executive secretary of the Fellowship of Reconciliation, John Swomley, met to discuss a call received from E. D. Nixon, head of the Montgomery chapter of the NAACP. Nixon expressed concerns and spoke of possible consequences for the boycott regarding rumors about Rustin's alleged ties with the Communist Party. The New York group also discussed possible ramifications if word got to Montgomery about Rustin's past arrest and conviction in Pasadena, California, for engaging in a public homosexual act. The short of it is that Rustin was advised by his New York colleagues to leave Montgomery. King reluctantly agreed, but arranged for him to be transported to Birmingham on February 29, 1956. Interestingly, King expressed no concern about Rustin's sexual orientation. Although this might suggest that homosexuality was not an issue for the Baptist preacher, Michael G. Long has shown in his recent excellent book on King and homosexuality that he might well have been ambivalent about it.[13]

Reflecting on his first visit to King's house, Rustin recalled seeing the armed guards outside the house and a loaded pistol in a chair inside the house. When Rustin questioned King about these weapons, he replied in a way that suggested that he was actually conflicted about it. "We're not going to harm anybody unless they harm us,"[14] King reportedly told Rustin. They would only act violently in retaliation to violence done to them. At that particular time, King clearly believed that blacks had a right to self-defense, according to Rustin. Indeed, many black and white men in the Deep South were known to carry guns and/or sharp knives or razors at that time. It was a southern

---

12. Bayard Rustin, letter to Carroll Bowen, in *I Must Resist: Bayard Rustin's Life in Letters*, ed. Michael G. Long (San Francisco: City Lights, 2012), 165.

13. See Michael G. Long, *Martin Luther King, Jr., Homosexuality, and the Early Gay Rights Movement: Keeping the Dream Straight?* (New York: Palgrave/Macmillan, 2012).

14. Quoted in Stewart Burns, *To the Mountaintop: Martin Luther King Jr.'s Mission to Save America 1955-1968* (New York: HarperSanFrancisco, 2004), 82.

custom to have weapons within easy reach. In the early 1940s, social scientist Gunnar Myrdal wrote of his amazement at the prevalence of guns and knives in the possession of southern black men: "This custom was taken over also by the Negroes during Reconstruction days. The writer has been astonished to see how firearms and slashing knives are part of the equipment of many lower class whites and Negroes in the South."[15] Because of the violence committed against blacks by white racists throughout the enslavement period and the Reconstruction years, blacks believed that they, more than anybody else in the country, had a right to self-defense. Indeed, I can attest to the fact that this was the stance of my late father and paternal uncles who had grown up in Pinson, Alabama. When they moved to the North, the guns and knives (razors) went with them, and they, like very many other black men who moved north, were not opposed to using these weapons for self-defense and defense of family. Tragically, however, both in the South and the North they too often found that they had to defend themselves not only against the violence of white racists, but of other black men as well.

Nevertheless, Rustin knew that there was no place for self-defense in Gandhi's doctrine of nonviolence. "Rustin responded that in this historic situation in Montgomery in 1956, such rights were trumped by a greater moral responsibility. A commitment to Gandhian nonviolence called for an unconditional rejection of retaliation, even in self-defense."[16] In his report to the War Resisters League on his visit to Montgomery, Rustin said: "All the leaders are clear that they will have no part in starting violence. There is, however, considerable confusion on the question as to whether violence is justified in retaliation to violence directed against the Negro community. At present there is no careful, non-violent preparation for any such extreme situation."[17] Many, including King, were not able to see the inconsistency between what they were preaching by day, while possessing guns or having easy access to them, a point corroborated by Glenn Smiley who reported to the FOR that King had good intentions and wanted to do the right thing but was possibly prevented by his youthfulness (at twenty-six years of age), and the fact that his bodyguards were armed. Smiley reported that King seemed to see the inconsistency of preaching nonviolence while having armed bodyguards, but he did not see clearly enough. "He believes and yet he doesn't believe,"[18] Smiley declared.

15. Gunnar Myrdal, *An American Dilemma: The Negro Problem and Modern Democracy* (New York: Harper & Brothers, 1944), 560.

16. Burns, *To the Mountaintop*, 82.

17. Stewart Burns, ed., *Daybreak of Freedom: The Montgomery Bus Boycott* (Chapel Hill: University of North Carolina Press, 1997), 209.

Smiley reported that when he asked King what he knew about Gandhi, he responded: "I know very little about the man, although I've always admired him."[19] What King knew or did not know about Gandhi at the time cannot be known with certainty. However, what both Smiley and Rustin discovered immediately about King was that he was quick of mind and a very quick study. Having passed on to King a number of books to read and study by and about Gandhi and nonviolence, including Richard Gregg's *The Power of Nonviolence*, for example, Smiley found that at the very next mass prayer meeting King's speech contained ideas from several of those books. Apparently King immediately set up a daily reading regimen that focused on the Gandhi materials given him by Smiley. In addition, Rustin recalled that around this time King began referring regularly to Gandhi by name in speeches and sermons. This too was an indication that King began reading the books almost immediately and was being influenced by ideas contained in them, as well as what he was hearing from Rustin and Smiley. In his report to the War Resisters League, Rustin asserted that King was "eagerly learning all that he can about non-violence and evidence indicates that he is emerging as a regional symbol of non-violent resistance in the Deep South."[20] This says something about King's brilliance of mind, as well as his level of commitment to providing the best possible leadership for the bus boycott.

Rustin recalled telling King that "it was precisely . . . because the followers will seldom, in the mass, be dedicated to [nonviolence] in principle, that the leadership must be dedicated to it in principle, to keep those who believe in it as a tactic operating correctly. But if, in the flow and the heat of battle, a leader's house is bombed, and he shoots back, that is an encouragement to his followers to pick up guns. If, on the other hand, he has no guns around him, and they all know it, they will rise to the nonviolent occasion of a situation."[21] Rustin recalled that they had a number of conversations like that. It looks like his explanation contributed much toward King's turning away from the retaliatory ethics of self-defense and moving toward the idea of nonviolence as a way of life. At least Rustin recalled that King was fascinated by what he had said in this regard.

As noted earlier, King had a sense, even in seminary, that the efficacy of Gandhian nonviolence might be affected by the location and context in which

18. *The Papers*, 3:20.

19. Quoted in Burns, *To the Mountaintop*, 89.

20. Burns, ed., *Daybreak of Freedom*, 209.

21. Bayard Rustin, *The Reminiscences of Bayard Rustin* (New York: Oral History Research Office of Columbia University, 1988), 140.

it is applied. In other words, sociocultural context is important, which means that the precise way that Gandhi applied nonviolence in South Afrika and India might not work elsewhere. Of course, King's thinking at the time was based on a pragmatic view of nonviolence. He saw nonviolence as a strategy that may or may not work in a given social struggle. In his thinking at the time, nonviolence was but one of a number of possible strategies. He was a long way from the mature Gandhian idea of nonviolence as a way of living and behaving in the world. What is important, however, is that even during his seminary days, King could see that nonviolence as a strategy to address social evil would have to be adapted to the particular context, since every society and/or community is different. This idea became solidified for him when he began applying Gandhian principles and techniques during the bus boycott and in subsequent nonviolent direct action campaigns. Even after the successful application of Gandhian techniques during the bus boycott, King told an interviewer in 1959 that they needed to "carefully explore the potentialities and limits of the kind of direct action which was successful in Montgomery."[22] This is evidence of his awareness that the application of the method of nonviolence needed to be adapted to the local context. What worked in Montgomery might not work as effectively (or at all!) in Albany, Georgia, or Birmingham, Alabama, or other places in the South. Even if nonviolence worked in the South, this was no guarantee it would work in the North without major adjustments. Consequently, it is not surprising that certain of Gandhi's ideas did not find their way into King's philosophy and practice of nonviolence. King did not just uncritically seek to apply Gandhi's principles and techniques to every situation in the Deep South and the North, but sought to adapt them to the local context.

KING AND GANDHIAN VOWS

Gandhi was a voluminous writer. His *Collected Works* exceed one hundred large volumes. While I am a long way from reading the entirety of each of these volumes, I have read enough of them, in addition to the six-volume *Selected Works of Mahatma Gandhi*, to know that there are at least eleven vows that were crucial to Gandhi's thinking and practice of nonviolence. Presently, I list these without explanation, although later in the chapter I examine in some detail the two that most influenced the development of King's doctrine of nonviolence, namely *satyagraha* and *ahimsa*. The eleven vows are:

- Satyagraha or Truth (or God)

---

22. *The Papers* (2005), 5:117.

- Ahimsa (or noninjury)
- Brahmacharya (chastity/purification)
- Nonstealing
- Nonpossession
- Control of the palate
- Fearlessness
- Removal of untouchability
- Bread labor
- Equal regard for all religions
- Swadesi (patronage of one's own neighborhood, district, and nation)[23]

Taken together, these eleven overlapping vows were the basis of self-discipline and self-purification in the Gandhian ashram. According to Gandhi, the purpose of the vows was for building the virtue of adhering to Truth, no matter how painful or difficult things happen to be.

Gandhi argued that one may be able to get around a rule, for example, the rule that the consumption of alcoholic beverages is not good for one's health. Where rules are concerned, one may always encounter an exceptional situation in which one opts to break the rule for medicinal or any number of reasons. As a rule, the nonconsumption of alcohol is good, unless at some point one needs it for medicinal purposes. But a vow is quite different and has an air of permanence or absoluteness about it. Accordingly, Gandhi contends that a vow is "unflinching determination, and helps us against temptations. Determination is worth nothing, if it bends before discomfort."[24] By definition, a vow means that there is to be no deviation, regardless. Vow-taking also suggests that one can only take vows that are based on "universally recognized principles."[25] Therefore, one cannot take a vow of racism, sexism, heterosexism, or sin.

Vow-taking, Gandhi held, is a sign of strength, not of weakness: "To do at any cost something that one ought to do constitutes a vow. It becomes a bulwark of strength."[26] One who makes a vow cannot then turn around and say that one will do what it prohibits, for example, tell the truth "as far as possible." One who does this, said Gandhi, "betrays either his pride or his weakness. . . . To do something 'as far as possible' is to succumb to the very first temptation."[27]

23. Shriman Narayan, ed., *The Selected Works of Mahatma Gandhi* (Ahmedabad: Navajivan, 1968), 4:213–44, 256–60.

24. Ibid., 4:248.

25. Ibid.

26. Ibid., 4:249.

27. Ibid.

One leaves an opening for breaking the vow when such language is used. Invoking the phrase, "as far as possible," gives one an out, the very thing that the vow, by definition, does not permit. One adheres to a vow regardless. It does not matter if one is confronted with a life-or-death decision or situation. One does not break a vow if one presumes to follow the Gandhian way. Is it any wonder that for Gandhi vows are the basis for self-discipline and self-purification in order to open oneself entirely to Truth or God?

I know of only one place where Martin Luther King explicitly used "vow" language regarding his commitment to nonviolence. In "The State of the Movement," an address to the SCLC staff retreat at Frogmore, South Carolina, November 28, 1967, King told those gathered: "I have taken a vow. I, Martin Luther King, take thee, nonviolence, to be my wedded wife, for better or for worse, for richer or for poorer, in sickness and in health, till death do us part."[28] In the posthumously published article, "Showdown for Nonviolence," he expressed vow language without using the term itself, saying that he was "committed to nonviolence absolutely," and that he had no intention of burning down buildings. "If nonviolent protest fails this summer," he said, "I will continue to preach it and teach it. . . . I plan to stand by nonviolence because I have found it to be a philosophy of life that regulates not only my dealings in the struggle for racial justice but also my dealings with people, with my own self. I will still be faithful to nonviolence."[29] Indeed, even earlier, at the Democratic National Convention in Atlantic City in 1964, King told Mississippi Freedom Democratic Party delegate and activist Hartman Turnbow that even if being nonviolent led him to the grave he would remain committed to it; that he would never approve of violence.[30] He was without question committed to nonviolence, regardless; absolutely. Indeed, there is nothing in the King corpus to support longtime King attorney, confidant, sometime fundraiser and speechwriter Clarence B. Jones's contention that depending on the situation, Martin would deviate from "his otherwise unwavering commitment to nonviolence . . .";[31] that in the face of the 9/11 tragedies "he

28. King, "The State of the Movement," Address to SCLC Staff Retreat at Frogmore, SC, November 28, 1967, King Center Library and Archives, 12.

29. King, "Showdown for Nonviolence," in *A Testament of Hope: The Essential Writings of Martin Luther King, Jr.*, ed. James M. Washington (New York: Harper & Row, 1986), 69.

30. Howell Raines, *My Soul Is Rested: Movement Days in the Deep South Remembered* (New York: G. P. Putnam's Sons, 1977), 266. Former SNCC activist Julian Bond told the story of how old Hartman Turnbow used to carry an automatic pistol in a briefcase. He would walk around dressed as the farmer he was in coveralls, boots, a large hat, and a briefcase. "And he opens the briefcase and nothing in it but an automatic" (quoted in ibid., 267). Virtually all black families that SNCC activists stayed with during their work in Mississippi owned guns.

would have reluctantly accepted that some kind of measured, military response was morally necessary."[32]

I have found no explicit reference to a vow of fearlessness and/or *brahmacharya* in King's published and unpublished writings, sermons, and speeches. Nor is there evidence that the King Papers Project has uncovered documents in which he actually cites the terms *ahimsa* and *brahmacharya*. However, there is clear evidence that King appeals to the concept or idea of ahimsa when he stresses the importance of noninjury when discussing and engaging in nonviolence. For example, in his February 2, 1959 Address at the Thirty-Sixth Annual Dinner of the War Resisters League in New York, King said that nonviolence prohibits "not only external physical violence but also internal violence of spirit. The nonviolent resister not only refuses to shoot his opponent but he also refuses to hate him. At the center of nonviolence stands the principle of love."[33] Nowhere in this and other speeches or writings does he use the term *ahimsa* to describe this concept, but the idea expressed is precisely what ahimsa means.

According to Gandhi, ahimsa literally means noninjury, or "not to hurt any living creature by thought, word or deed, even for the supposed benefit of that creature."[34] Of course, Gandhi acknowledged that absolute ahimsa is impossible since we humans invariably and unwittingly kill living beings such as insects. Moreover, Gandhi conceded that it is sometimes deemed necessary to kill poisonous spiders or snakes to ensure the safety of human beings.[35] Ahimsa seeks not only to avoid physical harm to human beings, but psychological harm, or that caused by lying, hatred, racism, thinking evil thoughts about a person or group, and wishing ill to others.[36] "The Gandhian concept of noninjury," said King, "parallels the Hebraic-Christian teaching of the sacredness of every human being."[37] King also declared that the nonviolent resister "must follow a consistent principle of noninjury,"[38] refusing all the while to inflict injury on an opponent, while willing to invite self-suffering rather than to inflict suffering on another. In both instances King was talking about ahimsa, but did not use the term.

31. Clarence B. Jones and Joel Engle, *What Would Martin Say?* (New York: HarperCollins, 2008), 166.

32. Ibid., 167.

33. *The Papers*, 5:124–25. See 505 where King names "noninjury" as one of Gandhi's weapons.

34. V. B. Kher, ed., *In Search of the Supreme* by M. K. Gandhi (Ahmedabad: Navajivan, 1961), 2:28.

35. Ibid.

36. Ibid., 2:26.

37. King, "The Ethical Demands for Integration," in *A Testament of Hope*, 124.

38. King, "Love, Law, and Civil Disobedience," in *A Testament of Hope*, 46.

King saw racism as a violation of ahimsa because it was a denial of the personhood of blacks, and thus a violation of their humanity. Similarly, King believed that "having to live in a community and pay higher consumer prices for goods or higher rent for equivalent housing than are charged in the white areas of the city"[39] was also a violation of ahimsa since it is a form of injury or violence done to human beings. Indeed, anything that violates human personhood is violence, and thus a contradiction of ahimsa.

When it comes to the term *satyagraha*, we have a different situation, for in more than one instance King explicitly cites the term. Even more frequently, he cites the meaning of the term—"soul force" or "love force." Satyagraha is from the roots "*satya*" (truth, love, or soul) and "*graha*" (force).[40] It means truth-force, love-force, or soul-force. Like Gandhi, King used all three of these characterizations when describing nonviolence.

Although at this writing we have no evidence that he used the term *brahmacharya*, King had a good sense that nonviolence as a way of life, or what he sometimes characterized as "pure nonviolence,"[41] was virtually impossible to the masses of people because it requires "extraordinary discipline and courage."[42] Gandhi used similar language when writing about brahmacharya. Accordingly, one develops such extraordinary discipline and courage by adhering to the criteria for observing brahmacharya. To this end Gandhi pointed to ten such criteria:

- Solitude
- Moderation in eating
- Reading good books
- Regular meditation
- Plenty of physical and mental exercise
- Abstaining from spicy and intoxicating food and drink
- Avoiding plays and shows that excite the sexual instinct
- Abstaining from sex
- Avoiding being alone with a woman or man
- Repeating Ramanama (God) or some other formula[43]

---

39. King, "A Testament of Hope," in *A Testament of Hope*, 327.

40. King, *Stride*, 96.

41. King, "The Social Organization of Nonviolence," in *A Testament of Hope*, 32.

42. Ibid.

43. Narayan, ed., *The Selected Works*, 5:449–50.

Gandhi held that adherence to these criteria are absolute for one who makes the vow of brahmacharya, the purpose of which is self-purification, which alone opens one to obedience to Truth, or God.

It is of interest to note that in a number of letters from friends, well-wishers, and former professors during the Montgomery bus boycott, Martin Luther King was advised to find time for solitude, silence, meditation, and reflection. These are not different from some of the criteria for obtaining brahmacharya. In a letter to Allan Knight Chalmers, one of King's former professors at Boston University, he expressed his frustration over the failure to find time to retreat, reflect, think, and relax.[44] He informed his teacher that upon his return from his trip to India, he decided to work in a day of silence and meditation each week. Wyatt Tee Walker, a close SCLC colleague of King's, described King's day of silence as one "in which he abstained from the distractions of daily life, including the telephone, television, and radio. That day was spent in prayer and meditation and in developing a rigorous discipline of 'think time,' which he devoted to mapping strategies for the nonviolent campaigns he led."[45] Although Walker implies that King experimented with the "Day of Silence" over a long period of time, King himself said that he tried it several times, but found that things began to pile up so much that he invariably found himself using the day set aside for silence and meditation to catch up. King lamented: "And so in a real sense I am in about the same position now as I was two or three years ago. But I know that I cannot continue to go at this pace, and live with such a tension filled schedule."[46] The challenge of making and giving ample time and space to self-care was a problem that King grappled with throughout his civil rights ministry, and was never able to bring it under his control. Self-care is critical in Gandhian ethics. Gandhi was adamant about adhering to the criteria for observing brahmacharya. In addition, silence and meditation were considered to be means of self-purification in preparation for nonviolent direct action campaigns.[47] But once again, we are cautioned to remember the difference in place and context where Gandhi and King are concerned. King knew that he needed at least a day of silence each week, but it was virtually impossible to partake of this more than a few times because of the pace of his involvement in the movement. Walker referred to King's

44. *The Papers*, 5:436.

45. Wyatt Tee Walker, Foreword to Lewis V. Baldwin, *Never to Leave Us Alone: The Prayer Life of Martin Luther King, Jr.* (Minneapolis: Fortress Press, 2010), vii.

46. *The Papers*, 5:436.

47. See Iyer, ed., *The Essential Writings of Mahatma Gandhi*, 416; and Mahatma Gandhi, *Christian Missions: Their Place in India* (Ahmedabad: Navajivan, 1941), 33, 181–82, 195.

day of silence as a "discipline," but in truth, King never actually developed the discipline of retaining the day of silence.

King knew the importance of regular periods of silence, meditation, and reflection. However, the differences in personality as well as sociocultural contexts between him and Gandhi made it virtually impossible for him to adhere strictly and regularly to some of the criteria for observing brahmacharya. As a Baptist minister, he believed strongly in prayer, and after the experience at the kitchen table one late night during the early weeks of the bus boycott he renewed his faith, trust, and absolute dependency on God. Thereafter he called on God regularly.[48] Although he fasted periodically, he did not, like Gandhi, do so consistently as part of his method for purifying one's self in preparation for nonviolent demonstrations.

Unlike Gandhi, King did not eat in moderation, and he was not a vegetarian. He loved soul food and generally looked for and found it during his travels throughout the country. He did not forego the consumption of alcoholic beverages, nor did he abstain from sex—marital or extramarital. Although King was periodically able to go to the YMCA for physical exercise when he was at home in Atlanta, it cannot be said that he got "plenty of physical exercise," which Gandhi advocated. Indicators are that King was desirous of this, but was often prevented from getting it as a result of his busy schedule of making speeches, engaging in fundraising activities, and a plethora of other movement-related activities.

Although King spoke of the need to undergo "a process of self-purification" at the beginning of the Birmingham campaign, he did not say what that entailed, other than initiating a series of workshops on nonviolence.[49] Interestingly, when King and other leaders talked with student Freedom Riders on May 31, 1961, he said that prior to continuing the ride the students would participate in a workshop "in order to purify themselves and in order to delve deeper into the meaning of the philosophy and method of nonviolence."[50] However, King did not mean the same thing by "purification" that Gandhi meant, since there is no evidence of the student activists undergoing all of the things that Gandhi generally engaged in prior to nonviolent campaigns, such as fasting, praying, silence, and so forth. Gandhi was talking about purifying mind, body, and spirit in preparation for the task ahead. More than anything else, perhaps, place and context made it impossible for King to implement all that a vow of brahmacharya required.

48. *The Papers*, 5:355.

49. King, *Why We Can't Wait* (New York: Harper & Row, 1964), 80.

50. King, Statement on Freedom Rides in Atlanta, May 31, 1961, King Center Library and Archives, 6.

Martin Luther King was most influenced by Gandhi's doctrines of satyagraha and ahimsa, and gave them a place of centrality in his philosophy of nonviolence. According to Gandhi, it is only in the self-purified state that one is able to build the virtue of adhering to the Truth under all circumstances. Although King did not expressly address brahmacharya or even use the term, we just saw that he occasionally sought to live by several of its criteria.

I know of no place where King refers to the vow of fearlessness, and yet there is much evidence that he saw clearly the importance of this for the ordinary human being as well as for one like himself, who was daily involved in a life-threatening ministry. King learned early during the Montgomery bus boycott how important it was to be able to manage the many threats to the lives of himself, his wife, and his children. Indeed, "manage" was about the most that could be expected, since the threats were ubiquitous. Gandhi saw the vow of fearlessness as "indispensable for the growth of the other noble qualities. How can one seek Truth, or cherish Love, without fearlessness?"[51] According to Gandhi, the vow of fearlessness means that one is free of all external fear. Only then is one free to pursue Truth or God. Gandhi seemed to believe that most human beings cannot achieve perfect fearlessness. However, he believed they should strive unrelentingly toward this goal.[52] The vows of nonpossession and nonstealing can aid in this process: "Fear has no place in our hearts," Gandhi maintains, "when we have shaken off attachment for wealth, for family and for the body."[53] We are admonished to enjoy such things, but without an attitude of possession or attachment. After all, Gandhi believed that none of these things belong to any human being, but to God only.

Martin Luther King was certain that fear is part of the human condition, and can serve as a warning that something is wrong. Consequently, he knew that there was no chance that human beings would ever be entirely free of all fears. Indeed, King himself admitted to being afraid for his life at times. But he came to see that by adhering to a number of principles, one could face her fears and live through them, rather than becoming incapacitated by them. He expressed these very ideas in the sermon, "Antidotes for Fear," a version of which was first preached in 1957. In a later version of the sermon, he observed that the point was "not to be rid of fear but rather to harness and master it."[54] But how does one do this? King provided a recipe of four overlapping ingredients.

51. Narayan, ed., *The Selected Works*, 4:232.

52. Ibid., 4:233.

53. Ibid., 4:234.

54. King, *Strength to Love* (New York: Harper, 1963), 110.

The first thing one must do is to be honest enough to admit that some fear is before him, and then "unflinchingly" face up to it. Second, one must then muster the courage to face and live through the fear, even if one cannot overcome it entirely. Courage makes it possible for one to avoid being overwhelmed by a certain fear to the point of becoming incapacitated. In this regard, King said: "Courage is an inner resolution to go forward in spite of obstacles and frightening situations. . . . Courage breeds creative self-affirmation. . . . Courage faces fear and thereby masters it. . . ."[55] Courage requires the power of will to face danger or fear and to press on, regardless. In this regard, King was much influenced by what "the existential philosophers would call 'the courage to be,' that 'in spite of' quality."[56]

A third way that one can master fear is through love; the kind of love that "confronts evil without flinching and shows in our popular parlance an infinite capacity 'to take it.'"[57] King observed that a fourth way to master one's fear is through a positive religious faith. Possession of such faith does not mean that one will not experience fear, pain, or suffering. "Rather, it instills us with the inner equilibrium needed to face strains, burdens, and fears that inevitably come, and assures us that the universe is trustworthy and that God is concerned."[58] In what was perhaps the most frightening experience he had during movement days in the Deep South, King told of the experience he had in Philadelphia, Mississippi on June 21, 1966, when he returned there to lead a memorial service for James Chaney, Michael Schwerner, and Andrew Goodman on the second anniversary of their brutal murders at the beginning of Freedom Summer. The three young civil rights activists were murdered near Philadelphia by Deputy Cecil Price and other Klansmen when they went there to investigate the burning of the Mount Zion Church. When King and marchers reached the courthouse, they were met by Deputy Price, "in customary cowboy hat, sunglasses, and short-sleeved shirt." By this time, a mob had formed and was taunting King and the demonstrators. When Price stopped the group from ascending the steps of the courthouse, King began to speak, telling Price that he knew he was the one who jailed Schwerner, Chaney, and

55. Ibid., 111.

56. King, "Why a Movement," Speech to SCLC Staff Retreat at Frogmore, SC, November 28, 1967, King Library and Archives, 6. Paul Tillich, on whom King wrote half of his doctoral dissertation, actually wrote a book titled *The Courage to Be* (New Haven: Yale University Press, 1952). King included this book in the bibliography of his dissertation.

57. King, *Strength to Love*, 112.

58. Ibid., 115.

Goodman. It was an extremely tense and frightening situation, but King turned and courageously addressed those present.

> "In this county Andrew Goodman, James Chaney, and Mickey Schwerner were brutally murdered. I believe the murderers are somewhere around me at this moment."
>
> "You damn right," King heard Price say, "they're right behind you."
>
> "They ought to search their hearts," King continued. "I want them to know that we are not afraid. If they kill three of us they will have to kill us all. I am not afraid of any man, whether he is in Mississippi or Michigan, Birmingham or Boston. I am not afraid. . . ."[59]

What King did in those moments was courageous beyond words, but he did not hesitate to say later, that that had been one of the most terrifying moments of his life. The atmosphere was so filled with fear that afternoon, it could be sliced with a butter knife. However, King managed to control the fear enough to say what needed to be said. All of this suggests that fearlessness, or the ability to control fear, had special meaning to King, even if he did not make an express vow of it.

Without doubt, Martin Luther King was aware of the importance of brahmacharya in the Gandhian ethic of nonviolence, even though the term does not appear in King's writings and speeches. Moreover, the fact that he attributes several paragraphs to a discussion on what he described as Gandhi's "absolute self-discipline" in his Palm Sunday sermon on March 22, 1959, (not long after he returned from India) bears this out.[60] That King did not cite the term *brahmacharya* does not mean he was not familiar with it and was not influenced by its meaning.

King believed that the result of his formal academic studies must be aimed at finding solutions to racial discrimination, economic injustice, and militarism, all of which caused his people almost unbearable suffering in an ostensibly free and democratic society. As a student, he read voraciously, searching for a sound formal theological foundation for his deepening and widening social conscience. Through formal study, King wanted to affirm whether his religion had something to say to otherwise Christian people who believed that

---

59. Quoted in Seth Cagin and Philip Dray, *We Are Not Afraid: The Story of Goodman, Schwerner, and Chaney, and the Civil Rights Campaign for Mississippi* (New York: Nation Books, 2006 [1988]), 382.

60. *The Papers*, 5:152.

Christianity had nothing at all to say about the massive mistreatment of human beings, other than to urge Christians to stay focused on spiritual matters. We saw in chapter four that while in seminary, King eagerly sought a formal theological foundation for his strong social conscience and convictions. He found this in the writings of the church historian-ethicist/social gospel leader, Walter Rauschenbusch. His search for a method to effectively address the problems of his people led him to the philosophy of nonviolence that was advocated and practiced by Gandhi. The remainder of this chapter focuses on Gandhian elements of nonviolence that influenced King, and how he melded these together with elements more specific to his experience as an Afrikan American Baptist social gospel minister who was reared in the Deep South and was committed to obtaining civil rights and freedom for his people.

Formal Elements of King's Philosophy of Nonviolence

The ethic of nonviolence that was developed and practiced by Martin Luther King is a creative blending of Christian, Hindu, and Afrikan American elements. While there may be additional aspects that others may identify, I find that the following six give us a good sense of the type of nonviolence developed and practiced by King. We will see that this doctrine of nonviolence is based on a sound theological foundation. Once one understands this important point, the Gandhi-King idea that nonviolence is a way of life, or a way of living in the world, is easy to grasp. For it means that this is one's mode of living and operating in the world, from which there are to be no deviations. One becomes for all intents and purposes an absolutist, inasmuch as one vows to live by nonviolence, regardless. What King thought about nonviolence and how human beings should behave in the world actually said a great deal about how he thought about God and God's expectations of us. The components of Kingian nonviolence to be examined include:

- Deep religious faith
- Conviction of the existence of an objective moral order and the idea that the universe hinges on a moral foundation
- Agape
- Sin
- Satyagraha
- Ahimsa

The last two elements are the expressly Gandhian or Hindu contributions, but as we have seen, these terms were not—like the other four elements—explicitly present in King's vocabulary and practice of nonviolence at the beginning of the Montgomery struggle.

Martin Luther King brought something unique to the first four elements in his philosophy and practice of nonviolence. This was quite possibly because he was Afrikan American and Christian and was reared in the Deep South. Therefore, the context in which he did his civil rights ministry was quite different from where and how Gandhi did his work, and consequently he had to treat those four elements as he did.

By the time Martin Luther King was *reintroduced* to Gandhian ideas during the bus boycott, he already had a clear understanding of the first four concepts: deep religious faith, morality of the universe, agape, and sin. He gathered a sense of the meaning and importance of each of these through home and church teachings, was formally introduced to each idea as a student at Morehouse College, and studied them systematically in seminary and during doctoral studies. As we have seen, King may have first heard the Hindu terms *satyagraha* and *ahimsa* at Morehouse, but learned more about them while he was a student in seminary. However, as seen earlier, indicators are that he first studied and applied these concepts in a serious and systematic way only after he met and was tutored by Bayard Rustin and Glenn Smiley during the early weeks of the bus boycott.

After meeting Rustin and Smiley, King read what Gandhi wrote about satyagraha and ahimsa and discussed their deeper meaning and practical implications with the two men. Although in practice he had to adapt Gandhi's ethic of nonviolence to the sociocultural context of the Deep South, King essentially expressed satyagraha and ahimsa in Gandhian terms without substantially altering the meaning these had in the Indian context. What follows is a discussion of the six elements of King's ethic of nonviolence, beginning with the important place of deep religious faith.

Deep Religious Faith

Admitting that he was afraid at times during the early days of the bus boycott, because of the threats against his life and that of his family, King went on to say that by the time his house was bombed he had had "a deep religious experience," and thus was "prepared for almost anything that occurred. I had come to feel, at that time, that in the struggle, God was with me, and through this deep religious experience, I was able to endure and face anything that came my way. Now, I think that still stands with me. After a long process of really giving my whole life to a religious way and to the will of God, I came to feel that, as we struggle together, we have cosmic companionship."[61] King was actually reflecting on the experience at the kitchen table and the vision of having heard a voice consoling and encouraging him to stand up for justice, and promising to be with him always.

Martin Luther King was fundamentally a man of deep religious faith, and was not ashamed of the fact. This is not to say that he was perfect by any means. He was not, and would be the first to say so. Nevertheless, from the time he was a little boy, religious faith and the church were integral parts of his life. King's deep religious faith and love for the church can be traced to his maternal great grandfather, his maternal grandparents, and his paternal grandmother. His parents and maternal grandmother lived a thoroughly Christian life and saw to it that King and his siblings received the best possible guidance toward learning the basic principles of the Christian faith, and the importance of the Christian love ethic in how human beings live and relate in the world. King and his siblings were frequently required to recite verses of Scripture at the dinner table during luscious family meals, and heard numerous biblical stories told by their grandmother. When the children were not at home they were, more often than not, in church, but never far from the long arm of adult supervision as provided by parents and extended family members, including church members. Church was important throughout King's life, in that it helped—despite its imperfections—to keep him centered and grounded. Not surprisingly then, the church played a central role in virtually all that he did in his civil rights ministry. He loved the church deeply, and yet as revealed in many of his sermons he was one of its staunchest critics. Indeed, for King there could be no deep disappointment regarding the church and its practices, where there is no deep love.[62] In addition, as far back as seminary he had said that religion and life were inseparable for him.[63]

From the start of the Montgomery movement, King incorporated the creative use of mass meetings, later called *prayer* meetings in order to keep the focus on the spiritual nature of their undertaking. Another reason for changing the name to "prayer meeting" was to soften the political connotation of the mass meeting, for word had gotten out that the city fathers were planning to outlaw mass meetings. In any event, leaders and supporters of the boycott were not merely engaged in a sociopolitical struggle. It was a struggle between the forces of good and evil. In fact, the Montgomery struggle signaled the importance of spiritual renewal, and the centrality of religious faith in all that

61. *The Papers* (2000), 4:298.

62. King, "Letter from Birmingham Jail," in *Why We Can't Wait*, 95.

63. *The Papers* (1992), 1:363.

the boycotters were seeking to do. Consequently, it was no accident that the prayer meetings were held in local black churches. The southern black church, indeed the prayer meetings, served to encourage spiritual renewal and "spiritual commitment" and provided the lifeblood that was needed to propel the people and the movement forward. King therefore introduced the practice of organizing each meeting around five prayers, "including one for the strength of spirit to be nonviolent."[64] Lewis V. Baldwin has written brilliantly on the significance of prayer for King, as well as the nation and the world.[65]

The prayer meetings remained a pivotal part of the practice of the nonviolent protest demonstrations until King's death. These prayer meetings, with King generally as the featured speaker, probably did more to encourage, energize, and mobilize the protesters than any other single activity. It was here, in the prayer meetings, that the people got fired up, energized, and were urged to endure racial slurs, and later (beginning with the Birmingham movement), high-powered water hoses, the vicious teeth of police attack dogs, rocks, bottles, and such. The prayer meetings helped to lift the spirits of the people and to provide them with that little extra something to encourage them to keep on keeping on, or as King liked to say, "to go on anyhow."

Generally, the prayer meetings followed a basic pattern that was familiar to the vast majority of protesters because they were used to something similar in their respective local churches. The pattern included "songs, prayer, Scripture reading, opening remarks by the president [King], collection, reports from various committees, and a 'pep talk.'"[66] The people usually began singing hymns long before the meetings formally began. Reflecting on the prayer meetings in Montgomery and the importance of singing, King said: "One could not help but be moved by these traditional songs, which brought to mind the long history of the Negro's suffering."[67] Some of those songs were old church hymns; some were Negro Spirituals. The inspirational talks were generally given by ministers representing different denominations. King encouraged this ecumenical dimension from the beginning. The goal was to encourage, energize, and raise the spirit and level of expectation of the people for the day-to-day struggle—to give them what they needed in order to stay in the struggle. Coretta Scott King recalled that the people generally left the meetings feeling renewed and rejuvenated. "And everyone would go home feeling good and

---

64. Taylor Branch, *Parting the Waters: America in the King Years: 1954-1963* (New York: Simon & Schuster, 1988), 178.

65. See Baldwin, *Never to Leave Us Alone.*

66. King, *Stride*, 87.

67. Ibid., 86.

inspired and ready to go back the next morning to a long day of hard work."[68] The prayer meeting fed them; gave them the sustenance to fight on, one more day. "It was something about that experience," said Mrs. King, "that gave all of us so much hope and inspiration, and the more we got into it, the more we had the feeling that something could be done about the situation, that we could change it."[69] At every meeting, the people were reminded to love rather than hate, and to work at developing the capacity to accept and endure suffering and violence rather than return an eye for an eye. Having followed closely the teachings of the Sermon on the Mount, it was not difficult for King to make the later transition to explicitly Gandhian teachings, for there was much that they had in common. For example, both the Sermon on the Mount and Gandhian teachings stressed love, as well as the importance of not returning blows for blows received. This brings up an interesting point. Weeks before King began introducing explicitly Gandhian language and ideas into the prayer meetings, the people were already committed to nonviolence in principle. Was this solely because of the love ethic of the Sermon on the Mount and the fact that all had been taught this at their respective churches? Was there something about the southern black church or black religion itself that caused blacks to be so receptive to the spirit of nonviolence? Was it a result of an amalgam of teachings from the Sermon on the Mount and the black church? Without question, one cannot deny the strong influence of Gandhian nonviolence. But as Nathan Huggins and Lewis Baldwin surmise, there seems to be something about the southern black church experience that made Montgomery blacks and others throughout the South more amenable to Gandhian nonviolence.[70] So Huggins thought that trying to understand nonviolence in relation to the black southern Christian was more interesting than viewing it in relation to the Gandhian connection. Be that as it may, the focus in this chapter is on the Gandhian influence, even as readers are challenged to remember that what happened in those prayer meetings in Montgomery most assuredly helped those in attendance to make the general Gandhian philosophy more easily accessible to them.

68. Quoted in Henry Hampton and Steve Fayer (with Sarah Flynn), *Voices of Freedom: An Oral History of the Civil Rights Movement from the 1950s Through the 1980s* (New York: Bantam, 1990), 30.

69. Quoted in ibid.

70. Nathan I. Huggins posed the issue in his article, "Charisma and Leadership," *The Journal of American History* 74 (September 1987). Here he wrote that Gandhian nonviolence "worked in the southern setting because of the deep tradition of Christian stoicism in the black community" (480). Intrigued by this idea, Baldwin reflected on it at length in, *There Is a Balm in Gilead: The Cultural Roots of Martin Luther King, Jr.* (Minneapolis: Fortress Press, 1991), 185–88.

Mrs. King reflected further on the significant role of the songs in the prayer meetings. They seemed to set the tone for the entire meeting, as well as provide the people what they needed to sustain them throughout the struggle.

> They had an order of service, and so sometimes they would do what you call the long meter. Someone would come and sing, without an instrument at all. Then they would have someone who played the piano or the organ, and they would start, just like they start at the church services. And they would sing the songs and the hymns of the church. "What a Friend We Have in Jesus," "What a Fellowship, What a Joy Divine, Leaning on the Everlasting Arm." They'd sing spirituals like "Lord, I Want to Be a Christian in My Heart," and "Oh, Freedom Over Me, Before I Be a Slave, I'll Be Buried in My Grave, and Go Home to My Lord and Be Free." Or they would sing "Go Down Moses, Way Down in Egypt Land."[71]

The songs, scriptures, and prayers were deliberately selected in order to reinforce the emphasis on nonviolence. They were also chosen for their potential for motivating, inspiring, and reassuring the protesters that God is the God of justice who is ever present with them and working cooperatively with them to achieve freedom and liberation.

The singing, in particular, seemed to hold the people together in the spirit of common cause. From the start, and progressively throughout the movement, especially through the labors of young SNCC activists (beginning) in Albany, Georgia in 1962 and beyond,[72] singing was among the most important aspects of the prayer meetings. From hymns to "Negro" spirituals, singing energized and lifted the spirits of the participants, as well as reminded them of the long history of black suffering (and overcoming!) in the United States, as King himself acknowledged in his book about the Montgomery struggle.[73] Indeed, by the end of the Birmingham campaign in 1963, King was referring to the "freedom songs" as "the soul of the movement."[74] Understandably, the freedom songs were quite valuable and inspirational to early youthful SNCC activists, since they were frequently the shock troops who were the first on the scene in some of the most dangerous places in the Deep South, such as the Mississippi

---

71. Quoted in Hampton and Fayer (with Sarah Flynn), *Voices of Freedom*, 30.

72. See Clayborne Carson, *In Struggle: SNCC and the Black Awakening of the 1960s* (Cambridge, MA: Harvard University Press, 1995 [1981]), 59, 64, 75.

73. King, *Stride*, 86.

74. King, *Why We Can't Wait*, 57.

Delta region, and Selma, Alabama. Leith Mullings and the late prolific Manning Marable remind us that the freedom songs "promoted solidarity, increased faith, expressed sorrow, and strengthened the wills of movement activists."[75]

At any rate, all aspects of the prayer meetings—even before Gandhian ideas were explicitly introduced—were calculated to inspire a sense of the spirit of nonviolent resistance in the attendees. In addition, every inspirational speaker was charged with making nonviolence the central theme of his speech. King was intentional and emphatic about this point, particularly as his own knowledge and understanding of Gandhian nonviolence deepened almost daily after meeting and being advised by Rustin and Smiley. At this writing, I have located no evidence that female inspirational speakers were presented at the prayer meetings. Surely the backstory of this screams to be told.

From the very beginning of King's civil rights ministry, Christian love was the regulating ideal, and remained so throughout. Therefore, King was insistent that all things be done with a certain spirit and attitude. They were to "never assemble with a feeling of a sense of bitterness," he said in a prayer meeting at the Day Street Baptist Church. "We always assemble with deep tones of love in our hearts."[76]

At each prayer meeting, King gave remarks as president of the MIA. He used this occasion to spread the gospel of nonviolence, and to inspire the people to a feeling that victory will come if they do their part and if they persevere. Because of the influence of Rustin and Smiley, every speech that King made at the prayer meetings revealed a deepening of his understanding of Gandhian nonviolence, how it worked, and what was required of proponents. There was also increasing depth to King's theology and his growing conviction that because God has created a moral universe, human beings do better in the world when they behave nonviolently. Implicit in this was his deepening faith that violence and evil only beget violence and evil. At one of the prayer meetings, King told the people in language that was unmistakably Gandhian: "We must meet the forces of hate with the power of love; we must meet physical force with soul force."[77] Of course, the first part of that statement is as much Christian (i.e., the Sermon on the Mount) as Gandhian. King reminded the protesters that their aim must never be to defeat or humiliate white oppressors, but to win their respect and friendship. This too was a Gandhian idea, for Gandhi sought quite intentionally, for example, to win the respect and friendship of the imperialist

75. Manning Marable and Leith Mullings, eds., *Let Nobody Turn Us Around: Voices of Resistance, Reform, and Renewal* (Lanham, MD: Rowman & Littlefield, 2000), 396.

76. *The Papers* (1997), 3:230.

77. King, *Stride*, 87.

British general, Jan Smuts, during the Indian struggle in South Afrika.[78] At the end of a nonviolent campaign, the work of a nonviolent protester is not over. One then has to be intentional about seeking reconciliation with one's opponent. Seeking to be reconciled with one's opponent after the struggle is won is part of the nonviolent process. As we will see, seeking both the respect and friendship of one's enemy is also language that is consistent with the agape love ethic that is so central to King's doctrine of nonviolence.

During the prayer meetings, Martin Luther King and the other pep speakers frequently reiterated the idea that nonviolence at its best is illustrative of Christian love in action. This made sense to those in attendance. Most of the attendees were Christians, and the vast majority of them were willing to at least adhere to nonviolence as a viable strategy for social change, even if they could not accept it as a way of life. Black Christians seemed to know almost instinctively that nonviolence was the Christian way. Besides, they were not generally taught—in the home or in church—to hate and/or be violent toward whites just because they were white, which was quite different from what whites were taught in the home and in too many white churches. This might well be another reason that Deep South blacks resonated so easily to the Gandhian type of nonviolence, for theirs was an ethic of respect for the dignity of human beings as such, rather than for select individuals or groups. Gandhian nonviolence requires such respect for persons.

Nevertheless, that blacks caught the spirit of nonviolence at the prayer meetings was a good beginning and an important first step toward accepting nonviolence as a way of living in the world. Not unlike Gandhi, King came to see that in the deepest sense "nonviolence is ultimately a way of life that men live by because of the sheer morality of its claim."[79] Those who adhere to such a stance are quite likely influenced by the personalistic, Jewish, Christian, Afrikan American stance that the universe itself is founded on morality, and therefore the world works best when people live in accordance with that conviction.

OBJECTIVE MORAL ORDER AND MORAL LAW

It seems to me that most scholars on Martin Luther King have placed far too little emphasis on the significance of this second element of King's doctrine of

---

78. See Mahatma Gandhi, *All Men Are Brothers: Life and Thoughts of Mahatma Gandhi as Told in His Own Words*, compiled and ed. Krishna Kripalani (New York: Columbia University Press, 1960), 97#50, from *The Mind of Mahatma Gandhi*, compiled by R. K. Prabhu and U. R. Rao (London: Oxford University Press, 1945), 46.

79. King, *Stride*, 89.

nonviolence, which focuses on the fundamental morality or goodness of the universe. To assert, as King did, that there exists an objective moral order, and that the universe hinges on a moral foundation, is to express the conviction and faith that things work best for human beings when they comply with moral law and how the universe is constructed. For if the universe is governed by the moral law of love and is founded on morality as King so staunchly believed—since it cannot be demonstrated rationally or proven—it then follows that all human behavior should be in compliance with this rather than with injustice, hatred, selfishness, violence, and oppression. The conviction that the universe is fused with value and therefore is friendly toward the achievement of good in the world, along with King's deep religious faith, are the theological grounding principles of the other elements of his doctrine of nonviolence. King was certain about his conviction that only a God who is fundamentally good and loving could (and would!) establish the world on a moral foundation. If God is the source and sustainer of goodness, justice, and love, and established the universe on a moral foundation, it then becomes possible to say that not only were human beings created for good—to be and to do good—but that things actually work best in the world when done nonviolently or without intentionally harming life in general and human life in particular. To say that we live in a fundamentally moral universe, as King staunchly believed, is to also suggest that we should be intentional about not causing harm to human life.

Although the idea of an objective moral order and moral law were also present in Gandhi's thought, these had a much more prominent place in King's theology generally, and more especially in his mature doctrine of nonviolent resistance to evil. Presently, the best discourse on the doctrine of an objective moral order and moral laws in King's thought is provided in my *God and Human Dignity: The Personalism, Theology, and Ethics of Martin Luther King, Jr.*[80]

King's conviction that reality hinges on a moral foundation,[81] and that there exists an objective moral order and moral laws, is fundamental for theologically grounding his social ethics in general and his ethics of nonviolence in particular. Two important things are implicit in this idea: 1) It provides reason to struggle against injustice and evil, since the grain of the universe is thought to be on the side of justice; and 2) It suggests that the universe is structured such that it provides cosmic companionship for those who wage the battle against injustice. That is, those who fight for freedom

---

80. Rufus Burrow Jr., *God and Human Dignity: The Personalism, Theology, and Ethics of Martin Luther King, Jr.* (Notre Dame: University of Notre Dame Press, 2006), ch. 7, 8.

81. King, "Recovering Lost Values," in *A Knock at Midnight*, ed. Clayborne Carson and Peter Holloran (New York: Warner Books, 1998), 10.

against oppression do not fight alone. If God created a moral universe it must also be the case that God will work cooperatively with intelligent life forms to eradicate injustice and establish justice. The forces of the universe are their daily companions, for freedom fighters.

To believe that the universe is fundamentally good or moral, as King did, is to suggest that human beings ought to strive for goodness, justice, and morality in the world because this is what the world is made for. It implies, moreover, that human beings exist for good and not evil; for justice, and not injustice, even when we choose to behave by doing evil and injustice. In such cases it means that we go against the grain of the universe. If God has established the universe on a moral foundation, it stands to reason that God expects that we will work relentlessly for the creation of goodness and justice in the world, and that we will do it in ways that cause the least harm to human life.

The idea that there is an objective moral order suggests that we need never feel that we are alone in the struggle for social justice and establishing the beloved community. We need not feel that the God of the universe is not concerned about our well-being in the world, for this is a God who is ever present and working with us in the struggle for good. In addition, this principle offers up the idea that the world works better when human beings strive to comply with moral law, more specifically the law of love. Before continuing, it will be instructive to consider the sources of King's conviction that the universe hinges on a moral foundation.

SOURCES OF KING'S CONVICTION ABOUT THE MORAL ORDER

The very fact that Martin Luther King or any human being engages in moral judgment implies that an objective moral order exists; exists independently of specific individuals whether they are aware of it or want it to exist or not. The individual does not make or invent this order, but discovers it. It is given. This is what it means to be an *objective* moral order. It does not just exist for or say something only about the individual making moral judgments. It is not just a psychological fact in a single individual, and thus to this extent is not subjective. It is objective in the sense that it exists independently of me and is discoverable and true for every rational being who consciously seeks to discover it, much like the scientist who endeavors to discover the laws of physics. Individual and group actions are frequently wrong or sinful in light of the moral law, and thus the latter does not reside in the individual or the group. Since law has meaning only for intelligence or mind (i.e., for personal beings), and is appreciated by such, it is conceivable that the source of moral law is a Supreme Mind, the giver or Source of moral law.

The first source of King's conviction that the universe hinges on moral order or a moral foundation is his interpretation of the Christian faith and his understanding of God based on that interpretation. Reared in the southern black Baptist church, King believed in a creator God whose nature is fundamentally love. As such, he believed all things created by God to be essentially good. Indeed, the biblical account of the creation affirms: "God saw everything that he had made, and indeed, it was very good" (Gen. 1:31). One may reason from this that as a loving and rational being, God created the world according to basic fundamental laws that were given, such as the physical law of gravity. One may surmise that because God wanted the world to operate in a certain way and because God's nature is love, moral law was inserted when God created the world. Because God is love, we may further surmise that the highest moral law is love. As such, God created the world that "was very good" to operate in ways consistent with love and goodness. Indeed, why would Love (God) create the world to operate in any other way?

One who accepts this line of reasoning, as Martin Luther King most assuredly did, must also believe that when decisions are made and actions engaged in that are contrary to this, bad things happen. Indeed, King frequently reminded his parishioners that God created the world to operate in a certain way. "There is a law in the moral world—which reminds us that life will work only in a certain way," he said. "The Hitlers and the Mussolinis have their day, and for a period they may wield great power, spreading themselves like a green bay tree, but soon they are cut down like the grass and wither as the green herb."[82] Arguing against the ethical relativism of Communism, King went on to say that "Christianity sets forth a system of absolute moral values and affirms that God has placed within the very structure of this universe certain moral principles that are fixed and immutable. The law of love as an imperative is the norm for all of man's actions."[83] King believed that at the center of the Christian faith is the belief in a God who is the source and ground of all there is and who created and sustains moral law and moral values.

This biblical, black church stance was confirmed for King during his student days at Morehouse College. Benjamin E. Mays recalled that often after his Tuesday chapel talks, King would remain to ask him questions and to discuss various things he had said. Undoubtedly, many of the things that Mays said in those chapel talks were informed by what he had written in his classic text, *The Negro's God as Reflected in His Literature* (1938). In this book, Mays determined

---

82. King, "Our God Is Able," in *Strength to Love*, 103.
83. King, "How Should a Christian View Communism," in *Strength to Love*, 95.

that according to black religious faith God is believed to be on the side of the oppressed, and that God will "eventually bring to judgment those who continue to violate His laws."[84] Historically, blacks lived by the conviction that no matter what happens, God is present and will take care of them. God is on the side of right, and thus "will bring things out victoriously,"[85] said Mays. Because God's laws are against the oppression and enslavement of blacks, God rejects these practices as contrary to the requirement that persons love others as they love themselves and God. King was most certainly exposed to these ideas through Mays's chapel talks, and in private conversations with him. As far back as his Morehouse days, then, King possessed a strong sense of the existence of an objective moral order and moral laws that govern the universe.

King sometimes reverted to religious and biblical language to further clarify his thinking about the objective moral order and moral law. That Easter followed Good Friday, for example, was proof to him that the universe is on the side of the forces of justice, goodness, and right. According to Christianity, King said, "Good Friday may occupy the throne for a day, but ultimately it must give way to the triumphant beat of the drums of Easter."[86] Since he believed that moral law is at the core of the universe, it was an easy move for him to conclude that love will have the final say, no matter what happens on a day-to-day basis in the world. Evil may occupy the throne for a day, but in the final analysis love–justice will prevail. For King, Christianity "says to us sometimes a vicious mob may take possession and crucify the most meaningful and sublime and noble character of human history. It says to us that one day that same Jesus will rise up and split history into A.D. and B.C. so that history takes on a new meaning."[87] Similarly, King conceded that even the satanic may have its day, but devilish wishes and practices must ultimately give way to the highest. "A mythical Satan," said King in a sentence that editors deleted from one of his published sermons, "through the work of a conniving serpent, may gain the allegiance of a man for a period, but ultimately he must give way to the magnetic redemptive power of a humble servant on an uplifted cross."[88]

Another source of King's conviction that the universe hinges on a moral foundation is his study of the philosophy of personalism. He first studied this philosophy under George W. Davis at Crozer Theological Seminary. Because

84. Benjamin E. Mays, *The Negro's God as Reflected in His Literature* (New York: Atheneum, 1969 [1938]), 126.

85. Ibid., 189.

86. *The Papers*, 6:288.

87. Ibid., 6:288–89.

88. Ibid., 6:506.

of his desire to study personalism systematically under Edgar S. Brightman, then the premier personalist philosopher in the United States, King chose to do doctoral work at Boston University. Under Brightman he studied the personalist approach to the philosophy of religion, and criticisms of it. When Brightman died unexpectedly, L. Harold DeWolf, a protégé and former student, became King's major professor and advisor. Under DeWolf, King studied personalism systematically, having enrolled in his class on personalism. Through his study, King learned that belief in the objectivity of value and in an objective moral order roots deep in the history of personalism. He studied and was influenced by several books written by Brightman that gave focused attention to the idea of an objective moral order. These include but are not limited to *Religious Values* (1925) and *Moral Laws* (1933).

In *Religious Values*, Brightman argued for the objectivity of value, saying that moral experience itself "give us clews [*sic*] to an objective and law-abiding value-order, which, in turn, can be real only in and for a personal God. In each case the ground for our belief in the existence of an objective order is the fact that there is experience given which is capable of being organized into a coherent system, in some sense common to all and accessible to all."[89] The very fact that we humans have moral experience "point[s] to a real objective order of value in the universe, just as truly as the laws of nature point to an objective natural order, and for the same sort of reason, namely, the appeal to the logical ideal of reasonableness."[90] Arguing for the objectivity of value and moral law, Brightman held that our experience of value, our conceptions of justice, love, truth, and so forth "point to and presuppose an ideal standard to which they ought to conform."[91] Values are as real as the laws of nature. As objective, values exist "as purposes of the Divine Mind."[92] Brightman develops similar arguments in his book *Moral Laws*.[93]

A personalist, King agreed with the idea that belief in an objective moral order and moral law opens the way to belief in God, "without whom that law would have no significant being. If we believe in the law we must also believe in the conditions which make the law possible."[94] According to King, God is the chief condition or source making moral law possible. As such, God guides, but does not coerce, human destiny and the destiny of the world. King argued

89. Edgar S. Brightman, *Religious Values* (New York: Abingdon, 1925), 110.

90. Ibid., 168.

91. Ibid., 169.

92. Ibid.

93. Edgar S. Brightman, *Moral Laws* (New York: Abingdon, 1933), 285–86.

94. David Elton Trueblood, *Philosophy of Religion* (New York: Harper & Brothers, 1957), 115.

that one who lives by this conviction and who believes that this same God "has planted in the fiber of the universe an inexorable moral law that is as abiding as the physical laws . . . will act like it."[95] One who claims to believe that God has established moral laws but then lives and behaves in a contrary way lives a lie.

Martin Luther King lived by the *faith* (for he knew it could not be proved with mathematical certainty) that we live in a moral universe, and that there are moral laws that are just as abiding and demanding of our compliance as physical laws (such as the law of gravity). Failure to comply with moral laws—the most significant of which is love—can have as detrimental and catastrophic consequences as the failure to comply with the physical laws of the universe. King argued that we do not doubt that there are physical laws that govern certain behaviors. For example, we don't—when we are in our right mind—jump from the summit of Mount Everest for the fun of it. The consequences for doing so will be devastating. Likewise, if we fail to adhere to the moral law of love we suffer harsh consequences. Indeed, the consequences of the enslavement of blacks in the U.S. continue to hound not only present-day blacks, but the sons and daughters of white enslavers. God "has placed within the very structure of this universe certain absolute moral laws," said King. "We can neither defy nor break them. If we disobey them, they will break us."[96] For proof of this, one need merely consider the humanly contrived devastating tragedies around the world, tragedies caused by hatred, greed, and exorbitant self-interest at the expense of other human groups, the environment, and so on. King believed that although the manifestations of various oppressions may seem to carry the day, the universe has been so constructed that "truth will ultimately conquer its conqueror."[97]

Martin Luther King was convinced that Easter was coming in race and class relations. He was also confident that Easter was coming in the relations between nations. This optimism was based on his fundamental conviction that the universe is built on a moral foundation, which is to say that goodness and justice will have the final say. This faith conviction easily led to King's strong belief that love makes the world go around, and is at the center of nonviolence. One who lives by such a conviction can only be committed to absolute nonviolence. Such a person permits no exceptions. This is a good segue to the third element in King's philosophy of nonviolence.

95. *The Papers* (2007), 6:171.
96. King, "Our God Is Able," in *Strength to Love*, 105.
97. Ibid.

AGAPE

Although Gandhi said much about love, it was Martin Luther King who more thoroughly defined and integrated the concept of agape into the theory of nonviolence in a way that gave it a more distinctly Christian flavor. This was relatively easy to do since he had begun his civil rights ministry by focusing on the love imperative in the Sermon on the Mount. It is reasonable to say that King's infusion of agape Christianized the doctrine of nonviolence, which is one reason he characterized nonviolence as Christianity in action. But perhaps even more important, agape gave nonviolence a more expressly theological grounding, for King understood God to be not only the source of agape, but agape itself, from which all of the various forms of love flow. Agape is also the means by which love is instilled into the hearts and souls of human beings. King was in full agreement with John's claim that God is love, and that human beings love precisely because God first loved us (1 John 4:7-19). "I have discovered that the highest good is love," King said in "Paul's Letter to American Christians." He went on to say: "This principle is at the center of the cosmos. It is the great unifying force of life. God is love. He who loves has discovered the clue to the meaning of ultimate reality. . . ."[98]

It is of interest to point out that although we find numerous discussions of the three types of Greek love (eros, philia, and agape) in King's speeches, sermons, and writings, the postdoctoral King does not credit the influence of Swedish theologian Anders Nygren (1890–1978) regarding his understanding of agape. Although as a doctoral student King wrote an essay for DeWolf's class in Systematic Theology that included a brief discussion on Nygren,[99] he primarily depended on a secondary source (Walter Marshall Horton, *Contemporary Continental Theology*, 1938), rather than Nygren's important massive classic text, *Agape and Eros*.[100] At this time, I know of no place where King expressly states that Nygren influenced his understanding of agape. Furthermore, I know of no place that indicates that King actually read Nygren, even though he referenced his name and book on a few occasions during his formal academic training. This is rather puzzling, considering that Smith and Zepp contend that Nygren's book was one of three supplemental texts in King's course with Smith in his senior year in seminary, Christianity and Society. Not unlike me, both men thought it "strange that King never mentions Nygren by

---

98. King, "Paul's Letter to American Christians," in *Strength to Love*, 133.

99. *The Papers* (1994), 2:127.

100. Ibid., 2:127–28. Here we find that all of King's citations on Nygren were from Walter Marshall Horton, *Contemporary Continental Theology: An Interpretation for Anglo-Saxons* (New York: Harper, 1938), 163–65.

name in any of his published works,"[101] especially since he frequently described agape in Nygrenian language. But unlike me, it seems that Smith and Zepp were not apprehensive about assuming that King actually read Nygren's book. After all, it was included as a supplemental text in Smith's course. It is therefore assumed that King read the book. Anyone who has taught in the theological academy as long as I have is aware that students generally do not read supplemental texts, unless the instructor requires an assignment(s) based specifically on such books. And even in such a case, it is naïve to assume that most students will read the entire text. In any event, King mentioned Nygren and his book in a paper written for Davis's course, Christian Theology for Today, but did not actually elaborate and discuss his ideas.[102] Had King actually read Nygren's book and pondered his view of agape, there is no question that his understanding of it would have been even deeper and richer, and his theological grounding of the idea would have been on an even more solid foundation. Before proceeding, it should be noted that it appears that King's postgraduate orations on agape, eros, and philia were much influenced by a Harry Emerson Fosdick book, *On Being Fit to Live With*.[103] The language that King uses in his own discussions of the terms is very similar to Fosdick's, but he does not inform the reader of this. Before going further, it will be instructive to discuss Nygren's understanding of agape.

NYGREN'S VIEW OF AGAPE

In his massive classic text, *Agape and Eros*, Nygren systematically and painstakingly discusses the relationship between the agape and eros motifs from the time of the early church, to Augustine's synthesis of the two in *caritas* (love to God), to Luther's smashing of that synthesis by radically reforming the Christian idea of love. So we may reasonably think of *Augustine as the great synthesizer*, and *Luther as the great reformer* of the Christian idea of love.[104] Nygren saw Luther's as a thoroughly theocentric idea of love. Accordingly he writes:

> *Against the egocentric attitude which had come to mark the Catholic conception of love, Luther sets a thoroughly theocentric idea of love.* When

---

101. Kenneth Smith and Ira Zepp Jr., *Search for the Beloved Community: The Thinking of Martin Luther King Jr.* (Valley Forge, PA: Judson, 1974), 63.

102. *The Papers* (1992), 1:267.

103. Ibid. (2007), 6:425n16.

104. Anders Nygren, *Agape and Eros*, trans. Philip S. Watson [single-volume edition] (Philadelphia: Westminster, 1953), 560, 681, 692.

Luther wishes to say what love in the Christian sense is, he draws his picture not from our love, not from the realm of human love at all, but from God's love, especially as this has been revealed in Christ. But this love is not an acquisitive love [as Augustine claimed all love to be], but a love that gives.[105]

God's love, according to Luther, is a thoroughly giving love, which implies that one is to focus little, if at all, on self-love. The real focus should be on God, not human beings. For Luther then, "the real subject of Christian love is not man, but God Himself."[106] Agape does not seek its own, as human love does. Rather, it is a thoroughly giving and self-sacrificing love, as represented in Paul's words in Rom. 5:8: "But God proves his love for us in that while we still were sinners Christ died for us," a text that Luther exploited to the fullest as he distinguished between human and divine love.

Therefore, human beings' relationship with God is solely on the basis of sin. Nygren contends that "in Luther a Copernican revolution takes place, and fellowship with God now becomes a fellowship on our human level. In an acutely pointed paradox, Luther's conception might be expressed by the formula, 'Fellowship with God on the basis of sin, not of holiness.'"[107] The basis of human fellowship with God is God's spontaneous love gushing forth, and "justification is the justification of the sinner, the Christian is 'simul iustus et peccator.' It is above all this last—Luther's assertion of the sinfulness remaining even in the justified man—which has caused offence in Catholic circles."[108]

At least six of Nygren's ideas about agape appear in numerous places in King's writings and speeches. I list these[109] before offering a more thorough discussion of agape.

- Since God is the source, and agape flows directly from God to the human heart, it is the love of God operating in the human heart (733–34). Consequently, the love that the Christian gives is only that which she has received from God (734). She is merely the conduit or channel through which God's love flows to her neighbor (735). It is a thoroughly self-giving love.

105. Nygren, *Agape and Eros*, 683.

106. Ibid., 734.

107. Ibid., 684.

108. Ibid., 690.

109. Unless otherwise noted, the numbers in parenthesis in this section are to Anders Nygren, *Agape and Eros*, trans. Philip S. Watson [single-volume edition] (Philadelphia: Westminster, 1953).

- Agape is spontaneous, free, and unmotivated (726–29). No human action is needed for God's love to come gushing forth. There is nothing that you or I can do to earn God's love. Agape has nothing to do with the object, as such, but finds its source in God alone. To be recipient of agape, fellowship with God is all that is required.
- Agape is overflowing, needing nothing (outside God) to set it in motion (730).
- Agape is not selective of its object, that is, it takes no thought of its object, of whether one is godly or ungodly, good or bad (730–31). Agape is the same, whether directed toward the godly or the ungodly. It is no respecter of persons. This is illustrated in the biblical text: "For he makes his sun rise on the evil and on the good, and sends rain on the righteous and on the unrighteous" (Matt. 5:45). In this sense, agape is *disinterested*, and thus is most supremely manifested in love for the enemy (731). It is therefore equivalent to enemy-love, an idea (we will see) that was important in Søren Kierkegaard's writings on love.
- Agape is unceasing. God does not cut it off (732), which means that it is always available to anybody who seeks and is open to receive it. It is available and flowing even before one asks for it; even if one never asks for it. One need merely place self in the path of agape and be open to receive it.
- Agape is primarily God's love. God is Agape (740). "Even when it is attributed to man, Agape is patterned on Divine love" (210). In John's first letter we are told that "love is from God," and "God is love" (1 John 4:7, 8). Because God is Agape, God alone brings about agape in the world. "Since God is Agape," Nygren writes, "everyone who is loved by Him and has been gripped and mastered by His love cannot but pass on this love to his neighbour" (216). Agape is not generated by human beings, "but it has come to us from heaven," (733) descending from God to human beings. So when Martin Luther King insists that love is at the center of nonviolence, he is saying something quite profoundly theological, for this love is of, and from, God. Indeed, this love *is* God. It is not far-fetched to say that God (Love) is at the center of the Kingian type of nonviolence. In any case, this love, according to Nygren—Christian love—"is through and through a Divine work" (734). Here we see the strong influence of Luther.

Although Nygren does not say it, we should remember that the idea of God as philia (or friend) is also found in the Second Testament. Therefore, despite what Nygren implies, what he says about agape should not be taken to mean that it is the only form of love in the Bible and the Christian tradition. Although scholars seem to believe that the preponderance of the evidence suggests a preference for agape, as the way to characterize God in the Second Testament, it is just as clear that philia, the type of love shared between friends, is also a prominent description of God in the Bible. According to some biblical scholars, it is not even clear that the Second Testament makes a precise distinction between agape and philia.[110] Consequently, there is biblical evidence of God as philia as well as agape. As far as we know, there is no evidence of eros (sexual love) in the Second Testament.[111] At the very least then, to say that God is agape means that God is the fundamental source, sustainer, and continuer of love in the world, such that the agape we humans practice in the world is derived solely from God. Human beings are but the conduits of such love, which flows down to us directly from God.

NYGREN THROUGH KING'S EYES

Martin Luther King liked Nygren's idea of agape as "a lost love." For even when deceived a thousand times, the conveyor of such love is obligated to keep seeking and loving those who persist in rejecting or turning away from love. King spoke and wrote similarly about nonviolence. No matter how many times the nonviolent resister is pelted with stones or otherwise treated violently and inhumanely, she is expected to stay the nonviolent course, accepting blows without retaliation; indeed preferring to receive blows than deliver them.

The concept of agape is central to the type of social ethics and nonviolence advocated and practiced by Martin Luther King. Although love is also prominent in Gandhian thought, it is *the* basic ethical category in Christianity. Nonviolence requires that one courageously confront and resist evil and injustice, and also that one do so in the spirit of love. The King type of nonviolence, then, is grounded in love. But as he so often said, it is not a weak or sentimental kind of love that is required. "It is a very stern love that would organize itself into collective action to right a wrong by taking on itself suffering."[112] Interestingly, Richard Gregg, author of *The Power of Non-violence* (1935, 1944, 1959), wrote similarly about the type of love that was central to how he viewed nonviolence. "This love must be strong and clear-sighted,

---

110. See Karl Paul Donfried, "Love," in *HarperCollins Bible Dictionary*, ed. Paul J. Achtemeier (New York: HarperCollins, 1996 [1985]), 625–27. Reacting to a lecture I was giving in my course, Prophetic and Ethical Witness of the Church, a student, Julie Osborne, called attention to the presence of philia in the Second Testament, arguing that agape was not the only biblical form of love.

111. Donfried, "Love," in *HarperCollins Bible Dictionary*, 625.

112. King, "My Trip to the Land of Gandhi," in *A Testament of Hope*, 26.

not mawkish or sentimental. It does not state or hint that it is going to 'do good to' the other person, nor does it make a parade of itself," he said. "It must be patient and full of insight and understanding and imagination. It must be enduring, kind and unselfish."[113] Although King would have agreed with this characterization of the love that was central to his thought and practice of nonviolence, he would not have agreed with Gregg's claim that this type of love was not "exceedingly rare," but quite prevalent in the world.[114] The major difference between the two men's thinking about love is that King saw it as grounded in the God of his faith. Gregg did not think of love theologically to the extent that King did.

The love that is required, that is at the center of Kingian nonviolence, is agape. It is precisely this that makes the Christian ethic so very difficult to live out in practice, for as King said during the Montgomery movement, "[I]t [Christianity] demands a dangerous and costly altruism"—not just love of self, but love of the neighbor.[115] It is this type of love that makes Christianity serious business indeed. One need not look long and far to see just how difficult it is to live out the true meaning of Christian love for the neighbor. Christian agape, according to King, is the highest good, "the most durable power," and the "heartbeat of the moral universe."[116] King knew that it is quite possible for one to engage in pragmatic nonviolence without possessing the spirit of love; without even believing in God. However, one who is committed to nonviolence as a way of life understands that agape is the key element and the agape spirit must be exhibited throughout.

Long before reading Gandhi, Martin Luther King knew much about love and what it requires. It was the chief principle on which the Montgomery bus boycott was based from beginning to end, and continued to be the regulating ideal in every civil rights campaign led by King. Indeed, after reading about Gandhi's doctrine of satyagraha, King concluded that agape was implicit in it, which may be another reason that Gandhian nonviolence so easily appealed to southern blacks. It had a ring of familiarity to it. King broadened and deepened the concept of nonviolence, giving it a more Christian character by placing agape at the center. Furthermore, so central is agape to King's doctrine of nonviolence that he often does not discuss it without also discussing the meaning of love.

113. Richard Gregg, *The Power of Non-Violence* (New York: Fellowship Publications, 1944 [1935]), 52.

114. Ibid.

115. *The Papers*, 6:252.

116. Ibid., 6:291.

We have seen that the deepest roots of King's thinking about agape may be traced to his family upbringing and his experience in the black church. More specifically, one of his earliest encounters with agape—that love that takes no thought of its object and expects nothing in return—was when, at age six, his mother placed him on her lap; gave him his first race relations history; told him that he was as good as anybody; and admonished that he was bound by Christian teachings to return love for hate. One must love the other, regardless of who he is and what he has done. The young boy was to love those racist white parents who caused him so much pain by taking away his boyhood friend. This was an impossible task for a child, but it was one of King's earliest lessons on the deeper meaning of love and its requirement of giving, self-sacrifice, and redemptive suffering.

Like Nygren, King viewed agape as disinterested love, which means that it gives no thought to *who* the object is, and it expects nothing in return. It has no concern for *who* the neighbor is. It loves regardless, and it does so spontaneously. "Christian love," according to Nygren, "is the same whether it is directed to the godly or the ungodly, 'just as the gold remains gold whether the good or the bad get it.'"[117] Agape is not determined or limited by the object, whether one loves or hates. It is available regardless, even to white racist parents who forbid their children to be friends with black children because of race. This is the type of love that King's mother taught him about when he was a boy.

The epitome of disinterested love is thought to be found in the concept of *enemy-love*. One who possesses this kind of love knows that he can expect nothing in return from his enemy. Disinterested love, said King, "is a love in which the individual seeks not his own good, but the good of his neighbor (1 Cor. 10:24). *Agape* neither begins nor ends by discriminating between worthy and unworthy people, or any qualities that people possess. Rather, it begins and continues by loving others *for their sakes*. It is an entirely 'neighbor-regarding concern for others,' which discovers the neighbor in every man it meets."[118]

King's characterization of agape as *disinterested love* was much influenced by the late Paul Ramsey whose text, *Basic Christian Ethics*, was required reading in the course on Christianity and Society with Kenneth Smith in the spring term of King's senior year in seminary.[119] According to Ramsey, the Christian ethic is based, not on one's own, but the good of one's neighbor (1 Cor. 10:24), and the ideal of neighbor love as expressed in the parable of the Good Samaritan

117. Nygren, *Agape and Eros*, 730.

118. King, "An Experiment in Love," in *A Testament of Hope*, 19.

119. Smith and Zepp, *Search for the Beloved Community*, 62.

(Luke 10:29-37). Ramsey argued that the parable tells us nothing about the neighbor as such. Rather, the real subject of the text is neighbor love. The focus is on the questioner becoming a neighbor, not whether one is worthy of being loved. This took the focus off the nature of the object to be loved, and placed the emphasis on expressing love for the neighbor. The parable is significant for Ramsey because it "actually shows the nature and meaning of Christian love which alone of all ethical standpoints discovers the neighbor because it alone begins with neighborly love and not with discriminating between worthy and unworthy people according to the qualities they possess."[120] One who discriminates in this way cannot pass the test for disinterested love.

Paul Ramsey was inspired by Søren Kierkegaard's discussion on the idea of a completely unselfish or disinterested love.[121] To test the presence of such love, one need only be attentive to how one behaves toward an enemy, or even more, the dead. Generally one expects nothing from an enemy, and the deceased can give absolutely nothing in return, can "make no repayment," said Kierkegaard, who writes further:

> If one wants to make sure that love is completely unselfish, he eliminates every possibility of repayment. But precisely this is eliminated in the relationship to one who is dead. If love nevertheless remains, it is in truth unselfish. . . .
>
> If, therefore, you wish to test for yourself whether or not you love disinterestedly, note sometimes how you relate yourself to one who is dead.[122]

King argued that "the best way to assure oneself that love is disinterested is to have love for the enemy-neighbor from whom you can expect no good in return, but only hostility and persecution."[123] This is precisely the type of love that King's doctrine of nonviolence requires of its proponents.

In any event, Anders Nygren argued that agape is superior to all other forms of love and is the "most powerful and creative force in the universe," a point that King readily adopted. It is a love that is not produced by human beings, but has its fundamental source in God, and thus comes down to humans from heaven. This is a love that is totally outpouring, whether its objects

120. Paul Ramsey, *Basic Christian Ethics* (New York: Charles Scribner's Sons, 1950), 93.

121. See ibid., ch. 3; and Søren Kierkegaard, *Works of Love*, trans. Howard and Edna Hong (New York: Harper Torchbooks, 1962), ch. 9.

122. Kierkegaard, *Works of Love*, 320, 322.

123. King, "An Experiment in Love," in *A Testament of Hope*, 19.

are the victims of the Virginia Tech tragedy on April 16, 2007; the Aurora, Colorado theater massacre of June 2012; the mass murders of twenty elementary school children and seven adults in Newtown, Connecticut on December 17, 2012; the murders and severe injuries caused by the Boston Marathon bombers in 2013; or whether the object is the perpetrator of those tragedies. Theologically, God intends for *every* person to be a recipient of God's ever-flowing, inexhaustible love—regardless. It is up to us to decide whether or not to receive that love and to live in ways that are consistent with it.

While the Montgomery bus boycott was still under way, in 1956, Martin Luther King described agape as "that high type of love" that exemplifies "understanding good will," "seeks nothing in return," and "loves the person who does the evil deed," while hating the deed.[124] Not only is agape understanding goodwill for all human beings and seeks nothing in return, but it is also "redemptive love," the "love of God working" within human beings. One who possesses this love doesn't love because there is something about the object as such, as in the case of eros. Rather, for King, one loves self or the neighbor simply because "God loves them." One loves self and the neighbor because she is of inestimable worth to God, because God loves her, and because God loves those she loves as well as those she may not love. Agape is directed even toward that which is deemed unlovable or behaves as if it has no value, such as the perpetrators in the aforementioned shooting massacres and bombing, and the racist thugs who violently assaulted nonviolent demonstrators on the civil rights trail. Only agape seeks out the sinner, and loves her! This is truly an unbelievable love, albeit the one to which King was thoroughly committed.

Indeed, the nature of agape is such that in reaching out to an object it actually imbues it with value. King believed that "this is the type of love that can redeem. It is a transforming love. . . . It is a love that can change individuals. It can change nations. It can change conditions."[125] The point of significance for King's doctrine of nonviolence is that agape *loves in spite of*; it loves because every person is a child of God, and it loves even those who behave like the enemy or haters of humanity. It does not calculate the worth or lack of worth of the object. Agape loves the William Gayles (mayor of Montgomery during the bus boycott), the Bull Connors (commissioner of public safety during the Birmingham campaign), the racist hooligans who severely beat the Freedom Riders in Anniston, Alabama and blew up their bus; as well as the Alabama state police and Sheriff Jim Clark and his deputized thugs who brutally beat and tear-gassed nonviolent demonstrators on the Pettus Bridge in Selma in what came

124. *The Papers* (1997), 3:306.
125. Ibid., 3:327.

to be known as "Bloody Sunday"; loves them even as it requires that justice be done.

Agape seeks out the other. It is not passive; does not wait for the victims to reach out for help. It sees the injustice being done and spontaneously begins the process of engaging it. It is, according to Emil Brunner's interpretation of Nygren, "like a spring gushing out or coming forth."[126] Agape is that love which spontaneously floods toward the other, and takes no thought of whether he is righteous or unrighteous, worthy or unworthy. To this extent agape is disinterested, and thus expects nothing in return. It is purely divinely inspired and caused.

One does not fully understand the significance of agape for Martin Luther King's doctrine of nonviolence if one does not understand his agreement with Nygren *and* the black church tradition: that because God's love for persons is unselfish, free, unmotivated, unceasing, spontaneous, overflowing, takes no thought of its object, and is supremely manifested in love for one's enemies, it is incumbent upon human beings to love each other in the same way.[127] The logic of agape pushes us to accept the corollary—that we are to love persons just because they are persons, belong to, and are loved by God.

This is a much different type of love than that expressed in Jean-Paul Sartre's play, *Dirty Hands*. Here we find a dialogue between the characters Hugo and Hœderer in which the former wonders why he should love others when they do not love him. He then declares that it is not what human beings are that interests him, "but what they can become."[128] This prompts Hœderer's response: "And I, I love them for what they are. With all their filth and all their vices."[129] Agape is expressed in neither stance when taken by itself. However, when the two are taken together it becomes a view that moves in the direction of agape. Agape is the love that requires us to love human beings *both* for who they are right now, and for who and what they can become when they strive toward the best and the highest. In the agape sense, this is in part what it must mean to love persons just because they are persons and are loved by and belong to God. Agape requires that we love persons both for who they are, and just as importantly for who they can become. We love them with all their filth and vices (as Hœderer put it), but agape drives us to believe that they can be better than they are. So we love them also for what they can become. Because persons

---

126. Emil Brunner, *Faith, Hope, and Love* (Philadelphia: Westminster, 1956), 64.

127. Nygren, *Agape and Eros*, 727, 730, 731.

128. Jean-Paul Sartre, *Dirty Hands*, in *No Exit and Three Other Plays* (New York: Vintage, 1949), 225.

129. Sartre, *Dirty Hands*, 225.

are conduits of God's agape, God expects that they will both convey and *do* love to each other.

According to Martin Luther King, one *can* love his enemies, and those who have treated him unjustly. One can do this because of the love of God within him and the love of God within the enemy. Therefore, blacks can love whites who are racists precisely because of God's agape (or the love of God in blacks *and* in white racists). Love in this sense is "the highest Good," "the *summum bonum*," "the most durable power in the world," as King liked to say.[130]

Agape was for King a thoroughly communal or relational principle. That is, persons are not created to exist in isolation. Instead, they are created by Agape, that is, the God who is Love. Love is a relational category, and thus human beings are created in and for relationship and community with God and each other. Agape always seeks to create, preserve, and enhance community. Moreover, agape goes hand in hand with satyagraha and ahimsa in that all three concepts focus on a kind of strict self-discipline and a willingness to intentionally avoid causing harm to another.

Although King once preached a sermon, in 1962, in which he named and discussed six levels of love,[131] there is no question that for him agape is the far superior type. He also understood the value of eros and persons' desire to be loved just because they are persons. For King, self-love was a significant part of agape, necessarily included in it.

Agape is not an easy kind of love to consistently apply and live. Indeed history, as well as Reinhold Niebuhr, have shown that it is virtually impossible to achieve all that agape requires in interpersonal, let alone in group or corporate relations. Agape is a costly and dangerous sort of love, inasmuch as it willingly risks everything, including one's life, to save the neighbor, as in the parable of the Good Samaritan.[132] This is not the type of love to which the weak and faint of heart will consistently adhere. King learned this early in his civil rights ministry. This is why it was so essential for would-be nonviolent protesters to undergo intensive training *before* being allowed to participate in the nonviolent demonstrations. They had to be taught and trained—as far as possible—to love their opponents, while at the same time not retaliating when violence of any kind was done to them.

---

130. King, "Paul's Letter to American Churches," in *Strength to Love*, 133.

131. See King's sermon, "Levels of Love" in *The Papers*, 6:437–45. The six types of love he preached on are: Utilitarian, Eros, Motherly Love, Philia, Humanitarian, and Agape.

132. King, "On Being a Good Neighbor," in *Strength to Love*, 19.

King's Disagreement with Nygren

Martin Luther King did not uncritically accept the totality of Nygren's view of agape. For example, he was in sharp disagreement with Nygren's rejection of self-love[133] and his stance that agape "starts with the conviction of one's own lack of worth."[134] Although Nygren presented the idea that eros begins with the conviction of the worth of the soul, he then rejected this type of love as inferior to the fundamentally Christian type.[135] He thus repudiated the idea of self-love. King rejected the Nygrenian view that agape excludes self-love, that the Christian ethic "does not recognise self-love as a legitimate form of love,"[136] and that agape begins with one's lack of conviction of one's own worth.[137] King did not accept Luther's (and John Calvin's!) teaching that self-love is sinful.[138] Perhaps because of his black southern heritage, his deep rootedness in the black church, and his firsthand experiences of racism, he understood the Christian message differently. King was too much of a personalist to downplay the importance of self-love, and particularly for a people whose sense of humanity was so frequently terrorized that many seemed to lack self-love.

Philosophically, King believed every person to be sacred and of infinite worth in herself. *Theologically*, he declared that persons as such possess inherent worth and are sacred because they have etched into their being the image of God. They are precious and sacred because they belong to and are precious and sacred to God. Affirming the inalienable sacredness of every person, King said: "Every man is somebody because he is a child of God. . . . Man is a child of God, made in His image, and therefore must be respected as such."[139] On this view, God is unquestionably the source of human sacredness and worth. Each person has inviolable worth, and therefore must love self as they love the neighbor. Indeed, how does one love the neighbor rightly when he does not have a healthy sense of love of self? Jesus admonished that we love the neighbor as we love self (Matt. 22:39). From this, it appears that love for the neighbor and for the self are not antithetical or mutually exclusive. Erich Fromm put it thus: "If it is a virtue to love my neighbor as a human being, it must be a virtue—and not a vice—to love myself since I am a human being too. There is no concept of man in which I myself am not included."[140] King sided with

---

133. Nygren, *Agape and Eros*, 217.

134. Ibid., 222.

135. Ibid., 222.

136. Ibid., 217.

137. Ibid., 222.

138. Ibid., 710, 711, 716.

139. King, "A Christmas Sermon on Peace," in *A Testament of Hope*, 255.

Erich Fromm's psychological line of reasoning in this regard, and also agreed with his view that "the right kind of self-love and the right kind of love of others are interdependent."[141] These are not contradictory or disjunctive, Fromm contends, but conjunctive. Other-regarding and self-regarding love are not alternatives, but are integrally and intricately connected. "Love, in principle, is indivisible as far as the connection between 'objects' and one's own self is concerned."[142] King would not have disagreed with Fromm's further point: "The affirmation of one's own life, happiness, growth, freedom, is rooted in one's capacity to love, i.e., in care, respect, responsibility, and knowledge. If an individual is able to love productively, he loves himself too; if he can love only others, he can not love at all."[143] King must have thought about the importance of self-love when he periodically lamented the growing incidents of black-against-black violence and homicide in black communities in Montgomery, Chicago, Cleveland, Los Angeles, and other urban centers.

Although King did not mention Nygren in his critique, it is in fact a clear repudiation of Nygren's stance against self-love and his sense of the absence of worth in human beings. King's understanding of the Christian ideal, his personalism, his religious upbringing, his experiences of racism and whites' systematic attempts to dehumanize and destroy him and his people would not allow him to agree with any claim that love of self is not a legitimate form or part of Christian love. Moreover, King knew better than most how important it was (indeed is!) for blacks to love themselves, especially after being subjected to several hundred years of dehumanizing slavery and discrimination. Indeed, one of the reasons for the high incidence of intracommunity black violence and homicides, King believed, was to a large extent due to the lack of self-love among many of his people, not exorbitant love of self. If anything, King implied, blacks need more love of self, not less.

For King the personalist, Nygren's rejection of self-love (following Martin Luther[144]) was a thoroughly anti-personalist stance, and therefore he rejected it. King's upbringing in the black church made it easy for him to agree with his personalist forebears that both eros and agape each has an important place in Christian ethics. "To reject the *eros* idea, to exclude self-love and duties

---

140. Erich Fromm, *Man for Himself: An Inquiry into the Psychology of Ethics* (New York: Rinehart & Company, 1947), 128–29.

141. King, "Antidotes for Fear," in *Strength to Love*, 111. See also "Three Dimensions of a Complete Life," in ibid., 69.

142. Fromm, *Man for Himself*, 129.

143. Ibid., 130.

144. See Nygren, *Agape and Eros*, 710.

to self as non-Christian, and to limit Christian love to an 'unmotivated' love to others is to create an abstract Christian ethic and fall into a sentimental immoralism."[145] The personalist Albert C. Knudson broadened this critique of Nygren's interpretation of agape in a way that King would have approved, when he wrote:

> In so far as this theory completely eliminates moral worth from the objects of the divine grace and in so far as it entirely excludes duties to self from the Christian ethic, it de-moralizes and de-personalizes the Christian life. It leaves both the divine grace and the law of brotherly love without a rational basis. Blind faith takes the place of moral insight. We affirm the divine love and the duty of brotherly love, but without any rational ground for either. If the individual has no inherent worth, the affirmation of the divine grace leads to an unmoral predestinationism, and the inculcation of brotherly love leads to an unmoral sentimentalism. If, on the other hand, we acknowledge the worth of others as a basis for our love of them, it is clear that we cannot deny a similar value to ourselves, nor can we deny duties to self.[146]

Although King nowhere explicitly cites Knudson's critique, he was very likely aware of it, since *The Principles of Christian Ethics* (where Knudson's critique appears) was required reading in Kenneth Smith's course at Crozer, Christianity and Society.[147] A major written assignment for the course was a critical review of Knudson's book, which means that King most likely did a thorough reading of it, or at least read it carefully enough to understand Knudson's critique. In addition, it is likely that having studied the History of Personalism under DeWolf at Boston University, King had the opportunity to revisit Knudson's critique. Presently, there is no documentary proof that this occurred. However, it is known that in DeWolf's course on History of Christian Doctrine, King wrote a paper titled "A Comparison and Evaluation of the Theology of Luther with That of Calvin" in which he cited Knudson's book, *Basic Issues in Christian Thought*.[148] The significance of this is that Knudson also includes in that book a discussion and critique of Nygren's view of agape and his rejection of self-

145. Albert C. Knudson, *The Principles of Christian Ethics* (New York: Abingdon, 1943), 132.

146. Ibid., 137.

147. Smith and Zepp, *Search for the Beloved Community*, 63.

148. *The Papers* (1994), 2:174–91. Although King received a grade of A, DeWolf commented that the paper's title was "awkwardly worded" (174).

love.[149] It is at least within the realm of possibility that King read and was familiar with that discussion.

We also see in a number of places King's own critique of the limitation in the position advocated by Nygren, and that it is quite similar to Knudson's critique. In addition, King's understanding of the Bible, as well as his own experience as a systematically oppressed person in the United States, convinced him of the absolute necessity of love of self, most particularly among the oppressed. More than anything, it was necessary for oppressed people to have high regard and love for themselves, their cultural contributions, and so forth. King knew that this was especially important for his own people who were not far removed from the inhumanity of enslavement and who were still systematically discriminated against and treated like subhumans. Self-love was a necessity for his people. King understood the difficulty of loving others in a healthy way if one did not love self. He therefore stressed self-love no less than other-regarding love. In his sermon "Three Dimensions of a Complete Life," he stressed that "every person must have a concern for self and feel a responsibility to discover his mission in life."[150] This is the "length of life," which King held in dialectical relation with the "breadth of life" or the need to love and think highly of the other,[151] a clear indication of the importance of both self-love and other-regarding love for King. Unlike Nygren, he saw an integral interdependency between the two types of love.[152]

SIN

Martin Luther King hoped and worked unrelentingly for the actualization of the beloved community. However, because of his experience with an obstinate federal government that insisted on escalating the war in Vietnam while virtually ignoring the plight of the poor of all races in the United States, as well as the seriousness with which he took the prevalence and power of sin, King believed that we may expect to *approximate* the attainment of the community of love through human and divine cooperation, and the method of nonviolence. The realistic elements in King's theology, that is, his sense of the depth and persistence of sin in individual and group relations; his realization of the limitations of human reason and imagination, and the egregious selfishness

149. See Albert C. Knudson, *Basic Issues in Christian Thought* (New York: Abingdon-Cokesbury, 1950), 189–91.

150. King, "Three Dimensions of a Complete Life," in *Strength to Love*, 69.

151. Ibid., 71.

152. *The Papers*, 6:539.

and virtual inability to see the interests of others as clearly as one's own, should remind us that we will not likely achieve all that the Christian love ethic requires of us. Nor will we achieve a perfect form of society or a perfect form of the beloved community. Consequently, any adequate discussion on King's doctrine of nonviolence must also include a consideration of his understanding of sin. In this regard, his theology was quite realistic at some points, although I wonder about the consistency of his stance, particularly as it relates to specific manifestations of sin such as racism and inequality between white and black people and whether these may be permanent forms of sin. I revisit this important point in chapter ten.

King's social gospel ministry was grounded in the love ethic of the Sermon on the Mount. However, consistent with the social gospel in the black religious tradition, he took just as seriously the presence, prevalence, and depth of sin—especially in group relations—and how it operates effectively to alienate groups from each other and from God. The emphasis on sin is one of the elements of realism in King's theology and doctrine of nonviolence. Among other things, the sin element provides strong reason to resist injustice and other forms of oppression rather than passively accepting them, awaiting a messiah figure, or some kind of miraculous divine intervention.

Sin, King held, militates against establishing even a semblance of the beloved community. The menacing and obstinate presence of sin makes it difficult, if not impossible, for human beings in their collective relations to do what God requires of them: to do justice and righteousness and to liberate the oppressed from the hands of oppressors. For King, nonviolence is both the Christian and the most reasonable way of resisting social evil and injustice, especially for one who lives by the faith that reality hinges on a moral foundation; who believes that God is both *axiogenesis* and *axiosoteria*, the source of goodness, and the preserver and enhancer of goodness, respectively.[153]

Unlike many liberal social gospel advocates, the mature King's interpretation of the Christian love ethic was not based on sentimentality or an overly optimistic attitude regarding human nature and human destiny. Like his teacher, the personalist Brightman, King knew that in addition to the presence of goodness and value in the world there is also the shadow of a cross at the very center of human existence.[154] This too is evidence of the realism in King's thought, for he did not pretend that social evil was somehow an illusion,

153. See Edgar S. Brightman's discussion of these terms in *A Philosophy of Religion* (New York: Prentice Hall, 1940), 204n, 217, 230, 372.

154. Edgar S. Brightman, *An Introduction to Philosophy* (New York: Henry Holt & Company, 1925), 364.

or was not real. Disvalue and evil are as real as the evidences of good and value in the world. King also agreed with Brightman that the tragedies of life must be faced and challenged, and that in doing so one should remember that the tragic elements are not all that define human existence. "There is tragedy," said Brightman, "but there is also meaning; and meaning includes and transforms the tragedy."[155] King tried unceasingly to transform the tragedy of racism, economic injustice, and militarism through persistent nonviolent resistance. This understanding and his spirit of resistance added a strong realistic component to his doctrine of nonviolence, thereby allowing him to retain a balance between human beings' capacity for goodness and for evil. The effort to achieve a balance between these was how King generally avoided the criticism of being either overly optimistic or overly pessimistic in his doctrine of human nature and what he believed could be actually accomplished in history.

In the discussion on the formal intellectual influences on King's thought, we saw how important Reinhold Niebuhr's doctrine of sin was to him. Because of the extensive nature of that discussion what follows will be briefer, and will also serve as a reminder that Niebuhr's Christian realism was not a minor influence on King's thought and practice. Indeed, the prevalence of sin served as a constant reminder to King of the need for organized nonviolent resistance against the social forms of sin such as injustice.

NIEBUHR REVISITED

By the time King completed doctoral studies at Boston University, he had carefully examined Niebuhr's doctrine of human nature and human destiny as found in the two volumes of *The Nature and Destiny of Man* and in *Faith and History*.[156] By then, King no longer believed as he did at one point in seminary that persons, especially in their collective relations could, through conscious choice and hard work, overcome their sin once and for all.[157] Rather, sometime between 1954 and 1960 he arrived at the conclusion that a basic assumption of the Christian faith is that there is something "fundamentally wrong" with human nature,[158] and that Christianity and the Bible are unmistakably clear in pointing out that there are "tragic dimensions of the gone-wrongness of human nature."[159] King therefore came to argue against liberal theology's notion that

155. Ibid.

156. King was clearly influenced by these volumes in his presentation to the Dialectical Society during his doctoral studies. See King's paper, "The Theology of Reinhold Niebuhr," in *The Papers*, 2:256–79.

157. *The Papers*, 6:96, 97.

158. Ibid., 6:381.

159. Ibid., 6:382.

human beings are capable of reaching a sinless state, whether through human effort, or even divine grace.

King's homespun realistic view of human nature was temporarily overshadowed by the strong liberal teachings to which he was exposed in the first two years of seminary—teachings that opened him to a more optimistic view of human nature and human destiny, even as he grappled with the Christian realist view that not only acknowledged the ubiquity of sin, but took it seriously, especially in its group or communal forms.

Niebuhr gave King a more sophisticated theological framework through which to think about and grapple with sin and its manifestations, as well as its prevalence on every level of human achievement. For example, one sees the influence of Niebuhr in King's view that the basic fact of Christianity and of human beings is that we are sinners. His contention that "sin is an ever present shower that sprinkles every one of us" also exhibits the influence of Niebuhr.[160] Sin therefore is a persistent menace, which can only mean that there is always room for improvement in human relations—individually and collectively. To King (and to Niebuhr), this meant that one must be ever vigilant in attempts to approximate the requirements of agape as far as possible; that one should not settle once for all for what may be accomplished in a nonviolent demonstration, since there will likely be more to be done or accomplished. King often found himself in this precise situation, and this left him open to the frequent criticism that not all, or even enough, was achieved in this or that campaign, whether in Albany, Birmingham, Selma, Chicago, or elsewhere. But we should recall that in part, at least, this had to do with the fact that King was instinctively an alliance builder; one who sought to do things democratically with the inclusion of as many voices as possible. Such an approach invariably leads to decisions informed by a great deal of compromises. Effectively, this means that participants, including King, inevitably find themselves settling for less than they hoped to gain. The lesson from Niebuhr is that King and others who fight for freedom and justice must not passively accept gains colored by so much compromise. One accepts what one can achieve, but recognizes that love requires more. The war against injustice must continue to be waged. While Niebuhr left open the door to violence as an option, King closed and deadbolted that door. For him, nonviolent resistance was the only reasonable means to resisting injustice and seeking to establish justice.

According to King, sin is a revolt against and alienation from God, an attempt by human beings to usurp God from the throne and to occupy it

160. Ibid., 6:99.

themselves. King therefore held that "the gravest sin that one can committ" [*sic*] is "the sin of feeling that one has risen above the capacity for sin."[161] Sin, then, is the unwillingness and failure of human beings to accept their status as creatures, preferring instead—and doing all they can—to become God. King believed, not unlike Niebuhr, that sin in its collective dimensions "rises to even more ominous proportions"[162] than the sins of individuals. It is virtually impossible for the group to see the mote in its own eye as easily and clearly as it sees the defects in other groups and nations, "and individuals find it difficult enough," Niebuhr declared in *Moral Man*.[163] And more so, try as we may, we never quite see the interests of others as clearly as we see our own, and history and experience have shown rather conclusively that it is a virtually impossible accomplishment for the group.[164] Furthermore, Niebuhr argued that "human groups, classes, nations, and races are selfish, whatever may be the moral idealism of individual members within groups. . . . No nation, race, or class sacrifices itself. Human groups make a virtue of the assertion of self-interest and will probably do so until the end of history."[165] This is an important component of Niebuhr's realism, which he characterized as "the disposition to take all factors in a social and political situation, which offer resistance to established norms, into account, particularly the factors of self-interest and power."[166] The emphasis is on what is, not what ought to be, in social and political reality. Because of the prominence he gave divine grace, and how he understood agape love, King would have softened Niebuhr's claim, but he would not have disagreed with him entirely. Racial discrimination is a manifestation of sin and must be resisted through organized nonviolent direct action.

The truth of Niebuhr's claims means that there will always be clashes between group interests, which become especially problematic when a group possesses exorbitant and unchecked wealth, power, and privilege—the *occasion* for injustice.[167] This inevitably raises the possibility that one or more groups will want to resist the more disproportionately powerful group. Experience

161. Ibid., 6:200.

162. Ibid., 6:386.

163. Reinhold Niebuhr, *Moral Man and Immoral Society* (New York: Charles Scribner's Sons, 1932), 107.

164. Reinhold Niebuhr, "Can the Church Give a Moral Lead?," in *Essays in Applied Christianity*, ed. D. B. Robertson (New York: Meridian, 1959), 75.

165. Ibid., 79, 83.

166. Niebuhr, "Augustine's Political Realism," in *The Essential Reinhold Niebuhr: Selected Essays and Addresses*, ed. Robert McAfee Brown (New Haven/London: Yale University Press, 1986), 123.

167. Niebuhr, *Moral Man*, 49, 114, 163.

and history taught King that those who possess massive unchecked power and privilege do not generally share these voluntarily with the oppressed. Human nature being what it is, and because sin is present on every level of human progress, there will always be occasions for groups to behave badly toward other groups, especially if they possess the power to get away with it. This implies that groups will always be confronted with the question of *how* to resist injustice and oppression, a question that King answered once and for all for himself.

As sinners, human beings are always in need of divine grace or mercy, but this should not be taken to mean that they will ensure that people will ever overcome sin and evil permanently. Indeed, such a view implies that as long as there are human beings in the world there will be sin, and as long as sin persists, particularly in groups, there is need to resist it. On this point, King was in complete agreement with both Rauschenbusch and Niebuhr.[168]

Martin Luther King was much appreciative of Reinhold Niebuhr's view that the massive disproportion of power and privilege is the underlying occasion for social injustice throughout the world. While King continued to believe—to the dismay of Niebuhr—that agape can change nations,[169] his belief was tempered by Niebuhr's doctrine of the intransigence of group pride and stubbornness, especially when the group possesses inordinate power and privilege. Whether he agreed entirely with Niebuhr or not, King unquestionably understood his point about the inevitability of group egoism and selfishness, and the relevance of applying agape to overcome it. "The moral obtuseness of human collectivities makes a morality of pure disinterestedness impossible," said Niebuhr. "There is not enough imagination in any social group to render it amenable to the influence of pure love."[170] King got this, and yet he was realistic enough to know that the love that can change groups and nations is not some sentimental type of love, but only the tough agape type of love at the center of the universe. This, for King, is the love that finds its expression in nonviolent resistance to social evil and injustice. In other words, for King, agape requires that social evil be resisted, and thus that justice be done. Nonviolence, accordingly, is the most effective and most moral means to this end.

By now, we know that for Martin Luther King the *method of all methods* to address and eradicate social evil and injustice (as far as possible) is nonviolent

168. See Walter Rauschenbusch, *Christianizing the Social Order* (New York: Macmillan, 1926 [1912]), 126; and Niebuhr, "Must We Do Nothing?," in *The Christian Century Reader*, ed. Harold Fey and Margaret Frakes (New York: Association Press, 1962), 226.

169. *The Papers*, 3:327.

170. Niebuhr, *Moral Man*, 272.

direct action, what Gandhi called *satyagraha*. The point is not that nonviolent resistance to evil can eliminate evil or sin in a permanent sense. Nothing, King believed, can do that this side of the grave. However, what organized nonviolent resistance can do, in King's estimation, is reduce the effects of specific manifestations of sin, for example, instances of racism, economic exploitation, and militarism, thereby opening the way to more nearly approximate the beloved community.

Satyagraha

While in seminary, King quite possibly heard or saw the terms *satyagraha* and *ahimsa* in courses on Christian Theology, and Christianity and Society, under George W. Davis and Kenneth L. Smith respectively. In the case of Davis, King included Gandhi's name in an assignment outline of case studies of important religious leaders. In the assignment for Smith he included one sentence about Gandhi, but said nothing substantive about him or his work.[171] In both courses, it appears that King received only a cursory introduction to Gandhi, although it is known that a number of faculty members at Crozer were familiar with, and influenced by the work of Gandhi.[172]

Satyagraha may be characterized as *soul-force*, *love-force*, or *truth-force*, or, as Gandhi said, "the Force which is born of Truth and Love or non-violence. . . ."[173] Unlike "passive resistance" or "nonresistance," satyagraha involves conscious, sustained action to remove social evil, injustice, or dehumanization. It requires that we "meet the forces of hate with the power of love; we must meet physical force with soul force," said King.[174] We saw this very idea—meeting hate with love—in the discussion on agape, so there is an obvious link between nonviolence and love.

Satyagraha requires of proponents an enormous amount of courage and discipline, as well as a *disposition* and a *way of life* that stress and respect the dignity and sacredness of every human being. Satyagraha points to and demands *absolute nonviolence* or *noninjury*, which does not only apply to physical injury, but to psychological and emotional injury as well. The latter emphasis implies an integral connection with ahimsa, as we will see subsequently. For now, suffice it to say that in Gandhian nonviolence one is not even permitted

171. *The Papers*, 1:435.

172. Smith and Zepp, *Search for the Beloved Community*, 48.

173. Gandhi, *Satyagraha in South Africa*, in *The Selected Works of Mahatma Gandhi*, ed. Shriman Narayan (Ahmedabad: Navajivan, 1968 [1928]), 3:151.

174. King, "An Experiment in Love," in *A Testament of Hope*, 17.

to think ill of another, let alone to speak ill, or to do physical injury of any kind. King himself was in total agreement with this idea.

Satyagraha is "a direct corollary of nonviolence and truth."[175] Truth or love "is the spiritual . . . basis of nonviolent resistance."[176] Nonviolence is therefore "an extremely active force" and provides no room for cowardice and weakness. The satyagrahi must courageously confront the opponent and not run away. King approvingly quoted Gandhi, saying that he preferred "violence to cowardice."[177] Nonviolence "is a way not for the weak and cowardly but for the strong and courageous,"[178] King said. In November 1956, King told those gathered at a mass prayer meeting at the Holt Street Baptist Church, that "if cowardice was the alternative to violence, I'd say to you tonight, use violence. . . . Cowardice is as evil as violence."[179] The way of nonviolence means a willingness to resist, suffer, sacrifice, and go to jail if necessary.[180] One does not passively accept suffering, for there is nothing redemptive in this for King. Rather, one resists unearned suffering and its cause(s) nonviolently with all one's might. For King, there was nothing redemptive as such about the suffering occasioned by systematic oppression. Instead, the suffering is *made* to be redemptive by the determination to resist to the death the oppression and its causes. In this regard, full-blown nonviolence is a method only for the strong and courageous. Accordingly, King said: "If one uses this method because he is afraid or merely because he lacks the instruments of violence, he is not truly nonviolent."[181]

One must be able to choose not to react violently, rather than be compelled (for fear of being overpowered, for example). Therefore, nonviolence is not a method for the weak and passive, but for the strong. Such a person receives blows without even the thought of retaliating. This takes a tremendous amount of courage and discipline. As King so often said, "[T]he strong man is the man who will not hit back, who can stand up for his rights and yet not hit back."[182]

The nonviolent resister does not submit to evil or unjust power, but confronts it with the power of love and the conviction that it is better to accept

175. Gandhi, *All Men Are Brothers*, compiled and ed. Krishna Kripalani (New York: UNESCO/ Columbia University Press, 1969 [1958]), 99.

176. Smith and Zepp, *Search for the Beloved Community*, 49.

177. Gandhi, *All Men Are Brothers*, 93.

178. *The Papers* (2005), 5:504.

179. Ibid., 3:430.

180. King, *Stride*, 216.

181. King, "An Experiment in Love," in *A Testament of Hope*, 17.

182. *The Papers*, 3:430.

violence when engaging in a just cause than to inflict it on one's opponents.[183] This was most difficult to teach would-be nonviolent demonstrators, but it is what the nonviolent workshops and socio-drama sessions (discussed in the next chapter) were designed to do. Nonviolence, according to Gandhi, "is the summit of bravery," and it "cannot be taught to a person who fears to die and has no power of resistance."[184] From Montgomery to Memphis, this was an important principle in King's doctrine and practice of nonviolence. Those who lacked the indomitable will and courage to remain nonviolent as violence was being inflicted on them were not allowed to join the ranks of the nonviolent demonstrators. They could contribute to the struggle in other ways, but were not permitted to march.

Nonviolence, therefore, is built on truth or love, but not love of the sentimental type. It is built on agape. In addition, for the satyagrahi who believes in a personal God as King did, the foundation or source of nonviolence is God. For if God is Agape, as proclaimed in the Bible, by King and the black church, and by other philosophers and theologians, then it is reasonable to say that nonviolence is built on God, that God is its source. It is also reasonable to say that God has constructed the universe such that things function best in the world when nonviolence has the right of way. Logically, this leads to the idea that God expects that harm and injury will not be done to human beings in the world. Therefore, nonviolence ought to be the sole morally acceptable way of living in the world. The satyagrahi derives his power from his faith in God. Steadfast obedience, faith, and dependence on God will help him to develop the courage and fearlessness needed to wear down his opponents in the social struggle through the use of love.

An important point to keep in mind is that the effectiveness of satyagraha is not dependent upon the number of people involved in a nonviolent demonstration. Nor is it dependent upon the attitude and moral sense (or lack thereof) of the opponent. Rather, the effectiveness of nonviolence depends primarily upon the degree of commitment and determination of the satyagrahi. Consequently, if just a handful, yea, one person, commits to the true spirit of nonviolence as a way of life, the ultimate outcome of a civil rights demonstration can only be victorious. The real concrete victory in this case is that such a person was unswerving in living the nonviolent faith.

Once proponents of nonviolence catch the spirit of satyagraha, they are willing to die at the hands of opponents without attempting to defend themselves through violent means. As noted before, satyagraha is *active* in the

183. King, "My Trip to the Land of Gandhi," in *A Testament of Hope*, 26.
184. Gandhi, *All Men Are Brothers*, 93.

sense that it requires direct confrontation of, and resistance to, injustice and social evil. But it is also *dynamic*, in the sense that the satyagrahi is always engaging in mental and spiritual training and self-discipline in order to be prepared to do what soul force requires. In Gandhian nonviolence, this means that the satyagrahi is committed to the vow of brahmacharya, which seeks complete control over all the senses, appetites, and emotions, and especially the sexual appetite and the palate. As we saw earlier in this chapter, this particular vow is not prominent in King's doctrine of nonviolence, although he utilized some of its elements, for example, prayer, meditation, and periodic fasts, in order to procure the purification of the self in preparation for nonviolent demonstrations.

Nonviolence is directed, not against the opponent, but against the evil or injustice. It is impossible to do this without committing self to "a continuous process of self-purification," which Gandhi did religiously. In "Letter from Birmingham Jail," King included self-purification as one of the four basic steps in preparation for nonviolent campaigns.[185] Unfortunately, he did not go on to say what this entailed. Even if King did not frequently fast and adhere to long periods of silence, as Gandhi did, as a Christian minister he most certainly devoted time to prayer on a regular basis in preparation for demonstrations. We know, of course, that on a number of occasions, King fasted and prayed while in jail. For Gandhi, on the other hand, the self-purification process meant long periods of fasting, prayer, meditation, and silence. He believed that such discipline and purification made it possible to avoid inflicting suffering on the opponent, and also cleared the path to Truth or God. Indeed, King, like Gandhi, invited and endured unearned suffering in support of a just cause. These are some of the redemptive qualities of satyagraha.

After King's visit to India in 1959, he said that he was convinced more than ever that nonviolence "is the most potent weapon available to oppressed people in their struggle for freedom."[186] He believed it to be the most reasonable and moral means of addressing and eradicating injustice and establishing the beloved community. Because of the extraordinary discipline and courage required, neither King nor Gandhi expected that vast numbers of people would subscribe to pure nonviolence or nonviolence as a way of life.[187] King was convinced that a small number of people in a given community who are

---

185. King, *Why We Can't Wait*, 79; *Playboy* Interview, in *A Testament of Hope*, 376. The other three elements are *fact gathering, negotiation,* and *direct action.*

186. King, "My Trip to the Land of Gandhi," in *A Testament of Hope*, 25.

187. See King, "The Social Organization of Nonviolence," in *A Testament of Hope*, 32; *Stride*, 218; *Why We Can't Wait*, 168; and Gandhi, *An Autobiography, or The Story of My Experiments with Truth*

"unswervingly committed to the nonviolent way, can persuade hundreds of others at least to use nonviolence as a technique and serve as the moral force to awaken the slumbering national conscience."[188] His confidence was in the "creative minority," to use Henry David Thoreau's term, who are the true believers in nonviolence as a way of life. Because of King's conviction that the universe hinges on a moral foundation, he was convinced that nonviolence is the *only* method that is consistent with how the universe operates. Consequently, one might say that in the long run the universe is friendly to all acts of nonviolence, even when it appears in a given moment or circumstance that the desired results were not achieved. The advocate of satyagraha consciously avoids engaging in violence of any sort, whether physical, emotional, or spiritual. King declared that the type of nonviolence he advocated is much more than a strategy or technique to which one adheres only as long as it produces the desired results. Rather, it is fundamentally that way of life to which one adheres precisely because of the morality of the approach.

Ahimsa

Although both King and Gandhi maintained that ahimsa essentially focuses on *human* life, Gandhi also applied it to nonhuman life forms. He knew instinctively, however, that it was virtually impossible to avoid killing insects and certain poisonous animals that might harm human beings. The term *ahimsa* literally means *noninjury*. Under no circumstance would Gandhi or King want to harm a human being physically, emotionally, or psychologically. Therefore, the doctrine of ahimsa means that one is to avoid not only doing physical injury to a person. One must also avoid thinking ill of another, as well as using words that may hurt, harm, or demean in some way. This is the deeper meaning of ahimsa. It means that one must not even think evil thoughts of a human being, let alone subject her to physical injury.

When King wrote and spoke about the necessity of noninjury, he was referring to human beings. And yet, we know that he also expressed a fondness for nature and nonhuman life forms.[189] Not unlike his personalist forebears, King had an appreciation for nature and nonhuman life forms. From the time of the father of American personalism, Borden P. Bowne (1847–1910),

(Ahmedabad: Navajivan , 1927), 392; Raghavan Iyer, ed., *The Essential Writings of Mahatma Gandhi* (Delhi: Oxford University Press, 1990), 74.

188. King, *Stride*, 218.

189. See Clayborne Carson, ed., *The Autobiography of Martin Luther King, Jr.* (New York: Warner Books, 1998), 28. Here King writes about communing with nature, and finding God there.

personalists exhibited the need to respect the plant and animal kingdoms and to acknowledge the duty of human beings to them. Bowne admitted, however, that most people of his day failed to recognize their duty in this area, and that there was need for expansion of the moral sphere in this regard, "not less for the sake of man himself, than for the sake of the animals."[190]

King would not have disagreed with Bowne's claim, but in light of the experience of Afrikans in Diaspora he would also insist on the acknowledgment of duties to them because their inherent dignity ought to have the right of way. The King type of personalism unquestionably requires that one respect the dignity of life as such, but that one also affirm that there are gradations of worth or value that must be acknowledged. Bowne rejected the view that because God is thought to be immanent in all things—which is not the same as saying that God *is* all things—they are of equal value. Instead, Bowne argued that "there is nothing in the dependence of all things on God to remove their distinctions of value."[191] King would be in strict agreement with this stance. There was no way that he, or any other right-thinking person, could accept the view that dogs and human beings are, generally, of equal value. To a large extent, because of the historical treatment of his people in the United States, King's focus was on human beings and the need to do all in one's power to preserve and enhance the dignity of his people in particular, and all human beings in general. Because, historically, his people had been treated like nonpersons or subhumans, it made sense to King to focus unabashedly on the dignity of human beings above all else.

In any event, while King did not write much about the dignity of animals and other nonhuman aspects of creation, he recognized that they all possess intrinsic worth by virtue of being created by God. Gandhi, on the other hand, devoted a great deal of energy and attention to these aspects of creation. Nevertheless, even Gandhi concluded that he was "not able to accept in its entirety the doctrine of nonkilling of animals."[192]

Martin Luther King had a good sense that the idea expressed in ahimsa does not fail. That is, although one who consciously strives to practice what ahimsa requires may not succeed in carrying out all of its requirements, or may do so but not experience the intended results, ahimsa as such will not have failed. One may not live to see the perfect realization or manifestation of ahimsa, but it does not fail, since what is required is that one *intends* through one's actions to uplift and enhance rather than to cause harm to the opponent. Everything about a

190. Borden P. Bowne, *The Principles of Ethics* (New York: Harper & Brothers, 1892), 150.

191. Borden P. Bowne, *The Immanence of God* (Boston: Houghton Mifflin, 1905), 130.

192. Gandhi, *Non-Violence in Peace & War* (Ahmedabad: Navajivan, 1949), 2:67.

person's being says that injury must not be done either to self or to others. To understand ahimsa is to know that it can do nothing but succeed, particularly in a world believed to hinge on a moral foundation.

Right or wrong, both King and Gandhi believed that human beings have been evolving toward ahimsa—and thus away from violence—at least from the time human beings began recording history. This is not to say that either man believed that violence on a massive scale did not exist in his day, or in other eras of history. Each lived by the conviction that because God is love and creates persons out of love and community in order that they may live lovingly and justly in communal relations, it must be the case that human beings—if they will work at it—will gradually come to the reality that what is required of them, in part, is the noninjury of human beings. Over the course of thousands of years, human beings seem slowly to be coming to this realization. King had this in mind when he wrote: "Man was born into barbarism when killing his fellow man was a normal condition of existence. He became endowed with a conscience. And he has now reached the day when violence toward another human being must become as abhorrent as eating another's flesh."[193] Gandhi wrote similarly, and King likely was influenced by it.

> [I]f we turn our eyes to the time of which history has any record down to our own time we shall find that man has been steadily progressing towards *Ahimsa*. Our remote ancestors were cannibals. Then came a time when they were fed up with cannibalism and they began to live on chase. Next came a stage when man was ashamed of leading the life of a wandering hunter. He, therefore, took to agriculture and depended principally on Mother Earth for his food. Thus, from being a nomad, he settled down to civilized stable life, founded villages and towns, and from member of a family he became member of a community and a nation. All these are signs of progressive *Ahimsa* and diminishing *Himsa*.[194]

Himsa means the destruction of life. Ahimsa means the noninjury and the nondestruction of life, and thus points to the necessity for nonviolence. Ahimsa is a comprehensive principle that is grounded in the idea of the unity of *all* life. Therefore, the term includes concern not only for human life, but for life as

---

193. King, *Why We Can't Wait*, 169. See also Shriman Narayan, ed., *The Selected Works of Mahatma Gandhi* (Ahmedabad: Navajivan, 1968), 6:155–62.

194. Gandhi, "The Law of Human Species," in *The Selected Works of Mahatma Gandhi*, 6:161.

such. And yet, it remains true that for King the focus was on avoiding doing injury to human beings.

King came early to the idea of the unity and interrelatedness of all life as a result of the values instilled in him as a child. The theological and moral significance of these ideas is that everything that is done affects every person—including the divine Person—either directly or indirectly. This is why it is important in the social struggle to attack not the persons who are oppressors, but the injustice or institution. The logic of the concept of the unity of all life is that a violent counterattack on the opponent is also an attack on one's self, other persons, and God. King was quite in agreement with Gandhi's affirmation that "we are all tarred with the same brush, and are children of one and the same Creator. . . ."[195] He also saw clearly some of the similarities between other Gandhian ideas and Christianity. For example, in 1963 he said: "The Gandhian concept of non-injury [ahimsa] parallels the Hebraic-Christian teaching of the sacredness of every human being."[196] At this writing, I have not found the term *ahimsa* in King's writings and speeches, although he frequently expressed the meaning of the term.

Like Gandhi, King argued that nonviolence must avoid not only physical violence, "but internal violence of spirit. The nonviolent resister not only refuses to shoot his opponent but he also refuses to hate him. At the center of nonviolence stands the principle of love."[197] Agape is the core principle of pure nonviolence, which led King to the view that "[t]he nonviolent resister would contend that in the struggle for human dignity, the oppressed people of the world must not succumb to the temptation of becoming bitter or indulging in hate campaigns. To retaliate in kind would do nothing but intensify the existence of hate in the universe."[198] King believed that only agape makes it possible to avoid this.

According to Gandhi, "In its positive form, *ahimsa* means the largest love, greatest charity. If I am a follower of *ahimsa*, I *must love* my enemy."[199] Here we see the presence of the element of disinterested love or enemy-love that King encountered in his study of Paul Ramsey.[200]

---

195. Gandhi, *All Men Are Brothers*, 80.

196. King, "The Ethical Demands for Integration," in *A Testament of Hope*, 124.

197. King, "An Experiment in Love," in *A Testament of Hope*, 19.

198. Ibid.

199. Gandhi, *All Men Are Brothers*, 84.

200. See King, *Stride*, 104–5. Smith and Zepp tell us that one of the two required books for Kenneth Smith's course on Christianity and Society during the spring term of King's senior year in seminary was

Two key elements of ahimsa are *truth* and *fearlessness*, which are also key components of satyagraha. Just as one cannot be a satyagrahi if he is a coward, one cannot practice ahimsa if he is a coward. One can practice ahimsa only because he possesses the greatest courage. Not only must such a person love his enemies. He must also refuse to do physical or bodily harm to them, and must not even harbor an evil thought about them. Lying, exhibiting ill-will, hatred, or holding a grudge against a person are all contradictions of the ethics of ahimsa.

Only when one grasps the meaning and significance of the six components of King's doctrine of nonviolence—*deep religious faith, the existence of an objective moral order and moral laws, agape, sin, satyagraha,* and *ahimsa*—will one be able to understand the true meaning of his doctrine of nonviolent resistance to evil, and why, to the end of his life, he vowed to be wedded to nonviolence. Absolute nonviolence demands well-trained, well-disciplined, relentlessly committed, loyal, and courageous individuals.

The elements of nonviolence discussed in this chapter converge and are interrelated in the thought and practice of Martin Luther King. In its full-blown sense, King's doctrine of nonviolence is more than a strategy for social change. It is a philosophy or a way of relating and living in the kind of world King believed God created. For example, one fails to gain a full understanding of the meaning of satyagraha if one does not also consider the meaning of ahimsa and how it is related to the practice of nonviolence and how one thinks about and treats the opponent. But in addition, implicit in these two concepts is agape, which both ahimsa and satyagraha presuppose and include. This implies that the truth of these concepts is grounded in a particular way of thinking about the universe or reality itself. For Martin Luther King, of course, the universe is situated on a moral foundation and therefore is thought to operate best when intelligent life forms behave and live in ways that are consistent with this. According to King's view, behaving nonviolently is what the universe requires, and this applies to the need to resist the various forms of injustice and oppression as well.

In 1952, while still a doctoral student, King said that we are not to take advantage of opportunities to defeat our opponent, but instead, should love our enemies and let them know that we love them, an idea based on his interpretation of Matt. 5:43-44, which stresses the obligation to love one's enemies, noting that God makes the sun to rise on the evil and the good, and

---

Paul Ramsey, *Basic Christian Ethics* (see Smith and Zepp, *Search for the Beloved Community*, 62). In that text, Ramsey developed the concept of disinterested love, which King later appropriated.

sends rain on the just and the unjust.[201] Unknown to King at the time, this statement about loving one's enemy was also a Gandhian principle.[202] King was not a proponent of absolute nonviolence when he made this statement in graduate school, for at the time he limited nonviolence to relations between individuals and small groups. He did not apply it to races and nations at the time. Instead, he declared: "This would not follow with all out war between nations."[203] At the time, he believed that nonviolence simply would not work in situations involving nations on the verge of war. However, this limited stance on nonviolence changed for King, especially after he was awarded the Nobel Peace Prize in December 1964. By that time, he was moving in the direction of an international and absolute stance on nonviolence. Indeed, even by March 1956, there were signs that King was moving in that direction. At that time, he told his Dexter congregation: "I believe absolutely and positively that violence is self-defeating."[204]

Periodically, reference has been made to the need to stress the actual practice of the type of nonviolence that influenced Martin Luther King, and from which he incorporated elements that made it his own brand. What has not been addressed as yet, is how King and his disciples actually trained would-be demonstrators to behave nonviolently when being called names, spat upon, hit with rocks, bottles, clubs, burned with electric cattle prods, having police attack dogs sicced on them, and having their skin torn off by high-powered fire hoses, all without retaliating violently. The next chapter explores this important aspect of King's *practiced* ideas and philosophy of nonviolence.

201. *The Papers*, 6:128, 324.

202. See King, *Why We Can't Wait*, 49–50; and Gandhi, *Autobiography*, 345, 391–92, and *The Collected Works of Mahatma Gandhi* (Ahmedabad: The Publications Division Ministry of Information and Broadcasting, Government of India, 1967), 22:415–21.

203. *The Papers*, 6:128.

204. Ibid., 3:208.

9

Training in Nonviolence

An important feature of the application of nonviolence, beginning in Montgomery, and in subsequent civil rights campaigns, had to do with training. Generally, would-be demonstrators did not know how to behave nonviolently when verbally or physically attacked by racist opponents. Nor did they know how to assume a nonviolent self-defensive posture when physically attacked. This too required training. As Martin Luther King became more familiar and comfortable with Gandhian ideas and techniques through the counsel and advice of Rustin and Smiley and during the day-to-day incidents pertaining to the bus boycott, he realized the importance of training the protesters how to carry themselves when insulted by white racists. This was significant not only during the boycott, but even more so once it was over and the people returned to the buses. To get at the issue of training, then, King expanded the prayer meetings to include a training component at the end that incorporated early stages of role-playing (or socio-drama), a training method that CORE actually put into practice during the sit-ins in 1960, and the Freedom Rides in 1961. James Lawson, a Vanderbilt University divinity school student, who had spent time in India studying the ideas and method of Gandhi, also included role-playing in his nonviolent workshops where he trained Nashville student activists such as Diane Nash and John Lewis. Lawson would later train SCLC staffers and others associated with King and his organization. But this all happened a few years after King's first training sessions were held in Montgomery.

King actually began including training sessions in nonviolence not long after Rustin and Smiley started tutoring him in Gandhian ideas and techniques. To get the emphasis on training started, Smiley sought permission from King and the MIA to show a fifteen-minute FOR documentary film on nonviolence: "Walking to Freedom."[1] In addition, it was Smiley who provided instruction on how to do actual training in nonviolence. Such training was absolutely essential. It could not be assumed that the boycotters would automatically know how to respond nonviolently when accosted or otherwise attacked by white racists. Because many of the males were proponents of self-defensive violence, their first inclination would have been to strike back at verbal and physical abuse. Indeed, even Gandhi learned a valuable lesson when he failed to provide training for the people of the Kheda district in India who were to engage in a noncooperation campaign. Confessing his error, what he characterized as a "Himalayan miscalculation," Gandhi said: "I had called on the people to launch upon civil disobedience before they had thus qualified themselves for it, and this mistake seemed to me of Himalayan magnitude."[2] Gandhi had not put in the time and effort to properly train the people for that particular nonviolent campaign. Teaching, then, is an important aspect of the training for nonviolent resistance demonstrations. It cannot be presumed that would-be demonstrators automatically know what is expected of them in such campaigns or even how best to defend themselves nonviolently. Most of the guesswork is removed if they are trained beforehand. Implicit in this is also the important principle of satyagraha—that one who disobeys even unjust civil laws during noncooperation campaigns must also willingly submit to arrest and imprisonment. The novice is not likely to know such things. Thus, teaching and training are absolutely essential for those who volunteer to participate in nonviolent direct action campaigns. Gandhi knew from long experience of leading civil disobedience campaigns in South Afrika and in India what King would learn less than two decades later: The teaching and training in nonviolent techniques is one of the toughest, but most important challenges to be addressed by the leaders of protest movements.

What did the early King-led training sessions in nonviolence look like? After the Supreme Court ruled against Montgomery's and Alabama's segregation ordinance, in *Browder v. Gayle*—but before the ruling actually took effect—King decided that it was time to begin preparing blacks to return to the buses on a desegregated basis. Such training was necessary because there would surely be incidents on the desegregated buses; as all seats were now to be occupied on a first-come first-served basis, there would be whites who would take out their anger on black passengers. Human nature being what it is, King also knew that even among oppressed blacks there would likely be those who would be inclined to lord the Court's decision over whites, and this too could

1. Stewart Burns, ed., *Daybreak to Freedom: The Montgomery Bus Boycott* (Chapel Hill/London: University of North Carolina Press, 1997), 254, 292.

2. M. K. Gandhi, *An Autobiography or The Story of My Experiments with Truth* (Ahmedabad: Navajivan, 1927), 392.

lead to racial incidents. King wanted to avoid both types of behaviors. It was important, King said, that blacks respond with dignity, no matter what whites said or did. He reminded them that their objective all along was not to defeat the bus company and white people. "We are not out to defeat or to humiliate the white man," he told the forty-seventh Annual NAACP Convention on June 27, 1956. "We are out to help him as well as ourselves."[3] The training was to prepare blacks how to respond appropriately and nonviolently to the anticipated behavior of whites. The training would be tough for many blacks because they were smart enough to know that such training put the moral onus once again on them to behave cordially to racists whose behavior might be in violation of the Court's decision. It would require that blacks endure more suffering, even after the landmark judgment against segregated buses took effect.

King knew full well that many whites would be angry about the Court's ruling, and that this would likely be reflected in their behavior toward blacks. He also knew that nonviolence would not immediately change the hearts, attitudes, and disposition of many whites. Nonviolence is a process, and as such it would take years for such change to actually occur in most people. Because blacks had gone through the training and discipline necessary to carry out the boycott, which lasted for more than a year, and had participated regularly in the mass prayer meetings, King expected that unlike white opponents, the hearts and souls of his people[4] would be positively affected; that they would develop a new sense of self-dignity, as well as respect for the dignity of others, including white oppressors. In this, he was not disappointed, as he frequently reflected on the evolution of the new sense of dignity in his people as a result of their determination to sustain the boycott until justice prevailed.

On October 3, 1956, the FOR film about the bus boycott, "Walking to Freedom," premiered at the mass prayer meeting at Hutchinson Street Baptist Church where about eight hundred persons were reportedly in attendance.[5] After the brief film, King led the first training exercise in nonviolence to prepare the people to return to desegregated buses.

Understandably, the first training session was not very sophisticated. King asked for two volunteers to stand and state—for all to hear—how they planned to behave once they returned to the buses, and in the event they sat next to a white person who was hostile and insulting toward them, or who may even

3. Clayborne Carson et al., eds., *The Papers of Martin Luther King, Jr.* (Berkeley: University of California Press, 1997), 3:305.

4. Martin Luther King, Jr., *Stride Toward Freedom* (New York: Harper & Row, 1958), 219.

5. William Robert Miller, *Martin Luther King, Jr.: His Life, Martyrdom, and Meaning for the World* (New York: Avon, 1968), 63.

shove them physically. Considering the contributions that black women had made to that point, it should come as no surprise that two women volunteered. The first woman said that she would be upset at such treatment, but that she would not move. Her inclination would be to ignore the person and just let others observe that person's ignorant behavior. However, were she shoved, she said, she might be inclined to respond in kind. To this there were many murmurs of disapproval from others in attendance. King thanked the woman for her honest response, and then proceeded to cross-examine her by asking her what would be achieved by shoving the person. The woman seemed to be in agreement when the audience said that nothing would be gained that would help the cause. Not convinced that she was truly in agreement, King pressed her further. If she truly agreed that nothing would be achieved, he inquired, then why would she respond in kind? The woman replied that it really would not be the thing to do.

The second woman was somewhat philosophical, remarking that it was important for them to remember that whites do not know blacks as well as blacks know them. "It isn't going to do any good to get mad and strike back, 'cause that's just what some of them *want* us to do." She said that they fought too long and hard to desegregate the buses, and that it was important for them to behave with dignity and act "like good Christian ladies and gentlemen. . . ."[6] King informed the group that there would be many more sessions like this before they returned to the buses.

As we can see, there was nothing formal or sophisticated about the first training sessions in nonviolence and how the people were to respond. Indeed, King was feeling his way through. There was a call for volunteers who were then asked how they would respond to various situations they might encounter on the buses. The leader, as well as others present, reacted to the answers and pressed with more questions and clarifications for why they would react a certain way. That first session was but a prelude to the much more precise *socio-drama* demonstrations of what might actually happen to protesters and how they should respond to racial insults and other forms of violence.

Training sessions occurred regularly after King led the first one. Increasingly, his understanding of the socio-drama component and what the training sought to do deepened as he continued to be advised by Smiley (who remained in Montgomery after Rustin was advised to leave). Writing in *Stride Toward Freedom* (1958), King gave a thorough description of what they sought to do in the training sessions and explained the method involved.

6. See Burns, ed., *Daybreak of Freedom*, 293.

We lined up chairs in front of the altar to resemble a bus, with a driver's seat out front. From the audience we selected a dozen or so "actors" and assigned each one a role in a hypothetical situation. One man was driver and the others were white and Negro passengers. Both groups contained some hostile and some courteous characters. As the audience watched, the actors played out a scene of insult or violence. At the end of each scene the actors returned to the audience and another group took their place; and at the end of each session a general discussion followed.

> Sometimes the person playing a white man put so much zeal into his performance that he had to be gently reproved from the sidelines. Often a Negro forgot his nonviolent role and struck back with vigor; whenever this happened we worked to rechannel his words and deeds in a nonviolent direction.[7]

The object was for the actors to portray their roles as realistically as possible, a point that many of the people apparently took to heart since some periodically played their roles too well and were subjected to mild criticism by the group. The entire session was a teaching occasion in that weaknesses could be pointed out and suggestions made as to how better to respond in the real-life situation. The performance of each actor is evaluated by the group. Each actor contributed to the teaching as well, since they responded to questions about why they reacted in a certain way. This helped the audience to understand why opponents and proponents behaved as they did. Such give-and-take also helped the actors to understand why they reacted in a certain way. It also gave them a sense of what they might expect in actual situations on the buses. This could be an important element in the later step of the process when efforts are made to reconcile with the opponent.

CORE utilized something like socio-drama as early as the 1940s when, in conjunction with the Fellowship of Reconciliation, it offered training in nonviolence. Socio-drama is a means of addressing intergroup conflict, with the group members portraying the various roles. Some portrayed the role of demonstrators or sit-in activists; others played the role of white racists, thugs, and policemen.[8] The aim was to train participants how to adhere to nonviolence no matter what opponents said or did to them. Socio-drama was

---

7. King, *Stride*, 163.

8. See the illuminating discussion on socio-drama and its use by CORE activist Gordon Carey (a white New Yorker) in Fred Powledge, *Free at Last?: The Civil Rights Movement and the People Who Made It* (New York: HarperPerennial, 1992), 214–15, 220, 230, 254, 261.

"the basic combat training" of the would-be satyagrahi. "It is as vital to him as bayonet drill or target practice is to the recruit in infantry training."[9] Of course, one can be trained and taught how to respond to what is said or done, but one becomes a satyagrahi only by actually behaving in the nonviolent way *and* in the spirit of agape. Let us not forget Gandhi's statement to Benjamin Mays: that one does not gain training in nonviolence through teaching and preaching, but by actually practicing it. The real training comes through the actual living or practice of nonviolence and all that one experiences and gains in the process. One's best training in nonviolence comes by actually being in the fray; by actually having mustard and catsup squirted all over one's face and clothing, being spat upon, clubbed, and called everything but a child of God by racist hoodlums. To respond nonviolently *and* in the spirit of love to such degrading actions is evidence that one is adequately trained in nonviolence. Short of actually being in the fight, however, the training provided during the socio-drama sessions was the best substitute for being in actual situations where one is beaten and otherwise harassed for participating in a nonviolent demonstration. In any case, the teaching and training are necessary, but the trainee must also be made aware that this alone does not qualify them as a bona fide satyagrahi. One has to face the opponent and actually endure—in the spirit of agape—the slings and arrows that will surely come one's way.

Completely sold on the idea of the need for training in nonviolence, King and SCLC co-sponsored the first Southwide Institute on Nonviolent Resistance to Segregation in Atlanta, July 22–24, 1959 with the FOR and CORE. It was recommended that such institutes and workshops be held nationally, regionally, and locally as often as deemed necessary, and also that a handbook of principles and techniques of nonviolence be developed and made available to individuals and groups upon request.[10] Although it would not be the same as participating in workshops on nonviolence that included heavy dosages of socio-drama, making such handbooks available to would-be student and other activists was better than nothing.

In addition to the contributions of Smiley, King learned much from the socio-drama technique of CORE. James Lawson included a version of socio-drama in his nonviolent workshops with the Nashville student activists—making them the best-trained of the early student activists—as they prepared to do sit-ins at local businesses. Socio-drama became a significant part of training workshops in nonviolence sponsored by SCLC, and Lawson

9. William Robert Miller, *Nonviolence: A Christian Interpretation* (New York: Association Press, 1964), 165.

10. *The Papers* (2005), 5:262.

was a key instructor. Social psychologist Kenneth B. Clark interviewed King in 1963 and asked him how he accounted for the fact that the nonviolent demonstrators in Birmingham and elsewhere tended, on the whole, to be as disciplined and "dignified" as they were in the face of such hatred and violence. King responded that education and training in both the theory and practice of nonviolence was the key. He also cited the importance of the socio-drama component. "We even have courses where we go through the experience of being roughed up," King said, "and this kind of sociodrama has proved very helpful in preparing those who are engaged in demonstrations."[11] In addition, King responded affirmatively to Clark's query about whether children were included in the training and workshop sessions. He said that even children as young as seven years old who participated in the demonstrations also went through the training; they could not be in the demonstrations if they did not first go through the training.

A number of people who grew up in Birmingham recalled that when they were growing up they were taught by their parents to hit back if they were physically attacked. Larry Russell was one such person, although on reflection he said that once they got involved in the planned children's campaign they accepted the training in nonviolence, though it was difficult to accept.[12] Mary Gadson also grew up in Birmingham and recalled how black youths were rigorously trained in nonviolence techniques. She characterized the socio-drama part of the training much like King did: "They trained you to be disciplined. They would get up into your face and say all kinds of things, like 'Nigger sit down!' and 'Nigger move!' You'd have to stand there and take it. You were being disciplined to take the harshness. The training was to control. I wouldn't let them get to me. I would not allow the person who was doing the shouting to be in control."[13]

By the time of the Birmingham campaign in 1963, the nonviolent training sessions sponsored by SCLC were much more sophisticated than those early sessions near the end of the Montgomery bus boycott. They included much more dramatic role-playing. White participants portrayed the exact behavior of white racist onlookers during the nonviolent protests. As King told Kenneth Clark, the socio-drama sessions often meant that participants would be "roughed up," much like they would be during the actual demonstrations.

11. Kenneth B. Clark Interview in *A Testament of Hope: The Essential Writings of Martin Luther King, Jr.*, ed. James M. Washington (New York: Harper & Row, 1986), 337.

12. Ellen Levine, *Freedom's Children: Young Civil Rights Activists Tell Their Own Stories* (New York: G. P. Putnam's Sons, 1993), 60.

13. Ibid., 61.

Both blacks and whites were instructed on how to respond to such treatment. Anyone who wanted to participate in the demonstrations, from Birmingham onward, had to go through this training. In further description of what happens in the training sessions, King said:

> The focus of these training sessions was the socio-dramas designed to prepare the demonstrators for some of the challenges they could expect to face. The harsh language and physical abuse of the police and the self-appointed guardians of the law were frankly presented, along with the nonviolent creed in action: to resist without bitterness; to be cursed and not reply; to be beaten and not hit back. The S.C.L.C. staff members who conducted these sessions played their roles with the conviction born of experience.[14]

Wyatt Walker reacted angrily to James Forman's criticism of his and Dorothy Cotton's ecstatic reaction to Bull Connor calling out the dogs on young people in Birmingham. SCLC had actually been counting on such a misstep by Connor, since this would guarantee massive media coverage. Moreover, the very purpose of the workshops in nonviolence was to prepare participants in the most realistic sense for what they could expect from racist onlookers, including Bull Connor.

Potential white demonstrators were made to understand that they could expect worse treatment during Freedom Rides, sit-ins, or demonstrations because racist opponents were particularly repulsed by their support of blacks. Although John Lewis and other black Freedom Riders were beaten severely when their bus was bombed outside Anniston, Alabama, the severity of the beating of Professor Walter Bergman and James Peck was almost indescribable. Bergman was beaten so badly that he later suffered a stroke and paralysis. In the minds of the white racist thugs, these two men were "the kind of northern white 'nigger lover' responsible for agitating southern blacks."[15] A black freedom rider, Isaac Reynolds, reported later that the attackers were especially brutal in their beating of Bergman, Peck, and other white Riders who were attacked.[16] Peck was beaten so badly that he required dozens of stitches to close deep gashes in his head.

---

14. King, *Why We Can't Wait* (New York: Harper & Row, 1964), 60.

15. See Seth Cagin and Philip Dray, *We Are Not Afraid: The Story of Goodman, Schwerner, and Chaney, and the Civil Rights Campaign for Mississippi* (New York: Nation Books, 2006 [1989]), 110.

16. See Powledge, *Free at Last?*, 256.

By 1963, King and SCLC required potential demonstrators to sign a pledge card indicating that they would adhere to nonviolent principles during the demonstrations, and that they would always follow the directions of their captain. Looking back, Myrna Carter, who was twelve when she participated in the 1963 Children's Crusade in Birmingham, remembered that participants had to take an oath and agree to be nonviolent.[17] It is significant that they were not turned away merely because they felt they could not endure insults and physical violence. However, they were not allowed to march in the demonstrations either. Since King's experience taught him that everybody had something positive to contribute to the movement, those who did not believe they could retain their composure in the ranks of the demonstrators were invited to answer telephones, type, file papers, do mailings, or run errands, but everybody could join and play a significant part in the nonviolent army. Indeed, King saw it as one of the greatest advantages of nonviolence, namely that anybody could join and play a significant role.

Even though King understood that most participants in the nonviolent demonstrations would not reach the point of being committed to nonviolence in an absolute sense, he knew that training in the techniques of nonviolence was essential. Because of his commitment in this regard, there were seldom incidents within the ranks of demonstrators. Generally demonstrators were disciplined, well mannered, and nonviolent.

SELF–DEFENSIVE NONVIOLENCE

Because many would surely experience some type of harassment or violence during the demonstrations, the trainers also spent time in the workshops addressing the matter of self-defense. We have seen that King was an adherent of the ethics of physical self-defense when he arrived in Montgomery, and that through the counsel, advice, and example of Rustin and Smiley he relinquished the idea of retaliatory self-defense and devoted himself to nonviolence as the most reasonable way of living in a world that hinges on a moral foundation. However, nothing in the Gandhian or Kingian doctrine of nonviolence requires that one give up self-defense or self-protection entirely. It requires only that one find another way to protect one's self, but that one be nonviolent at all times during participation in a demonstration.

As William Robert Miller rightly pointed out, participants in the training sessions had to "learn the gymnastics of receiving blows—chewing gum in order to relax tensions and so ease the impact when struck, clasping hands

17. See Levine, *Freedom's Children*, 86.

behind the neck and shielding the face with one's arms, drawing the knees up to protect the abdomen when lying down and being kicked, learning how to fall down gracefully when it is impossible to remain sitting or standing. These and other techniques must be both memorized and practiced."[18] It is human nature to want to somehow protect one's body as much as possible from blows or objects intended to cause harm. To this end participants were taught how to lie in a fetal position and cover their heads and faces with their arms and hands to avoid more damage to their bodies than necessary, when they are subjected to cannon bursts of water from high-powered fire hoses, or when they are being beaten with clubs or bats.[19] They were taught other things to do to protect themselves as far as possible, but always nonviolently. Under no circumstance were they to respond violently. Self-defense was acceptable only if it was a type of self-protective nonviolent resistance such as that just mentioned.

The idea of self-defensive nonviolence is quite consistent with Kingian ethics. Indeed, the fundamentally personalist, Christian, and Afrikan American conviction of the inviolable dignity of persons as such actually looms large in this regard. We have seen that philosophically, King believed that every person, as person, is an end in herself and not a means only, and thus should be respected and treated accordingly. Theologically, King argued that the God of the Hebrew prophets and Jesus Christ is the source of human dignity; that every individual person is inestimably sacred and precious because loved into existence by God and imbued with the image of God. We also saw in chapter eight that in part King rejected a portion of Anders Nygren's doctrine of agape precisely because of Nygren's failure to acknowledge the worth or value of the individual. Nygren rejected self-love, claiming that agape starts with the conviction that the soul has no value.[20] King judged this to be a thoroughly anti-personalist, anti-Christian, anti-black stance. In addition, he recognized that any human being is also a part of humanity and thus must be as valuable and precious as any member of humanity. This most assuredly is the case as human beings stand before God. Every single one is inviolably precious to God, or none is. Moreover, King agreed with Erich Fromm that "my own self must be as much an object of my love as another person. . . . If an individual is able to love productively, he loves himself too; if he can love *only* others, he cannot love at all."[21] King interpreted this to mean that "the right kind of self-love and

18. Miller, *Nonviolence: A Christian Interpretation*, 166.

19. See Powledge, *Free at Last?*, 573–74.

20. See Anders Nygren, *Agape and Eros*, trans. Philip S. Watson [single-volume edition] (Philadelphia: Westminster, 1953), 217, 222.

21. Erich Fromm, *The Art of Loving* (New York: Harper & Brothers, 1956), 62.

the right kind of love of others are interdependent."[22] This, for Martin Luther King, is the truly personalist, Christian, Afrikan American stance.

What this all means for our purpose is that just as the would-be nonviolent demonstrator is required to receive insults and blows from opponents without retaliating in kind and thus injuring them in any way, so too is he obligated to defend his own personhood and body as best he can, albeit through nonviolent actions such as those mentioned above. The nonviolent demonstrator recognizes that as a human being and member of the human family he is as infinitely and inalienably valuable before God as any other person; that in order to love his opponents properly he must also possess a healthy love of self. Therefore, he is obligated to apply all acceptable nonviolent measures to defend himself from physical attacks by opponents. After all, it is the entire person—mind *and* body—that is sacred and must be defended as best as one can.

Years later, when Clark Olsen reflected on his experience during the Selma, Alabama campaign in 1965, he recalled how he and fellow Unitarian Universalist ministers James Reeb and Orloff Miller were attacked by racist thugs after the second Selma march on March 9. Olsen recalled that his colleagues had been instructed upon arrival that if physically attacked they were "to fall down on your knees, huddle down, with your hands over your head, protecting your head with your arms."[23] Unfortunately they were attacked from behind and were not able to assume the self-defensive posture. Reverend Reeb did not survive the attack.

Most discussions on King and nonviolence fail to mention, let alone stress, the importance of the self-defensive component and its relation to the significance of self-love in Kingian ethics. It is important to remember that King's was not only an other-regarding ethic, but a self-regarding one as well. Thus the nonviolent exponent is as morally obligated to defend self nonviolently as to resist the violent opponent nonviolently. She respects and seeks to defend the image of God not only in the other, but in herself as well. This means that the training in the techniques of nonviolence must focus not only on how to respond nonviolently to physical and verbal attacks, but also how to defend oneself nonviolently.

22. King, "Antidotes for Fear," in *Strength to Love* (New York: Harper & Row, 1963), 111. See also "Three Dimensions of a Complete Life," in ibid., 69.

23. Quoted in Henry Hampton and Steve Fayer (with Sarah Flynn), *Voices of Freedom: An Oral History of the Civil Rights Movement from the 1950s through the 1980s* (New York: Bantam, 1990), 232.

INFLUENCE OF MORAL JIU-JITSU

Although in chapter eight I referred to Richard Gregg's book *The Power of Nonviolence*, and alluded to its importance for Martin Luther King, I did not elaborate. When it was first published in 1935, this book was required reading for pacifists like Rustin and Smiley.[24] Anybody who has more than a cursory knowledge of King's philosophy of nonviolence knows that the idea of knocking opponents off balance morally is an important aspect of his doctrine. This element of nonviolence was developed systematically by Gregg, who was actually inspired in this regard by Gandhi. King was introduced to Gregg's book in Montgomery, when Glenn Smiley included it among several other books on and about Gandhi and nonviolence.[25] Although dubious, the claim was made by one of King's seminary professors that King read Gregg's book in preparation for a paper he wrote on Gandhi.[26] Nevertheless, at whatever point King may have read all or a portion of Gregg's book, it is unquestionable that he was familiar with and influenced by at least one major idea in the book. In a number of his writings, speeches, sermons, and interviews, King indicated familiarity with Gregg's concept of *moral jiu-jitsu*. The concept is intended to illustrate what happens when the nonviolent resister (i.e., the power of love) is meanly confronted by a violent antagonist.

The ancient art of jiu-jitsu is based on balance. The aim is to disrupt that balance without engaging in violence of any kind. Gregg imagines what will happen when a thoroughly disciplined nonviolent resister who is familiar

24. Aldon D. Morris, *The Origins of the Civil Rights Movement: Black Communities Organizing for Change* (New York: Free Press, 1984), 159.

25. Stewart Burns, *To the Mountaintop: Martin Luther King, Jr.'s Sacred Mission to Save America 1955-1968* (New York: HarperSanFrancisco, 2004), 89.

26. John Ansbro uncritically accepts the claim of Kenneth Smith and Ira Zepp Jr. that King read the 1944 edition of Gregg's book in seminary. (See Ansbro, *Martin Luther King, Jr.: The Making of a Mind* [Maryknoll, NY: Orbis, 1982], 147.) Kenneth Smith claims that he actually read the paper King wrote on Gandhi in seminary, and that although he remembered nothing about the contents of the paper, he remembered that Gregg's book was in the bibliography. It is very hard to know what to make of this since it has not been possible to corroborate this claim. Both authors and King are deceased, and the King Papers Project has not yet produced the paper to which Smith and Zepp refer. (See Smith and Zepp, *Search for the Beloved Community: The Thinking of Martin Luther King, Jr.* [Valley Forge, PA: Judson, 1974], 48.) Nor has other evidence surfaced to support the claim that King read Gregg's book in seminary. Furthermore, this writer has known too many instances in which his own seminary students have included books in a bibliography for a paper but exhibited no evidence of familiarity with basic arguments or main points in the text, which suggests that students did not read those books. Until substantive evidence appears to support the claim of Smith and Zepp, I think the better part of wisdom suggests that we accept the claim with a grain of salt.

with the method of nonviolence is attacked by a violent assailant. The attitude of the nonviolent resister "is fearless, calm, steady, and because of a different belief, training or experience he has much self-control. He does not respond to the attacker's violence with counter-violence."[27] What he does do, however, completely catches the violent opponent by surprise, thus knocking him off balance morally. If the opponent strikes out in violence, the nonviolent resister receives the blows in the spirit of love and out of respect for the attacker. "He states his readiness to prove his sincerity by his own suffering rather than by imposing suffering on the assailant, through violence."[28] He accepts any and all blows thrown at him without showing signs of fear and resentment. He even seems to invite the blows, while staunchly and bravely bearing the excruciating pain, all of which further confounds, confuses, and throws the opponent off balance, causing him to feel at a loss as to what to do. He does not know how to respond to the nonviolent resister, one who will not under any circumstance fight back. From all of this, Gregg determines that what we actually have is an example of moral jiu-jitsu in practice. He illustrates the concept in a more detailed way.

> The non-violence and good will of the victim act like the lack of physical opposition by the user of physical jiu-jitsu, to cause the attacker to lose his moral balance. He suddenly and unexpectedly loses the moral support which the usual violent resistance of most victims would render him. He plunges forward, as it were, into a new world of values. He feels insecure because of the novelty of the situation and his ignorance of how to handle it. He loses his poise and self-confidence. The victim not only lets the attacker come, but, as it were, pulls him forward by kindness, generosity and voluntary suffering, so that the attacker quite loses his moral balance. The user of non-violent resistance, knowing what he is doing and having a more creative purpose and perhaps a clearer sense of ultimate values than the other, retains his moral balance. He uses the leverage of a superior wisdom to subdue the rough direct force or physical strength of his opponent.[29]

27. Richard Gregg, *The Power of Non-Violence* (New York: Fellowship Publications, 1944 [1935]), 42.
28. Ibid.
29. Ibid., 43.

Gregg points to the disadvantages of moral jiu-jitsu to the antagonist,[30] as well as the advantages to the thoroughly disciplined, trained, and committed nonviolent resister. We will see subsequently that the way Gregg characterized moral jiu-jitsu is precisely the way King articulated the concept, even though he seldom cited the term.

From Montgomery onward, King frequently appealed to three of the advantages named in Gregg's book, although without explicitly linking them to his concept of moral jiu-jitsu. The proponent of moral jiu-jitsu possesses "superior position, poise and power" because: 1) She has taken the moral initiative, thus surprising and confusing the opponent; 2) She exhibits sincerity and deep conviction, a willingness to receive unearned blows and suffering; and 3) Her refusal to return violence for violence implies a deep respect for human personality in general, and that of the opponent in particular. Such respect for human personality implies the conviction that at bottom, human beings are fundamentally decent "and have in their hearts at least a spark of good spirit which can eventually be aroused and strengthened into action."[31] Respect for human personality is a Christian and personalist principle that was instilled in King from the time he was a child, and was reinforced during formal academic studies from Morehouse to Boston University.

Respect for personality is fundamental to King's theology and his doctrine of nonviolence. King was in one accord with Gregg's claim that respect for human personality "gradually tends to put the violent attacker to shame and to enhance the respect of any onlookers toward the gentle resister."[32] My own sense is that the first part of this claim is generally true, that is, many, even most, violent assailants may, over time, experience a sense of shame. However, one wonders about individuals like Adolph Hitler, Benito Mussolini, and even those cutthroat rugged individualists who have amassed huge wealth and privilege at the expense of countless workers whose labor was essentially stolen from them during the period of U.S. slavery. Indeed, one wonders about the Ku Klux Klansmen and White Citizens Council members who unconscionably terrorized and murdered both blacks and well-meaning whites who fought for the civil rights and freedom of blacks. Where is the evidence that such people, who all too often go to their graves filled with hatred and total disregard for the humanity and dignity of human beings who happen to be black, actually exhibited shame because blacks and their supporters respected human personality and resisted their violent acts nonviolently? Many years of

30. Ibid., 44–46.
31. Ibid., 87.
32. Ibid., 48.

experience tell me that there are far too many people whose moral sensibility is at such a low stage of development—or even nonexistent—that they are not influenced in the least by the knowledge that the other respects human personality.

Nevertheless, the claim that the thoroughgoing nonviolent resister respects persons as such, and possesses superior poise and power, implies that such a person is also the bearer of strength of character. Gregg observes that five qualities are characteristic of such an individual. First and foremost, this person is driven by the *agape love* that is central to King's theology and doctrine of nonviolence and that may also be seen as the source and foundation of the other four qualities: a deep faith in the potential of human beings; "a courage based upon a conscious or subconscious realization of the underlying unity of all life and eternal values or eternal life of the human spirit";[33] respect and love for truth; and "a humility which is not cringing or self-deprecatory or timid but rather a true sense of proportion in regard to people, things, qualities and ultimate values."[34] These five qualities (love, faith, courage, truth [or honesty], and humility) are also central to how King viewed the committed nonviolent resister. In "Nonviolence and Racial Justice," King discussed five elements of nonviolence that are strikingly similar to those found in Gregg. According to King, nonviolence resists, and thus is not a method for cowards; it is based on humility, and does not seek to humiliate the opponent, but to befriend and reconcile with him; it respects persons, and thus attacks the forces of evil, not persons; at the center of nonviolence is agape, that is, understanding goodwill; and at bottom nonviolence is based on the conviction that the universe hinges on a moral foundation, and thus is friendly to and supports the achievement of good and value in the world.[35] Because the universe is on the side of justice, the nonviolent resister may reasonably have faith in the future, which in turn enables such a person to endure physical blows and suffering without retaliating in kind. In addition, and not unlike Gregg, King believed that while persons are not born with these qualities, most are capable of developing them through rigorous training and discipline. But we have seen that King, like Gandhi, believed that only a small minority of persons are ever likely to reach the stage of commitment to absolute nonviolence as the way God intends for human beings to live in the world. However, many more can, when properly trained and disciplined, be much more committed to nonviolence than the vast

33. Ibid., 51.

34. Ibid.

35. King, "Nonviolence and Racial Justice," in *A Testament of Hope: The Essential Writings of Martin Luther King, Jr.*, ed. James M. Washington (New York: Harper & Row, 1986), 7–9.

majority of people, and thus are able to help in leading nonviolent campaigns against social injustice. Indeed, King himself was aware that believers in nonviolence as a strategy need not necessarily view it as a way of life; that they could, indeed did, do much good in the struggle for civil rights. Although many of the young people in the movement, for example, the Nashville student activists, saw the value of nonviolence in the deeper spiritual sense that King did, huge numbers—such as many of the northern latecomers to SNCC—did not.

EVIDENCE OF MORAL JIU-JITSU IN KING

We see the influence of Richard Gregg's concept of moral jiu-jitsu in many of King's writings, sermons, and speeches. In *Stride Toward Freedom*, King wrote that nonviolence (or the power of love) may cause a sense of shame to develop in violent opponents, "and thereby bring about a transformation and change of heart."[36] In the commencement address given at Lincoln University in Pennsylvania in 1961 ("The American Dream"), we find him emphasizing the same principle, while also stating the effect of nonviolence on both the opponent and the nonviolent resister.

> The practical aspect of nonviolent resistance is that it exposes the moral defenses of the opponent. Not only that, it somehow arouses his conscience at the same time, and it breaks down his morale. He has no answer for it. If he puts you in jail, that's all right; if he lets you out, that's all right too. If he beats you, you accept that; if he doesn't beat you—fine. And so you go on, leaving him with no answer.[37]

This is precisely the idea that we saw in Gregg's elaboration of the doctrine of moral jiu-jitsu, but we also saw that in this writer's mind, at least, the idea about the arousal of the conscience of the opponent should not be accepted uncritically. We should at least be aware that sustained nonviolence may not have (indeed has not had!) this effect on every opponent. And yet, it is important to remember that King was a thoroughgoing personalist and Christian in the sense that he believed that there is a core of goodness in every human being even if we see no concrete evidence of it in the way specific individuals behave and live. Consequently, it follows for such a person that there is at least a reasonable chance that the power of love will somehow affect the

---

36. King, *Stride*, 99.

37. King, "The American Dream," in *A Testament of Hope*, 214.

moral sensibility of violent opponents. In any event, this was the unwavering conviction by which King lived and did civil rights ministry.

In *Why We Can't Wait* (1964), King shows how sustained nonviolence confuses and discombobulates racist antagonists and throws them completely off balance morally—precisely the aim of *moral jiu-jitsu*.

> When, for decades, you have been able to make a man compromise his manhood by threatening him with a cruel and unjust punishment, and when suddenly he turns upon you and says: "Punish me. I do not deserve it. But because I do not deserve it, I will accept it so that the world will know that I am right and you are wrong," you hardly know what to do. You feel defeated and secretly ashamed. You know that this man is as good a man as you are; that from some mysterious source he has found the courage and the conviction to meet physical force with soul force.[38]

Asked by *Playboy* interviewer Alex Haley in 1965 what he meant by "militant nonviolence," King replied that it was both a powerful and just weapon. He then said, once again illustrating the concept of moral *jiu-jitsu*: "If you confront a man who has long been cruelly misusing you, and say, 'Punish me, if you will; I do not deserve it, but I will accept it, so that the world will know I am right and you are wrong,' then you wield a powerful and a just weapon. This man, your oppressor, is automatically morally defeated, and if he has any conscience, he is ashamed."[39] As in a number of instances, the latter part of King's statement—the insertion of "if"—indicates his awareness that there may be exceptional cases in which conscience may be absent in opponents or so underdeveloped that they are less susceptible to the influence of the power of love. But, as in the case of the Bull Connors, Laurie Pritchetts, and Jim Clarks that King and SCLC encountered along the civil rights trail, a bad seed here and there was not enough to stop the power of love. For King, the universe itself is so structured that in the long sweep of things love will have the last say. Indeed, King believed there is a power in love that the world has never truly discovered. Jesus and Gandhi discovered it, but the mass of men and women have not, so committed are they to striking back when struck, of appealing to an eye for an eye, a tooth for a tooth, and hate for hate.[40] We should remember that for King, the God of the Hebrew prophets and Jesus loves every human

38. King, *Why We Can't Wait*, 19.

39. King, *Playboy* Interview, in *A Testament of Hope*, 348.

40. *The Papers* (2007), 6:428n20.

being—regardless. Consequently, one who subscribes fully to the King type of nonviolence must love even the Cecil Prices and Adolph Hitlers of the world, even as they also resist their dastardly treatment of human beings with all the power they can wield through nonviolence and a determined desire for human dignity and human rights.

Arguably, King's best illustration of moral jiu-jitsu appears in the sermon he preached at the Detroit Council of Churches on March 7, 1961, "Loving Your Enemies." Reacting to the tendency to hamper blacks' progress in the area of civil rights, he said:

> We will match your capacity to inflict suffering by our capacity to endure suffering. We will meet your physical force with soul force. Do to us what you will, and we will still love you. We cannot in all good conscience obey your unjust laws because non-cooperation with evil is as much a moral obligation as is cooperation with good. And so put us in jail, and we will go in with humble smiles on our faces, still loving you. Bomb our homes and threaten our children, and we will still love you. Send your propaganda agents around the country and make it appear that we are not fit morally, culturally, and otherwise for integration. And we will still love you. Send your hooded perpetrators of violence into our communities at the midnight hours, and drag us out on some wayside road and beat us and leave us half dead, and we will still love you. But be assured that we will wear you down by our capacity to suffer. And one day we will win our freedom, but not only will we win freedom for ourselves, we will so appeal to your heart and conscience that we will win you in the process. . . . This seems to me the only answer and the only way to make our nation a new nation and our world a new world.[41]

It did not take long for Martin Luther King to understand the significance of the difference between nonviolence as a strategy or tactic for social change, and nonviolence as a philosophy or way of life. As a strategy, one appealed to nonviolence only as a means to social change as long as it worked. As a philosophy or creed, one is committed to nonviolence as a way of life in all things, no matter what. One committed to this degree believes that the world functions best as God intends only through nonviolence or the power of love, which for King is the only absolute. Bayard Rustin helped King to understand

41. Ibid., 6:428.

and accept Gandhi's doctrine of nonviolence as a way of life, and before long came to see King as "a devotee" to nonviolence.[42]

King was a quick study. Within a month's time of having met and worked with Rustin and Smiley, "he had become an articulate advocate of Gandhian methods."[43] It was around this time that the *Baltimore Afro-American* newspaper characterized him as "Alabama's Gandhi."[44] Two months later, King himself was declaring that Gandhi's influence was at the center of the movement. Indeed, later, in September 1960, King summarized the message of the nonviolent resister as follows:

> [W]e will take direct action against injustice without waiting for other agencies to act. We will not obey unjust laws or submit to unjust practices. We will do this peacefully, openly and cheerfully because our aim is to persuade. We adopt the means of non-violence because our end is a community at peace with itself. We will try to persuade with our words, but if our words fail, we will try to persuade with our acts. We will always be willing to talk and seek fair compromise, but we are ready to suffer when necessary and even risk our lives to become witnesses to the truth as we see it.[45]

We have seen that King's emphasis on the love ethic of the Sermon on the Mount has much in common with Gandhian principles. Because of his dependence on Christian love and his insistence from the beginning that theirs would be a method of persuasion and protest rather than intimidation and violence, King learned quickly from Rustin and Smiley. "The glorious thing," Rustin said, "is that he came to a profoundly deep understanding of nonviolence through the struggle itself, and through reading and discussions which he had in the process of carrying on the protest. . . ."[46] King unquestionably learned much from the literature by and about Gandhi, but the day-to-day practice of living nonviolence and making necessary adjustments to his practice during the boycott is what solidified the learning and compelled him to see nonviolence as something more than a strategy for social change.

42. Bayard Rustin, *The Reminiscences* (New York: Columbia University Oral History Library, 1988), 356.

43. *The Papers*, 3:21.

44. Ibid., 3:20.

45. Ibid., 5:504.

46. Rustin, *The Reminiscences*, 138.

Always the man of ideas and ideals, King gleaned the theoretical meaning of nonviolence through intensive reading, reflection, and conversation with Rustin, Smiley, and Lawson. However, the true meaning of nonviolence was gained only as his reading, thinking, and conversing about it converged with the day-to-day efforts to actually do, that is, to put into practice what nonviolence required. Ideas and practice, or *practiced ideas*, are what made nonviolence live for King and convinced him beyond all measure that this is the best means to establishing the beloved community.

When we remember that King was a Christian and a thoroughgoing personalist, it would be a stretch to say that he valued ideas as much as he valued human beings. And yet, there is no doubt that he loved ideas for what they can contribute to making persons and the world better than they are. Indeed, we have seen that throughout his intellectual journey toward nonviolence the ideas that King himself brought to the table were in constant dialogue with those he encountered through study of personalism, Rauschenbusch, Gandhi, Niebuhr, Hegel, existentialists such as Paul Tillich and Jean-Paul Sartre, and a host of others. A truly eclectic thinker in the best sense, King came to see that ideas do not belong to any single individual, since we are always building on what went before. In this regard it makes sense to say that ideas are communal—that they belong not to a single individual, but to the community.

In any event, Martin Luther King was also one who had the courage to change or tweak his ideas and practice when such change seemed called for by experience or current events, and when he learned new things about his people, his country, and/or the world. This is precisely what happened when, influenced by a recommendation from Marian Wright (now Edelman), he decided to launch the Poor People's Campaign.[47]

When Martin Luther King took his branch of the movement north to Chicago in 1966, he discovered once again the challenge of trying to apply nonviolence in a new context. It was one thing to move in and out of cities in the Deep South with the nonviolent way, an area of the country that had a slower pace and rhythm and where cities were not as congested as a Chicago or Cleveland. In the South, nonviolent campaigns could virtually bring businesses and cities to a halt. But in Chicago, this was not possible unless significant changes were made in how nonviolence was applied. King discovered not that

47. Taylor Branch, *At Canaan's Edge: America in the King Years 1965-68* (New York: Simon & Schuster, 2006), 641. King wanted a means to "dramatize poverty from remote Mississippi or Alabama," and thus welcomed Wright's suggestion. "Wright got the gist of her idea from Robert Kennedy, who told her after the hearings in Mississippi that Congress would address such misery only if someone made it more uncomfortable not to" (641).

nonviolence could not work in northern cities like Chicago, but that it needed to take on a radically different look. They had arrived at a new stage of struggle, which meant that a new nonviolent tactic was needed than what was utilized in the South. Virtually after the fact, when it was too late to impact Chicago, King saw that the new face of nonviolence had to be mass civil disobedience, with which the SCLC had not yet experimented.

Mass civil disobedience was particularly needed regarding something as big as the massive poverty and economic injustice that he wanted to address. The Poor People's Campaign would be primarily about jobs and income. Intellectually and practically, King knew that in the North, in Washington near the halls of Congress and the White House, movement strategy had to be such that it could bring those places to a standstill, such that the machinery of business and government could not function. For this to happen, nonviolence had to be implemented on a grand scale, the likes of which King and others had not experienced in the United States.

Nonviolence had to be radically adapted to the urban conditions of the North. King implied as much in his "State of the Movement" address to the SCLC staff retreat at Frogmore, South Carolina, on November 28, 1967: "Non-violent protest must now mature to a new level, to correspond to heightened black impatience and stiffened white resistance. This high level is mass civil disobedience."[48] King argued that it must be an open process, operated by massive numbers of the nation's poor of all races. "Mass civil disobedience as a new stage of struggle, can transmute the deep anger of the ghetto into a creative force. To dislocate the functioning of a city without destroying it can be more effective than a riot because it can be longer lasting, costly to the largest society, but not wantonly destructive. It is a device of social action that is more difficult for the government to quell by superior force."[49] For only a tactic of this magnitude could disrupt the workings of government to the extent that politicians and other powers would be forced to both listen to and to think very seriously about honoring their demands.

CONCLUSION

Martin Luther King's children were made to understand that he sometimes had to go to jail to help people, such as making it possible for children of all races to be admitted to places like Funtown in Atlanta. There is sometimes humor in the

48. King, "The State of the Movement," address to SCLC Staff Retreat at Frogmore, SC, November 28, 1967, King Center Library and Archives, 4.

49. Ibid., 5.

304 | Extremist for Love

honesty and forthrightness of children. When Coretta King tried to explain to their daughter Yolanda why she could not go to Funtown, and that her daddy sometimes went to jail to make it possible for her to go, she responded: "Well, that's fine Mommy. Tell him to stay in jail until I can go to Funtown."[50]

We are now at the point of asking what all this means concretely for us today, nearly fifty years after Martin Luther King was assassinated. King insisted that nonviolence is the only reasonable and moral means to achieving the beloved community. Having seen how deep are the family roots of King's commitment to resisting social injustice and engaging in nonviolent direct action, how he loved ideas for what they could provide toward making human beings and human communities better, and how he unswervingly and unrelentingly practiced those ideas in civil rights campaigns from Montgomery to Memphis, we can now ask: Did he leave openings for hope that things could be better than they are at this moment? In part, King's legacy to us is that we should not only study and grow to love ideas and ideals, but should put them to use in establishing the community of love; that community in which the dignity of every person will be respected and each one will be treated accordingly just because they are persons.

No honest person will deny that nearly fifty years after King's death, the racial discrimination that hounded and tormented his people in his day continues to do so even today. Indeed, King thought that the problem of racism was just as acute in Congress, if not more so, than in the rest of the country. In this he was not deceived. Just months before he was assassinated, he said that "Congress, more than the American people, is running amok with racism."[51] This statement is just as true today, if not more so, since racism is frequently masked by right-wing rhetoric about family values, and people are being judged on the basis of the content of one's character on a playing field that is nowhere near level. And yet, we know that right up to the end King held out *hope* for the day when the problem of racism would be resolved and his people would be admitted to full equality. However, none understood better than King just how difficult a challenge this would be, knowing as he did how endemic racism is in the very fabric of this nation. Indeed, King knew that this nation was born in racism, and that even the most liberal white persons did not know how deeply implicated they were in racism. Today we know that many of the most sensitive and "enlightened" white liberals are not in touch with their

50. Quoted in Lewis V. Baldwin, *There Is a Balm in Gilead* (Minneapolis: Augsburg Fortress Press, 1991), 147.

51. King, "The Crisis in America's Cities," address to SCLC Conference in Atlanta, August 15, 1967, King Center Library and Archives, 3.

own unearned privilege and how much they benefit from racism, even though they themselves are not racists and do all they can to eradicate racist practices.

Considering all of the sacrifices and contributions of King and many others who were committed to movement work, is there reason to hope that we can get any closer to establishing the beloved community—not a perfect community to be sure, but one that is constitutionally based on a racism-free society and full equality for all? In the spirit and witness of Martin Luther King it must be our hope that this can be done if groups of creative minorities of people are willing to make the necessary sacrifices. So the question before us is: What can be done to achieve this end? King himself left clues. What are some of these? What elevated his level of hope, and may thus contribute to elevating ours? This is the subject of chapter ten, the final chapter of this book.

PART 5

Where Do We Go from Here?

Although Martin Luther King experienced moments of discouragement when it seemed that progress toward the attainment of civil rights and equality was not occurring quickly enough, or the changes that were occurring were not deep enough to make a real and lasting difference in the lives of the vast majority of blacks and the poor of all races, he believed fundamentally—right up to his last speech the night before he was assassinated—that racial equality and the beloved community were on the horizon and were in fact achievable. Remember his words that night at Masonic Temple in Memphis? Repeating words he uttered in a sermon in early 1957, when twelve unexploded sticks of dynamite were found on the porch of his house, King told the huge crowd that he had been to the mountaintop; that he had looked over and seen the Promised Land (or beloved community). Because of the level of hatred and moral insensitivity in the nation, along with the increasingly credible threats against his life, King went on to say to the crowd that he might not get to the Promised Land with them, but that he wanted them to know that as a people they would get there.[1] King was assuming that even in his absence from the

1. After twelve sticks of unexploded dynamite were found on the doorsteps of his house in early 1957 (approximately one year after his house was bombed), King preached a sermon in which he anticipated the "mountaintop" and "Promised Land" language of his very last speech in Memphis the night before he was assassinated. The *Pittsburgh Courier* (February 9, 1957) reported him saying: "Tell Montgomery that they can keep shooting and I'm going to stand up to them; tell Montgomery they can keep bombing and I'm going to stand up to them. If I had to die tomorrow morning I would die happy because *I've been to*

scene blacks would continue on the path to freedom and equality, and would also continue to do those things, such as engage in organized nonviolent direct action campaigns, that would ensure the actualization of racial equality in a racism-free society. All of this, he believed, would contribute to saving the soul of the nation.

Having read deeply in the King corpus of published and unpublished papers, speeches, and sermons, I have seen nothing to suggest that King believed that white people in the United States would not admit blacks to full equality, and that racism would not be a permanent fixture. But as I say this, I want to be careful not to imply that this was because King possessed an overly optimistic view of human nature in general, or that he was naïvely optimistic about the possibilities of human beings' achievements in the area of human relations, more specifically, race relations. I most certainly do not want to imply that King was unduly or uncritically optimistic about whites' intentions regarding the race problem. Nor do I want to suggest that King had such trust and faith in white people that he was convinced that they would eventually do the right thing in the matters of race and equality. He was much more realistic than that, and he learned a great deal from experience, history, and current events. He knew, for example, that it did not matter which political party controlled the White House, for historically, presidential administrations have consistently betrayed blacks, Native Americans, other people of color, and the poor. He knew that whether Democrats or Republicans controlled Congress, the traditionally left out and excluded in the nation remained left out and excluded. The only difference, King knew, was that one or the other political party—usually the Democratic one since the era of Franklin D. Roosevelt—shelled out more crumbs for the historically excluded, and not more than that. However, neither party was committed—then or now—to admitting them to full equality and living-wage employment. Indeed, Martin Luther King knew that white religious people and their pastors, not unlike most white people generally, were committed to going only so far in the struggle for equality of the races; that their commitment was not to total equality between the races and a racism-free society. King was realistic enough to know that as human beings white people—like all other human beings—had their own interests, and as finite and limited beings they were as susceptible to missing the moral mark as every other group. Therefore, it was not that Martin Luther King possessed an uncritical faith and trust in white people to do the right thing. He

the mountaintop and _I've seen the Promised Land_, and it's going to be here in Montgomery" (quoted in James Cone, _Martin & Malcolm & America: A Dream or a Nightmare_ [Maryknoll, NY: Orbis, 1991], 125, my emphasis).

did not. And yet, his optimism about the achievement of racial equality and the beloved community remained strong to the end of his life. Why? If the answer is not to be found in faith and trust in white people, or even black people, then where?

Martin Luther King wrote about his position even in his posthumously published article, "A Testament of Hope," where he said that his optimism was high even during the pessimistic times they had been experiencing in recent years. What critics of his optimism fail to understand, he said, was that he had seen and had been motivated and inspired by the changes that occurred since the Montgomery struggle. He had gotten a clear glimpse of what could happen when people of goodwill worked cooperatively and determinedly together in common cause. To be sure, the changes were not enough, and there was no evidence that they went deep enough to ensure that future generations of black people would not have to fight many of the same battles again and again. The successful boycott did not end racial discrimination in Montgomery. The agreement with Birmingham businessmen did not end racial discrimination, the race bombings, and other vicious acts of the Klan and the White Citizens Council against blacks. The march from Selma to Montgomery, and even the passage of the 1965 Voting Rights Bill, did not end racial segregation in Selma and the Mississippi Delta and did not ensure that blacks would not be discriminated against at the polls. Nevertheless, King had witnessed what individual black and white people *could* achieve when they *trusted* each other enough to work cooperatively, creatively, courageously, and tenaciously together. He had lived through a time when whites and blacks together had been physically brutalized and murdered—for example, Bob Zellner, James Peck, John Lewis, Jim Zwerg, Walter Bergman, Jonathan Daniels, Sammy Younge Jr., Herbert Lee, Viola Liuzzo, James Reeb, Michael Schwerner, James Chaney, and Andrew Goodman, Jimmy Lee Jackson, and many more. Even so, King had also seen numerous instances in which individual blacks and whites rose to the occasion and continued the fight even though they were aware that any one of them could well be the next casualty. But he had seen well-meaning people fight through their fears and uncertainties, exhibiting the attitude that human beings and freedom are too precious to give up fighting for civil rights. This, to King, was not only indicative of the human spirit in general, but was representative of the best of what it meant to be a citizen of the United States of America. That spirit and determination enhanced King's own level of optimism, expectation, courage, and confidence in the possibility of what can be achieved when human beings are allied together in common cause and refuse to give in to complacency, passivity, and fear. He had seen that human beings, regardless of race-ethnicity, or whether they were southerners or northerners, could be better than they were when they *chose* to be.

The very fact that such people resisted injustice with all their might and were willing to sacrifice their lives so that others might be free inspired Martin Luther King's sense and level of hopefulness. The fact that there were white people at all in a fundamentally racist nation who were willing to fight and die in order to actualize freedom and equality for all people inspired King and was, for him, reason enough to continue the struggle while continuing to believe that racial equality could be achieved. This is all the more striking when it is remembered that the idea of the *inequality* (not equality!) of the races was actually assumed by the drafters of the Constitution.

In "A Testament of Hope," King said that naysayers "fail . . . to perceive the sense of affirmation generated by the challenge of embracing struggle and surmounting obstacles."[2] In some sense a victory was won precisely at the point that one actually took on the challenge of struggling against obstacles to equality and freedom. King then went on to say something that few have paid much if any attention to. What he said needs to be examined very carefully if we are to really understand what might be characterized as the *sheer madness of his optimism* in a nation where white people have historically kept (and keep) racism alive, no matter how hard and long black and well-meaning whites and others have struggled against it; no matter how many lives have been lost because of it; no matter how many laws and policies have been developed and enacted to outlaw it. We find in what King said the real reason and driving force behind his optimism. To those who wondered why he continued to be optimistic, he said: "They have no comprehension of the strength that comes from faith in God and man. It is possible for me to falter, but I am profoundly secure in my knowledge that God loves us; he has not worked out a design for our failure."[3] Notice what King said: "the strength that comes from faith in God *and* man." While it would be erroneous to say that King had no faith and trust in human beings, it would be an even more egregious error to say that the deepest source of his optimism was his faith and trust in human beings. Any faith and trust that King had in human beings was derivative; a derivative of his underlying faith, trust, and absolute dependence on the God of the Hebrew prophets, Jesus Christ, and his parents and grandparents. This God, King held, was relentlessly faithful, compassionate, caring, trustworthy, and just. King

---

2. Martin Luther King Jr., "A Testament of Hope," in *A Testament of Hope: The Essential Writings of Martin Luther King, Jr.*, ed. James M. Washington (New York: Harper & Row, 1986), 314.

3. Ibid.

made this very discovery early in the Montgomery struggle, and it strengthened and carried him forward in the movement.

It will be recalled that one late night during the early weeks of the Montgomery bus boycott King went to bed after a particularly taxing day. Just as he was dozing off to sleep the telephone rang. King reported that the caller was crude and vulgar, saying essentially that the good white people of Montgomery were fed up with his troublemaking and that if he and his family did not leave town within a week their house would be blown up. This was not the first call of this sort that he had received, but on that particular night, perhaps because of the lateness of the hour and his deep fatigue, he simply could not get to sleep. As he recounted the incident many times in ensuing years, he got out of bed, went to the kitchen, made a pot of coffee, and sat at the kitchen table. As he thought about the ugliness of what the caller had said, his sense of humanity took over as he began to think about the safety and well-being of his wife and infant baby. Naturally, this led to thoughts about his role in the Montgomery campaign and how he could somehow bow out gracefully, but without appearing to be a coward. He then began reflecting on the conceptions of God he had studied in seminary and during doctoral studies, hoping that he could find some comfort therein. However, he found that not one of them was sufficient for his need as he sat at the kitchen table wondering what to do.

King knew in that instant that he needed to call on the God that his parents and maternal grandmother told him about when he was a boy. It was no longer sufficient for him to know that his parents had told him about this God, that they themselves utterly trusted and depended on this God, and constantly held their son in their prayers. Now, in a moment of deep despair and troubled soul, he had to find and experience this God for himself. Having come to the end of his own means and self-dependence, the young minister turned his entire being toward God in prayer. Reminding God that he was trying to do the right thing by fighting to end segregation on the buses, he confessed that he was at his wits' end, that he knew not what to do. He was turning it all over to God on whom he would depend absolutely from that point forward. Having made his confession and opened himself to God, King said that he experienced the presence of the Divine as he never had before. His fear and sense of despair left him almost immediately, as he sensed God's voice admonishing him to stand up for justice and righteousness, and assuring him that God would be with him forever. At that point King decided to put his ultimate faith and trust in God.

King referred to his experience that night as his "vision at the kitchen table,"[4] his "deep religious experience" as he called it in a 1957 interview.[5] "I had come to feel, at that time, that in the struggle, God was with me, and through this deep religious experience, I was able to endure and face anything that came my way."[6] This experience, he reflected, prepared him for almost anything that might come, including the bombing of his house three nights later. Reflecting on the vision experience in a sermon one year later, he told his Dexter Congregation: "Since that morning I can stand up without fear. So I'm not afraid of anybody this morning."[7] That experience also taught King something about the power of prayer. What his parents and maternal grandmother earlier taught him about prayer and God's unrelenting compassion and faithfulness became real for him perhaps for the first time in his twenty plus years as a Christian. Lewis V. Baldwin provides instructive words on what King gleaned from the vision at the kitchen table.

> King found new life in prayer, was reminded that prayer indeed mattered, and began to believe anew in how the sovereign work of the Almighty was being manifested in both his own life and in the bus protest. Moreover, the experience deepened his sense of what it meant to follow Jesus Christ as a passionate disciple, and he came to see that prayer would be a vital dimension of that which enabled him sufficiently to carry out his work. In a general sense, the experience in the kitchen further equipped King to speak from experience and thus authoritatively about the saving power of prayer.[8]

4. See Cone, *Martin & Malcolm & America*, 125. When biographer David J. Garrow writes of this experience, the reader is left with the sense that this was an all-defining moment for King; that it was the equivalent of a religious conversion experience for him that settled once and for all any doubts or tendencies to doubt, that night and beyond. (See Garrow, *Bearing the Cross: Martin Luther King, Jr., and the Southern Christian Leadership Conference* [New York: William Morrow, 1986], 56–58, 89.) My own sense is that this was indeed a significant early experience for King that strengthened his faith and resolve, and in that moment, at least, comforted him to the point that he was able to manage any fears and doubts that would surely arise later. King was a finite and limited being, and thus the fears and uncertainties would most assuredly arise again and again, as long as he was on this side of the grave and continued to be faithful to his calling. King would (and did!) call on this experience at other difficult moments, but having gone through all he had gone through each time, I would think that he had much more to draw upon than the vision experience only, important as that was. My point is, we cannot (or should not) minimize the importance of the "successes" along the way, for these too King could remember during the difficult and depressing periods as the movement advanced.

5. Clayborne Carson et al., eds., *The Papers of Martin Luther King, Jr.* (Berkeley: University of California Press, 2000), 4:298.

6. Ibid.

7. Quoted in L. D. Reddick, *Crusader without Violence: A Biography of Martin Luther King, Jr.* (New York: Harper & Brothers, 1957), 166.

King recounted the vision experience on a number of subsequent occasions when things were not going well for him and the movement. It was a reminder to him of God's promise to be faithful and present to him as he lived out God's calling on his life. It was also a reminder that neither he nor any other human being was really in charge, but that it was God's world, and ultimately the world and all that is in it belong to God who, like a loving and caring parent, watches over it all. It was a reminder of who he had vowed to hold onto and trust that night at the kitchen table in a moment of deep faith crisis. On that night, at the kitchen table, he vowed to trust in the God of the Hebrew prophets, Jesus Christ, his parents and grandparents—the God who was able to make a way out of no way.

So in the most fundamental sense, Martin Luther King's faith and trust was in the God he discovered that late night at the kitchen table, and each day thereafter. This was the faith that would sustain him when it seemed that the movement was faltering or that even his closest colleagues and allies were forsaking him. This and this alone was the source of any faith and trust he developed in human beings of any race. Moreover, that King agreed unconditionally with the Jewish and Christian teaching that every person is imbued with the image of God and therefore has something of God in her or him must also mean that one who accepts such teaching must also have some confidence in the capacity for human beings to do that which is noble and good. We saw earlier that as a doctoral student King studied and was much influenced by Brightman's doctrine that God is *axiogenesis* and *axiosoteria*[9] (the source of good and the conserver and continuer of goodness). This idea is not inconsistent with the creation stories in the book of Genesis, where we are told that God created all that there is and declared that it was good, indeed, "very good" (Gen. 1:31). This must necessarily mean that God considers human beings to be very good, fundamentally, notwithstanding the inclination to sin by choosing to do other than what God requires.

If human beings are fundamentally good, it is reasonable that one such as Martin Luther King would have faith in their capacity to do the right thing. King was not naïve about this, however. He had witnessed and experienced racism enough to be realistic in his thinking about human beings and human destiny. He developed this strong sense of realism about human capabilities early, a point that is often overlooked by critics who claim that he had too much

8. Lewis V. Baldwin, *Never to Leave Us Alone: The Prayer Life of Martin Luther King, Jr.* (Minneapolis: Fortress Press, 2010), 69–70.

9. See Edgar S. Brightman's interesting discussion of these terms in relation to God in his book, *A Philosophy of Religion* (New York: Prentice-Hall, 1940), 204n, 216–17, 230, 372.

faith or trust in white people and thus was uncritically optimistic about what can be achieved in race relations.

King was not an uncritical idealist. Rather, he sought in his practice to be consistent with his best ideas and highest ideals. But in doing so he never lost sight of the harsh realities of the sheer pervasiveness of racism and the elusiveness of racial equality. He acknowledged that as a human being he might "falter," might come up short, but he was "profoundly secure" in the knowledge that God's love and compassion for human beings is unswerving, and that God would not have constructed the universe in a way that human beings would be guaranteed to fail in their efforts to do God's will.

This is where Martin Luther King's faith lay—in God. Because of this basic faith he could also trust that human beings, when they will to do so, can be better than they are, whether regarding the race question, economic inequality, or war. If we keep this in mind we can avoid the tendency of some critics to charge that in the matter of racial equality and the attainment of the beloved community King was unduly optimistic. It is important to remember the fundamental source of his optimism, how he perceived reality (as infused with value), and where he turned in moments when even he was not able to see that progress was being made toward eliminating racism and establishing the community of love.

There is much to be said for James Cone's claim that while early on in King's civil rights ministry he tended to trust more in human beings—blacks because of their nonviolent direct actions in the struggle, and many whites because of their commitment to formal equality—as the movement continued into the turbulent 1960s he was forced to return to his deep commitment, trust, and hope in God. Contrasting King's earlier and later hope and trust in human beings and God, Cone writes: ". . . Martin's hope in the last years was not based upon the backing he received from whites or even blacks. Rather, his hope was grounded almost exclusively upon his faith in the God of the biblical and black traditions, which told him to stand up for right even if it would cost him his life."[10] However, because King's hope was fundamentally grounded in his faith in God—which dated back at least to the vision at the kitchen table—Cone's statement should not be taken to mean that in the later years King had no hope or trust in human potential when human beings were at their best. Nor should Cone's statement be taken to mean—and I don't think he intended it to mean—that at some point after the kitchen table experience King lost faith and trust in God, recapturing it only in his last years. King's trust in God

10. Cone, *Martin & Malcolm & America*, 236.

also included his strong sense that God imbued human beings with the divine image. Because of the trace of God in human beings it must also be the case that they have the capacity—even if they too often lack the inclination—to strive for higher ground; to respect the humanity and dignity of persons. In light of this, I have a difficult time seeing a too sharp dichotomy between King's earlier and later hope in God and in human beings. Besides, King's hope and trust in human beings was always based on what he believed they were capable of at their best. By the same token, it makes sense that his faith and hope in God would deepen over the years, especially as he witnessed so often the tendency of human beings to prefer the low road.

To the end, Martin Luther King remained committed to the dialectical method of obtaining the highest truth and the best solutions to the problems that plagued his people. This was no different regarding his thinking about human nature in general and what is achievable in race relations. He was not a racial idealist *or* racial realist. Consistent with his propensity to dialectical thinking it is reasonable to say that he was both. We see evidence of dialectical thinking in numerous places in his writings, speeches, and sermons. In "A Testament of Hope," we find King saying:

> Man has the capacity to do right as well as wrong, and his history is a path upward, not downward. The past is strewn with the ruins of the empires of tyranny, and each is a monument not merely to man's blunders but to his capacity to overcome them. While it is a bitter fact that in America in 1968, I am denied equality solely because I am black, yet I am not a chattel slave. Millions of people have fought thousands of battles to enlarge my freedom; *restricted as it still is progress has been made.* This is why I remain an optimist, though I am also a realist, about the barriers before us. Why is the issue of inequality still so far from solution in America, a nation that professes itself to be democratic, inventive, hospitable to new ideas, rich, productive and awesomely powerful? The problem is so tenacious because, despite its virtues and attributes, America is deeply racist and its democracy is flawed both economically and socially.[11]

Because human beings have been created such that they can choose to do good or evil, right or wrong, King had reason to have confidence that those who happened to be white could, if they choose, do the right thing and admit blacks to full equality. As he read history, it seemed evident that humanity was

---

11. King, "A Testament of Hope," 314 (my emphasis).

on an upward path in human relations. The changes were not coming solely because of any moral sensitivity on the part of white oppressors, but because of the determined and cooperative struggles of blacks, along with committed whites. What was important to King was the clear evidence of such upward progress, even though much of it occurred only at a snail's pace. He took encouragement and inspiration from the very fact that conscious, determined struggle and sacrifice were a key to at least opening the door to equality, as well as eliminating some of the worse forms of human degradation, for example, chattel slavery and denial of the vote.

It is true, King acknowledged, that in 1968 he and his people lacked equality and full freedom. However, as he surveyed U.S. history and the moral shape of the country he had also to admit that the changes that occurred were a result of not only the struggles of blacks, but of many white people struggling in conjunction with them in every era of the nation's history (even though most of the changes were not deep and lasting, and others were superficial and fleeting at best). King was saying that by the late 1960s much more should have been accomplished in the struggle for freedom and equality, and yet it was also true that progress had been made, and this was why he continued to retain a sense of optimism. But his optimism or idealism in this regard was balanced by his realism and his ability and willingness to see things as they were; to see, despite his optimism, that racism and economic exploitation are endemic to this society and all of its institutions, and that nothing that has happened historically suggests a willingness of the vast majority of white people in any era—including these early years of the second decade of the twenty-first century—to eradicate policies and practices that guarantee chronic misery in Afrikan American communities.

Make no mistake about it. As optimistic as Martin Luther King was about the coming of the beloved community, he was also a *racial realist*,[12] as evidenced by what he said in an interview with Alex Haley in 1965: "The concept of

---

12. The concept of "racial realism" is associated with the writings of the civil rights activist-legal scholar, the late Derrick Bell (1930–2011). The idea is captured in Bell's claim that "just as death is inevitable and inherent in life, so racism in America, while not inherent, is intractable. It is socially constructed, but no less real. We must deal directly with American racism, just as we do with death. Civil rights advocates and their organizations must face the unavoidable truth that this nation's social stability is built on a belief in and a determination to maintain white dominance. Racism is the manifestation of this deeply entrenched determination" (Derrick Bell, "The Racial Preference Licensing Act," in *The Derrick Bell Reader*, ed. Richard Delgado and Jean Stefancic [New York/London: New York University Press, 2005], 52. Reprinted from Foreword: The Final Civil Rights Act, 79 *California Law Review* [1991]. For systematic and provocative discussions on racial realism see 55–96 in *The Derrick Bell Reader*).

supremacy is so embedded in the white society that it will take many years for color to cease to be a judgmental factor."[13] King was not deceived or naïve about the existence and prevalence of racism among whites. This was not a problem among merely a few white people. Rather, in 1968 King declared that "the largest portion of white America is still poisoned by racism which is as native to our soil as pine trees, sagebrush and buffalo grass. Equally native to us is the concept that gross exploitation of the Negro is acceptable, if not commendable. Many whites who concede that Negroes should have equal access to public facilities and the untrammeled right to vote cannot understand that we do not intend to remain in the basement of the economic structure. . . ."[14] This is why equality continues to be elusive, but to his credit King saw unquestionably the structural barriers to achieving equality and a racism-free society. And yet his sense of optimism about what can be achieved remained, which is why he could acknowledge on one hand that racism is so endemic to the structures of this society that it will be many years before it is eliminated, and immediately thereafter say that "it is the keystone of my faith in the future that we will someday achieve a thoroughly integrated society [inclusive of full equality for all]. I believe that before the turn of the century, if trends continue to move and develop as presently, we will have moved a long, long way toward such a society."[15] There is no question that as I write these words more than four decades after King's assassination we are a long, long way from actualizing such a society. Nevertheless, we can see in King's statement that despite his realism about the depth and endemic nature of racism in this country, his last word was one of hope that racism would be eradicated and full equality established. However, there is no evidence on the horizon that either of these is forthcoming.

What, then, are we to think and do? Chapter 10, the final chapter of this book, is an exercise in trying to provide answer to this question. In order to do so we will have to make sense of why it appears that regardless of the legal changes that occur, the substantive condition of black people seems only to worsen. Why does racism, with its devastating consequences, endure fifty years after King's famous "I Have a Dream" speech? Is there reason to hope that racism will be eradicated and equality for blacks become a reality for the first time in the history of this nation?

13. *Playboy* Interview, in *A Testament of Hope*, 375.

14. King, "A Testament of Hope," 316.

15. *Playboy* Interview, in *A Testament of Hope*, 375.

10

Enduring Racism: What Can Be Done to Keep Hope Alive?

Early in his civil rights ministry, Martin Luther King made it crystal clear that the goal was to save the soul of the nation and to establish the beloved community. He did not understand this to be a perfect community, or that it would be a one-to-one correspondence in all details with the kingdom of God ideal. The beloved community acknowledges the absolute dignity of all members and is structured such that the basic needs of all are met before any is allowed to have extras. For the theist like King, this meant that the community is essentially humanized by the ethical principles of Jesus. This idea is not unlike the view of the social gospel advocate Walter Rauschenbusch whose work left an indelible mark on King when he was in seminary. Rauschenbusch himself wrote explicitly about the beloved community ideal but only to the extent that he discussed and criticized Josiah Royce's meaning of the term. Royce saw the beloved community, which he equated with the church, as the great problem in Christianity. According to Rauschenbusch, it was largely problematic that Royce viewed the church as the central idea of Christianity, rather than Christ. This, he felt, was "one of the most unsatisfactory elements in Royce's thought."[1]

When considering King's thought about the beloved community one is left with the sense that he had in mind a radically transformed society; a society that was different even from what Rauschenbusch wrote about regarding the Christianizing of the social order. The latter did not mean requiring that all persons be converted to Christianity, or that the name "Christian" appear in the leading political documents of a nation. Clarifying the point in 1912, Rauschenbusch wrote:

---

1. Walter Rauschenbusch, *A Theology for the Social Gospel* (New York: Macmillan, 1917), 127.

Some descendants of the Scotch Covenanters still refuse to vote or hold office under our government because Jesus Christ is not formally acknowledged as the head of our nation. But in the present state of our life that would only be one more act of national hypocrisy. Moreover Jesus himself does not seem to have cared much about being called "Lord, Lord," unless there was substance to the word. To put a stop to child labor in our country would be a more effective way of doing homage to his sovereignty than any business of words and names.[2]

We have seen that what Rauschenbusch actually meant by Christianizing the social order was taking the highest moral principle of humanity and applying it toward humanizing and reshaping all societal institutions. This would mean not allowing inequality and graft to be embodied in the Constitution of the United States, for example. Foundational principles such as equality and honesty should characterize such a document. This does not mean that rulers will consistently and fairly implement and enforce such principles, for human beings are who they are, and sin is present on all levels of human achievement. Rauschenbusch pointed to slavery as "the one great social institution contradicting the democratic principle which was able to secure recognition and protection in the federal Constitution. It long jutted into our American life as a disturbing remnant from an earlier and evil age. From the terrible sacrifice which it cost our nation to get rid of it we can learn the difference between a suppression of human rights that is supported by the fundamental law, and a frustration of human rights that circumvents the law."[3] Rauschenbusch would have done well to acknowledge the "terrible sacrifice" that enslavement cost blacks, the ones who actually suffered and endured the injustices and indignities, but he did not.

Martin Luther King would have agreed with Rauschenbusch's idea of Christianizing the social order as far as he went. The difference, however, is a major one. An important and necessary criterion for King in a nation with the United States' history of race relations is that the idea of Christianizing the social order should be thoroughly infused and informed by the principle of democracy and equality for all, or for none.

Lewis V. Baldwin, interpreting King's August 16, 1964 address, "Revolution and Redemption," contends that a central idea therein is that followers of Jesus should not be seeking to "Christianize" the world, but to humanize it.[4] One can agree that Christians should not be trying to Christianize

2. Rauschenbusch, *Christianizing the Social Order* (New York: Macmillan, 1926 [1912]), 124.
3. Ibid., 151–52.

in the sense of proselytizing. However, if one means by this term what Rauschenbusch and King seem to have meant, then Christianizing is not a bad thing. Although presently, no evidence has been uncovered to suggest that King read Rauschenbusch's book *Christianizing the Social Order*, we know from a letter he wrote to Mr. M. Bernard Resnikoff in 1961 that his understanding of Christianizing the social order was similar to that of Rauschenbusch. "When I referred to America becoming a Christian nation," he told Resnikoff, "I was not referring to Christianity as an organized institutional religion. *I was referring more to the principles of Christ, which I think are sound and valid for any nation and civilization.*"[5] Moreover, in the sermon, "Transformed Nonconformist," King cited approvingly the Apostle Paul's idea of "the responsibility of Christians to imbue an unchristian world with the ideals of a higher and more noble order."[6] This sounds like what is meant by "Christianizing the social order." As noted above, except for conservatives and fundamentalists, it has nothing to do with requiring that all citizens be Christians or that the name "Christian" be inserted into major political documents. Nor does it have to do with the old idea of establishing a theocracy ruled by the church and making Christian belief and worship compulsory for all.[7] Rather, it has to do with bringing society under the ethical principles of Jesus; of humanizing in the best sense. To Christianize means not that a social order can be perfect, which is impossible as long as human beings are human beings and sin exists. It means, rather, that the basic structure or foundation of society can be brought under the humanizing principles and ideals of Jesus. King's beloved community ideal fits in well with this idea.

4. Lewis V. Baldwin, "Introduction" in *"A Single Garment of Destiny": A Global Vision of Justice*, ed. Lewis V. Baldwin (Boston: Beacon, 2012), 3. See page 20 where King clarifies what he means by "evangelism." It has less to do with proselytizing, and even sending food baskets abroad. Indeed, King admonishes: "It is not even enough to build schools and hospitals. If the millions are to be fed, clothed and housed, the resources of the nations must be put to the task. . . . Christians must encourage, yea demand that their governments act as though the financial and technical resources entrusted to them belong to God, and that these resources are used to the Glory of God for the care of God's children wherever they may be in need." For King, the emphasis of evangelism was more on humanizing than making Christians of everybody. Moreover, he rejected the tendency to identify Christianity and the West.

5. See "I Have Never Been a Religious Bigot," in *"A Single Garment of Destiny": A Global Vision of Justice*, ed. Lewis V. Baldwin [Foreword by Charlayne Hunter-Gault] (Boston: Beacon, 2012), 197 (my emphasis).

6. Martin Luther King Jr., "Transformed Nonconformist," in *Strength to Love* (New York: Harper & Row, 1963), 9.

7. Rauschenbusch, *Christianizing the Social Order*, 124.

James Cone was not wrong when he asserted that Martin Luther King
was a theologian of action, a liberation theologian in the best sense.[8] Any
formal papers that King wrote on theology were written while he was in
seminary and during doctoral studies. Once he was installed as senior pastor at
Dexter Avenue Baptist Church in Montgomery, and elected as president of the
Montgomery Improvement Association shortly thereafter to provide leadership
for the historic bus boycott,[9] there was no time to pursue any postgraduate
scholarly interests he might have had to write abstract theological tracts and/
or to give formal lectures on academic theology before students and professors
of theology. This did not mean that King was no longer a man of ideas and
ideals. But it did mean that he was increasingly a man of *practiced ideas* in every
nonviolent direct action campaign in which he participated.[10]

From what we have learned about Martin Luther King as man of ideas and
lived ideas in nonviolent direct action demonstrations, we can do nothing but
agree that were he among us today he would not want to let the various levels
of government off the moral-economic-political hook regarding the condition
of massive numbers of poor people in the United States, and would insist that
as citizens in an ostensibly democratic society, black people should expect the
support of their tax dollars to help solve their problems, many of which are
the consequence of long years of systematic race discrimination and economic
deprivation. Indeed, we have seen that King challenged governments at all
levels to be responsive to the needs of all citizens. He believed that ultimately
a great nation is a compassionate nation.[11] This is determined by how well
a nation treats its citizens, especially those among the poorest and left out.
And yet there is no question that King was also devoted to the determination
and self-determination of his and other oppressed people and the importance
of taking their problems into their own hands and doing all they can to
cooperatively solve them. By doing so, they send the message that they are

8. James H. Cone, *Martin & Malcolm & America: A Dream or a Nightmare* (Maryknoll, NY: Orbis, 1991), 123.

9. Stewart Burns has written of the little-known two-year boycott of public trolleys by blacks in Montgomery in 1900, barely four years after the famous Supreme Court ruling in *Plessy v. Ferguson* (the case that made "separate but equal" the law of the land). In response to the mandated segregated seating on the trolleys, black ministers in Montgomery urged their parishioners to boycott. "The protest forced the streetcar firm to suspend segregation, though Jim Crow seating resumed after the boycott died down" (Burns, *To the Mountaintop: Martin Luther King, Jr.'s Sacred Mission to Save America 1955-1968* [New York: HarperSanFrancisco, 2004], 460n37).

10. Here my use of the term *practiced* is borrowed from James Cone. See his use of *practiced word* in *Martin & Malcolm & America*, 123.

11. King, *Where Do We Go from Here: Chaos or Community?* (Boston: Beacon, 1967), 178.

neither willing nor interested in uncritically placing their well-being entirely into the hands of those who have historically contributed so much to the cause of their socio-economic predicament in the first place. Even so, to the end King recognized that the powers—in all areas and at every level—are so implicated in the problems that oppress black people that they too must be made to shoulder the responsibility for solving problems that undermine their humanity and sense of dignity as well as their life-chances. This is an absolute necessity if there is to be legitimate hope of solving the systemic aspects of the problem. However, without intentionally minimizing the importance of systemic change in any way, in what follows I focus on what blacks themselves must do, even if it means adhering to what King referred to as "a temporary separation of the races" in the March 25, 1968 conversation he had with Jewish rabbis.[12] I return to this important and provocative idea subsequently. For now, suffice it to say that what follows focuses on how blacks should be thinking about and pursuing equality and a racism-free society, even when indicators are that racism in the United States has an air of permanence about it.

ENDURING RACISM AND HOPE

By 1968, Martin Luther King was pulling no punches. If he had doubts in previous years, he was convinced by now that the vast majority of white people were not willing to admit blacks to full equality and integration *with* power. It is not that he lost all hope that this could happen, for even by 1967 he believed that there was at least a minority of whites who were committed to actualizing authentic equality for blacks.[13] Indeed, right up to the last months of his life he referred to the need to honestly acknowledge the disappointments, while clinging to hope.[14] Hope. This is a significant term in Kingian theology and ethics, and anyone who truly wishes to understand King and his theological project must be aware of this, at all times. None have written more forcefully on the place and importance of hope in King's thought than James H. Cone:

> Martin King's greatest contribution was his ability to communicate a vision of hope in extreme situations of oppression. No matter how difficult the struggle for justice became, no matter how powerful were the opponents of justice, no matter how many people turned

12. See "Conversation with Martin Luther King, Jr.," in *A Testament of Hope: The Essential Writings of Martin Luther King, Jr.*, ed. James M. Washington (New York: Harper & Row, 1991 [1986]), 666.

13. King, *Where Do We Go from Here*, 11.

14. King said this to SCLC staffers at the Frogmore, SC retreat, "The State of the Movement," November 28, 1967, King Center Library and Archives, 8.

against him, King refused to lose hope, because he believed that ultimately right will triumph over wrong. He communicated that hope to the masses throughout the world, enabling them to keep on struggling for freedom and justice even though the odds were against them.[15]

Indeed, at the National Cathedral in Washington, D.C. on March 31, 1968, just four days before he was assassinated, King declared that he would "not yield to a politic of despair," but that he would retain a strong sense of hope.[16]

Nevertheless, King made it clear that the progress that was made as a result of efforts to achieve desegregation in education and other areas of society had been obtained at cut-rate prices. The heaviest costs, in terms of deprivation, were paid by those who were denied access to quality education. Essentially, the nation paid nothing. King knew that in order to do what really needed to be done it was going to be expensive in monetary and other terms, although he was not deceived into thinking that the nation would (even if it could!) ever fully repay blacks for several hundred years of stolen labor and discrimination during and after enslavement.

One also gets the sense that the King of this period, while still insisting on the need for desegregation and eventual integration, was just as adamant about the need for quality education for black students; not one or the other—desegregation *or* quality education—but both. King's position in this regard was different from that of civil rights lawyers who focused primarily on desegregation, believing that this would be the most important gain for black students. King's stance was also different from that of W. E. B. Du Bois, who argued as far back as 1935 that the NAACP's plan to launch a massive legal assault against segregated schools was really not the most important issue concerning black children in public schools. Du Bois argued neither for desegregated nor segregated schools for black children. Rather, he argued for *quality education*, whether the school was desegregated or segregated.

Civil rights activist-lawyer Derrick A. Bell (1930–2011) also uncritically bought into the NAACP desegregation approach. However, years later, after he was appointed as the first black person to the Harvard Law School faculty in 1969, Bell came to believe that the Du Boisian approach was more important than the desegregated school approach; that quality education was more

15. James H. Cone, "Martin Luther King, Jr., and the Third World," in his *Risks of Faith: The Emergence of a Black Theology of Liberation, 1968-1998* (Boston: Beacon, 1999), 94.

16. King, "Remaining Awake Through a Great Revolution," in *A Knock at Midnight*, ed. Clayborne Carson and Peter Holloran (New York: Warner, 1998), 222.

reasonable for black students in the face of enduring racism. Bell came to see that the Supreme Court's landmark *Brown* decision in 1954 was more in the self-interest of whites than to the benefit of blacks. Bell quoted NAACP staff attorney Lewis M. Steel approvingly in this regard. Writing and reflecting on the Court's decisions, including *Brown*, during Earl Warren's tenure as Chief Justice, Steel said in an article that cost him his job:

> Never in the history of the Supreme Court had the implementation of a constitutional right been so delayed or the creation of it put in such vague terms. The Court thereby made clear that it was a white court which would protect the interests of white America in the maintenance of stable institutions.
>
> In essence, the Court considered the potential damage to white Americans resulting from the diminution of privilege as more critical than continued damage to the underprivileged. . . . Worse still, it gave the primary responsibility for achieving educational equality to those who had established the segregated institutions.[17]

On this view, those who benefited most from decisions like *Brown* were not blacks, but whites. Under the Warren Court, the argument continues, the decisions "were profoundly conservative and protected the economic and political status quo by responding to the pleas for justice by blacks and other severely disadvantaged groups just enough to siphon off discontent, thereby limiting the chances that the existing social order would pay more than minimal costs for the reforms achieved."[18] Bell came to agree with Steel, Du Bois, and others that such civil rights decisions must be understood in light of their perceived benefits to whites. The Court's order that the *Brown* decision be implemented "with all deliberate speed" was most certainly more beneficial to whites than to blacks.

In any event, Du Bois believed that as long as racism existed—and like this writer he saw no evidence that it was abating[19]—there was absolutely a need for separate black schools, and no more so than today. These were

17. Quoted in Derrick Bell, *And We Are Not Saved: The Elusive Quest for Racial Justice* (New York: Basic Books, 1987), 60. From Lewis M. Steel, "Nine Men in Black Who Think White," *New York Times Magazine*, October 13, 1968, 56.

18. Quoted in ibid., 61. From Arthur S. Miller, "Social Justice and the Warren Court: A Preliminary Examination," *Pepperdine Law Review* 11 (1984): 489.

19. W. E. B. Du Bois, "Does the Negro Need Separate Schools?," in *Du Bois on Education*, ed. Eugene F. Provenzo Jr. (Walnut Creek, CA: AltaMira, 2002), 135.

the places where black students would likely receive the best, highest-quality education, assuming that those schools had the best-qualified black teachers who received the same pay as white teachers, as well as the same up-to-date quality equipment, books, and other resources that white schools received. Black teachers would not only love, respect, and appreciate black students and their culture, but would *want* to teach them black history and other subjects that teachers in white districts historically had not taught, and did not—and do not—want to teach. In a word, Du Bois argued for quality education, not desegregation, although by his own admission he would have preferred both in a racist nation.

Martin Luther King was without question influenced by the desegregation argument of the NAACP, but dialectical thinker that he was, he was no less influenced by Du Bois's insistence on the highest-quality education for black students. King cited two reasons for the failure of the American educational system. In these we can see the influence of the classroom desegregation model of the civil rights lawyers of the NAACP, in addition to the quality education argument of Du Bois.

> Schools have to be infused with a mission if they are to be successful. The mission is clear: the rapid improvement of the school performance of Negroes and other poor children. If this does not happen, America will suffer for decades to come. Where a missionary zeal has been demonstrated by school administrations and teachers, and where this dedication has been backed by competence, funds and a desire to involve parents, much has been accomplished. But by and large American educators, despite occasional rhetoric to the contrary, have not dedicated themselves to the rapid improvement of the education of the poor.[20]

King went on to say that the other major hindrance to the failure to adequately address the education problem is the issue of desegregation. Many whites claimed that desegregation of the classroom actually diminished the quality of education for white students, a criticism, according to studies of the U.S. Office of Education, that defied all evidence.[21]

Martin Luther King loved ideas and ideals, and distinguished himself by living or practicing them in nonviolent direct action demonstrations for freedom, justice, and civil rights throughout his civil rights ministry. We in

20. King, *Where Do We Go from Here*, 195.
21. Ibid.

turn must consider what we should be doing forty-five years after King's assassination when all evidence points to enduring racism and inequality of opportunity between whites and blacks. We should understand by the way that Martin Luther King was well aware that racism was not the only problem facing this country and the world, and that blacks were not the only group in need of justice.[22] King was equally aware that the problem of race was far from being solved at home in the United States, as well as around the world. It was the problem that dogged and hounded his people, and was exacerbated by other major social ills such as economic injustice, classism, and militarism. This is why even when King turned to addressing labor concerns, economic exploitation, and the Vietnam War, he insisted that he had not moved racism to the back burner. In fact, when critics charged that by joining the peace movement and criticizing the Vietnam War he was no longer focusing on race, he declared that this was a "misconception." In a 1967 "Face to Face" television news interview, he said: "I don't spend that much of my time on the peace question or on Vietnam. Because ninety-five percent of my time is still spent in the civil rights struggle."[23] That he saw the interconnections between those problems did not mean that he would focus less on matters of race, especially when racism continued to be among the most glaring problems confronting his people.

King knew that racism was still alive and very well, and thus he had to keep working to eradicate it. He was not naïve but realistic when he declared that there had never been a time in U.S. history when there has been "a single solid determined commitment on the part of the vast majority of white Americans on the question of genuine equality for the black man."[24] King challenged his audience to see that "the plant of freedom has grown only a bud and not yet a flower."[25] Although writing about King's view of death, Michael G. Long is not wrong in his claim that King was in the best sense "a realist full of Christian hope."[26] No matter what other social issues King addressed, he knew that they were in some way connected to racism. Understanding this, King said in his address at the SCLC staff retreat at Frogmore, South Carolina on November 28,

22. King, "Revolution and Redemption," in *"A Single Garment of Destiny,"* 20.

23. See "Face to Face," television news interview in *A Testament of Hope*, 408.

24. King, "Transforming a Neighborhood into a Brotherhood," Address to the National Association of Radio Announcers in Atlanta, August 11, 1967, King Center Library and Archives, 8.

25. Ibid., 7.

26. Michael G. Long, "Transforming Death: Life's Ultimate Tragedy and Hope for the Dawn," in *The Domestication of Martin Luther King, Jr.: Clarence B. Jones, Right-Wing Conservatism, and the Manipulation of the King Legacy*, ed. Lewis V. Baldwin and Rufus Burrow Jr. (Eugene, OR: Cascade Books, 2013), 234.

1967, that he was not completely optimistic about racism and other problems in the country, but neither was he ready to accept defeat.[27] He retained his sense of hope, which he said has an "in spite of" quality about it.[28] Hope "involves the recognition that what is hoped for is already here, it is already present in the sense that it is a power which drives us to fulfill that we hope for."[29] Justice is not here in the everyday concrete sense, and yet it is present as long as there are individuals who hope for it and do all in their power to actualize it. As long as there is hope, justice is in some sense already present. In the final analysis, King said, hope is "a final refusal to give up."[30] There is no doubt that King had hope, right up to the end. This was the case despite his sense that racism was everywhere present in the United States, not least in the halls of Congress.[31]

The remainder of this chapter will focus on forces and ideas that King believed gave reason to *hope* in the struggle for civil rights and the establishment of the beloved community. In an atmosphere of enduring racism, what can be done to keep hope alive? According to King, at least three forces created the opening for such hope: 1) Black determination and self-determination; 2) Arousal of the conscience of the nation; and 3) Awareness of the church that it has failed in the area of race. For our purpose two additional things, also suggested by King, need to happen: 4) a revolution of values; and 5) efforts to form what he called a "Grand Alliance." There are other things that need to happen as well, but the focus of the following discussion will center on these five. No single one of these or any combination of them has received much attention since King's assassination, but I think that each continues to be viable and has the potential, particularly when taken together, of helping us to more nearly approximate the type of society that King envisioned. All of these imply the education factor, that is, the need for people to learn the value and importance of each element, and to practice them. An important key is to get people to see that to truly understand the importance of any one or all of these factors is to live or practice them in day-to-day living. This is consistent with the Kingian way. If I truly understand the value of arousing the conscience of the nation, I must, from wherever is my station or vocation in life, do whatever

27. King, "The State of the Movement," address to SCLC staff retreat at Frogmore, SC, November 28, 1967, King Center Library and Archives, 3.

28. King, "See You in Washington," speech to SCLC staff retreat in Atlanta, January 17, 1968, King Center Library and Archives, 11.

29. Ibid.

30. Ibid.

31. King, "The Crisis in America's Cities," SCLC Conference in Atlanta, August 15, 1967, King Center Library and Archives, 3.

I can to actualize this, and where possible to unite with others in common cause. If I understand the importance of the church being aware that it has failed in the area of race and being an advocate for justice, I must take steps to inform it of this fact and what may be the consequences if it does not do what God expects of it. The same holds true for the other three areas. I'm saying that to know, to truly understand, is to *do* what is known or understood, for we learn from Kingian ideas that it is in the doing, the practicing, not the speaking alone, that we know what one truly believes. So the stance advocated here is that in the best sense one does what one believes. I begin by discussing the need for a radical change in values, for to do that which consistently enhances and uplifts human beings one has to be fundamentally driven by the ideal of humanity and dignity, rather than material things. Persons, human values, must be seen as more important than property rights and other impersonal objects. When this happens one focuses on doing those things that enhance and uplift human beings, instead of expending precious energy and resources to protect wealth, property, and other impersonal objects.

NEED FOR A REVOLUTION OF VALUES

Martin Luther King believed that the United States, the strongest, most powerful, and wealthiest nation in the world, could lead the way toward a revolution of values; toward moving from a "thing-oriented" society to a "person-oriented" society;[32] to viewing human beings as the most important *subjects*; to seeing them as beings of innate, infinite, inviolable worth or absolute dignity. A revolution of values would consist of turning the present system of values on its head, such that where priority was once given the accumulation of wealth and property and protecting and hoarding them at all costs, focus would now be on acknowledging and even enhancing the worth of human beings. This very idea implies that all social, economic, political, and other policies that have bearing on human life-chances would have to be formulated and implemented in ways that honor and respect human beings first and foremost, regardless of their race-ethnicity, class, gender, age, or sexual orientation. Such policies would be more people-friendly than property- or object-friendly. The focus would be more on protecting human rights than property rights. A radical revolution of values would mean that every able-bodied willing adult would be able to find not only a job, but a job that guarantees a living wage, thus making it possible to have a sense of dignity about one's work, as well as to meet all basic

---

32. King, *Where Do We Go from Here*, 186.

needs and to save a percentage of one's wages for future emergencies, family vacations, retirement plans, and such.

King believed that there was no real reason the United States, as the wealthiest, most powerful nation in the world, could not do those things that would be indicative of a nation whose policies and practices were based on a revolution of values, which would mean that the nation's top priority is the building up of human beings, giving all people the opportunity to achieve their most important goals. Failure of citizens in this regard would be caused by only a lack of desire, will, creativity, and sacrifice. Writing about the nation's ability in this regard, King said:

> There is nothing to prevent us from paying adequate wages to schoolteachers, social workers and other servants of the public to insure that we have the best available personnel in these positions which are charged with the responsibility of guiding our future generations. There is nothing but a lack of social vision to prevent us from paying an adequate wage to every American citizen whether he be a hospital worker, laundry worker, maid or day laborer. There is nothing except shortsightedness to prevent us from guaranteeing an annual minimum—and *livable*—income for every American family. There is nothing, except a tragic death wish, to prevent us from reordering our priorities, so that the pursuit of peace will take precedence over the pursuit of war. There is nothing to keep us from remolding a recalcitrant status quo with bruised hands until we have fashioned it into a brotherhood.[33]

King believed that if the nation had the will to do such things it could find a way to do them. In my own experience as a seminary professor for three decades, I know full well that seminaries affiliated with the American Theological Schools (ATS) that come to decision about eradicating lily-white faculties and remaking themselves in the image of the multiracial-ethnic world that God created can do so once they actually decide to do it, and then apply the will, persistence, and resources to get it done. It is not easy, even then. But if they truly want it to happen, *decision* and *will* are necessary prerequisites. It can be done if faculties, administrations, and trustee boards truly want to do it. One who adheres to the Kingian ethic can only conclude that those ATS seminaries that have not done it at this juncture in history, which is the vast majority of them, simply do not want to do it, no matter what excuses or rationales they

33. Ibid., 188–89.

put forth to the contrary. People and the institutions they manage can be better than they are if they choose and will to be. They can find a way(s), an idea that Martin Luther King never relinquished.

The nation and individual citizens who are committed to undergoing a revolution of values know the importance of retaining a healthy tension and balance between the values of "I" and the values of "Thou"; of "self" and "other." King was convinced that a revolution of values had to occur both at the individual and collective levels. We saw above what this means for the state or nation. In a number of speeches and sermons—even the night before he was assassinated—King told the biblical story of the Good Samaritan as an illustration of what happens to the individual who undergoes a revolution of values. Unlike the Priest and the Levite who traveled down the curvaceous and dangerous Jericho road in the days of Jesus, who looked on a certain man who had been beaten and robbed and went on their way as if they had seen nothing, a third man, a certain Samaritan, himself a member of an outcast group, stopped, dismounted from his animal, tended to the man's wounds, and paid for his care at a local inn, promising to provide anything else that might be needed.

King reasoned that the difference between the behavior of the Priest and the Levite and the Samaritan was that the two former men were operating on the old truncated value system that placed self above and before others. They functioned according to a value system that was "I" or "me" centered rather than "thou" or "other" centered. King said that the Samaritan transformed the traditional "I-centered" ethic into a "thou-centered" one, which led him to ask a different question than the Priest and the Levite likely asked: "If I stop to help this man in need, what will happen to me?" Instead, motivated by a fundamentally different way of seeing things, the Samaritan (in King's imagination) asked an entirely different question, placing the emphasis on the well-being of the victim, or the other: "If I do not stop to help this man in need, what will happen to him?" And yet King knew, as we must know today, that important as the actions of individual good Samaritans are, it is equally important that "the whole Jericho Road must be transformed so that men and women will not be beaten and robbed as they make their journey through life."[34] The structures of society need to be embodied with and thoroughly infused with the radical ideal of what King called a "dangerous unselfishness,"[35] indeed, "an eternal, dangerous and sometime costly altruism."[36]

34. Ibid., 187.

35. King, "I See the Promised Land," in *A Testament of Hope*, 284.

36. Clayborne Carson et al., eds., *The Papers of Martin Luther King, Jr.* (Berkeley: University of California Press, 2000), 4:250.

Even this implies the need for a new sense of values as we work toward solving major problems and working toward the beloved community.

Realistically, we know that reaching this stage is a long, long way off for a large complex group like a society or nation. Much energy and effort in the way of teaching and education must be expended at the individual level, even as attempts are made on the collective level to radically transform unjust structures. Ideally, working at the individual level involves a socialization process that usually begins at the family level. Early in life, children should be taught the value of human life generally, and human life in community, in particular. Much of this teaching should be by example; by the way parents and other mature members of the family live in relationship with others. Often when I observe how young parents engage in parenting today, I am convinced that they somehow believe that children are born knowing how to behave in a civilized manner, including how to treat and respect others; that somehow they will magically mature into knowing (without responsible parental supervision and example) how best to live respectfully and responsibly in community. Most children are not taught such things today, essentially because their parents and teachers were not taught those things, and thus did not—because they could not—teach them to their children and students. One cannot teach what one does not know intellectually and through her lived experience. If one is a good citizen and knows the importance of children being taught to value self and others, one must also want to teach children those same values. In the case of the family setting, this means that parents and extended family members who are old enough and mature enough must be vigilant in teaching and modeling for children what it means to respect self and others; what it means to be good citizens.

The teaching efforts of the family must then be augmented by those of the church or other religious institutions. At least this should be the case for families that have chosen to be members of a local church, synagogue, or mosque. In such cases their behavior will be informed by religious teachings. Beginning with religious education for children, religious institutions should be devoted to teaching and modeling for children and young people the importance of human values and helping them to grasp the practical significance of the idea of the image of God imbued in each individual. This should be regularly reinforced by sermons and through religious education and youth activities, including summer camp experiences and all-night lock-ins. This means that religious leaders at all levels will have to be on the same page and in agreement about the role of the church, synagogue, or mosque in teaching children how to be good citizens who respect not only themselves and members of their in-group, but others throughout society. However, even when these things are done diligently and well, reinforcement will be needed.

If taught well, children should know by the time they reach middle school that they and their group are not the center of the universe; that not all of life revolves around them and their desires; that because they live in community and attend a school community, they should not expect to have everything their way or everything they want. By this time, they should understand that in a communal environment one's own wants and desires must be weighed in light of the wants and desires of others. Schools have a key role to play in this process of ongoing socialization. They can teach specific courses, such as civics and history, in ways that highlight the importance of human values in community, rather than focusing on the value of impersonal objects. In physical education (for the very small number of schools that still include this in their curricula) and sports activities, schools can contribute further in this regard by teaching and modeling for students the importance, not of winning at all costs (as they are presently taught), but of working together as a team to accomplish something of value to the team or larger group—win or lose. Moreover, when the emphasis is taken off of winning and placed on the contributions of each member of the team, every member learns something about the value of self as well as the value of each team member and her contributions. In this approach the emphasis is on making better persons, rather than winning trophies and other awards. Without question the focus today is on the latter, but a revolution of values would require that the emphasis be removed from winning and placed on making human beings and the world better than they are. Only when this type of work has been done over several generations will a society or nation be positioned to lead a revolution of values. We are naïve to assume that just because ours is the most powerful and wealthiest of nations, it is capable of leading other nations in developing a new sense of values.

Martin Luther King was convinced of the need for a radical restructuring of the basic institutions and structures of the United States. In this regard he argued that "[f]or its very survival's sake, America must reexamine old presuppositions and release itself from many things that for centuries have been held sacred. For the evils of racism, poverty and militarism to die, a new set of values must be born. Our economy must become more person-centered than property- and profit-centered. Our government must depend more on its moral power than on its military power."[37] This is what a revolution of values entails, and it takes a special human being to be beneficiary of injustices and other

37. King, *Where Do We Go from Here*, 133.

wrongdoings done to others to be willing to renounce such benefits and to declare their willingness to fight and even die for the equal treatment of all.

New Sense of Determination and Self-Determination

Martin Luther King insisted on pressure and black self-determination as the best way for blacks to overcome problems that plague their community, including problems associated with racism. In late 1967 he told the National Association of Radio Announcers in Atlanta that "somewhere we must come to see that we must rise up and stand on our own two feet and say to our white brothers that we are determined to be men. . . . We're somebody. We are determined to gain our freedom and we are going to start with ourselves, by freeing our own psyche, our own souls."[38] King knew better than most, that many of the problems crushing the black community were not caused by blacks but were derivative. Too often, the source was to be found in racism and economic deprivation. And yet, he was insistent that as moral agents it was in blacks' power to decide *how* to respond to the issues they confronted. They could respond apathetically and passively, or they could respond through organized pressure and resistance.

In light of a particularly tragic phenomenon that has plagued urban centers, many middle-class suburbs, as well as rural areas of this country at least since the 1980s, I have often wondered about the relevance of King's legacy regarding it. The phenomenon to which I refer is *black-against-black violence and homicide* among young Afrikan American males (which is not to say that young Afrikan American females are not also victims of this tragedy, but the overwhelming majority are males). In 1985 the Centers for Disease Control declared that the leading cause of death among young black males is homicide, and little has happened in ensuing years to mitigate that finding. Indeed, at this writing the most glaring example of this tragedy is in Chicago, Illinois, where the south side of that city is like a virtual war zone.

To be sure, there are underlying systemic problems, not least the enduring racism and economic injustice that contribute greatly to the cause and perpetuation of this tragic phenomenon and the difficulty eradicating it. But I have long wondered about the role of individual self-determination and moral agency in addressing this and other problems that make life so difficult in many black communities. That is, I have pondered what individuals can do in spite of the structural problems that support the phenomenon of intracommunity violence and homicide.

38. King, "Transforming a Neighborhood into a Brotherhood," 12.

Can the individual actually do something to mitigate or even contribute to eradicating this tragedy? For at the end of the day it is absolutely necessary to address the structural issues involved, for example, substandard housing and education, violent and unsafe neighborhoods, poor to nonexistent healthcare, no job training, no jobs, a racist and classist police force and judicial system, and so on. However, it is just as necessary to address the role that individuals can play. For the systemic problems cannot be addressed and solved without individuals, and individuals will not be around long enough to address the structural problems if they fail to take *decided* steps to put an end to a tragedy such as intracommunity violence and homicide. Do individual members of communities have a role to play in stemming the tide of violence in the face of systemic changes that occur at a snail's pace, if at all?

Generally, when the call for black self-determination arises regarding such issues there are loud cries of "foul play," and the charge is often made that the victim is being blamed. As a theological social ethicist trained in the tradition of personalist social ethicists such as Walter G. Muelder[39] and Martin Luther King, I understand that social problems will more likely be adequately addressed and solved when strategies focus on systemic causes as well as choices and actions taken by individuals. Moreover, it is important to remember that as staunchly as King criticized the unjust structures of this society and called for a revolution of values, he also criticized the lack of self-determination on the part of many oppressed people, including his own, and it is in that spirit that I want to talk about the need for blacks themselves to step up in the face of tragedies such as intracommunity violence and homicide in black communities.

Martin Luther King was critical of any tendency of blacks to shirk their duty to be responsible citizens in black communities and throughout the nation. Even though victimized by systemic problems that made their lives a virtual hell, King saw this as no excuse for not doing all in one's power to decide and act against such things as crime, including, he told his people, the practice of too often inflicting violence and homicide on each other.[40] In this respect he said: "We must not let the fact that we are the victims of injustice lull us into abrogating responsibility for our own lives."[41] Acknowledging that

---

39. Muelder, a third-generation personalist under Edgar S. Brightman, was dean of Boston University School of Theology when King was a doctoral student. Although he had no courses with Muelder, King was mentored by him, and it was Muelder who helped him make sense of Niebuhr's critique of Gandhi's nonviolence. Muelder was also my teacher when I was a doctoral candidate in social ethics at Boston University in the late 1970s.

40. King, "Second Anniversary of Protest: President's Address," Montgomery, Alabama, December 5, 1957, King Library and Archives, 12.

systemic "external factors" such as racial discrimination and economic injustice make life miserable for blacks and insisting that these must be eradicated, King nevertheless demanded that blacks "must work within the community to solve the problem while the external cause factors are being removed."[42]

King insisted that blacks had to work relentlessly and simultaneously on two fronts: "On the one hand we must work to remove this system which is the causal basis for our ills. . . . But we have another job. And that is to work to improve these standards that have been pushed back because of the system of segregation."[43] King was saying that as a moral agent, each individual is responsible for doing his part to make low-income black communities decent and civilized places to live. Consistent with his dialectical way of thinking and problem solving, King would not let either individuals or unjust social systems off the moral hook, an important lesson for all who still possess hope in the creation of the beloved community.

King agreed with his close friend Rabbi Abraham Joshua Heschel that "[f]ew are guilty but all are responsible."[44] This is another way of saying that although Afrikan Americans are not guilty of the fundamental causes of black-against-black violence and murder, they are absolutely responsible for how they respond to this phenomenal tragedy and the causes of it. Do they apathetically accept what is being done to them, or do they muster plans and available resources to do all in their power to eradicate the problem, and then contribute to radically transform things such that they more nearly approximate King's ideal of the beloved community? Whatever is decided, individual blacks are responsible for the decision made, and no decision *is* a decision. One does not have the luxury of not deciding. Similarly, women—of all races—are not guilty of the causes of gender discrimination against them and the glass ceiling put in their path to upward mobility, but they alone are responsible for how they respond to such things. Do they accept things as they are, or do they find ways to overcome and to eradicate the life-destroying debris in their way? Lesbian, gay, bisexual, and transgendered people are not guilty of the causes of discrimination against them, but they are without question responsible for how they respond to it. You get the point. We are responsible for the personal response made to whatever is done to us, King admonished.[45]

41. King, *Stride Toward Freedom* (New York: Harper & Row, 1958), 223.

42. *The Papers* (2000), 4:471.

43. King, "Second Anniversary of Protest: President's Address," Montgomery, Alabama, December 5, 1957, King Library & Archives, 11.

44. Abraham J. Heschel, *The Prophets* (New York: Harper & Row, 1962), 16.

45. *The Papers* (2007), 6:142.

For Martin Luther King, young people, like adults, are self-determining, autonomous beings, capable of choosing or deciding for themselves how to respond to the injustice and racism that they experience every day right along with their parents and other black adults. Even during the Montgomery bus boycott King sensed that children and young people understood that their freedom was being denied solely because of their race. It was therefore reasonable that they be allowed to participate in demonstrations to obtain their freedom, although the SCLC's first organized effort to do this would not occur until the Children's Crusade in the Birmingham movement in 1963.

Anyone who reads U.S. history with eyes open knows that many of the social maladies that still hound and harass the black community are directly related to the consequences of the enslavement era and the ongoing phenomenon of race discrimination. Critics in and outside the black community have been quick to blame residents for being unemployed and underemployed in such large numbers; for producing such high dropout rates in junior high and high school; for having such high crime and homicide rates; for living in substandard housing and unsafe neighborhoods. Others have been just as quick to answer such criticisms by citing evidence that convincingly suggests the systemic causes of such problems and thus the need for massive assistance through federal aid programs to solve them. For his part, King pointed to both environmental and individual causes of those problems and noted the role that each plays in undermining the humanity of blacks. Blacks were not the cause of enslavement, discrimination, and all of the resulting harsh consequences, for example, the astronomically high unemployment and crime rates. There was no doubt in King's mind about this. However, he was just as insistent that blacks were responsible for how they responded to the things done to them. Because of the new sense of dignity and determination that developed among blacks during the civil rights movement, King believed there was every reason to be hopeful that they would rise to the occasion and take matters into their own hands in pursuit of their civil rights and freedom. Indeed, it was "the determination of the Negro himself" that gave King reason to be hopeful about the future.[46]

As difficult as it must have been—for it was like criticizing blacks while they were down—Martin Luther King did not hesitate to challenge his people when their behavior indicated that they were on the wrong path. He wanted blacks to be both determined and self-determined to overcome their apathy around the matter of voting and of protesting injustice. He wanted them to be

---

46. Kenneth B. Clark interview in *A Testament of Hope*, 339.

better stewards of their money, better caregivers of what little property they had, and less violent toward each other. Pointing to segregation as an important external cause of blacks' "lagging standards," as far back as 1958, King lamented:

> Yet Negroes must be honest enough to admit that our standards do often fall short. One of the sure signs of maturity is the ability to rise to the point of self-criticism. Whenever we are objects of criticism from white men, even though the criticisms are maliciously directed and mixed with half-truths, we must pick out the elements of truth and make them the basis of creative reconstruction. We must not let the fact that we are the victims of injustice lull us into abrogating responsibility for our own lives.[47]

King was not browbeating his people. He was writing not long after the "successful" bus boycott, and had seen throughout their struggle that blacks exhibited a new sense of humanity and dignity, as well as a new sense of determination to rise up from the predicament in which they had been forced since the time of American enslavement.

King had been in Montgomery long enough to know the areas in which growth was needed in the black community. Just as he called out the powers-that-be, he felt compelled to challenge his own people about their personal standards. He acknowledged that they were the victims of American enslavement and long years of segregation and deprivation, but even as they endured and suffered so much they remained moral agents, and therefore still had the capacity to act—which was obvious from the types of detrimental actions many tended to engage in. Although he had no desire or intention of letting the powers off the moral hook, King saw it as his job as a son of the black community and as one of its chief leaders to remind his people that they could engage in more self- and community-making actions than previously was the case. So he went on to cite what he considered to be other areas needing improvement:

> Our crime rate is far too high. Our level of cleanliness is frequently far too low. Too often those of us who are in the middle class live above our means, spend money on nonessentials and frivolities, and fail to give to serious causes, organizations, and educational institutions that so desperately need funds. We are too often loud and boisterous, and spend far too much on drink. Even the most poverty-

---

47. King, *Stride*, 223.

stricken among us can purchase a ten-cent bar of soap; even the most uneducated among us can have high morals.[48]

As far back as 1957, King chided his people about black-on-black violence and homicide, saying that "we kill each other too much. We cut up each other too much."[49] King insisted that blacks could work on such matters and resolve them. But it would take conscious effort and an indomitable will. These were not easy criticisms for King to make, especially in the public arena for all to hear or read about. He knew that so much of the self-destructive behavior in black communities was connected to external factors that blacks could not control. But even so, he felt that too much was at stake for him to try to protect the image of the black community by remaining silent. The criticisms had to be made, and he could not, indeed would not, leave it to chance that someone else would do it. Throughout King's civil rights ministry, he called for a "massive move toward self-determination,"[50] what he sometimes referred to as a "determined refusal to be stopped."[51] King's point was that there are some things that oppressed people must exert the will to do for themselves.

Today, more than ever before, the Kingian prophetic critique needs to be heard and appropriately responded to in the black community as well as the nation at large. Without question there are things that blacks themselves can do to break the unacceptable cycle of black-against-black violence and homicide; the unacceptably high dropout rate among secondary students; the still too high teen pregnancy rate; and the almost total disregard and disrespect that too many black youths have for senior citizens. At the center of this is the need for blacks to do some of their first works over again.

Literary artist James Baldwin said that in his church—"which is not at all the same church to which white Americans belong—we were counseled, from time to time, to do our first works over."[52] Doing one's first works over means intentionally going as far back as possible, preferably to the beginning, and looking anew and critically at everything that happened on the way to where one is now. In the process, one should be mindful of what happened at each step and then be willing to tell the unadulterated truth about it—all of it. Baldwin put it bluntly: "Go back to where you started, or as far back as you can, examine all

48. Ibid.

49. *The Papers*, 4:336.

50. King, "The State of the Movement," 4.

51. Ibid., 8.

52. James Baldwin, "Introduction: *The Price of the Ticket*," in his *The Price of the Ticket: Collected Nonfiction 1948-1985* (New York: St. Martin's/Marek, 1985), xix.

of it, travel your road again and tell the truth about it. Sing or shout or testify or keep it to yourself; but *know whence you came.*[53] Know how you got to where you are now, and have the character and guts to tell the truth about it, and then do something about it. This is all-important for black people because so much has happened to them since they were ripped from the Afrikan continent and forced into one of the most dehumanizing forms of enslavement known to civilized human beings. So blacks have to be willing to do the hard work of doing their first works over and then developing the courage and determination to make the necessary adjustments in order to move forward in ways that honor them as human beings and children of the One God of the universe.

When blacks do their first works over, they will find that at an earlier time of their presence in this country they were taught by their parents and grandparents the importance of honoring, respecting, and obeying their parents and other adults in their extended family and community. Indeed, doing those first works over and reexamining them will make it clear that something of utmost value and importance has been lost, and needs to be recaptured and kept before every family in the community as the ideal toward which to strive. Respecting and obeying one's elders and other adults in the family and community, for example, was in fact a life-saving value, especially for black youths in the enslaved community, and afterward in the segregated Deep South. Historian John W. Blassingame reminds us of how important it was for black children to obey their parents in the slave community:

> In the face of all of the restrictions, slave parents made every effort humanly possible to shield their children from abuse and teach them how to survive in bondage. One of the most important lessons for the child was learning to hold his tongue around white folks. This was especially true on those plantations where the masters tried to get the children to spy on their parents. Sam Aleckson pointed out that as a child he "was taught to say nothing" about the conversations in the quarters. Frequently mothers had to be severe with their children to prevent them from breaking this important rule. Elijah P. Marrs, for example, declared: "Mothers were necessarily compelled to be severe on their children to keep them from talking too much. Many a poor mother has been whipped nearly to death on account of their children telling white children things. . . ."[54]

53. Ibid., xix (Baldwin's italics).
54. John W. Blassingame, *The Slave Community: Plantation Life in the Antebellum South*, revised & enlarged edition (New York: Oxford University Press, 1979 [1972]), 186–87.

To disobey a parent's command to be silent or to behave a certain way around white people, including white children, could, and often did, lead to severe consequences. Because it was a matter of life and death, black parents in those days gave new meaning to the biblical verse: "Those who spare the rod hate their children, but those who love them are diligent to discipline them" (Prov. 13:24). Indeed, sparing the rod on the plantation and virtually everywhere else in the Deep South could easily have meant risking the loss of a child, or a child or parent being severely beaten.

Today, in far too many homes, black children and youths have no sense of the importance of respecting and obeying their parents and respecting the old ones in the community. To a large extent this is not the fault of the children, for children cannot raise children to be responsible, civilized people who know what it means to live in community. Children cannot educate children about proper boundaries and social graces; cannot educate themselves and other children about the importance of balance between freedom or permissiveness and discipline. King himself argued against the all-too-common practice of those parents who essentially allow children to do what they want, when they want, under the pretext of not wanting to break the will of the child. Such children, King said, are "permitted to almost terrorize the home for fear of having [their] individuality repressed."[55] Children must be trained in the art of cooperative living within the family and the community. Without this, they have no way of knowing what are their own responsibilities, and too often the tendency is to live as if the needs and desires of others need not be taken into consideration. It does not require much effort to see what this can lead to in and outside the home. Indeed, we can see the consequences everywhere we look, and I for one am convinced that the failure to raise and discipline children is linked to the growing tragedy of black-on-black violence and homicide and a myriad of other problems linked to young people.

AROUSE THE CONSCIENCE OF THE NATION

Throughout his civil rights ministry, Martin Luther King believed that a primary role was to awaken and arouse the conscience of the nation regarding the plight of black people and the role that the nation itself must play. This too was one of the forces he believed gave reason for hope that things would get better along the civil rights trail. Individual whites, especially well-meaning ones, and the nation generally were being made more aware of racism and its debilitating effects not only on blacks, but on whites as well. The conscience

---

55. *The Papers,* 4:374.

of many was aroused when they saw the violent actions of white racists perpetrated against the nonviolent demonstrators sitting-in, riding buses for freedom, and marching for their civil rights. The first time this got national and international media attention was when Bull Connor ordered his men to use high-powered fire hoses and police attack dogs on nonviolent demonstrators, including children. Such actions led to a deluge of criticisms directed toward Birmingham authorities from around the nation and the world.

Since King's assassination, we are nearly two generations removed from the civil rights movement. Many young people have attended desegregated public schools. Because they did not live through civil rights protests and marches, and because this part of the nation's history was not (and is not) often taught in civics and U.S. history courses, many of these young people, regardless of race-ethnicity, are ignorant about it and assume that there is no race problem. In fact, I have met many white *and* black students who claim that what they learned about Martin Luther King and the civil rights movement in high school was that their efforts led to the eradication of the race problem. Many did not even hear about King and the movement in their college classes. And why would they, since many had heard that racism was little more than a figment of the imaginations of disgruntled blacks and white liberals, since it was known that King and others solved the race problem?

My experience in the theological academy convinces me that many whites, including, and perhaps particularly, professors and administrators, are of the opinion that racism is of declining significance, so thorough a job did activists presumably do in the 1960s to eradicate it. Indeed, when a Midwestern seminary reached its goal of a certain percentage of women, blacks, and other people of color on its faculty, a number of younger white faculty members argued strongly, as more experienced ones remained silent, that since the goal had been reached there was no longer reason to retain the written policy that required such balance in the faculty. For those white faculty members, there was no longer need for institutional vigilance and effort in this regard. Because for them race was surely no longer a problem, they naïvely assumed that those who did the hiring would always do the right thing to ensure that there was race and gender balance in the faculty and student body. They also assumed that without a policy in place, any new administration hired would take it upon itself, out of its deep sense of morality, to ensure racial-ethnic-cultural balance on the faculty. Sadly, and most troublesome, they seemed to have no sense of how deeply ingrained racism still is in the very fabric of this society and all of its institutions, including seminaries and other religious institutions.

During my first seven years at Christian Theological Seminary, I was the only person of color to hold a full-time faculty appointment. To its credit the administration, under the leadership of the late Thomas Jackson Liggett, worked hard and vigilantly in efforts to improve racial understanding at all levels in the seminary community. One method used to get at this was the fishbowl approach where black students, other students of color, along with the few staff members of color and the lone black professor would essentially gather in a circle, which would be encircled by the larger circle of white administrators, faculty, staff members, and students. The role of the outer circle was to observe and listen, without interruption. Those in the inner circle were asked to talk freely about their experience of racism in the seminary community and the wider society. The process was at least slightly cathartic for those in the inner circle, and served to some extent to educate those in the outer circle as to how they and their behavior were perceived by their colleagues of color. Essentially those in the inner circle told their stories of how they experienced racism and what it felt like.

I always knew that the fishbowl approach was a good first step toward racial understanding in educational communities. But I also knew that this was not nearly enough; that ways had to be found to allow whites in the community to publicly name their unearned advantages (I didn't know the "privilege" language at the time); how they thought they came to have such advantages; whether they saw anything wrong with it, and why; whether they thought they should do something about it, and when. In short, I knew way back then that racism was as much about white people as those who were its victims. Therefore, we needed to hear the stories and conversations of both groups. Unfortunately, for a long time we were not able to get beyond the fishbowl approach with people of color in the inner circle.

When the language of "white privilege" was finally introduced in the late 1980s by Peggy McIntosh of Wellesley College, Robert Jensen of the University of Texas at Austin, and others, many of us saw this as evidence that the all-important second phase had finally begun. Some of us began referring to white privilege as "the other side of racism." Now, we naïvely thought, when we resume race sensitivity training in the seminary, the focus will primarily be on white privilege and what, if anything, whites intend to do about it. In early sessions it seemed to me that most of the time was once again focused on blacks and other people of color telling their stories of how they experienced racism while whites passively listened. Early on I and a few others were frustrated about this and did not want to attend the sessions (although attendance was mandated by the president), since we believed that it was time for white people to start breaking their silence and owning up to their unearned privilege and begin talking publicly about what this meant to them, how it was manifested in the life of the school, and what, if anything, they intended to do about it. At this writing we have not yet progressed to this stage, nor is there reason to believe that it will happen in the immediate future.

I share this story about the experience of race sensitivity training at the seminary where I have spent my entire career because during the more recent sessions I learned something firsthand about how some members of a younger generation of whites think about race relations; how they seem to have little to no sense that racism is a problem. When I said in one of the sessions that there was no longer need for blacks to continue telling their stories of how they experienced racism, because by now white people know full well that racism continues to be a problem, I remember a young staff member approaching me after the session. She was in tears as she insisted that she had grown up in a race-sensitive home, a desegregated neighborhood, attended desegregated public schools, a desegregated college, and an all-white church. Very little to no energy and attention was devoted to race history in the schools she attended. In addition, race was not discussed in the home or at church. Thus she did not have a historical sense of race relations in this country. I had never heard anything like this before, but as I listened to her story I began reflecting on some of the things I'd heard younger white students say in my classes; things that suggested they had no clue about race relations. It then occurred to me that the young staff member had been right. It was not entirely her fault that she was ignorant about race relations. I now know that blacks' stories about their experiences are still important in race sensitivity training sessions, although I will continue to insist that the group, particularly the whites, should be made aware in the clearest possible language how frustrating this is to an older generation of blacks who have already expended much time and energy telling white people how they have experienced racism. It is imperative that whites be told that many blacks, especially in my generation, have no desire to do this anymore, but that some may do it in the hope that more progress may be made in the matter of race. Most important of all, the group should be made to understand that the primary focus of such sessions should be on white privilege; that whites themselves must be willing to break silence and talk openly about their privilege, how they understand it, what they intend to do about it, and when. It would be both admirable and encouraging if upper-echelon administrators and senior faculty members exhibited leadership by beginning the process of talking about white privilege as they experience it, as well as what they intend to do about it.

What is clearly needed at this juncture, are efforts to increase the awareness, to arouse the conscience of those who have little to no historical sense of menacing racism. Essentially, I learned from that young white staff member that the schools, churches, and too many families failed to instruct her generation on matters of race. Although I confess that my gut and my own experiences tell me that at least some among the younger generations (especially white people) are disingenuous when they claim to have no sense of the existence of racism, I am now convinced that at least some of them, because they attended desegregated schools and all the rest, simply do not know, or do not have a realistic view of race relations. For my money, those who do not know and those who prefer not to know, should know. It is the responsibility of those who take King's legacy seriously to see to it that they know. So it is critical that we endeavor to find ways to once again arouse the conscience of the nation regarding the matter of race.

Churches, mosques, synagogues, and educational institutions in general can play a significant role in this regard. Based on what I have experienced and witnessed in the church and the academy, there is little evidence that these institutions have been willing to undertake this challenge. By and large, most of the leaders have not come to terms with their own privilege, indeed, have not even acknowledged it and named it! Until this happens and they are willing to be self-critical about it, there is little hope that the institutions they lead will contribute significantly to educating and arousing the consciences of people regarding the new faces of racism.

I think the real key to this is to be found in young people themselves. Those who have been awakened, like that young white staff member, will need to find each other and start a movement to educate and arouse the consciences of others like themselves. Since there are also large numbers of blacks and other youths of color who attended desegregated schools and possess no historical sense of racism, even in their own lives, the numbers of those participating in such a movement should swell substantially. Such a group should aim to educate itself about historic racism as well as the myriad ways that racism manifests itself today. Because of their particular set of experiences in desegregated schools such knowledge should position them well to do the all-important anti-racism and pro-reconciliation work. But for an exception here and there, I see no reason to hope that my generation—and most especially the generation ahead of mine—will do this work in a way that will allow us to do anything but continue stagnating in race relations, or to even digress. Indeed, it is a sad fact that I have never heard a white colleague anywhere in the theological academy admit that racism is a sin; that racial discrimination is a sin, and thus is un-Christian. I have never heard a white colleague confess his unearned privilege, and how this gave him advantages that continue to elude Afrikan Americans.

A student in my course on Martin Luther King once asked if I thought that King believed one could be a racist and Christian at the same time. I responded that it was easy to answer this question since King was quite clear about the matter. Theologically, one cannot be racist and Christian at the same time. "I do not feel that a man can be a Christian and a staunch segregationist simultaneously," King said. "All men, created alike in the image of God, are inseparably bound together. This is at the very heart of the Christian Gospel. This broad universalism standing at the center of the Christian Gospel makes segregation morally evil. Racial segregation is a blatant denial of the unity which we have in Christ. . . . Segregation is utterly unchristian."[56] Surely white theologians know this! And yet I have never heard one of them say it publicly (or privately for that matter). If racism is to ever be eradicated it will be necessary for whites to acknowledge its incompatibility with Christianity; confess their racism and unearned privilege; ask for forgiveness; and vow to work to dismantle the structures of privilege and racism. Even as I write these words, I am convinced that the younger generation will have to step up to the plate, much like those courageous, energetic young freedom fighters who initiated the sit-ins, continued the Freedom Rides, and engaged in nonviolent demonstrations for civil rights and freedom in some of the most dangerous places in the nation such as Mississippi and Selma. For just as young people in movement days played an important role in arousing the conscience of the nation and helped to remove the blanket of fear covering the nation,[57] so too can present-day youth.

But the responsibility of arousing the nation's conscience regarding racism and white privilege should not be borne by well-meaning young people alone. Schools and religious institutions need also to step up and provide race relations and race sensitivity education to students and members, with a focus on understanding white privilege and what will be needed to overcome it. Any school system, college or university, and religious institution that claim to be committed to more humane race relations and full equality between the races will find ways to address this. The others will go on doing what they have always done.

56. Ibid., 4:281.
57. King, "The State of the Movement," 7.

RELIGIOUS INSTITUTIONS' AWARENESS OF MISSING THE MARK

Another force that Martin Luther King believed to be at work to ward off some of the backlash toward civil rights gains, thus providing hope for a brighter tomorrow, was the awareness of religious institutions that they had not done their job in the area of race relations; had not followed the gospel mandate to seek justice; had not consistently and forthrightly spoken out against racism and racial discrimination; had not even supported the landmark Supreme Court decision in *Brown v. Board of Education of Topeka, Kansas* (1954). Nor were most white churches forthcoming in support of local civil rights demonstrations throughout the South, beginning with the bus boycott in Montgomery. Looking back, King found that time and time again he had been disappointed with the response of local white pastors and their churches regarding the nonviolent demonstrations. Reflecting on the response of both secular and religious white moderates during the Montgomery bus boycott, King said that historians looking at this era would have to say that "the greatest tragedy of this period of social transition was not the strident clamor of the bad people, but the appalling silence of the good people. Our generation will have to repent not only for the acts and words of the children of darkness but also for the fears and apathy of the children of light."[58] King concluded that Montgomery white ministers as a group, from whom he "had naïvely expected so much, gave so little."[59] Acknowledging that there were individual exceptions, he lamented that during the boycott "the white ministers as a group had been appallingly silent. . . ."[60] He had hoped that white religious leaders would be among the strongest allies of the struggle for civil rights. Writing from a Birmingham, Alabama jail cell in 1963 he said: "Instead, some have been outright opponents, refusing to understand the freedom movement and misrepresenting its leaders; all too many others have been more cautious than courageous and have remained silent behind the anesthetizing security of stained-glass windows."[61] Indeed, King was just as disappointed with the response of white ministers, priests, and rabbis in Birmingham and other places, believing that "every minister of the

58. King, *Stride*, 202. King's use of the "children of darkness" and "children of light" imagery is reminiscent of Reinhold Niebuhr, who incorporated the phrases into the title of a book, *The Children of Light and the Children of Darkness: A Vindication of Democracy and a Critique of Its Traditional Defense* (New York: Charles Scribner's, 1944). It is known that King was familiar with this book, as well as the scriptural passage on which the book's title is based: "The children of this age are more shrewd in dealing with their own generation than are the children of light" (Luke 16:8).

59. King, *Stride*, 202.

60. Ibid., 169.

61. King, *Why We Can't Wait* (New York: Harper & Row, 1964), 94.

gospel has a mandate to stand up courageously for righteousness. . . ."[62] King had heard many white pastors instruct their members to obey a desegregation decision by the courts because it is the law. From ministers of the gospel he expected much more. He had hoped that they would have gone much further and pointed them to their religious and moral duty to obey such decisions because "integration is morally right and because the Negro is your brother."[63] In this, his experience was no different from Daddy King's and his maternal grandfather, A. D. Williams. White religious leaders were a disappointment regarding matters of race.

Martin Luther King loved the church, and that love was at the root of his strong criticisms of it. Few ministers, indeed few people in any profession, were (are) willing to be self-critical and even critical of others in their profession as was King. He lamented the fact that so many of his ministerial colleagues consistently violated the Christian command to be nonconformists. Like the prophets of old, King called them out.

> We preachers have also been tempted by the enticing cult of conformity. Seduced by the success symbols of the world, we have measured our achievements by the size of our parsonage. We have become showmen to please the whims and caprices of the people. We preach comforting sermons and avoid saying anything from our pulpits which might disturb the respectable views of the comfortable members of our congregations. Have we ministers of Jesus Christ sacrificed truth on the altar of self-interest and, like Pilate, yielded our convictions to the demands of the crowd?[64]

King was deeply disappointed with the church, not as one of those critics who seem always to be looking for something wrong with the church. He expressed his disappointment as one who was called to ministry, was literally raised up in the church and who loved it. He acknowledged that he was "nurtured in its bosom," "sustained by its spiritual blessings and . . . will remain true to it as long as the cord of life shall lengthen."[65] King went on to say that there could be no deep disappointment where there was no deep love.

Racism has always had social, economic, and political aspects. However, King rightly argued that in the most fundamental sense racism is a theological

---

62. King, *Stride*, 208.

63. King, *Why We Can't Wait*, 94.

64. King, "Transformed Nonconformist," in *Strength to Love*, 12.

65. King, *Why We Can't Wait*, 94.

and moral issue. In part he was influenced by Swedish social scientist Gunnar Myrdal's contention in his massive, seminal study *An American Dilemma*, that racism is the United States' greatest moral dilemma—that it "is a problem in the heart of the American. It is there that the interracial tension has its focus. It is there that the decisive struggle goes on. . . . Though our study includes economic, social, and political race relations, at bottom our problem is the moral dilemma of the American—the conflict between his moral valuations on various levels of consciousness and generality."[66] King was able to see that this greatest of moral dilemmas presented a real challenge to the church and its leaders. The way that King read and interpreted the Bible led him to the conviction that there is "a broad universalism" at the center of the gospel that makes racism and segregation contradictions to that gospel, and thus as morally unjustified and unacceptable. "Racial segregation is a blatant denial of the unity which we have in Christ," King declared, "for in Christ there is neither Jew nor Gentile, bond nor free, Negro nor white."[67]

King most assuredly did his part in helping the church to see that it had failed in the matter of race and that it had a biblical mandate to instruct all on the truth of the gospel regarding racism. And yet, at this writing very few churches and ministers seem to have a sense of what they should be doing—if anything—about enduring racism. Sunday after Sunday, their sermons are silent on the issue. It is no different in seminary chapels where, week after week, administrators, faculty members, and students preach, but seldom if ever say anything significant about Christians' responsibility in race relations. In fact, many pretend that they don't even know that racism continues to be an issue. Of course, all they need to do is examine the massive amount of social science data that point to the continuing racial dilemma, and/or listen to blacks who are honest and courageous enough to tell the truth about the racism that continues to undermine their sense of humanity and dignity. Furthermore, they could also read the daily and/or weekly newspapers. I am as convinced as Martin Luther King was that if all white ministers in any given denomination would collectively raise their voices against racism and its tragic systemic manifestations, the path to its eradication and to racial harmony would be a lot smoother than has been the case.[68]

All of this is to say that if there is to be renewed hope of moving in the direction of the beloved community in the twenty-first century, it will

66. Gunnar Myrdal, *An American Dilemma: The Negro Problem and Modern Democracy* (New York: Harper & Brothers, 1944), xlvii.

67. King, *Stride*, 205.

68. Ibid., 210.

be necessary for ministers and religious institutions to lead the way in race relations; to declare with strong and determined voice what "thus says the Lord" about racism and any other negative -*ism* that alienates human beings from each other and from God. It would help immensely if the theological seminaries were committed to requiring that students preparing for ministry learn about the Hebrew prophets and their unrelenting message about God's expectation that justice and righteousness be done. Most churchgoers very seldom hear prophetic preaching, primarily because their pastors do not preach prophetic sermons; sermons that call us back to our original purpose as the people of God, and that remind us to remember what God requires of us, namely to do justice in righteous ways, to love kindness, and to walk humbly with God. Baptist minister and seminary professor Marvin McMickle is most assuredly right when he says: "The fiery words of the prophets . . . go unspoken in most pulpits across America. There is very little likelihood that the vast majority of those who hear sermons today will come out of their churches saying to one another, 'The land is not able to bear all his words'" (Amos 7:10).[69] McMickle is right in his contention that most seminary-trained pastors fail to have a sense of urgency about preaching the message of the prophets because the seminaries that trained them did not impose that sense of urgency upon them.

Prophetic preaching does not require that one preach from one of the books of the prophets in the First Testament. Rather, such preaching "occurs when the preacher seeks to bring the will of God to the attention of the people of God and then . . . to challenge them 'to trust their [God] in all circumstances and to obey him with willing and grateful hearts.' Prophetic preaching happens when the preacher has the courage to speak truth to power not only inside the church building but also in the streets and boardrooms and jail cells of the secular order."[70] Unless they have their own self-centered ministerial agenda, for example, building mega-churches and placing themselves at the center of ministry, most pastors who avoid preaching prophetic sermons do so because they lack the courage. It is true that there have been rare instances in which pastors have been asked to leave because they preached prophetically on a regular basis. But even this is no reason for a pastor to forego prophetic preaching. The minister who is obedient to God's calling must preach such sermons on a regular basis, since God expects justice to be done.

---

69. Marvin McMickle, *Where Have All the Prophets Gone?: Reclaiming Prophetic Preaching in America* (Cleveland: Pilgrim, 2000), 7.

70. Ibid., 10.

Need to Form a "Grand Alliance"

Adam Fairclough rightly contends that Martin Luther King was by nature and philosophy "a coalition builder."[71] From the beginning to the end of his civil rights ministry, King stressed the importance of democratic process and alliance building. This often meant that he could not come to decisions as quickly as many would have liked. Indeed, he was at times criticized for being "indecisive." In reality, he was simply being true to his sense that important decision making should include the voices and input of as many people as possible. But when one utilizes such an approach it invariably takes more time—than would be the case of an individual—to come to decision. It also means that one will likely have to do more compromising than one would otherwise like. These are inherent hazards of the truly democratic and coalition approach.

Martin Luther King was not a political wimp. He understood that power and the holders of it generally understand nothing short of power. Power is generally what gets the powerful to move, and most especially in a direction they would rather not. Moreover, the powerful generally concede their position only to a more powerful entity; they almost never make other people or groups powerful.[72] In a discussion on rules about power in his (quite possibly forgotten but still important) massive text, *The Black Power Imperative: Racial Inequality and the Politics of Nonviolence* (1987), Theodore Cross (himself a white liberal progressive lawyer) made the point very well, and because of the influence of Reinhold Niebuhr and his own experience of racism Martin Luther King would have agreed with Cross's assessment:

> Superior positions are almost never surrendered except to superior power. This rule is no less true of the behavior of progressives than of conservatives. Most liberals, for example, will happily spend billions of dollars of government money authorizing job training grants, "innovative" housing programs, food stamp programs, and other efforts that protect the weakness of the poor. Antipoverty warriors, whose politics may be described as progressive, may be counted on to work endless hours in shaping social experiments to improve the lives of the less fortunate and, in the process, smother them

---

71. See Adam Fairclough, Foreword to *The Domestication of Martin Luther King, Jr.: Clarence B. Jones, Right-Wing Conservatism, and the Manipulation of the King Legacy*, ed. Lewis V. Baldwin and Rufus Burrow Jr. (Eugene, OR: Cascade Books, 2013), xv.

72. See the massive book by Theodore Cross, *The Black Power Imperative: Racial Inequality and the Politics of Nonviolence* (New York: Faulkner, 1987), 24.

with the kindness of a close and sincere embrace. *But one may rest assured that traditional liberals and other "concerned" groups have very little interest in empowering blacks or other powerless groups.* In fact, the most dedicated progressive voters will conscientiously instruct blacks to abjure power and seek aid. With a few notable exceptions—voting rights for blacks and a brief experiment with poverty law services and community self-determination initiatives—virtually every social program ever devised in this country to alleviate the condition of blacks or the poor confirms the proposition I have stated.[73]

King knew that black people did not possess the type of power that wealthy and powerful white people do. However, he learned early on the civil rights trail that there are many different kinds of power, and that the type most readily available to black and other oppressed people is found in large organized numbers of people. There is power in numbers, King liked to say, but in practice he added the other necessary element, namely organization. According to King, then, the power formula for those who have been traditionally and historically kept from the table for various reasons is numbers plus organization boldly aimed at addressing and resolving a specific problem.

Since King understood that economic injustice, racial, and cultural insensitivity were directed not only at blacks, but at Indians, Puerto Ricans, Mexican Americans, and poor whites, he argued vigorously and unrelentingly for the formation of what he often referred to as a "grand alliance" between these traditionally excluded groups. He was not interested in forming a social club, as are many people when they talk about the need to develop a coalition with one or more groups. The type of alliance that King had in mind was about the business of politics and taking on the powers-that-be in order to achieve a common goal. Because some inroads were already being made in this regard with labor and trade unions, as well as with white liberals who not only were committed to democratic principles but were willing to fight side by side with black people in their quest for freedom and justice, King saw even more reason to hope that things would get better for the historically left out.

In the multiracial-ethnic society like the United States, no group with insufficient economic resources could make it without the assistance of others. Martin Luther King understood this important fact. In the case of blacks he said that even if they pooled all of their resources and made purchases only from other blacks, this would not be enough to "create the multiplicity of new jobs and provide the number of low-cost houses that will lift the Negro

73. Cross, *The Black Power Imperative*, 45 (my italics).

out of the economic depression caused by centuries of deprivation. Neither can our resources supply quality integrated education. All of this requires billions of dollars which only an alliance of liberal-labor-civil rights forces can stimulate."[74] So King urged blacks to form "constructive alliances" with well-meaning people in the majority group. Even so, he also knew that the alliance would have to be broadened to include others who were victims of massive unemployment, racism, and impoverishment, for example, Puerto Ricans, Mexican Americans, Indians, and Appalachian whites.[75]

Notwithstanding the importance of forming political coalitions, it must be remembered that historically both blacks and Indians have been betrayed time and again by the white majority. Rayford Logan wrote a well-known book, *The Betrayal of the Negro*, in which he chronicled four decades of betrayals of blacks in this country by white decision-makers.[76] Vine Deloria Jr. did something similar in *The Trail of Broken Treaties*, where he documented the frequent betrayals of Indians.[77] This obviously raises the question of trust. Can blacks trust whites enough to do what King suggests regarding alliance building? Any black person who has lived for sixty years and has had his eyes and ears open knows very well the seriousness of this question. But we recall that King was a realist. He was aware that the historical relationship between whites and blacks is filled with instances in which blacks were betrayed by presumed white allies. He was also cognizant of the many betrayals of the Indians, as well as attempts to wipe them from the face of the earth.[78] King was therefore among the first to say that there are white people who cannot be trusted enough to form effective alliances with blacks, and in such instances blacks should not relax their "vigilance against halfhearted associates or conscious betrayers."[79] The element of suspicion among blacks, therefore, is understandable. However, King was convinced that "[o]ccasional betrayals do not justify the rejection of the principle of Negro-white alliance."[80] That some whites, or even most whites, cannot be trusted does not mean that this

---

74. King, *Where Do We Go from Here*, 50.

75. Ibid., 132.

76. See Rayford W. Logan, *The Betrayal of the Negro: From Rutherford B. Hayes to Woodrow Wilson*, new, enlarged edition (New York: Collier, 1965 [1954]).

77. Vine Deloria Jr., *Behind the Trail of Broken Treaties* (Austin: University of Texas Press, 1974). See also his instructive chapter, "Laws and Treaties," in his *Custer Died for Your Sins: An Indian Manifesto* (Norman/London: University of Oklahoma Press, 1988 [1969]), ch. 2.

78. See King, *Why We Can't Wait*, 130–31, and *Where Do We Go from Here*, 80.

79. King, *Where Do We Go from Here*, 51.

80. Ibid.

applies to *all* whites. Although the better part of wisdom suggests that blacks be wise as serpents in determining which whites to unite with, and which not, the truth of the matter is that the effort toward coalition building must be made with whites, especially those known to be committed to democratic principles and willing to fight and even die along with blacks in the ongoing struggle for freedom. According to King, one of the best examples of this was the alliance building that occurred between black and white youths during the sit-ins, Freedom Rides, and the student activism in SNCC.[81] This work, in addition to nonviolent demonstrations in general, was seen by King as significant means to coalition building.[82] Against some black power advocates, King was adamant that blacks could not achieve economic and political power without alliances with whites.

Part of what drove Martin Luther King to insist on the need for a strong black-white coalition in the quest for civil rights and full equality for all was based on his strong intellectual and faith conviction that human beings are bound together in a single garment of destiny because of the interrelated structure of reality. This was unequivocally clear to him in the realm of ideas, and was supported by his philosophical and theological conviction that the whole of creation is relational or communal. This conviction was only strengthened by King's awareness of the very close, integral relation between blacks and whites in this country as a result of the former's forced enslavement. The numerous rapes of enslaved women by white enslavers caused a very real biological connection between the two races. In addition, it was impossible to avoid the mixing of cultural, religious, language, music, and other factors, making blacks "a true hybrid, a combination of two cultures."[83] Following James Baldwin, King said: "This is the dilemma of being a Negro in America. In physical as well as cultural terms every Negro is a little bit colored and a little bit white."[84] Whether either group likes it or not, blacks and whites are inextricably bound together. Historically, biologically, and sociologically this is the case because of enslavement and the rape of enslaved women by white men. Theologically, the two groups are bound together this way because this is how God created human beings; as one family under God, and thus as inextricably

---

81. King, "The State of the Movement," 7–8.

82. King, "See You in Washington," 9.

83. King, *Where Do We Go from Here*, 53. I would think that this intermixing also made whites a hybrid of sorts—an admixture of two cultures.

84. Ibid. King's wording is very similar to Baldwin's: "That's part of the dilemma of being an American Negro; that one is a little bit colored and a little bit white . . . " (in *The Negro Protest: James Baldwin, Malcolm X, and Martin Luther King Talk with Kenneth B. Clark* (Boston: Beacon, 1963), 6.

bound together in that single garment of destiny that King liked to talk about. And yet, because of the nature of the historical relationship between blacks and whites there was not a natural social or political alliance between them. Such alliance making has to be worked at persistently, which also means that issues of trust have to be worked out, and this will not be an easy task, even today.

By 1967, Martin Luther King believed that blacks had "reached the stage of organized strength and independence to work securely in alliances. History has demonstrated with major victories the effectiveness, wisdom and moral soundness of Negro-white alliance. The cooperation of Negro and white based on the solid ground of honest conscience and proper self-interest can continue to grow in scope and influence. It can attain the strength to alter basic institutions by democratic means."[85] King recognized that in order for blacks and whites to work together effectively in a coalition, blacks will need to be secure enough in themselves and to have reached a certain stage of self-confidence and in-group power to match the strength of the group(s) with which they seek to be in alliance. Although King seems to have thought in 1967 that blacks had actually reached the stage of organized strength, he himself questioned this about ten days before he was assassinated.

NEED FOR INTRACOMMUNITY ALLIANCE

During a conversation with Jewish rabbis on March 28, 1968 (barely seven days before he was assassinated), Rabbi Everett Gendler asked King to comment on Black Power advocates' call for segregation or separation of the races. In his response, King unfortunately used the terms *separation* and *segregation* interchangeably. It seems to me that the two are not necessarily the same thing. Moreover, when blacks hear the two terms they are not left with the same feeling. The "feel" is different. For me, the term *separation* implies that an individual or group has, on their own initiative, made a decision to remove themselves from another group, perhaps for a specified period of time. The term *segregation*, on the other hand, has the much heavier feel of being made to separate from another, with some kind of legal influence behind it, such that the segregated cannot on its own decide to unite with the group from which it was segregated. Blacks were free to separate from whites for political or other reasons, but did not (and do not) have the legal authority to segregate from whites. Moreover, the vast majority of blacks have never called for segregation of the races. Indeed, King elsewhere observed that black churches and black colleges are segregated institutions, but not segregating ones, since they would

85. Ibid., 52.

welcome anyone, regardless of race.[86] In my experience, most black communities are this way as well—segregated, but not segregating.

Many have forgotten that although King rejected—and saw as a negative—Black Power leaders' call for absolute separation of the races or separation as a goal, he was by this time convinced that from a political standpoint there are times when temporary black separation or intracommunity alliance building may be the best means to a position of strength that could enhance the group's bargaining position when it joins in alliance with whites and/or other groups. Such temporary separation was seen by King as a necessary step toward "a truly integrated society where there is shared power."[87] The truly integrated society may be likened unto the beloved community, for in that community power will not be doled out to blacks in teaspoons, but will be shared equally among all. In the conversation with the Jewish rabbis King asserted his belief that in order to get to this society of shared power and other resources, blacks needed to temporarily separate from the dominant white group, thus invoking a kind of temporary waystation ethic. This could allow blacks to unite intracommunally and combine resources in order to achieve among themselves a position of strength. This alone would put them in the best position to form an effective alliance with whites.

Based on the foregoing discussion, then, Martin Luther King did not believe that blacks were in a strong enough position to join in alliance with other groups, as he had previously claimed in 1967. He especially did not think that blacks were positioned to join in a real workable coalition with whites. He was certain that it was something that needed to be done, but he was just as convinced that blacks needed first to separate among themselves in order to work toward strengthening their position. They would not be able to even do this, however, until they did the hard internal work of helping the haves and the have-nots to find ways to unite and respect the dignity and potential contributions of each other. King was adamant that those who have can never be all they can be until those who have not can be all they can be. His declaration that "[t]he salvation of the Negro middle class is ultimately dependent upon the salvation of the Negro masses"[88] is as true today as in 1967. There is no question that the divide between blacks who are doing alright economically, and the masses of blacks who experience only hopelessness regarding their chances of moving beyond economic despair, is wider now than ever before—and widening. If there is to be any hope at all of adequately

86. *The Papers* (2005), 5:435.

87. "Conversation with Martin Luther King," in *A Testament of Hope* (1991), 666.

88. King, *Where Do We Go from Here*, 132.

addressing and resolving this problem, blacks will have to find ways of uniting around this issue as a race. I personally know of no instance in which this has been tried, but it seems to me that a good way to get started is for a small number of black civic and religious organizations to unite around the idea of engaging in a pilot project toward this end. Is it even reasonable to think that—with all of the intra-class suspicion—various segments of the black community can form a strong coalition to address a given problem that threatens every member? A pilot project might well be a means of finding out. Those involved in the project should come from every segment of the black community, especially those living in dire economic straits. The aim would be to work at uniting around some common goal that the group would address as a united front. This would mean they would have to work at overcoming class and other suspicions while working intentionally to build trust, which is necessary in political alliance building. Without question, each group would have its own interests, which would not be detrimental to those of others in the group, while the collective group would share some common interest, for example, the desire to eradicate racial discrimination and economic injustice. They would realize that the best means to this end is through their organized and persistent efforts.

King characterized the true alliance as being "based upon some self-interest of each component group and a common interest into which they merge. For an alliance to have permanence and loyal commitment from its various elements, each of them must have a goal from which it benefits and none must have an outlook in basic conflict with the others."[89] In order for there to be an effective alliance, it must be assumed that the participating groups essentially share similar values relative to the common goal to be pursued. It would be self-destructive, for example, for blacks to unite with fundamentalist groups (religious and secular), anti-abortion and anti-gun control groups, or any group that is not committed to democratic principles and rejects the idea of blacks as fully human.

In 1997, political sociologist and social analyst Manning Marable said that a major priority of the black community was strengthening ties with the Latino/a community, although since the late 1970s there had not been much success to that end.[90] Even Martin Luther King was aware of the significance of a black-Hispanic coalition. In 1967 he wrote of the need for blacks to form "new" coalitions. It was quite evident to him that Puerto Ricans should be included in such an alliance. King took notice of this fact when he wrote: "It is noteworthy

89. Ibid., 151.
90. Manning Marable, *Black Liberation in Conservative America* (Boston: South End, 1997), 255.

that the largest single civil rights action ever conducted was the New York school boycott, when nearly half a million Negroes and Puerto Ricans united in a demonstration that emptied segregated schools."[91] The boycott occurred in February 1964 and was organized by Bayard Rustin. More than 350,000 black and Hispanic students participated in the one-day boycott, which was deemed a success.[92] At any rate, it is not clear that King knew the prediction that by 2010 Hispanics would be the largest "minority" group in the nation. Nevertheless, he had a sense that something special could happen if blacks and Hispanics would unite around their common interests. Theodore Cross contends that if blacks and Hispanics could somehow put aside their differences and unite around common goals they could conceivably be the largest, most powerful political alliance in the nation. "Both groups," writes Cross, "have almost identical interests: full employment, breaking down racial segregation, welfare reform, restraints on racial bigotry, fuller minority participation in the political process, and quality schooling for the poor."[93]

Of the forces that King believed give reason to hope for a brighter tomorrow, the forming of coalitions shows much promise, even today. Before leaving this discussion, I want to comment briefly on three things that are pertinent to alliance building between blacks and Hispanics. These three things also suggest the very hard work and determination that will be required of each group if such an alliance is to have a real chance of being formed and sustained.

ISSUES THAT PREVENT ALLIANCE BUILDING

King himself pointed to the challenge involved in alliance politics, of actually getting two or more groups to unite in common cause.[94] At least six issues have generally made coalition building among blacks and Latinas/os difficult at best, despite their common causes:

- Many blacks believe that Latinos/as aspire to be white.
- Many Latinas/os believe blacks focus too much on race, "and a good number, especially among Mexican Americans, even harbor deep prejudice toward blacks."[95]
- Some black and Hispanic leaders foolishly engage in "promoting ethnic competition for jobs and elected posts in a variety of cities."[96]

91. King, *Where Do We Go from Here*, 150.

92. Daniel Levine, *Bayard Rustin and the Civil Rights Movement* (New Brunswick: Rutgers University Press, 2000), 158.

93. Cross, *The Black Power Imperative*, 597.

94. King, *Where Do We Go from Here*, 150–51.

95. Juan Gonzalez, *Harvest of Empire: A History of Latinos in America* (New York: Viking, 2000), 184.

- Immigration issues intensify the conflict between the two groups. "Some middle-class black leaders took the politically conservative view that undocumented Latino workers deprive poor blacks of jobs in the lowest wage sectors of the economy."[97] Some black leaders have supported legislation to block immigration.
- "English-only" referenda to impose language and cultural conformity on all citizens.
- It was accurately predicted that by or about 2010, Hispanics, as the fastest-growing group in the United States, would surpass blacks as the largest so-called minority group in the country, which could intensify the tension between the two groups in matters of education, housing, employment, political elections, and so on, unless they can figure out how to unite in common struggle for common goals.

BENEFITS OF UNITING OUTWEIGH THE DIFFERENCES

Now the second-largest "minority" group in the nation, blacks also share a number of key concerns with Latinos/as, such as full employment, racial segregation, welfare reform, addressing racial bigotry, quality schooling, and fuller participation and representation in the political process. It doesn't take much to see how advantageous it could be for the two groups and the nation at large if they would do what is necessary to unite in a strong political coalition. Theirs would most likely be a very powerful political alliance that would undoubtedly force a change in the way we see and do things in this country. Separated from each other, neither group is capable of achieving its goals because standing alone they possess insufficient power. United in a strong coalition, on the other hand, they would be a force to be reckoned with, and more important, would be strategically positioned to achieve their common goals. Each group—Hispanics and blacks—is guaranteed to fail if they choose to remain separate and to allow those who control their life-chances to bargain with each other separately rather than as a solid united front. Theodore Cross put it in a helpful way: "Mutually assured impotence for both ethnic groups is the expectable outcome of current conflicts where whites in industry, education, and government negotiate separately with blacks and Hispanics over the minor spoils of ethnic allotments."[98] It is long past due when Afrikan Americans and Latinos/as should make it absolutely, unequivocally clear to the powers-that-be, that an insult to one of them is an insult to both. The

96. Ibid., 183.
97. Marable, *Black Liberation in Conservative America*, 256.
98. Cross, *The Black Power Imperative*, 706.

consequence should be that the two groups present themselves as a powerful united front.

We have seen that blacks and Hispanics know from experience what can happen when they work together politically. King pointed to the overwhelming success of the boycott of segregated schools in New York City in 1964. Black mayoral candidates Harold Washington and Wilson Goode won elections in 1983 in Chicago and Philadelphia, respectively, as a result of strong Hispanic support. Washington, Goode, or any other black mayoral candidate stood no chance of winning without strong Hispanic support.[99] Goode's victory was a result of a strong Hispanic-black-liberal coalition. That was the good news. The bad news was that the alliance in each case was fragile at best, and came apart before too long. Hispanics and blacks were not vigilant in working to sustain the alliance. When Washington died unexpectedly in 1987 the Chicago coalition fractured and many Latino leaders who backed Washington supported the son of former mayor Richard Daley. The black-Latino/a alliance also ruptured in Philadelphia after supporting Goode for two terms.[100] Regardless, the two groups know without question the potential gains for both when they work together in alliance.

Without question, political alliance building is difficult work at best. Notwithstanding this, blacks and Latinas/os are better served when they work together rather than separately. Indeed, the forces pushing them toward alliance building are much stronger than those presently keeping them apart. Neither group will likely achieve its political goals without the strong support and assistance of the other.[101]

HOW TO MOVE TOWARD COALITION BUILDING

Presently, there is little proof of efforts to build a strong Hispanic–black alliance even though the evidence is overwhelming that the political advantages for the two groups require it. Although I do not pretend that it is as simple as this, at least three things need to happen to even get the process of alliance building started: 1) Make local efforts to build unity; 2) Meet in a formal political convention; and 3) Seek creative leaders.

A very good place to begin work on coalition building between blacks and Hispanics is at the local church level, possibly beginning with the pastors and then expanding to include church leaders. How difficult would it be for a black

---

99. Marable, *Speaking Truth to Power: Essays on Race, Resistance, and Radicalism* (Boulder, CO: Westview, 1996), 61.

100. Gonzalez, *Harvest of Empire*, 184.

101. Cross, *The Black Power Imperative*, 706.

pastor to phone a Hispanic counterpart to set a date for coffee or tea as a means of starting the process of getting to know each other? After a few such meetings one or the other could broach the subject of a small cadre of leaders from each church meeting for conversation and snacks at one or the other church, and so on. Before long the two congregations could be periodically worshiping together. And if the ministers and leaders are intentional and creative they can find ways of sharing common concerns and issues, which in turn could be the opening for exploring—not the combining of the two churches but—coalition building around common interests.

Already I have seen this type of thing happening among black and Hispanic seminary professors, encouraged in part by the American Theological Schools (ATS) through its program to bring black and Latina/o religious and theological scholars into dialogue. The ATS has brought these scholars together a number of times in Pittsburgh to get to know each other, to dialogue about common interests, as well as differences and strategies to address them. This experience has led to a number of instances in which the conversations between individual and small groups have continued well beyond the Pittsburgh meetings. There have also been instances of Hispanic and black scholars engaging in book projects together as a means of continuing the dialogue prompted by the ATS initiative. An example of this is the anthology co-edited by Anthony B. Pinn and Benjamin Valentin, *The Ties That Bind: African American and Hispanic American/Latino/a Theologies in Dialogue* (Continuum, 2001).

On the surface, the efforts of churches and scholars may seem a small thing, and it is. And yet each venture into dialogue with the other group can create openings for alliance making. We can see what can happen if such local ventures are multiplied over and over again in communities throughout the country.

Theodore Cross has suggested the much bigger project of Hispanics and blacks meeting together in a formal political convention as the first step toward developing a strong political alliance. The idea is a grand one, but we can see at the outset the amount of work that will need to be done, and the amount of trust needed in order to accomplish the goal. It is not impossible, but it will be a big challenge. Cross shares his sense of how such a meeting could proceed:

> The convention should begin by developing the usual ingredients of unity: a commitment to work together, to iron out differences, *to treat an attack on one group as an attack on the other*, and to develop tactics to prevent parties in power from creating divisions and

competition between blacks and Hispanics. The convention would then proceed to work out a common political plan and a strategy to accomplish agreed-on goals. The convention would address the difficult problems that cannot be resolved by the elementary rhetoric of cooperation. For example, convention leaders must agree on which political offices the minorities should seek and on who the candidates should be. Black candidates must be selected to run for some offices, Hispanics for others, each being firmly supported by the other. In any given city—such as New York City where blacks and Hispanics make up almost half the population—a black might be the sole minority candidate for mayor while an Hispanic candidate runs for city council president. In the next election year the roles would be reversed.[102]

Because of Martin Luther King's sense of the importance of a black-Hispanic coalition, he would undoubtedly agree with Cross that should such an alliance emerge, "the nation's ruling majority will face a political tidal wave."[103]

Reminding us that blacks and Hispanics can easily agree on a long list of issues, Marable was certain that real stumbling blocks to alliance building between the two groups were "mainstream leaders" on both sides who could not get beyond their traditionalism and parochialism in order to reach common ground. This led Marable to call for "creative, visionary leadership able to bridge the cultural, language, and ethnic divisions to begin a dialogue of mutual respect."[104] Marable could see, like Martin Luther King, that neither group can succeed without the other but together they stand the best chance of winning the fight for liberation, equality, and justice.

CONCLUSION

Martin Luther King was a man of practiced ideas that were honed on the dangerous civil rights trail from Montgomery to Memphis. He loved ideas and ideals for what they could do to make better persons and a better society and world. King was not an academic in the traditional sense. Rather, in the best sense he was a theologian of action, or as I prefer to put it, *an organic theologian of nonviolent resistance to evil.* A Christian and personalist, King believed that God created human beings in community in order to live in the community

102. Ibid., 707 (my emphasis).
103. Ibid., 599.
104. Marable, *Black Liberation in Conservative America,* 257.

of love where the absolute dignity of all people will be respected and honored in the way they are treated. Because of his staunch conviction that every human being is imbued with the image of God, and reality itself hinges on a moral foundation, King was convinced that in order for things to function according to God's expectations nonviolence as a way of life must be the means to addressing social injustices of all kinds. This is the legacy that Martin Luther King left for our very troubled world today.

Although I have said much about the importance of alliance building, particularly between the two largest so-called minority groups in the country—blacks and Hispanics—it is important that we remember that Martin Luther King was committed to the civil rights, liberation, and justice of all people, even though he always had the interests of his own people at heart as well. Although King believed that nationalism must ultimately give way to internationalism, he also held that a tinge of nationalism or group pride is fine as long as it is not at the expense of other groups or infringes upon their right to possess the same sense of group pride.[105] In the most fundamental sense, King was confident that God is concerned about the well-being of all human beings, and thus he believed this should be his—and our—concern as well.

We have seen that King saw much promise in coalition building among historically left-out groups. When he wrote and spoke of the need to form a "grand alliance," his hope was that blacks would unite with multiethnic/multicultural groups who shared similar interests and goals and would support and assist each other until those goals were achieved. Without question, the grand alliance that King had in mind was to be not only multiethnic and multicultural, but inclusive of poor whites who shared common goals, as well as liberal-progressive whites. Based on King's belief that blacks needed space and time to unite first among themselves in a kind of intracommunity coalition, my sense is that he would have wanted this to happen even before attempts at black-Hispanic coalition building. Moreover, in light of Hispanics' experiences in this country this would be a reasonable expectation of them as well. Afterward, they and blacks could begin the difficult work of uniting with each other, and then with others in the country.

Indeed, Juan Gonzalez's idea about developing a "Third Force" movement essentially expands on King's idea of the grand alliance. According to Gonzalez, a "Third Force" movement would strive "to build a genuinely multiracial, multiethnic civic majority. Its aim would not be just getting more people to vote, but getting them to participate actively in social and civic institutions,

105. *The Papers*, 6:133. Here King says: "So it is not the total concept of nationalism that I am condemning."

creating space and voice for citizens of all races and ethnic groups. Because such a coalition would reach out to those who so far have been alienated and disenfranchised, it would necessarily change the terms of national debate, providing an alternative to the corporate-conservative minority that has financed and run both major political parties for the past thirty years."[106] The "Third Force" would include a strong coalition of people of color—Latinos/as, blacks, American Indians, Asian Americans, and Pacific Island Americans. It would also include willing poor whites, liberal-progressive whites, as well as liberal-progressive GLBT folks, all who are as concerned about an enduring racism and how they benefit from it, as they are concerned about their own specific issue(s). This would be a grand alliance of which Martin Luther King would be proud.

106. Gonzalez, *Harvest of Empire*, 189.

Index